# SPEECH COMMUNICATION
## FOR THE
## CLASSROOM TEACHER

*Fourth Edition*

# SPEECH COMMUNICATION
## FOR THE
## CLASSROOM TEACHER

**PAMELA J. COOPER**
Northwestern University

GSP
**Gorsuch Scarisbrick, Publishers**
Scottsdale, Arizona

*To my parents —*
*who will always be my favorite teachers*

| | |
|---|---|
| Editor | John W. Gorsuch |
| Consulting Editor | Gerald R. Miller |
| Development Editor | Gay L. Orr |
| Production Manager | Carol H. Blumentritt |
| Sales & Marketing | Sandra Byrd |
| Cover Design | Cynthia Maliwauki |
| Typesetting | Publication Services |

ISBN 0-89787-344-0

10 9 8 7 6 5 4 3 2

# CONTENTS

# PREFACE

The content of this preface has changed little since the first edition of this text. That is, I believe, as it should be. My basic ideas about teaching have changed very little. I still believe teachers are the people who truly make a difference in the educational environment. The following poem, written by Patricia J. Anderson and Lester L. Laminack, speaks to this idea.*

## Remember When?

Remember when your mom bought your new pencils and notebooks?
When you had new school clothes?
And you were afraid you'd have the school's meanest teacher?
Remember when you worried about finding the bathroom?
When you wondered if you'd ever find your bus?
And thought about your best friend
who wasn't in your class?
Remember when?
Remember when you had to write a story
on what you did over summer vacation?
When you went to school and
couldn't find your new room?
And thought you'd never
make new friends again?
Remember when you got excited about
having new books assigned to you?
When you thought there was no way
you could eat lunchroom food?
And you wondered if the school
bully would pick on you this year?

---

* Reprinted with permission of the publisher, Early Years, Inc., Westport, CT 06880. From the August/September 1986 issue of *Early Years/K-8.*

Remember when?
Remember when a teacher
made a difference?

I remember teachers who made a difference for me. Even with all of the recent national reports expounding the problems in our schools and the problems of the teaching profession, I still believe teachers can and do make an important difference in the lives of their students. I hope what you learn in this text will help you make that difference.

This text is about communication—the very essence of teaching. It provides prospective and in-service teachers the means to analyze, develop, and facilitate their own and their students' communication behaviors. It is designed to be both theoretical and pragmatic, providing teachers with the rationale for using certain communication strategies and the practical means to utilize those strategies in the classroom. The book's discussions are supported by many and varied activities.

Many people have contributed to this fourth edition of *Speech Communication for the Classroom Teacher*. My students—particularly those in my teaching speech methods course and my classroom communication course—have influenced my ideas about teaching, and hence the book itself. They have challenged, criticized, and sometimes praised me. I am grateful for their insights and their enthusiasm for teaching as well as for learning.

My colleague Kathy Galvin has taught me a great deal. She continues to stimulate my thinking, challenge my ideas, and encourage me to "keep at it."

The staff at Gorsuch Scarisbrick, Publishers has been invaluable in assisting and encouraging me. The reviewers and editors made numerous helpful recommendations that enabled me to refine the manuscript for this edition.

Finally, my family—Rick, Jenifer, and Jamie—all deserve a very special thanks: Rick, for teaching me the real meaning of interpersonal relationships; Jenifer, for her youthful wisdom and beauty, which help to keep me young; and Jamie, because she's taught me a whole new meaning for the word "teacher."

*Pamela J. Cooper*

# 1 CLASSROOM COMMUNICATION

## OBJECTIVES

After reading this chapter and completing the activities, you should be able to:

- Define communication
- Describe the components of communication
- Describe the nature of communication
- Define the classroom as a system
- Distinguish classroom communication from other types of communication

## INTRODUCTION

Although many variables affect classroom learning, one variable most educators agree is paramount is communication. The essence of the teaching-learning process is effective communication. Without communication, teaching and learning would be impossible.

## COMMUNICATION: DEFINITION AND COMPONENTS

Communication scholars have long pondered the question, what is communication? The term *communication* is abstract, and like all words, has several meanings. For purposes of our discussion, classroom communication consists of the verbal and nonverbal transactions between teacher and students and between or among students.

In order for us to communicate, several components are necessary. We know from the previous definition of communication that we need *interactants* and a *message*. We also need *channels* (hearing, sight, and the other senses) through which the message can be sent and received. In addition, since the interactants in the communication event affect one another, feedback is also a necessary component. *Feedback* is the message sent in response to other messages. This feedback can be either verbal or nonverbal.

Another important component of the communication process is *noise*. Noise is any signal that disrupts the accuracy of messages being sent. Noise may be physical (someone tapping a pencil on the desk, chalk scraping on the blackboard) or psychological (daydreaming, personal problems, attitudes). These are all distractions that can cause inaccuracy in communication—preventing the message sent from being the message received. In the English classroom, for example, a source of noise could be a student's dislike for that subject. This dislike could function as noise by prohibiting the student from accurately receiving messages concerning, say, Shakespeare. Regardless of what messages the teacher sends about Shakespeare and his relevance today, the student will find it difficult to receive any messages that would enhance his liking for Shakespeare.

Finally, the *environment* in which the communication takes place is important. In the educational context, this environment is termed classroom climate. The climate is the atmosphere of the classroom. It is contingent on both verbal and nonverbal communication.

Much of what is discussed in this text concerns classroom climate—how to build a supportive classroom climate through communication. A supportive classroom climate is important because it promotes fuller development of a student's positive self-images and enhances self-concept.

I will be discussing ways to build a supportive classroom climate in various sections of this text. For now, keep in mind that a supportive classroom climate is one characterized by:[1]

- openness rather than defensiveness
- confidence rather than fear
- acceptance rather than rejection
- trust rather than suspicion
- belonging rather than alienation
- order rather than chaos
- control rather than frustration
- high expectations rather than low expectations

**ACTIVITY 1.1**

Define communication. You may want to choose a cartoon, quotation, or picture to make your definition clear.

## THE NATURE OF COMMUNICATION

Based on our definition of communication, several axioms or "truths" concerning communication are apparent: Communication is a transactional process which is complex, symbolic, and has both a content and a relational component. The next section discusses each of these in depth.

### Communication Is a Transactional Process

The transactional process nature of communication is depicted in figure 1.1[2] This perspective stresses that communication takes place between persons, not roles. In other words, if our communication is to be truly effective, I must think of you as a person, not just as another student. Similarly, you must think of me as a person, not just another teacher. This requires that we be person oriented rather than role oriented. What the transactional view suggests is that to be an effective communicator, I must not only concentrate on my performance as a teacher and be aware of you as a student, but I must also be aware of you as a person—treat you as an individual and not an object.

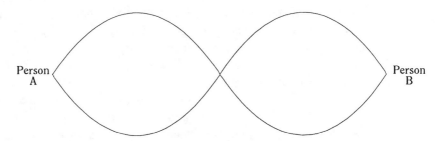

Person
A

Person
B

*Figure 1.1* *A transactional model of communication.*

   For example, your view of my lecture may not be the same as the student's sitting next to you, since you are two different people with different backgrounds, attitudes, and tastes that affect your perceptions of the lecture and me. In this situation, the transactional view emphasizes that not every student is the same as every other student. Thus, the transactional view stresses the simultaneous nature of sending and receiving messages. For example, as I lecture I send messages—both verbal (my words) and nonverbal (my posture, tone of voice, facial expression, etc.). At the same time, I receive messages from you (your posture, facial expression, etc.). Communication becomes complex, dynamic, and continuous—a process in which each individual gains identity from participation in the communication event. In other words, communication is a relationship we engage in; it is not something as simple as sending and receiving messages.

From a transactional process perspective, we are who we are in relation to the other person with whom we are communicating. In other words, when we say communication is transactional, we are saying that people adapt and change their own communication—even as it is occurring—based on how they perceive the other person is communicating to them. For example, when a teacher is pleased with students' work and communicates that pleasure, students are willing and eager to continue discussion, ask questions, etc. If, on the other hand, the teacher communicates displeasure, students "clam up"—are unwilling to continue discussion or ask questions.

Berlo defines process and some of the implications of viewing communication as a process:

> *If we accept the concept of process, we view events and relationships as dynamic, on-going, ever-changing, continuous. When we label something as a process, we also mean that it does not have a beginning, an end, a fixed sequence of events. It is not static, at rest. It is moving. The ingredients within a process interact; each affects the others.*[3]

Thus, not only does the teacher's behavior affect the student's behavior, but student behavior also affects teacher behavior. An infamous example of this is the story of the class who gave positive feedback to their instructor when he stood in one area of the room to lecture and withdrew that reinforcement whenever he moved to another area of the room. Soon the professor was lecturing from the area of the room from which he received positive reinforcement!

In 1971, Klein conducted a study indicating how student verbal and nonverbal behavior could affect the verbal and nonverbal behavior of the teacher. When students behaved positively, the teachers behaved in a positive manner. When the students behaved negatively, the teachers were negative.[4] For example, if the student disagreed with the teacher or did not pay attention to the teacher, the teacher reacted negatively (did not call on the student when her hand was up, walked away from the student, or did something to stop the student behavior).

Interestingly, what occurs in the classroom seems to deny this transactional process idea of communication. Arno Bellack and his colleagues devised a system to analyze classroom communication according to four moves commonly observed in teachers' behavior:[5]

1. *Structuring.* Structuring moves serve the pedagogical function of setting the context for subsequent behavior by either launching or halting—excluding interaction between students and teachers. For example, teachers frequently launch a class period with a structuring move in which they focus attention on the topic or problem to be discussed during that session.

2. *Soliciting.* Moves in this category are designed to elicit a verbal response, to encourage persons addressed to attend to something, or to elicit a physical response. All questions are solicitations, as are commands, imperatives, and requests.

3. *Responding.* These moves bear a reciprocal relationship to soliciting moves and occur only in relation to them. Their pedagogical function is to fulfill the expectation of soliciting moves; thus, students' answers to teachers' questions are classified as responding moves.

4. *Reacting.* These moves are occasioned by a structuring, soliciting, responding, or prior reacting move but are not directly elicited by them. Pedagogically, these moves serve to modify (by clarifying, synthesizing, or explaining) and/or to rate (positively or negatively) what has been said previously. Reacting moves differ from responding moves: while a responding move is always directly elicited by a solicitation, preceding moves serve only as the occasion for reactions. Rating by a teacher of a student's response, for example, is designated as a reacting move.

Bellack and his coworkers described the sequence of these communication moves in the classroom by describing the teaching cycles present. Of twenty-one possible cycles, six accounted for approximately 80 percent of the total:

1. SOL . . . . RES . . . . REA . . . . . . . . . . . . . . . . 26%
2. SOL . . . . RES . . . . . . . . . . . . . . . . . . . . . . 22.3%
3. SOL . . . . . . . . . . . . . . . . . . . . . . . . . . . . 9.7%
4. SOL . . . . RES . . . . REA . . . .REA . . . . . . . . . . . 9%
5. SOL . . . . REA . . . . REA . . . .RES . . . . .REA . . . 7%
6. STR . . . . SOL . . . . RES . . . .REA . . . . . . . . . 5%

SOL = soliciting; RES = responding; REA = reacting; STR = structuring

Eighty-five percent of all teaching cycles are initiated by the teacher. Thus, the style and sequence of communication used in the classroom leave the student a passive observer rather than an active participant.

Friedrich, in his synthesis of classroom interaction research, suggests that the patterns described by Bellack have great regularity—such patterns have existed in our classrooms since the earliest interaction research was reported in 1912.[6]

Albert Cullum, in his book *The Geranium on the Window Sill Just Died but Teacher You Went Right On*, speaks of the frustration many students must feel about these communication patterns.

"Good boys and good girls always listen.
To learn we must listen.
We must listen all the time.
Good boys and girls never talk,
but they always listen.
We should listen and listen and listen!"

To you, teacher,
and your words, your words, your words.
Your words, your words, your words,
your words![7]

## Communication Is Complex

It's been said that when two people interact, there are really six: my me, my you, my impression of the way you see me, your you, your me, and your impression of how I see you. Suppose two people—Penny and Rebecca—are communicating. The "people" in their communication transaction are diagrammed in figure 1.2. When we multiply this by thirty students and a teacher, we soon realize how complex classroom communication can be. All these "people" enter into the messages sent and received. No wonder communication problems arise! Remember also that in addition to these six "people" (and their attitudes, beliefs, moods) there are also factors such as time, place, and circumstances that affect communication and make it even more complex.

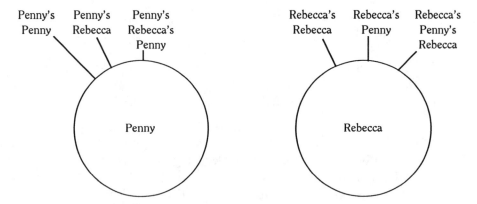

***Figure 1.2*** *The six "people" involved in a communication transaction.*
Adapted from *Dimensions in Communication: Readings,* edited by James Campbell and Hal Hepler. Belmont, CA: Wadsworth, 1965.

## Communication Is Symbolic

Communication is the symbolic means through which we relate our experiences and perceptions to others. The symbols we use are words (verbal messages) and behaviors (nonverbal messages). In order to relate our experiences and perceptions, we must share common meanings. The problem is that meanings are not transferable; only messages are. Stated in other terms, meanings are in people, not in words. For example, when you say to a student, "See me after class," the student provides the meaning. Thoughts such as "What did I do wrong?" or "Oh, no, she found out!" may go through the student's mind. The student doesn't know if you mean, "You've done something wrong" or "I think you did a great job and I want to compliment you." As Combs and his associates indicate, "The discovery of meaning . . . can only take place in people. . . . This is the human side of learning."[8] Just as words don't have a single meaning, neither do nonverbal aspects of communication. The clothes you wear, the expression on your face, the gestures you use may communicate different meanings than you intend.

## Communication Has Both a Content and a Relational Component

Whenever we communicate, we communicate on two levels—the content level and the relationship level. To clarify these two levels, consider the following example. A male student enters your office to discuss a problem he's having with an assignment. He knocks on your slightly opened door and asks, "Do you have a few minutes?" As you continue with your work, not even looking at him, you answer, "Yes. Come on in." Your content message indicates a specific behavior the student should perform—he should walk in. However, your relationship message states quite clearly that you don't wish to be disturbed. The relationship message can indicate how you view the other person, how you view yourself, and how you view the relationship between you and the other person.

The importance of the relationship message for teachers is evident. The relationships we create with our students affect us, our students, and the educational outcomes of our instruction. Much research suggests that when a teacher's communication response to student is one of "I accept you," the relationship is positive and learning is enhanced.[9]

---

### ACTIVITY 1.2

Read the following poem. What does it tell us about the two components of communication in the classroom?

Ideas are clean. They soar in the serene
supernal. I can take them out and look
at them, they fit in books, they lead
me down that narrow way. And in the
morning they are there. Ideas are straight—

But the world is round, and a
messy mortal is my friend.

Come walk with me in the mud. . . .[10]

## THE CLASSROOM AS A SYSTEM

Recent educational reports reflect the increasing role of communication in educational environments and the concept that the essence of teaching is communication—that teacher and student are linked in a *system* of simultaneous communication transactions.[11] Clark and her associates indicate the importance of viewing the classroom as a communication system:

> *The classroom must be managed as a complex, ever-changing communication system composed of a multiple of human variables; and these human variables must determine how communication skills can be employed for the clearest, most appropriate communication in a given situation, in class and out.*[12]

A system is a set of entities that interrelate with one another to form a *unique whole*. The underlying assumption when analyzing classroom communication from this perspective is that knowledge of the interrelationships and interaction among the components of the teaching-learning process is more important than knowledge of each alone. In other words, it's difficult and unproductive to talk about teachers without talking about students. In addition, it's necessary for teachers to achieve organized integration of all the components in the teaching-learning process, and a systems approach maximizes such an integration.

When we say that a system possesses the quality of *wholeness*, we mean that "a whole is more than the sum of its parts." The system possesses a unique quality that can't be understood by simply summing the parts. Every classroom is unique from every other classroom. This is true because of the second quality of systems—*interdependence*. The parts of a system interact mutually. Each element in your classroom—the students, the teacher, the environment, the teaching strategies—interact and mutually affect one another. Thus, a change in one part of the system will produce changes in the system as a whole. For example, suppose you decide to give your students a "pop" quiz. All other members of the classroom system are affected by your decision. If one student engages in disruptive behavior, the entire system is disrupted. Thus, all members of a system are affected by the actions of the other members.

Systems are *hierarchical.* The school is a subsystem of the community. The classroom system is a subsystem of the school in which it functions. Each student in the classroom is a subsystem of the classroom system. Thus, systems consist of a series of levels of increasing complexity.

Systems are *goal-oriented.* The primary goal of the classroom system is student learning. The parts of the system know if that goal has been achieved by examining feedback, such as test scores. The system regulates itself based on this feedback. For example, if test scores are low, the unit of instruction may have to be taught again.

Systems *interact with their environment.* The system is both affected by and affects its environment. Community variables, such as the amount of available educational funds, can affect the educational environment. On the other hand, watch what happens to a community when problems arise in the school or the basketball team wins the state championship! The more compatible the goals of the system are to the environmental needs, the more efficient the system.

In order to maintain itself, a system must "stay in balance." This state of balance is termed *homeostasis.* Paradoxically, a system must also be adaptable, be able to change to meet the needs of a changing environment. For example, it may be OK to dismiss school for a day so students can watch their team play at the state championship, but if the system is to remain in balance, students must return to the classroom soon and begin to work toward the goal of learning.

The final goal of the system can be accomplished in a variety of ways. This concept is called *equifinality.* For example, a teacher can teach the same content by a variety of methods and materials.

The system model in figure 1.3 exemplifies the qualities of a system.[13] Notice that a number of components comprise the classroom system. The system has numerous feedback mechanisms that allow it to regulate and change itself. Thus, each part of the system affects and is affected by every other part. The hierarchical nature of the classroom system is also evidenced in this model—the subsystem of the students and the suprasystems of the community and school influence the classroom.

When you view the classroom as a communication system, you are concerned with what the student is to accomplish and how the student is to accomplish it. You must be cognizant of all variables influencing the final outcome—learning— and how these variables relate to and interact with one another.

---

**ACTIVITY 1.3**

Look back at your definition of communication. Discuss how it relates to the system perspective.

---

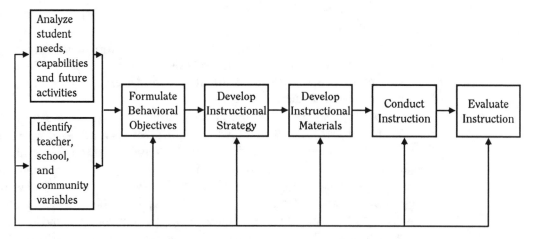

*Figure 1.3* *A system model of classroom learning.*

## CHARACTERISTICS OF CLASSROOM COMMUNICATION

Although communication in the classroom is similar to communication in any other context, there are characteristics of the classroom that make instructional communication somewhat unique. Four characteristics are notable.

One unique characteristic is that *roles are fairly limited and adhered to carefully*. Rowe found that students ask questions very infrequently.[14] Their role is to answer questions the teacher asks. The research reviewed by Friedrich cited earlier suggests the prominence and permanence of the pattern of a teacher's asking a question, the student answering the question, and the teacher reacting to the student's answer. Thus, the status differences are quite prominent. They are also complementary; that is, the teacher is in the primary position, and the student is subordinate to the teacher.

A second characteristic of classroom communication is that *most messages are informational* in nature rather than persuasive. Although persuasive messages are sent, the bulk of the communication is concerned with dispensing information and creating understanding. So many informational messages are presented to students in a given school day that they often suffer from "information overload"—more information is presented than the student can process.

A third characteristic is that the schools focus on *improving students' competencies*. In no other context is the emphasis on developing competencies so great. Students cannot progress from one level to another until certain competencies are developed. Most of the school day is spent in trying to develop these competencies.

Finally, a fourth characteristic of communication in the classroom is that *evaluation* is a major component of the educational environment. In this context, evaluation is an integral, constant component. From the very first day of class, teachers and students evaluate one another. This evaluation is not only of end products but is also present during the entire learning process. As students we evaluate the teacher's appearance, teaching methods, discipline procedures, and fairness in testing and grading—in fact, almost everything about the teacher is evaluated by students. As teachers we evaluate almost every aspect of our students—their intellectual, social, and personal characteristics. This evaluation on the part of students and teachers occurs throughout the educational environment—outside the classroom as well as inside it.

---

**ACTIVITY 1.4**

Read the following poem. How are the four characteristics of communication in the educational environment illustrated in this poem?

It's September again
—the time of jumping when you call,
doing cartwheels for you,
nodding yes.
It's September again
—standing on my head for you,
leaping high
hoping to please.
It's September again
—taking your tests,
finding my lost pencil,
losing ground.
It's September again
—hiding behind my reading book,
breathing quietly,
afraid![15]

---

**IN SUM**

This chapter has provided a basic introduction to classroom communication. The classroom as a communication system was discussed. The nature of communication as a transactional, complex, symbolic process involving both content and relational components was also discussed. Finally, four characteristics of classroom communication were outlined: that communication roles are limited and adhered to carefully; that messages are generally informational rather than persuasive; that schools focus on developing competencies; and that evaluation is a major component of the educational environment.

---

**ACTIVITY 1.5**                                                      **Term Project**

Keep a journal in which you enter notes from your readings, as well as observations, articles, poems, short stories, cartoons, and other materials on communication. The purpose of this journal is to help you analyze your own communication behavior and that of others. It should include anything that will help you meet this objective.

In your journal write on one of the following:

1.  When you think about teaching, what are your major concerns? Don't write what you think you should be concerned about, or what you think others are concerned about, but what concerns you. Be frank.
2.  Choose one of the following and write a brief opinion paper (one page):

    ■ The most critical issue in education is . . .
    ■ The most exciting challenge for teachers is . . .
    ■ Every teacher is a teacher of communication because . . .
    ■ Answer the question, "Why teach?"

---

## NOTES

1. See, for example, J. Goodlad, *A Place Called School* (New York: McGraw-Hill, 1984); A. Lieberman and L. Miller, *Teachers, Their World and Their Work: Implications for School Improvement* (Alexandria, VA: Association for Supervision and Curriculum Development, 1984); S. Lightfoot, *The Good High School* (New York: Basic Books, 1983); J. Herndon, *Notes from a School Teacher* (New York: Simon and Schuster, 1985); V. Purcell-Gates, "What Oral/Written Language Differences Can Tell Us about Beginning Instruction," *The Reading Teacher* (1989): 290–296; C. O'Neill, "Dialogue and Drama: The Transformation of Events, Ideas, and Teachers," *Language Arts* 66(2) (Feb. 1989):147–159; and C. Hillman, *Creating a Learning Climate for the Early Childhood Years* (Bloomington, IN: Phi Delta Kappa Educational Foundation, 1989).

2. J. Wenburg and W. Wilmot, *The Personal Communication Process* (New York: John Wiley, 1973).

3. D. Berlo, *The Process of Communication* (New York: Holt, Rinehart and Winston, 1960) 24.

4. S. Klein, "Student Influences on Teacher Behavior," *American Educational Research Journal* 8 (1971): 403–21.

5. A. A. Bellack, H. M. Kleibard, R. T. Hyman, and F. L. Smith, Jr., *The Language of the Classroom* (New York: Teachers College Press, 1967) 4.

6. G. Friedrich, "Classroom Interaction," *Communication in the Classroom*, ed. L. Barker (Englewood Cliffs, NJ: Prentice-Hall, 1982) 55–76.

7. A. Cullum, *The Geranium on the Window Sill Just Died But Teacher You Went Right On* (New York: Harlin Quist, 1971) 8.

8. A. W. Combs, D. L. Avila, and W. W. Purkey, *Helping Relationships: Basic Concepts for the Helping Professions* (Boston: Allyn and Bacon, 1971) 91.

9. See, for example, research reviewed in J. E. Brophy, "Classroom Organization and Management," *The Elementary School Journal* 83 (1983): 265–286; J. E. Brophy, "Teacher Behavior and Its Effects," *Journal of Educational Psychology* 71 (1979): 733–750; C. B. Cazden, "Classroom Discourse," *Handbook of Research on Teaching*, ed. M. C. Wittrack (New York: Macmillan, 1986): 432–463; I. L. Good, "Classroom Research: A Decade of Progress," *Educational Psychologist* 18 (1983): 127–144; A. Q. Staton-Spicer and D. H. Wulff, "Research in Communication and Instruction: Categorization and Synthesis," *Communication Education* 33 (1984): 377–391; M. L. Willbrand and R. Rieke, *Teaching Oral Communication in the Elementary School* (New York: Macmillan, 1983).

10. H. Prather, *Notes to Myself* (New York: Bantam Books, 1970).

11. See, for example, *The National Commission on Excellence in Education, A Nation at Risk: The Imperative for Educational Reform* (Washington, D.C.: U.S. Government Printing Office, 1983); "Tomorrow's Teachers: A Report of the Holmes Group" (East Lansing, MI: The Holmes Group, 1987); and "A Nation Prepared: Teachers for the 21st Century: Excerpts from The Report by the Carnegie Forum's Task Force on Teaching as a Profession," *Chronicle of Higher Education* (May 21, 1986): 43–54; G. H. Quehl, *Higher Education and the Public Interest: A Report to the Campus* (Washington, D.C.: Council for Advancement and Support of Education, 1988); T. R. Sizer, *Horace's Compromise: the Dilemma of the American High School* (Boston: Houghton Mifflin, 1984); "New Carnegie Report on Two Year Colleges," *Chronicle of Higher Education* 34(33), April 27, 1988, 1; and National Commission for Excellence in Teacher Education, *A Call for Change in Teacher Ed-*

*ucation* (Washington, D.C.: American Association of Colleges of Teacher Education, 1985).

12. M. Clark, E. Erway, and L. Beltzer, *The Learning Encounter* (New York: Random House, 1971) 3.

13. See other models by M. Dunkin and B. Biddle in *The Study of Teaching* (New York: Holt, Rinehart and Winston, 1974). Other adaptations appear in Friedrich, *Classroom Interaction* and W. Seiler, L.

D. Schuelke, and B. Lieb-Brilhart, *Communication for the Contemporary Classroom* (New York: Holt, Rinehart and Winston, 1984).

14. M. Rowe, "Wait Time: Slowing Down May Be a Way of Speaking Up," *Journal of Teacher Education* (Jan.-Feb. 1986): 43–48.

15. Cullum, *The Geranium on the Window Sill Just Died*, 7.

## SUGGESTIONS FOR FURTHER READING

Applebaum, D., and J. McClear. *Teacher, The Children Are Here.* Glenview, IL: Scott Foresman, 1988.

Baker, L., ed. *Communication in the Classroom.* Englewood Cliffs, NJ: Prentice Hall, 1982.

Bassett, R. E., and M. J. Smythe. *Communication and Instruction.* New York: Harper and Row, 1979.

Berliner, D. "On The Expert Teacher." *Educational Leadership* 44 (Oct. 1986): 4–9.

Berliner, D. "Simple Theories of Effective Teaching and a Simple Theory of Classroom Instruction." *Talks to Teachers.* Ed. D. C. Berliner and B. V. Rosenshine. New York: Random House, 1987, 93–110.

Book, C. "Communication Education: Pedagogical Content Knowledge Needed." *Communication Education* 38(4) (1989): 315–322.

Book, C. "Providing Feedback: The Research on Effective Oral and Written Feedback Strategies." *Central States Speech Journal* 36 (1985): 14–23.

Callahan, J., and L. Clark. *Teaching in the Middle and Secondary Schools.* 3rd ed. New York: Macmillan, 1988.

Cooper, J. M., ed. *Classroom Teaching Skills.* 3rd ed. Toronto: D. C. Heath, 1986.

Cooper, P., and K. Galvin, eds. *The Future of Speech Communication Education.* Annandale, VA: Speech Communication Association, 1989.

DeWine, S., and J. C. Pearson, "Communication Competence Among Teachers: The Ohio Solution." *Communication Education* 38(4) (Oct. 1989): 372–377.

Ennis, R. H., "Is Answering Questions Teaching?" *Educational Theory* 36(4) (Fall 1986): 343–347.

Fiordo, R. A. *Communication in Education.* Calgary: Detselig, 1990.

Franzwa, G. "Socrates Never Had Days Like This." *Liberal Education* (1984): 203–208.

Fulgham, R. *All I Really Needed to Know I Learned in Kindergarten.* New York: Villard Books, 1988.

Good, T., and J. Brophy. *Looking in Classrooms.* 3rd ed. New York: Harper and Row, 1984.

Herling-Austin, L., et al. *Assisting the Beginning Teacher.* Reston, VA: Association of Teacher Educators, 1989.

Kagan, D. M. "Teaching as Clinical Problem Solving: A Critical Examination of the Analogy and Its Implications." *Review of Educational Research* 58(4) (Winter 1988): 482–505.

Katula, R., ed. *Communication Quarterly Educational Supplement* 34(4) (1986). The entire issue is devoted to the topic of excellence in the speech communication classroom and includes profiles of outstanding speech communication teachers.

Kidder, T. *Among Schoolchildren*. Boston: Houghton Mifflin, 1989.

Levine, J. *Secondary Instruction: A Manual for Classroom Teaching*. Boston: Allyn and Bacon, 1989.

Littlejohn, S. *Theories of Human Communication*. 3rd ed. Belmont, CA: Wadsworth, 1989.

National Center for Research on Teacher Education. "Teacher Education and Learning to Teach: A Research Agenda." *Journal of Teacher Education* (Nov./Dec. 1988): 27-32.

Needels, M. C. "A New Design for Process-Product Research on the Quality of Discourse in Teaching." *American Educational Research Journal* 25(4) (Winter 1988): 503-526.

Nussbaum, J. "Effective Teaching: A Communicative Nonrecursive Causal Model." *Communication Yearbook 5*. Ed. Michael Burgoon. New Brunswick, NJ: Transaction Books, 1982. 737-752.

Nyquist, J. D., D. H. Wulff, and R. D. Abbott, "The Interface Between Communication and Instruction: Communication Foundations for a University Instructional Development Center." *Communication Education* 38(4) (Oct. 1989): 377-387.

Ornstein, A. "Research on Teaching: Issues and Trends." *Journal of Teacher Education* (Nov./Dec. 1985): 27-31.

Rubin, R., ed. *Improving Speaking and Listening Skills*. San Francisco: Jossey-Bass, 1983.

Shalaway, L. *Learning to Teach . . . Not Just for Beginners*. Cleveland, OH: Edgell Communications, 1989.

Staton-Spicer, A., and D. Wulff. "Research in Communication and Instruction: Categorization and Synthesis." *Communication Education* 33 (1984): 377-391.

Stewart, J. *Bridges Not Walls*. 5th ed. New York: Random House, 1988.

# 2 INTERPERSONAL COMMUNICATION

## OBJECTIVES

After reading this chapter and completing the activities, you should be able to:

- Define interpersonal communication
- Explain the importance of good interpersonal relationships in the classroom
- Define self-concept
- Define self-esteem
- Outline the process by which we receive our self-concept
- Explain how a teacher's self-concept can affect a student's self-concept and vice versa
- Define self-disclosure
- Explain the process of perception
- Describe techniques used by general semanticists

## INTRODUCTION

Carl Rogers[1] suggests that in our work with students it's the quality of our relationship with them, not the content we teach, that is the most significant element determining our effectiveness. We build these relationships through face-to-face communication with our students—through interpersonal communication. Interpersonal communication is a "people process rather than a language process."[2]

From a transactional perspective, this means that interpersonal communication is concerned with the relational as well as the content message of our communication. It is through communication that we develop, maintain, and terminate relationships. A teacher must possess a well-developed repertoire of interpersonal communication skills in order to establish, maintain, and promote effective interpersonal relationships in the classroom.

## RELATIONSHIP DEVELOPMENT

Several writers have analyzed the stages in developing and terminating relationships.[3] Although the number of stages and the terminology used to describe them vary from writer to writer, the basic stages of relationship development are initiating, experimenting, and integrating. The termination stages are deterioration and dissolution. Before examining each stage in relation to student-teacher relationships, a brief discussion of how communication changes as people progress through the stages is necessary.

### Communication Within Stages

Knapp[4] lists eight dimensions along which communication varies in the differing stages of a relationship. As we progress through the stages of relationship development, our communication becomes more:

1. *Broad*—more topics are discussed in more depth.
2. *Unique*—people are viewed as unique individuals rather than a stereotyped role.
3. *Efficient*—accuracy, speed, and efficiency of communication increase as we get to know the other person.
4. *Flexible*—the number of different ways an idea or feeling can be communicated increases—I may communicate my pleasure with a student's performance verbally, "Great job," as well as nonverbally—a pat on the shoulder.
5. *Smooth*—the ability to predict the other's behavior increases so that there is "greater synchronization of interaction."
6. *Personal*—we reveal more about ourselves—our fears, feelings, likes/dislikes, etc.—as we get to know another person.
7. *Spontaneous*—informality and comfort increase and we feel less hesitant about how to react, what topics to discuss, and how much can be said about a topic.

8. *Overt*—praise and criticism are less inhibited as we get to know another person.

Knapp speculates that as relationships deteriorate, communication becomes more narrow, stylized, difficult, rigid, awkward, public, hesitant, and overt judgments are suspended.

## Relationship Stages

### Initiating

This first stage is one of first encounters. On the first day of class we begin initiating our relationships with students. Much goes into this first stage. Our prior knowledge of the students and theirs of us, our mutual expectations, and our initial impressions all affect the initiation stage.

Much has been written in teacher education concerning the importance of the first day of class. First impressions have a great impact on how the student-teacher relationship progresses. First impressions are difficult to change. In addition, the first impression I have of a class or a student determines my expectations of how effective or pleasant future interactions will be.

"Getting off on the wrong foot"—either as a teacher or a student—can have very detrimental effects.[5]

### Experimenting

In this stage, students and teachers are "testing" one another and trying to discover the unknown. Students experiment with behaviors—"How much can I 'get away with'?" and "How can I please this teacher?" Teachers seek to find what teaching methods and classroom management techniques work best. Each person is trying to answer questions such as: Who are you? What do we have in common? What do you expect from me?

Much of the communication in this stage is stereotypical. Teachers aren't perceived by students as unique individuals, but only in their role as teachers. In like fashion, students are viewed in their role and not as individuals with unique ways of behaving or learning.

### Intensifying

In the intensifying stage, teachers and students communicate on a more interpersonal level. That is, communication is not role-to-role, but person-to-person. A larger variety of topics may be discussed and in greater depth than in the experimenting stage. Behavior is more easily predictable and explainable because teachers know students better and vice-versa. For example, at this stage of the student-teacher relationship, I will be able to predict how a particular student will react to humor or criticism and adapt my communication accordingly.

### Deterioration and Dissolution

We often consider termination of relationships as negative. However, in the student-teacher relationship, the termination stages of deterioration and dissolution are a natural phenomenon. Classes end and students leave. Patrick Walsh, in his book *Tales Out of School*, describes the feelings many teachers experience as the school year ends:

> *Nowadays I make my June farewells to students by writing them notes on the blackboard.*
>
> *A couple of years ago I was checking the roll for the last time when I suddenly got choked up. I made a quick exit, returned, but had to leave again. The next year, confident I'd be able to control my emotions, I started to tell a fourth-period how much I'd enjoyed teaching them. I got about five words out and had to stop.*
>
> *Another time I was collecting the last set of tests when it hit me that this would be the last time these kids would come together as "my" students. I could feel the tears starting, so I turned and pretended to look for papers on my desk. Finally, I grabbed some chalk and scribbled a note on the blackboard: "You've been one of the most talented, wild, fun classes I've ever taught. Thanks for a great year." As I finished writing, I thought of a line from T.S. Eliot: "It is impossible to say just what I mean."*[6]

## COMMUNICATION VARIABLES IN INTERPERSONAL RELATIONSHIPS

Several communication variables contribute to building a positive relationship between student and teacher—positive self-concept, effective self-disclosure, accurate perception, and shared language and meaning. In the remainder of this chapter, each of these variables will be examined.

### Self-Concept

Basic to all interpersonal communication is the question: Who am I? The answer to this question is a prerequisite to our ability to effectively communicate with others. Only when we know who we are can we proceed to communicate effectively with others. Rintye summarizes this idea when he states, "Trying to understand my communication behavior without understanding myself is like trying to perceive an iceberg by looking at the tip above the waterline."

### Definition

Your self-concept is your total description of yourself. It includes four parts:

1.  How you perceive yourself intellectually, socially, and physically
2.  How you would like to be
3.  How you believe others perceive you
4.  How others actually perceive you

Although I'll use the term *self-concept* throughout this chapter, it's important to remember that this term is somewhat misleading. Many self-concepts make up our general self-concept. For example, a student may have a concept of self as an athlete and a concept of self as a math student. Within each of these concepts, the student will possess the four parts listed above. You not only describe yourself, but you also appraise or evaluate yourself. This appraisal is your self-esteem. In other words, I have a concept of myself as a teacher—I am dedicated and hard working. If I value those qualities, I will have a high self-esteem. If I do not value my concept as a teacher, I will have low self-esteem. When people have high self-esteem, they feel likable, productive, and capable.

### Communication and Self-Concept

A reciprocal relationship exists between communication and self-concept: communication affects our self-concept and our self-concept affects how and what we communicate. A model by Kinch[7] demonstrates this reciprocal relationship (figure 2.1).

We can begin looking at this model at any of the four circles. Beginning with (P) our perceptions of how others see us influences our self-concept (S). Our self-concept determines our behavior (B).[8] Our behavior (B) in turn influences the actions of others towards us (A). These actions influence our perceptions of how others see us and we are back to the starting point again. Thus, as a teacher you can affect the self-concepts of students by the communication you initiate toward students. Several researchers have found support for this idea. For example Maehr et al.[9] found that when a significant other (someone important to the individual) reacted approvingly toward some attribute of the subject, the subject's self-concept of that attribute improved; if the individual perceived disapproval, the self-concept diminished. Webster and Sobieszek[10] report research indicating that the more positive the evaluation received, the more positive students felt about themselves and the more they talked in class. Cooper, Stewart, and Gundykunst[11] conducted studies that demonstrate that students with high and low self-concepts as a public speaker perceive messages differently and that these perceptions were related to changes in their self-concept, their motivation to achieve, and their rating of both the instructor and their relationship with the instructor. Thus, how we perceive the communication we receive from others influences our self-concept and our subsequent communication.

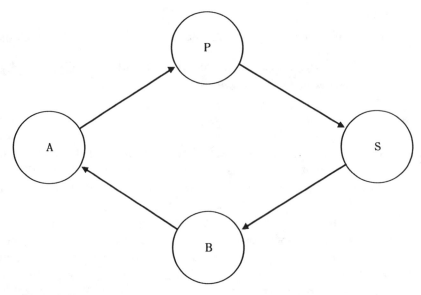

P = Perception of other's responses
S = Self-concept
B = Behavior
A = Actual responses of others

*Figure 2.1 Kinch's model of the relationship between self-concept and communication.*

One of the major ways self-concept affects communication in the classroom is through the self-fulfilling prophecy. Self-concept influences behavior. In other words, we behave in accordance with our self-concept. Consider the student who believes he is "dumb" in math. His attitude might be, "I don't do well, so why try." As a result, he doesn't do math homework, doesn't study for exams, and doesn't pay attention in class. Because of these subsequent behaviors, he fails math. He has fulfilled his own prophecy—"I don't do well in math."

In summary, self-concept affects communication because we communicate and behave in accordance with our self-concept. Our self-concept is formed, to a large extent, by the communication we receive from others.

### Self-Concept and Academic Performance

A logical question at this point is, what effect does self-concept have on academic performance? Purkey[12] outlined the characteristics of a student who demonstrated high academic achievement and Fitts[13] outlined the characteristics of a student who demonstrated low academic achievement (see table 2.1). Both researchers indicate that many of the variables that affect academic achievement are related to student self-concept.

A recent study by Mufson, Cooper, and Hall[14] supports this view. These researchers studied twenty-three seventh-grade students to identify emotional, social, or cognitive variables that might contribute to the lower than predicted scholastic performance of underachievers. Two groups of students, achievers and underachievers, were evaluated and compared through student, parent, and teacher interviews and questionnaires. The results of this study reveal that underachievers are less self-confident, less socially and emotionally mature, less able to focus on one concern at a time, less accurate in their perceptions about themselves and their work, and less hardworking.

In their review of classroom factors affecting students' self-evaluations, Marshall and Weinstein[15] concluded that a complex set of interactive factors were related to students belief about their competence in a particular classroom: task structure (the extent to which all students do the same task at the same time according to the same standards), grouping (purpose, frequency, and stability of grouping), locus of responsibility in learning and evaluation (the degree to which students have choices and self-evaluate their work), evaluation and feedback procedures, and information about ability (especially how public that information), and motivational strategies used by the teacher (extrinsic vs. intrinsic and cooperative vs. competitive). The reviewers concluded that students' self-evaluations are likely to be higher in classrooms with multidimensional tasks (i.e., the teacher communicates the affect that many abilities are valued and needed to perform tasks in the room and different students are doing different tasks at any given time) and cooperative atmospheres. Such findings are congruent with other research examining classroom structural factors.[16]

**Table 2.1** *Characteristics of students with high and low academic achievement.*

| Students with high academic achievement | Students with low academic achievement |
|---|---|
| 1. Have a high regard for themselves | 1. Have unfavorable attitudes toward school and teachers |
| 2. Are optimistic about their potential for success in the future | 2. Do not assume responsibility for learning |
| 3. Possess confidence in their competence as persons and students | 3. Have low motivation |
| 4. Believe they are hard workers | 4. Have low morale and are dissatisfied with school experience |
| 5. Believe other students like them | 5. Have low class participation rates |
| | 6. Act in ways to create discipline problems |
| | 7. Have high dropout rates |
| | 8. Have poor personal and social adjustment |

In general, teachers who appear to enjoy teaching, who include great student-to-student interaction, shared decision making, and positive student-to-teacher interactions foster more positive self-concepts in students.[17]

Interestingly, your self-concept as a teacher has also been found to relate to student achievement. Hamachek[18] reported that pupils of teachers whose self-concepts were high demonstrated higher academic achievement than did pupils whose teachers' self-concepts were low.

Your concept of self can greatly affect your teaching effectiveness. Jersild,[19] a pioneer in emphasizing the importance of a teacher's self-concept, suggests that for teachers to be effective, they need positive attitudes about themselves. In support of this view, Combs[20] found that effective teachers could be distinguished from ineffective teachers on the basis of their attitudes toward themselves. According to Combs, good teachers have a positive self-image. They (1) see themselves as identified with people rather than withdrawn or apart from others; (2) feel basically adequate and generally able to cope with problems; (3) feel trustworthy, reliable, and dependable; (4) see themselves as wanted rather than unwanted and as likable and attractive (in a personal, not a physical sense); and (5) see themselves as worthy, as people of consequence and integrity.

Teachers who possess the qualities outlined by Combs—teachers with positive self-concepts—have a flexibility that allows them to foster pupil autonomy and accept pupil ideas. Without this freedom from "self," teachers cannot perceive or address the needs and concerns of their students.[21] Research by Klein[22] suggests that student reactions indeed influence teachers' self-concepts. She found that positive behavior (agreement, attentiveness, cooperation) on the part of students elicited positive behavior from teachers. Based on what we know about the relationship between self-concept and behavior, it's probable that teachers engaged in the positive behavior because they felt positive about themselves.

Not only does positive student behavior affect our self-concepts as teachers, but negative student behavior can also influence the way we feel about ourselves as teachers. Recently I began teaching a class in communication and socialization. I had never taught the class before and I was somewhat nervous. One student began to argue with me about the requirements for the course and became quite hostile. Perhaps because I was not completely confident about this new course, I left class questioning my ability to teach this course effectively. As teachers we all have days when we don't get positive reactions from students. Often when we receive negative reactions, we feel inadequate. At this point, it is necessary to honestly reevaluate our teaching techniques and skills. However, it's just as important to keep things in perspective and not overreact to unpleasant situations. As I reflected on the student's hostile behavior and reevaluated what I wanted to accomplish in the course on communication and socialization, I decided I had been correct in my choice of requirements for the course. One student's negative behavior had "thrown me" temporarily, but a reevaluation of myself and the situation convinced me I was still adequate as a teacher.

## ACTIVITY 2.1

Mark on the scales below how you perceive yourself as a teacher.

| | | |
|---|---|---|
| Expert | :___:___:___:___:___:___:___: | Inexpert |
| Unintelligent | :___:___:___:___:___:___:___: | Intelligent |
| Qualified | :___:___:___:___:___:___:___: | Unqualified |
| Boring | :___:___:___:___:___:___:___: | Interesting |
| Nervous | :___:___:___:___:___:___:___: | Poised |
| Calm | :___:___:___:___:___:___:___: | Anxious |
| Honest | :___:___:___:___:___:___:___: | Dishonest |
| Bad | :___:___:___:___:___:___:___: | Good |
| Kind | :___:___:___:___:___:___:___: | Cruel |
| Undependable | :___:___:___:___:___:___:___: | Dependable |
| Powerful | :___:___:___:___:___:___:___: | Powerless |
| Bold | :___:___:___:___:___:___:___: | Timid |
| Silent | :___:___:___:___:___:___:___: | Talkative |
| Aggressive | :___:___:___:___:___:___:___: | Meek |
| Organized | :___:___:___:___:___:___:___: | Disorganized |
| Awful | :___:___:___:___:___:___:___: | Nice |
| Unpleasant | :___:___:___:___:___:___:___: | Pleasant |
| Irritable | :___:___:___:___:___:___:___: | Good natured |
| Cheerful | :___:___:___:___:___:___:___: | Gloomy |

## ACTIVITY 2.2

### Directions

Bring an object to class that typifies how you perceive yourself as a teacher or as a prospective teacher. In a dyad, disclose to the other person why this object typifies your perception.

How does your view of yourself affect the communication in your classroom?

## Self-Disclosure

Self-disclosure—voluntarily telling others information about ourselves that they are unlikely to know or discover from other sources—is important in the development of relationships. If we're going to communicate effectively with our students, we need to know how they view themselves (their self-concepts). Likewise, if our students are going to communicate effectively with us, they need to know how we view ourselves. The only way to really know how students view themselves is through their self-disclosures. The underlying assumption of interpersonal communication is that the more we know about another, the more effective our communication will be.

Although the focus in this chapter will be on verbal self-disclosure, you should remember that we disclose about ourselves nonverbally as well as verbally. The clothes you wear, the way you walk, your smile, all communicate things about you—your likes and dislikes, your emotional states, and so forth. We'll discuss nonverbal communication in chapter 4.

The more information you have about how students view themselves, the better able you'll be to see the world through their eyes and thus better understand their responses to you, to other students, and to the instructional process.

### Effective Self-Disclosure

A major characteristic of effective self-disclosure is appropriateness. Knapp[23] suggests appropriateness is dependent on many factors. To be effective communicators, we will want to consider the timing of our disclosure, the other person's capacity to respond, the short-term effects, the motives for disclosure, how much detail is called for, whether the disclosure is relevant to the current situation, and the feelings of the other person as well as our own.

Another characteristic of self-disclosure is that it occurs incrementally. It's unlikely a student will come into your office following the first day of class and tell you anything very personal. In order to self-disclose, we have to trust the other person, and it takes time to build trust in a relationship. We must believe that the other person will not reject us, but will accept us for who we are. In addition, we must trust that they will respect the confidentiality of the information. As soon as someone violates our trust, self-disclosure stops, or decreases significantly.

Self-disclosure is reciprocal. We disclose to the people who disclose themselves to us. It's primarily up to the teacher to begin this reciprocal process. If we are willing to share ourselves with our students, they'll be more willing to share themselves with us. The effect of this reciprocity is that a more positive classroom atmosphere can be developed and effective communication will be enhanced.

### Factors Influencing Self-Disclosure

Numerous factors influence self-disclosure. Self-disclosure occurs more readily under some circumstances than others. For example, audience size affects self-disclosure. The smaller the number of people, the more likely self-disclosure will occur.

Usually people are more comfortable disclosing information about themselves in a dyadic relationship than in a more "public" setting, such as a small group. Powell,[24] in his book *Why Am I Afraid to Tell You Who I Am?* indicates why self-disclosure is "scary": But if I tell you who I am, you may not like who I am, and it is all that I have.

Remember our discussion of communication complexity—complexity increases with each additional person. The more people that are present, the harder it is to "monitor" people's reactions to our disclosures. What happens if some people in a small group are accepting us and others aren't? Do we continue to disclose or do we stop? The decision is difficult. Thus, students are more likely to disclose to us on a one-to-one basis. To request disclosures in any other context may be unwise.

Children disclose more than adolescents or adults.[25] Elementary school teachers learn some rather interesting (and unsolicited) information concerning a student's home life, likes and dislikes, fears, and so on. However, children learn to "temper" their disclosures, so that by the time students reach adolescence, they are fairly secretive.

Females disclose more than males.[26] Men have traditionally been seen as the stronger of the sexes physically as well as emotionally. Many men don't cry or reveal their feelings, since this would seem to show weakness. As traditional sex roles are reevaluated, this tendency may well begin to disappear.

Finally, race and nationality affect self-disclosure. White students have been found to disclose more information than Black students. U.S. students disclose more than similar groups in Puerto Rico, Great Britain, West Germany, or the Far East.[27]

What does all this information on self-disclosure have to do with classroom communication? We know that academic as well as social experiences during school have direct effects on self-concept development.[27] Nussbaum and Scott's[28] research suggests that students perceive teachers as intentionally and unintentionally revealing information about themselves in the classroom. These self-disclosures are linked to affective learning and teacher effectiveness. Holladay[29] asked students to recall self-disclosures by teachers. These self-disclosures were most often about the teachers' education, experience as teachers, family, friends, beliefs and opinions, leisure activities, and personal problems. Downs and her associates[30] investigated the extent to which teacher self-disclosures are a part of teachers' regular classroom behavior. Teachers' classes were audiotaped, and the researchers categorized the self-disclosive statements as to general topic (teacher education, teacher experience, family, friends/colleagues, beliefs/opinions, leisure activities, personal problems, other) and purpose (not relevant to course content, clarify course content, and promote discussion). Seventy percent of the self-disclosive messages were used to clarify course content and the general topic of the disclosures was most often related to teacher beliefs/opinions. The researchers also report data that suggests that moderate amounts of self-disclosive statements are most effective.

Javidi and Long[31] found that experienced teachers used self-disclosive statements more often than inexperienced teachers. The researchers suggest this is true because more experience (which may be related to increased familiarity with course content, refinement of syllabi, and decreased tension due to increased classroom teaching time) may positively affect the use of self-disclosure.

Sorensen[32] was interested in the relationship between a teacher's self-disclosive statements and students' perceptions of the instructor's competence. She gave students 150 statements and asked them to evaluate the likelihood that a good (or poor) teacher would disclose each statement in the classroom. Disclosure statements that were (1) positively worded and (2) expressed sentiments that referred to caring were perceived by students to be used by good teachers. (For example, "I care about my students" vs. "I do not like people who smile all the time.") If teachers use these types of disclosive statements, it can be expected that they will increase students' affective learning.

Finally, we know that award winning teachers self-disclose more than non-award winning teachers. Most of the self-disclosures of award winning teachers are concerned with teaching experiences and are related to course content.[33]

Research has clearly demonstrated that the attitudes teachers hold toward students affect the quality and quantity of communication teachers have with students.[34] In addition, students' behavior toward you can affect how you feel about yourself as a teacher. This "feeling" can, in turn, influence your teaching, which can influence student learning. Remember the systems perspective—each individual in the system affects every other individual. Two poems, one from the students' perspective[35] and one from the teacher's perspective,[36] indicate the systems perspective as it relates to self-concept:

> Teacher, give me back my "I"– – –!
> You promised, teacher,
> You promised if I was good you'd give it back.
> You have so many "I's" in the top drawer of your desk,
> You wouldn't miss mine.

> _____

> Do you love your teacher, children?
> Do you think I'm important?
> Do you think I'm best?
> Tell me boys and girls, tell me:
> Am I the fairest one of all? . . .

**ACTIVITY 2.3**

To what degree have the teachers of your classes revealed themselves to you so that you may communicate effectively with them?

To what degree have you revealed yourself to your teachers so they may communicate effectively with you?

## Perception

Why is it that in a class of 20 students and a teacher there can be 21 different perceptions or descriptions of that class? The answer is that we select, organize, and interpret the stimuli we gain through our senses into a meaningful picture of the world around us. This process is called perception and is the basis of our communication. In addition, our perceptions of others affect how we relate to them. W. V. Haney suggests, "We never really come into contact with reality. Everything we experience is a manufacture of our nervous system."[37] Haney indicates that what we perceive may not be reality. In other words, through symbolic interactions, each of us constructs his or her reality such that my reality is not necessarily the same as yours. However, I communicate from my reality and you communicate from yours. An experiment will make this idea clear.

Examine figure 2.2 on the next page. How old do you think the person is? Some people see a woman of twenty; some see a woman of eighty. Although this stimulus is the same for everyone, not everyone perceives similarly. Each person constructs his or her own reality.

### Differences in Perception

What causes these differences in perceptions? John Steinbeck suggests one reason in the following passage from *Travels with Charley:*

> *I've always admired those key reporters who can descend on an area, talk to key people, ask key questions, take samplings of opinions, and then set down an orderly report very much like a road map. I envy this technique and at the same time do not trust it as a mirror of reality. I feel that there are too many realities. What I set down here is true until someone else passes that way and rearranges the world in his own style. In literary criticism the critic has no choice but to make over the victim of his attention into something the size and shape of himself. So much there is to see, but our morning eyes describe a different world than do our afternoon eyes, and surely our wearied evening eyes can only report a weary evening world.*

*Figure 2.2 Testing Perception: A young woman or an old woman?*

Perception begins with our senses. Some people see better than others, hear better than others, smell better than others, and so forth. Our senses can make our perceptions different from other people's.

Steinbeck also suggests another limiting factor to our perceptions—differing internal states. How we feel, our past experience, our opinions, values, and beliefs can all affect our perceptions.

Finally, differing environments can affect our perceptions. A good example of this problem is the generation gap. Other examples include communication between the sexes, and interracial and cross-cultural communication. Because of differing environments, people may perceive people and/or events differently. In terms of teacher-student communication, the classroom is perceived differently by each person in it. Student teachers often comment, "Boy, it really gives you a different perspective when you're the teacher! I always thought teachers had it easy and only students worked!"

If communication is to be effective, we must be aware that our perceptions are not reality, but our view of reality. Haney suggests that perception can be equated with a window. This window is the only means by which we can see the world. Inherent in this analogy is the realization that the window has limitations (our senses, internal states, past experiences, environment, etc.), and that what we can see from our window is not exactly the same as what someone else can see from their window. The outside world may not be different, but our perceptions (our view through our window) may be different from other people's.

### The Process of Perception

How does this process of perception work? There are basically five steps in the process.

1.  We observe the available data in our environment.
2.  We choose what data we see/hear/feel/smell/taste and process it (selective perception).
3.  We define the person or event and build expectations of future behavior.
4.  Our expectations help determine our behavior toward the person.
5.  Our behavior affects the other person's perceptions.

Obviously, the data we select from all the available data is affected by our personal experiences, our psychological states, and our values. Selective perception in the classroom affects both teachers and students. We make judgments concerning students based on those perceptions and communicate accordingly. Students do the same. If either students or teachers "misperceive," or interpret reality differently, communication problems may result.

---

ACTIVITY 2.4                                          Teacher-Student Paradox[38]

*Objectives*

To increase your awareness of the impact that the roles of "teacher" and "student" have in shaping the communication process and to develop greater skills at bridging the gaps between "teachers" and "students."

*Procedure*

The instructor will divide the class into groups of five or six. As a group, select two people to act as "teachers" and one person to act as "observer." The rest of the group will act as "students." The "teachers" will be assigned a lesson to teach the students. During this process, the observer will fill out Form A, noting specific verbal and nonverbal cues on the part of the "teachers" and the "students."

1.  How did your perception of the roles of "student" and "teacher" affect your ability to communicate in this situation?
2.  Describe some barriers that currently exist between you and teachers (or students) in general. Analyze ways to overcome these barriers as you continue to communicate with your teachers (or students).

*Observer Form*

During the teaching activity, note specific verbal and nonverbal cues given by "teachers" and "students" that begin to erect barriers to the communication process.

| *Teachers* | *Students* |
|---|---|
| Examples of: | Examples of: |
| Teaching strategy that caused mistrust: | Response to teaching strategy used that caused mistrust: |
| Teaching strategy that improved trust: | Response to teaching strategy used that improved trust: |
| Nonverbal cues that helped or hindered communication: | Nonverbal cues that helped or hindered communication: |

---

Warr and Knapper[39] outline three components of perception—the attributive, the expectancy, and the affective. The attributive component consists of those characteristics we attribute to the person or object. These characteristics may or may not be present. However, based on our past experiences, we perceive them as being there. We may view students as hard-working, eager, and intelligent. Or, we may view them as lazy, unmotivated, and unintelligent.

The expectancy component consists of the expectations we have of the things we perceive. We expect a college professor to read different kinds of books than a construction worker. We also expect them to dress differently. Based on the characteristics you attribute to students, you'll expect certain behaviors. For example, if you view students as hard-working, eager, and intelligent, you'll expect them to complete assignments on time, get "As," and contribute to class discussions.

Finally, we have feelings about the objects and people we perceive—the affective component of perception. The feelings are derived from our past experiences with whatever we're perceiving, the characteristics we attribute to whatever we're perceiving, and from our expectations concerning whatever we're perceiving. If you have the first view of students presented above, you'll probably feel positively toward students. If you have the second view, you'll no doubt dislike students.

### Perceptions and Classroom Communication

Kelley[40] conducted an experiment that demonstrates how our perceptions can affect our classroom communication. Students were given a brief biographical note concerning a lecturer they were about to hear. Unknown to the students, half of them received this biographical note, "People who know him consider him to be a rather warm person, industrious, critical, practical, and determined." The other half of the class received this brief note, "People who know him consider him to be a rather cold person, industrious, critical, practical, and determined." Following the lecture, the lecturer left the room, and students were asked to evaluate him. Students who received the "warm" description perceived the lecturer as social, popular, and informal; those who received the "cold" description perceived the lecturer as formal and self-centered. Among those students receiving the "warm" description, 56 percent participated in classroom discussion. Only 32 percent of those students receiving the "cold" description participated. Thus, our perceptions of others can determine the kind of communication that takes place as well as how much communication takes place.

### Improving Perception Skills

The effective teacher knows that students are individuals bringing with them a multitude of perspectives. This leads to unpredictability in the classroom. As Shulman reminds us, "the uncertainties inherent in any simple act of tutoring are multiplied enormously as one attempts to teach a room full of 30 mindful bodies."[41] All students bring their own perceptions, and since the classroom is a system, the myriad of perceptions are interdependent.

As a teacher, it's imperative that you begin to improve your perception skills. The more accurate your perceptions, the more effective your communication. Perhaps the best way to improve your perception skills is to "look before you leap." The following excerpt from Sir Arthur Conan Doyle's Sherlock Holmes adventure, "A Scandal in Bohemia," emphasizes the importance of this suggestion. Dr. Watson relates:

> *I could not help laughing at the ease with which he explained his process of deduction. "When I hear you give your reasons, " I remarked, "the thing always appears to me to be ridiculously simple that I could easily do it myself, though at each successive instance of your reasoning I am baffled until you explain your process. And yet, I believe that my eyes are as good as yours.*
>
> *"Quite so, " he answered, lighting a cigarette, and throwing himself down into an armchair. "You see, but you do not observe. The distinction is clear. For example, you have frequently seen the steps which lead up from the hall to this room."*
>
> *"Frequently."*
>
> *"How often?"*
>
> *"Well, some hundreds of times."*
>
> *"Then how many are there?"*
>
> *"How many? I don't know."*
>
> *"Quite so! You have not observed. And yet you have seen. That is just my point. Now, I know that there are seventeen steps, because I have both seen and observed."*

Draw your conclusions based on the best evidence available. Remember that our perceptions should be conditional. We should be open to changing them as new evidence becomes available.

Make a commitment to "accurate" perception. Unless you really want to increase your perception skills, you never will. Making a commitment to "accurate" perception involves making a conscious effort to seek out all possible information. It means being open—allowing others to disclose themselves to you and being willing to disclose yourself to them, realizing that this disclosure adds information needed in order for you to perceive accurately. Making a commitment to "accurate" perception involves a willingness to expend the time such a commitment necessitates. It's much easier to make snap judgments than it is to hold off judgments until more information is gathered. The danger in snap judgments is illustrated in the following excerpt from Sunny Decker's *An Empty Spoon.*

> *It's not all that hard to do the right thing. But it takes so much effort to think of the kid first, especially when you really need to explode. Arthur Wesson sat in my class for a month and never opened his mouth.*

*One day when I was feeling ugly, I asked him a question about the book we were reading. He didn't say a word. I thought of all the things I should have done, but no—I had to get belligerent. I asked the question again. Then I waited for an interminable length of time. Nothing.*

*"If you can't answer when you're spoken to, you can leave."*

*I hated the way I sounded. But I was too wrapped up in my own frustration to cope with anything Arthur might feel. He left. And I had to find out from a far more patient teacher than I that there wasn't anything personal in the kid's apathy. He couldn't read. His mother was insane, and there was no place to send her. The two babies at home hadn't eaten in a couple of days. I was just a very small ugliness in Arthur Wesson's ugly world. At least he'd found someone in school he could cry to. Except for selfishness, it might have been me. Everytime I saw him, I hated myself all over again. I was too ashamed to look him in the eye.*[42]

---

**ACTIVITY 2.5**

Mark on the scales below how you think the ideal teacher should be perceived.

| | | | | | | | |
|---|---|---|---|---|---|---|---|
| Expert | : ____ | : ____ | : ____ | : ____ | : ____ | : ____ | : Inexpert |
| Unintelligent | : ____ | : ____ | : ____ | : ____ | : ____ | : ____ | : Intelligent |
| Qualified | : ____ | : ____ | : ____ | : ____ | : ____ | : ____ | : Unqualified |
| Boring | : ____ | : ____ | : ____ | : ____ | : ____ | : ____ | : Interesting |
| Nervous | : ____ | : ____ | : ____ | : ____ | : ____ | : ____ | : Poised |
| Calm | : ____ | : ____ | : ____ | : ____ | : ____ | : ____ | : Anxious |
| Honest | : ____ | : ____ | : ____ | : ____ | : ____ | : ____ | : Dishonest |
| Bad | : ____ | : ____ | : ____ | : ____ | : ____ | : ____ | : Good |
| Kind | : ____ | : ____ | : ____ | : ____ | : ____ | : ____ | : Cruel |
| Undependable | : ____ | : ____ | : ____ | : ____ | : ____ | : ____ | : Dependable |
| Powerful | : ____ | : ____ | : ____ | : ____ | : ____ | : ____ | : Powerless |
| Bold | : ____ | : ____ | : ____ | : ____ | : ____ | : ____ | : Timid |
| Silent | : ____ | : ____ | : ____ | : ____ | : ____ | : ____ | : Talkative |
| Aggressive | : ____ | : ____ | : ____ | : ____ | : ____ | : ____ | : Meek |
| Organized | : ____ | : ____ | : ____ | : ____ | : ____ | : ____ | : Disorganized |
| Awful | : ____ | : ____ | : ____ | : ____ | : ____ | : ____ | : Nice |
| Unpleasant | : ____ | : ____ | : ____ | : ____ | : ____ | : ____ | : Pleasant |
| Irritable | : ____ | : ____ | : ____ | : ____ | : ____ | : ____ | : Good natured |
| Cheerful | : ____ | : ____ | : ____ | : ____ | : ____ | : ____ | : Gloomy |

Compare the results of this questionnaire with the questionnaire results in Activity 2.1. What might you do to make yourself more like what you perceive the ideal teacher to be?

## SHARED LANGUAGE AND MEANING

*Each man lives within his own Tower of Babel. Forming the highest reaches is the myth through which he looks out on life. To evolve into something near his potential he must interlace this myth with the feelings which are his founda-tions—to let things reveal themselves to him, to "talk of their nature, and be able to respond to them, to answer." Yet he cannot do this alone. To know what he means he must talk and listen to others whose revelations are different.*

### Characteristics of Language

This quotation[43] suggests that we need language in order to communicate, but language can also be a barrier to communication. This paradox exists because language is symbolic. (Remember our discussion of this idea in chapter 1.) Words "stand for" or symbolize things; they are not the actual things. Words, therefore, can have several meanings. Consider the word *frog*, for example. What comes to your mind? A tailless amphibian? A hoarseness in your throat? A small holder placed in a vase to hold flower stems in position? An ornamental fastening for the front of a coat? A mass of elastic, horny substance in the middle of the sole of a horse's foot? It should be obvious that what you thought of when you heard the word *frog* may not be the same as what another person might think of.

---

**ACTIVITY 2.6**

Consider the words *student* and *teacher*. List as many meanings of these two words as you can. Compare your list of meanings with other students' lists in class.

---

Not only are words symbolic, they are also arbitrary. Words have no meaning in and of themselves. They derive their meaning from the people who use them. There is nothing inherent in a chair that necessitates us calling it by that name. We could call it anything we desire. Figure 2.3 illustrates the symbolic, arbitrary nature of words.[44]

A symbol (lower left-hand corner) is a word. The apex of the triangle is the thought—the concept you have of an object or event. The referent (lower right-hand corner) is the actual object. For example, you see a chair and say "chair." The word you speak is the symbol, the thought is your image of the chair, and the referent is the actual chair. Notice that the line connecting the symbol and the referent is broken. This indicates that the symbol and the referent have no connection except what you make in your mind—in your thoughts.

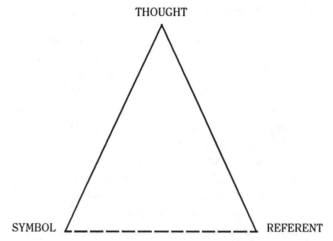

*Figure 2.3 The triangle of meaning.*

## Meanings and Perception

The symbolic and arbitrary nature of words suggests that words don't mean, people do. In other words, meanings are in people, not in words. Notice the confusion that can result because of this axiom of communication.

> *Here the Red Queen began again. "Can you answer useful questions?" she said. "How is bread made?"*
>
> *"I know that!" Alice cried eagerly. "You take some flour—."*
>
> *"Where do you pick the flower?" the White Queen asked. "In a garden or in the hedges?"*
>
> *"Well, it isn't picked at all," Alice explained, "it's ground—."*
>
> *"How many acres of ground?" said the White Queen. "You mustn't leave out so many things."*

We may tie this "meanings are in people" concept back to our discussion of the three components of perception. Our perceptions of things are influenced by the words we use to label them. If you are labeled a teacher, certain characteristics are attributed to you, certain behaviors are expected from you, and certain feelings are generated toward you. If you are labeled good, these characteristics, expectancies, and feelings will be different than if you are labeled bad. Remember, however, that your meaning for good and mine may not be the same, and our attributions, expectancies, and feelings about good teachers may differ because meanings differ. Thus, perception, language, and meaning are interdependent.

## General Semantics

When we discussed perception, we found it was impossible to focus on all the stimuli that bombard us; we have to zero in on certain stimuli if we are to make sense of our environment. Similarly, we must organize and order our language in order to classify things into general categories, thus helping make our world predictable. This is called the process of abstraction. For example, we classify some people into the category of student. We abstract from each of these people the characteristics they have in common. This abstraction notes the similarities and overlooks the differences among students. Based on this abstraction of student, we make predictions about what they might do to get an "A," how they'll behave during exams, and whether they are trustworthy.

However, abstraction can cause problems in interpersonal communication. We often overlook the differences in people and things simply because they fall into the same category. If we respond to the stereotype or the abstraction rather than to the person with whom we are trying to communicate, we can become very ineffective communicators.

General semanticists (people interested in how humans use their language and how language relates to behavior) present us with some devices to aid us in avoiding the dangers inherent in abstraction. The first device is called dating. A popular song of several years ago suggests the reason for dating—"The Times They Are 'A Changing." People, objects, events—everything is constantly changing. Thus, *you* in 1990 is not the same as *you* of 1970 or 2001. *Pam* 1985 is not *Pam* 1990. Even *Pam* 10:00 is not *Pam* 11:00. If you mentally attach a date to such statements as, "Pam is grouchy" (by saying "Pam is grouchy now"), you'll keep from assuming that Pam is always grouchy. You'll refrain from communicating as if people and events are static. Remember that one thing can be different at two different times.

Indexing is closely related to dating. Indexing helps us to account for individual differences. People, as well as objects and events, differ from one another. Thus, *Student 1* is not *Student 2*. If we index, we keep from making such generalizations as, "All students are lazy." If you've seen one, you haven't seen them all!

Both indexing and dating point to the fact that the verb *is* should be used with care. When we say *is*, we imply a static, unchanging phenomenon. This negates the concept that communication is a dynamic, continuous, and ever-changing process. There's a difference between saying, "That student is cheating," and "That student appears to be cheating." When we say that the student "is" cheating, we leave ourselves open for misevaluation.

Finally, the use of mental quotation marks reminds us that meanings are in people, not in words. When you say, "We're going to have a quiz on Tuesday," you may mean an evaluation instrument of fifty questions. Your students may think of a quiz as fifteen items. That difference in meaning could cause problems! If you use mental quotation marks—"quiz"—you'll be reminded that your students may need that term clarified.

The importance of perception, language, and meaning to teachers is perhaps best illustrated in the following poem:

*Frightened Students*

see
the frightened students
in a wilderness of words,
trying hard
to get the point,
pretending they have heard
the all-impressive symbols
that professors
love to sing
in well-intentioned monotones.
hear
the echoes ring
from the ivy-covered fortress
where the golden books
are stored
to tradition-coated
lecture halls
where students, ever bored
still
look intently back
into foggy, learned eyes

while
all the aged wisdom
of the great GOD of the skies
falls
around them
to confound them
and instruct their living span.
come in and learn
o little ones,
surely
you can understand
the way of love
well hidden here
underneath
the published text,
when will you
learn to live it
and
who will be the next
to graduate?[45]

---

**ACTIVITY 2.7**

*Directions*

Think about a communication problem or misunderstanding you've had with a teacher or student lately. Briefly describe the problem. How might your awareness and use of the techniques discussed here—dating, indexing, mental quotation marks, and using the word *is* sparingly—have helped in resolving the problem or avoiding it altogether?

## IN SUM

Teaching is not simply talking, just as learning is not simply listening. Rather teaching and learning involve a communication relationship. As a teacher you need to understand that self-concept, perception, language, and meaning are all integral parts of the communication process in the classroom. Hamachek, in an article entitled "Characteristics of Good Teachers and Implications for Teacher Education,"[46] reviews research suggesting that good teachers differ from poor teachers in the following five ways:

1. They have generally more positive views of others—students, colleagues, and administrators.
2. They are less prone to view others as critical, attacking people with ulterior motives; rather they see them as potentially friendly and worthy in their own right.
3. They have a more favorable view of democratic classroom procedures.
4. They have the ability and capacity to see things from the other's point of view.
5. They don't see students as persons "you do things to" but rather as individuals capable of doing for themselves once they feel trusted, respected, and valued.

Hamachek summarizes by saying that good teachers are able to communicate what they know in a way that makes sense to their students. They are good also because they view teaching as primarily a human process involving human relationships and human meanings.

## NOTES

1. C. Rogers, "The Interpersonal Relationship: The Core of Guidance," *Harvard Education Review* 32 (Fall 1962): 46.
2. J. Gibb, "Defensive Communication," *Interpersonal Dynamics*, ed. W. Bennis, E. Schein, F. Steele, and D. Berlew, 2nd ed. (Homewood, IL: Dorsey Press, 1967) 606.
3. See, for example, J. DiVito, *The Interpersonal Communication Book*, 4th ed. (New York: Harper and Row, 1986); J. DiVito, "Teaching as Relational Development," *Communicating in College Classrooms*, ed. J. Civikly (San Francisco: Jossey-Bass, 1986) 51-52; I. Altman and D. Taylor, *Social Penetration: The Development of Interpersonal Relationships* (New York: Holt, Rinehart and Winston, 1973); and M. Knapp, *Interpersonal Communication and Human Relationships* (Boston: Allyn and Bacon, 1984).
4. M. Knapp, 13-20.
5. G. Friedrich and P. Cooper, "First Day," *Teaching Communication: Methods, Research, and Theory*, ed. J. Daly, G.

Friedrich, and A. Vangelisti (Hillsdale, NJ: Erlbaum, 1990) 237–247.

6. P. Walsh, *Tales Out of School* (New York: Viking, 1986) 211.

7. Adapted from J. Kinch, "A Formalized Theory in Self-Concept," *American Journal of Sociology* 68 (January 1963): 481–486.

8. A. W. Combs, D. L. Avila, and W. W. Purkey, *Helping Relationships: Basic Concepts for the Helping Professions* (Boston: Allyn and Bacon, 1971) 39.

9. M. Maehr, J. Mansing, and S. Fafzger, "Concept of Self and the Reaction of Others," *Sociometry* 25 (1962): 353–357.

10. M. Webster and B. Sobieszek, *Sources of Self-Evaluation: A Formal Theory of Significant Others and Social Influence* (New York: John Wiley, 1974).

11. P. Cooper, L. Stewart, and W. Gundykunst, "Relationship with Instructor and Other Variables Influencing Evaluation of Instruction," *Communication Quarterly* 30 (Fall 1982): 308–315.

12. See R. Bassett and M. J. Smythe, *Communication and Instruction* (New York: Harper and Row, 1979) 30.

13. Bassett and Smythe, 31.

14. L. Mufson, J. Cooper, and J. Hall, "Factors Associated with Underachievement in Seventh Grade Children," *Journal of Educational Research* 83 (1989): 5–11.

15. H. Marshall and R. Weinstein, "Classroom Factors Affecting Students' Self Evaluations: An Interactional Model," *Review of Educational Research* 54 (1984): 301–325.

16. E. Cohen, *Design Group Work: Strategies for the Heterogeneous Classroom* (New York: Teachers College Press, 1987); and L. Nucci, "Knowledge of the Learner: The Development of Children's Concepts of Self, Morality and Societal Convention," *Knowledge Base for the Beginning Teacher*, ed. M. C. Reynolds (New York: Pergamon Press, 1989) 117–128.

17. Research reviewed in *Instructor* 99 (Feb. 1990): 39.

18. D. Hamachek, "Characteristics of Good Teachers and Implications for Teacher Education," *Learning to Teach in the Elementary School*, ed. H. Funk and R. Olberg (New York: Dodd, Mead and Co., 1975) 24–33.

19. A. T. Jersild, *When Teachers Face Themselves* (New York: Columbia University, 1955).

20. A. W. Combs, *The Professional Education of Teachers* (Boston: Allyn and Bacon, 1965) 70–71.

21. J. M. Civikly, "Self-Concept, Significant Others, and Classroom Communication," *Communication in the Classroom: Contemporary Theory and Practice*, ed. L. Barker (Englewood Cliffs, NJ: Prentice Hall) 146–168.

22. S. Klein, "Student Influence on Teacher Behavior," *American Educational Research Journal* 8 (1971): 403–421.

23. M. L. Knapp, *Interpersonal Communication and Human Relationships* (Boston: Allyn and Bacon, 1984), 13.

24. J. Powell, *Why Am I Afraid to Tell You Who I Am?* (Niles, IL: Argus, 1969) 20.

25. See research reviewed in L. Stewart, A. Stewart, P. Cooper, and S. Friedley, *Communication Between the Sexes*, 2nd ed. (Scottsdale, AZ: Gorsuch Scarisbrick, 1990).

26. See research reviewed in DeVito, *The Interpersonal Communication Book*, 4th ed. (New York: Harper and Row, 1986).

27. E. Pascarella, J. Smart, C. Ethington, and M. Nettles, "The Influence of College in Self-Concept: A Consideration of Race and Gender Differences," *American Educational Research Journal* 24 (Spring 1987): 49–77.

28. J. Nussbaum and M. Scott, "The Relationship among Communicator Style, Perceived Self-Disclosure, and Classroom Learning," *Communication Yearbook 3*, ed. D. Nimmo (New Brunswick, NJ: Transaction Books, 1979) 561–584; J. Nussbaum and M. Scott, "Student Learning as Relational Outcome of Teacher-Student Interaction," *Communication Yearbook 4*, ed. D. Nimmo (New Brunswick, NJ: Transaction Books, 1980) 533–552.

29. S. J. Holladay, "Student and Teacher Perception of Teacher Self-Disclosure," master's thesis, U of Oklahoma, 1984.

30. V. Downs, M. Javidi, and J. Nussbaum, "An Analysis of Teachers' Verbal Communication within the College Classroom: Use of Humor, Self-Disclosure, and Narratives," *Communication Education* 37 (April 1988): 127–141.

31. M. Javidi and L. Long, "Teachers' Use of Humor, Self-Disclosure, and Narrative Activity as a Function of Experience," *Communication Research Reports* 1 (1989): 47–52.

32. G. Sorensen, "The Relationship Among Teachers' Self-Disclosive Statements, Students' Perceptions, and Affective Learning," *Communication Education* 38 (July 1989): 259–276.

33. M. Javidi, V. Downs, and J. Nussbaum, "A Comparative Analysis of Dramatic Style Behaviors at Higher and Secondary Educational Levels," *Communication Education* 37 (Oct. 1988): 278–288.

34. T. Good and J. Brophy, "Behavioral Expression of Teachers' Attitudes," *Journal of Educational Psychology* 63 (1972): 617–624.

35. A. Cullum, *The Geranium on the Window Sill Just Died But Teacher You Went Right On* (New York: Quist Press, 1978) 52.

36. A. Cullum, *Blackboard, Blackboard on the Wall Who Is the Fairest One of All?* (New York: Quist Press, 1978) 52.

37. W. V. Haney, *Communication and Organizational Behavior: Text and Cases* (Homewood, IL: Richard D. Irwin, 1967) 51–77.

38. Reprinted from J. E. Jones and J. W. Pfeiffer, eds., *The 1973 Annual Handbook for Group Facilitators* (San Diego, CA: University Associates, 1973). Used with permission.

39. P. B. Warr and C. Knapper, *The Perception of People and Events* (New York: John Wiley and Sons, 1968).

40. H. Kelley, "The Warm-Cold Variable in First Impressions of Persons," *Journal of Personality* 18 (1950): 433.

41. L. Shulman, "The Wisdom of the Practitioner," *Talk to Teachers*, ed. D. Berliner and B. Rosenshine (New York: Random House, 1987) 382.

42. S. Decker, *An Empty Spoon* (New York: Harper and Row, 1969) 79–80.

43. C. Brown and P. Keller, *Monologue to Dialogue* (Englewood Cliffs, NJ: Prentice Hall, 1979) 133–134.

44. C. K. Ogden and I. A. Richards, *The Meaning of Meaning* (New York: Harcourt Brace, and London, Routledge and Kegan Paul, 1927) 11.

45. B. Comeau, *Fragments from an Unknown Gospel* (Boston: United Church Press, 1970) 72–73.

46. Hamachek, "Characteristics of Good Teachers," 341–345.

## SUGGESTIONS FOR FURTHER READING

Beane, J. A., and R. P. Lipka. *Self-Concept, Self-Esteem, and the Curriculum.* Wolfeboro, NH: Teachers College Press, 1986.

Brousseau, B., C. Book, and J. Byers. "Teacher Beliefs and the Culture of Teaching." *Journal of Teacher Education* (Nov./Dec. 1988): 33–40.

Byrne, B. M., and R. J. Shavelson. "Adolescent Self-Concept: Testing the Assumption of Equivalent Structure Across Gender." *American Educational Research Journal* 24(3) (Fall 1987): 365–385.

Canfield, J., and H. Wells. *100 Ways to Enhance Self-Concept in the Classroom.* Englewood Cliffs, NJ: Prentice Hall, 1974.

East, P. L. "Early Adolescents' Perceived Interpersonal Risks and Benefits: Relations to Social Support and Psychological Functioning." *Journal of Early Adolescence* 9(4) (Nov. 1989): 374–395.

Furman, E. "What Is a Good Teacher?" *Instructor* (Feb. 1990): 18.

Hurt, H. T., and T. Gonzalez. "Communication Apprehension and Distorted Self-Disclosure: The Hidden Disabilities of Hearing Impaired Students." *Communication Education* 37 (April 1988): 106–117.

McCroskey, J. C., and J. A. Daly, eds. *Personality and Interpersonal Communication*. New York: Sage, 1987.

Marsh, H. W. "Verbal and Math Self-Concepts: An Internal/External Frame of Reference Model." *American Educational Research Journal* 23(1) (Spring 1986): 129–149.

Nussbaum, J. F., M. E. Comadena, and S. J. Holladay. "Classroom Verbal Behavior of Highly Effective Teachers." *Journal of Thought* 22 (1987): 73–80.

O'Keefe, P., and M. Johnston. "Perspective Taking and Teacher Effectiveness: A Connecting Thread Through Three Developmental Literatures." *Journal of Teacher Education* 40(3) (1989): 20–26.

Petronio, S., J. Martin, and R. Littlefield. "Prerequisite Conditions for Self-Disclosing: A Gender Issue." *Communication Monographs* 51 (1984): 268–273.

Powell, R., and R. Arthur. "Perceptions of Affective Communication and Teaching Effectiveness at Different Times During the Semester." *Communication Quarterly* 33 (1985): 254–261.

Rubin, R., and J. Feezel. "Elements of Teacher Communication Competence." *Communication Education* 35 (July 1986): 254–268.

Rubin, R., and J. Feezel. "Teacher Communication Competence: Essential Skills and Assessment Procedures." *The Central States Speech Journal* 36 (Spring/Summer 1985): 4–13.

Sparks, G. "Research on Teacher Effectiveness: What It All Means." *Perspectives on Effective Teaching and the Cooperative Classroom*. Ed. J. Reinhertz. Washington, D.C.: National Education Association, 1984. 8–13.

Spitzberg, B., and T. Hurt. "The Measurement of Interpersonal Skills in Instructional Contexts." *Communication Education* 36 (Jan. 1987): 28–48.

Wheeless, V. E., W. R. Zakahi, and M. B. Chan. "A Test of Self-Disclosure Based on Perceptions of a Target's Loneliness and Gender Orientation." *Communication Quarterly* 36(2) (Spring 1988): 109–121.

# 3 LISTENING

## OBJECTIVES

After reading this chapter and completing the activities, you should be able to:

- Define listening
- Designate reasons why good listening is important
- List, define, and provide examples of three types of listening
- Discuss the barriers to effective listening
- Discuss active listening
- Improve your own listening skills

## INTRODUCTION

Ms. Sawyer is lecturing to her students about the fall of the Roman Empire. The students know this is an important lecture. The information is not available in the text, and Ms. Sawyer has indicated the information will be included in the unit exam.

One of Ms. Sawyer's students, Rosa, has had a difficult week. She has problems at home and she just found out she did not make the list of finalists for a scholarship. Rosa is certain she has an "A" in Ms. Sawyer's class and that she doesn't need to worry about the upcoming exam. In addition, the room is hot and stuffy.

Rosa begins by trying to concentrate on Ms. Sawyer's lecture. However, as Ms. Sawyer lectures, Rosa begins to daydream, mentally planning what she needs to get done this weekend.

Suddenly, Rosa is jolted back to the present when Ms. Sawyer asks her to summarize the major points of the lecture.

---

### ACTIVITY 3.1

Discuss the following:
1.  What is the basic problem in this situation?
2.  What circumstances caused the problem to occur?
3.  How could the communication problem have been prevented or minimized?
4.  What can be done to remedy the situation as it now stands?
5.  What could Ms. Sawyer and Rosa do to prevent this type of situation from recurring?

---

Obviously, Rosa has been "caught in the act" of not listening. She, like many of us, needs to improve her listening skills. In this chapter, we will discuss not only methods of improving our listening, but also the importance of listening, types of listening, and barriers to effective listening. Before beginning our discussion, check your knowledge of listening by completing the short questionnaire in Activity 3.2.

---

### ACTIVITY 3.2

Mark each statement "true" or "false."

|  | *True* | *False* |
|---|---|---|
| 1.  Listening is the same as hearing. | _____ | _____ |
| 2.  Listening is a natural activity and therefore cannot be taught. | _____ | _____ |
| 3.  Listening is a basically concealed, internal activity. | _____ | _____ |
| 4.  In the communication process, talking is more important than listening. | _____ | _____ |
| 5.  The average person spends more time talking than listening. | _____ | _____ |

If you answered false to all these statements, you have a better idea of what listening involves than most people do. If you answered true to any of these statements, don't feel that you're alone. Most people have some misconceptions about listening. These misconceptions can greatly affect our effectiveness as listeners and, therefore, should be eliminated.

## WHAT IS LISTENING?

*Student:* What do you mean the unit test is today? I thought you said it was Friday! We always have unit tests on Fridays!

*Teacher:* As we discussed last week, the test is today because we have an assembly scheduled during this period on Friday. I know you heard me explain that!

The teacher involved in this conversation is operating under the misconception that hearing and listening are the same activity. However, listening is much more than just hearing. Hearing is only the first step in the listening process—the physical step when sound waves hit your eardrums. After hearing sounds, three more steps must be completed before the listening process is complete—the interpretation of the sound waves (leading to understanding or misunderstanding), the evaluation of what was heard (when you decide how you'll use the information), and finally, the response step (reacting to what you heard).

Listening, then, is a four-step process. If any of the four steps is not completed, effective listening has not occurred. There are no shortcuts to effective listening. It is an active, difficult, time-consuming activity.

## THE IMPORTANCE OF LISTENING

Why is effective listening important? First of all, we spend a great deal of time listening.[1] Research demonstrates that 70 percent of our waking time is spent in participating in some form of communication.[2] Of that time, 11 percent is spent writing, 15 percent reading, 32 percent talking, and 42 to 57 percent listening.

Interestingly, although listening is the type of communication we engage in the most and learn first, it is the skill we are taught the least. The following chart shows the order in which we learn the four types of communication, the degree to which we use them, and the extent to which we are taught how to perform them:[3]

|         | Listening | Speaking   | Reading   | Writing |
|---------|-----------|------------|-----------|---------|
| Learned | 1st       | 2nd        | 3rd       | 4th     |
| Used    | 45%       | 30%        | 16%       | 9%      |
| Taught  | Least     | Next least | Next most | Most    |

In the classroom, listening is the main channel of instruction. Estimates of the amount of time students are expected to listen range from 53 to 90 percent of their communication time.[4] When such a large portion of time is spent listening, ineffective listening can be quite costly to students. Research suggests that most of us are inefficient listeners, retaining only about 20 percent of what we hear.[5]

Finally, listening is important because it is a survival skill. For example, in the business community, listening is cited as one of the top ten skills necessary for effective performance.[6] We acquire knowledge, develop language, increase our communication ability (the good listener is also a good speaker), and increase our understanding of ourselves and others through listening. Listening, then, is an important skill to develop and improve since we cannot be effective in our relationships or our professions without it.

---

**ACTIVITY 3.3**                                                  **Listening Log**

Maintain a communication log for one day. Construct a time chart divided into fifteen-minute intervals. Code your communication as speaking (S), writing (W), reading (R), and listening (L). If you engage in more than one type of communication during a fifteen-minute interval, code that interval according to the type of communication you engaged in the majority of the time. At the end of the day, tabulate the percentage of time you spent in each type of communication. What do your results tell you about the importance of listening?

|  | *Percentage* |
|---|---|
| Reading | _____ |
| Writing | _____ |
| Speaking | _____ |
| Listening | _____ |

---

## TYPES OF LISTENING

There are basically three types of listening—appreciative, informative, and therapeutic. However, these categories are not mutually exclusive. We may engage in all three in any given communicative situation.

We engage in appreciative listening when we listen for enjoyment. We may simply want to gain a sensory impression of the tone, mood, or style of another person. For example, we've all heard teachers or speakers we like to listen to because their voices are pleasant or because they are stylistically unique.

Much of the listening we do is informative listening. Whenever we listen to gain and comprehend information, discriminate between fact and opinion, or evaluate whether to accept or reject ideas, we are engaging in informative listening. Obviously, this type of listening is particularly important in the classroom. Errors in informative listening can be extremely detrimental to classroom learning.

The final type of listening is therapeutic. In this type of listening we are listening for the feelings of another person. Often we are simply sounding boards; people say, "Thank you for listening. I guess I just needed someone to talk to." Thus, in therapeutic listening we may not be asked to provide any service other than just listening. This should indicate how important listening is. And when we need someone to listen to us, how grateful we are when that person gives us the full attention we seek.

As we become more familiar with students we will find ourselves increasingly utilizing therapeutic listening. I remember a high school student who came to me for some personal advice on a problem she was having at home. She talked and talked. I probably said ten words. Suddenly, she jumped up and said, "Thanks, Ms. Cooper, for all your help. I know now what I need to do!" She had thought through her problem and had come to a solution with no other input from me except that I was willing to let her verbalize her thoughts and feelings.

## BARRIERS TO EFFECTIVE LISTENING

It's no wonder most of us are poor listeners. The factors that keep us from listening as effectively and efficiently as we could are numerous. These factors fall within four major categories: factual distractions, semantic distractions, mental distractions, and physical distractions.

### Factual Distractions

Factual distractions occur because we listen for facts rather than for the main ideas and feelings behind the message. As a result, we fail to integrate what we hear into a whole, or lose sight of "the big picture." Students sometimes have a problem pulling together facts into a coherent whole, particularly in essay exams, because they listen for facts but fail to analyze how the facts fit together. The same problem often occurs when students take notes. Thus, repeating only the main points of our lectures can help students integrate facts into a complete framework.

## Semantic Distractions

Semantic distractions occur when the other person uses unfamiliar terminology or when we react emotionally to words or phrases. Both of these semantic distractions result from the fact that meanings are in people, not words.

The following exchange illustrates the confusion that can result if someone is using a term in a manner unfamiliar to you:

### What Did You Knott Say?

Hello, who's speaking?
*This is Watt.*
I'm sorry. What's your name?
*Yes, Watt's my name.*
Is this a joke? What is your name?
*John Watt.*
John What?
*Yes. Look, who's this? Are you Jones?*
No, I'm Knott.
*Will you tell me who you are?*
Will Knott.
*Why not?*
My name is Knott.
*Not What?* [7]

## Mental Distractions

In addition, when we hear words that carry emotional overtones for us, our anger, frustration, or resentment can impair our ability to listen. For some students, the word *math* has a negative connotation. If students have not done well in math, they may continue to fail because they feel failure is inevitable and therefore they do not listen in class.

Mental distractions result from intrapersonal factors. One form of mental distraction occurs when we focus on ourselves. We may be formulating what we will say when it's our turn to speak; we may be engrossed in our own problems or needs; we may be concentrating on our own goals and plans; we may be simply daydreaming.

Mental distractions can also occur when we focus on the other person, allowing our preconceived attitudes toward the other to prematurely determine the value of what the person is saying. For example, we often listen more closely and with more interest to those we perceive as attractive. If the person belongs to a group we value, we may listen more closely and more positively. Other nonverbal factors such as vocal cues can also affect our listening.

Most of us stereotype others at sometime or another. Often we aren't as tolerant of those who fit a stereotype we don't value. For example, if I stereotype a student as a "low-level" student, and I don't find any value to students with low academic ability, I will be reluctant to listen to the student's ideas. To be effective listeners, we have to consciously "unteach" ourselves prejudices and stereotypes—or at least understand that they may be affecting the extent to which we are willing to listen to others.

Finally, focusing on the status of the other person can cause a mental distraction that keeps us from listening. Sometimes we fail to listen critically to those we view as of a higher status. The ideas of a teacher may be accepted simply because he is an "expert." Similarly, we rarely listen to those we perceive as having lower status. "Jane received a 'D' last term. She doesn't really understand this material. Let's ask Maria for help. I think she got an 'A' last term."

## Physical Distractions

The final barrier to listening—physical distractions—can take many forms. The color of the room, the time of day, uncomfortable clothing, and noises can all be physical distractions that interfere with your ability to listen.

---

**ACTIVITY 3.4**                                    **Analyzing Barriers to Listening**

Return to the case study presented at the beginning of this chapter. Analyze the barriers to listening—factual, semantic, mental, and physical—that Ms. Sawyer and Rosa encountered.

---

## IMPROVING LISTENING SKILLS

There are several behaviors that can help you improve your listening skills. Some are fairly easy to master. Others will take a great deal of effort on your part. However, all of them can help you increase your listening proficiency.

The first suggestion for improving listening is to remove, if possible, the physical barriers to listening. You might simply move to another room, or move the furniture in the room, turn the thermostat up or down, or close the door to your classroom. Manipulate your environment to fit your needs.

The second suggestion is to focus on the speaker's main idea. You can always request specific facts and figures later. Your initial purpose as a listener should be to answer the question: What is this person's main idea? Third, listen for the intent, as well as the content, of the message. Ask yourself: Why is this person saying this?

Fourth, give the other person a full hearing. Don't begin your evaluation until you've listened to the entire message. When a student tells you that his homework is not finished, allow the student to complete his explanation before you respond. Too often as listeners we spend our listening time creating our messages rather than concentrating on the content and intent of the other's message.

Fifth, remember the adage that meanings are in people, not in words. Ask for clarification when necessary. Try to overcome your emotional reactions to words. Focus on what you can agree with in the other's message and use this as common ground as you move into more controversial issues.

Finally, concentrate on the other person as a communicator and as a human being. All of us have our own ideas, and we have deep feelings about those ideas. Listen with all your senses, not just with your ears. The old admonition to "stop, look, and listen" is an excellent one to follow when listening. Focus on questions such as: What does she mean verbally? nonverbally? What's the feeling behind the message? Is this message consistent with those she has expressed in previous conversations? Perhaps the following poem summarizes this suggestion best:

### He Came to Me

He came for a large gift,
but he came to me.
Yes, a large gift, but I had it to give,
for he asked for that
which all men have to give,
the gift of attention.
And he came to me!
He wanted "a little hunk of life,"
my life.

I gave him only half a gift,
for I was only partly present to him.
My thoughts wandered, my attention wavered;
I made other plans, I looked past him,
I ran ahead and away from him,
I wanted him to leave!
I wonder if he knew how I robbed him that day,
cheated him, betrayed him in his trust.
I wonder, is he hungry still?
I can only say, Good Lord, forgive.
Forgive, and grant me a "next time."[8]

**ACTIVITY 3.5**                                    **Improving Your Listening Skills**

Consider a recent classroom transaction in which you engaged in poor listening. Briefly describe the communication transaction, the listening skills you used, and what you could have done to eliminate your poor listening behavior.

*Description of communication transaction:*

*People involved:*

*Topic:*

*Environment in which transaction took place:*

*The listening skills you used:*

*Ways to improve your listening in this transaction:*

## ACTIVE LISTENING

The process of listening isn't completed until you have made some active response—verbal and/or nonverbal—to the other person. Your response can have an important impact on the communication climate.

**ACTIVITY 3.6**

Think of someone who is a good listener. What characteristic does that person possess?

*Characteristics of a Good Listener*

1.

2.

3.

4.

5.

No doubt somewhere on your list in Activity 3.6 is a characteristic that relates to the person's ability to demonstrate that he is truly interested in you. One of the ways another person demonstrates this interest is through *active response*.

The concept of active listening has been around for a number of years. The main idea of active listening is that the listener must get involved in the communication transaction. In other words, listening is not passive; rather, it is as active and behavioral as speaking. And, of course, the primary indicator of active listening is active responding.

Two methods of active response are paraphrasing and perception checking. Both methods can help you make certain that what you heard was actually what the other person meant.

## Paraphrasing

Paraphrasing is a restatement of both the content and the feelings of another person's message. It is not, however, simply parroting another's words. Often, understanding a speaker's feelings is even more important to understanding her message than simply comprehending the actual words spoken. Thus, paraphrasing restates both the content and the feeling components of the message.

Suppose a student says to you, "I don't see how I can possibly finish this report by tomorrow. I have two major tests tomorrow. Boy, I've really gotten myself into a bind." Your paraphrase might be something like, "It sounds like things are really hectic for you and you feel frustrated."

If paraphrasing sounds trite, uncomfortable, or clumsy to you, keep in mind two important ideas: (1) Anytime you learn a new skill, it initially feels funny. Remember how clumsy you felt when you first were learning to ride a bike? Remember, also, that with practice, riding a bike became easier and very natural. The same is true of paraphrasing. The more you practice and utilize the skill, the easier it will become. (2) Paraphrasing is not always appropriate or necessary. If someone says to you, "Wow, what fantastic weather!" there's no need for paraphrasing. Paraphrasing should be used to help you avoid confusion and misunderstanding. The overuse of the paraphrasing technique is just as detrimental to effective communication as its underuse.

---

**ACTIVITY 3.7**                                    **Paraphrasing Practice**

To help you become more comfortable with paraphrasing, write paraphrasing responses for the following situations:

"I really feel uncomfortable talking to large groups of people. I wonder if I could get Mr. Amtson to let me present my speech for him alone rather than for the entire class."

"I really hate this school. Everyone here tells me what to do. I don't have any freedom."

## Perception Checking

A second technique of active responding is perception checking. Perception checking is similar to paraphrasing—both seek to clarify the speaker's meaning. But a perception check, unlike paraphrasing, is not limited to the last utterance of the speaker. Perception checking refers to behavior over an extended period of time.

A perception check consists of stating three ideas: (1) sensory data that describes what you have heard and seen to lead to your conclusion, (2) the conclusion you've drawn, and (3) a question that asks the other person whether your conclusion is accurate.

Suppose you are a science teacher and one of your students has, for the past week, been late for class every day, been extremely disruptive, and failed to hand in homework. You have decided to call the student into your office to talk. How might you use perception checking?

You might say, "Martin, I am aware that you've been late every day this week, you have ridiculed other students when they answer questions, and your work has not been up to par. I suspect all this might mean you are having a problem—either with this class or at home. Is there any truth to that?"

The basic purpose of perception checking is to clarify our perceptions of another's thoughts, feelings, or intentions. Since it's impossible to communicate with others without making some inferences, it's important that we check out those inferences in order to make our communication as effective as possible.

---

**ACTIVITY 3.8**                    **Teaching Students to Listen to Teacher Talk**

Read the following article. Discuss with your classmates whether or not Bozik's suggestions would be helpful.

When working to develop student listening skills, one area worthy of special attention is teaching students to listen to teacher talk. Lessons are more meaningful if they relate to real-life situations in students' lives. Preparing students to be successful in-class listeners provides clear motivation for student learning and an opportunity for immediate and relevant application.

Effective comprehensive listening requires that listeners ask themselves questions. By learning to ask the right questions, students can be taught to anticipate the type of evaluation the teacher may use and thus make a more accurate assessment of what materials need to be remembered and studied. Any questions that cannot be easily answered should prompt the student to ask the teacher a question.

Encourage students to ask themselves the following questions when listening to a lecture or other teacher presentation. Use your own lectures to demonstrate the technique, stopping to discuss how the questions relate to what you are saying. For example, stop occasionally to ask the class, "What idea am I talking about now?" Discuss how students can phrase and ask appropriate questions if the answer to any of the questions is, "I don't know." Teach students that teachers are usually pleased to be asked questions and view them as a sign of student interest and desire to learn.

### Questions and Comments

1.  What is the teacher talking about? Keep reminding yourself what the topic is. If you can't easily answer the question, raise your hand and ask, "Can you remind me what topic this relates to?"

2.  What is the main idea? The teacher has something to say about the topic; keep focusing on the message. If in doubt, ask, "What is the main thing we should remember about this?"

3.  What ideas or details has the teacher said two or more times? Repetition is one technique teachers use to emphasize important concepts and to be sure students understand important ideas and information. These are items that are most likely to be on tests.

4.  When does the teacher stop to ask if there are any questions? Asking for questions usually indicates the teacher is particularly concerned you understand the material just presented. This material is likely to appear on a test.

5.  What is an example of the idea the teacher is talking about? Teachers often give examples; write these in your notes. If you cannot think of an example, ask the teacher for one. Asking for examples is a common test item.

6.  How does what the teacher is talking about relate to yesterday's topic? You should see a connection between the two topics; there may be none, but that would be rare. If you cannot state to yourself how the two ideas are related, ask the teacher, "How does this relate to what we talked about yesterday?"

7.  How does this topic relate to the course subject? Remind yourself of the connection between the small idea of today's class and the big idea of the course. For example, "What do 'causes of the Civil War' have to do with American History?"

8. What did I learn today? Review in your mind what was new to you. Things you already know, you will remember. New material will require study.

9. If I were the teacher, what would I ask on a test? You might write a few test questions at the end of your notes. For example, "Name four causes of the Civil War." Put a star next to likely test material in your notes. Do the same for material on handouts.

By learning to listen carefully and think about the relationship between the lecture and the evaluation, students can begin to study immediately and prepare themselves for successful performance on a test or other evaluation tool.

By Mary Bozik. From Pamela Cooper, ed. *Teacher Talk*, vol. 7 (Spring 1989): 2.

---

**ACTIVITY 3.9**                                    **Teachers, Evaluate Yourselves**

Check the box below that most accurately describes your behavior for each statement.

| | Frequency | | | | Evaluation | |
|---|---|---|---|---|---|---|
| | Always | Sometimes | Seldom | Never | I am satisfied | I need to improve in this area |
| *As a Planner:* | | | | | | |
| 1. I realize students have difficulty listening attentively for long periods of time. | | | | | | |
| 2. I plan my sequence of learning activities with variety so that listening is a pleasant and not overly lengthy task. | | | | | | |
| 3. I plan my presentation carefully so students listen to one thing at a time. | | | | | | |
| 4. My instructions are planned with clarity so students can easily understand them. | | | | | | |
| 5. My explanations are carefully, clearly, and concisely given. | | | | | | |

*(Continued)*

| | Frequency | | | | Evaluation | |
|---|:---:|:---:|:---:|:---:|:---:|:---:|
| | Always | Sometimes | Seldom | Never | I am satisfied | I need to improve in this area |
| 6. I plan more than one way to say something, so if students do not understand the first time, I am prepared with an alternative. | | | | | | |
| 7. I plan some times during the day when students may individually talk with me. | | | | | | |
| 8. I work to establish a rapport that encourages oral sharing and listening. | | | | | | |
| *As a Presenter:* | | | | | | |
| 1. I encourage good listening by limiting the amount of talking I do. | | | | | | |
| 2. I use changes in pitch, tempo, and volume when speaking. | | | | | | |
| 3. I manipulate these paralinguistic elements to hold the student's attention. | | | | | | |
| 4. I consciously use kinesics (body movement and gestures) to add richness to my speech. | | | | | | |
| 5. I give students time to think when I ask a question. I endure some "empty spaces" while students cope with the verbal problem I have presented. | | | | | | |
| 6. Silence doesn't threaten me, so I don't feel I have to fill it up with talk. | | | | | | |
| 7. I wait to get the attention of all the students before I begin to speak. | | | | | | |
| 8. I have eye contact with the majority of the listeners before I begin to speak. | | | | | | |
| 9. I remember to give some positive responses to each speaker *without needlessly summarizing or paraphrasing* what she or he has said. | | | | | | |
| 10. I make sure that when only one student has difficulty understanding, I clarify for that individual later rather than interrupting the train of thought. | | | | | | |

*(Continued)*

| | Frequency | | | | Evaluation | |
|---|---|---|---|---|---|---|
| | Always | Sometimes | Seldom | Never | I am satisfied | I need to improve in this area |
| 11. My speech is free of repeated expressions or phrases that are unnecessary or offensive. (Common among teachers are "You know...," "Listen...," "Are you ready?" "Get out your books," "Pass your papers to the right," and so on.) | | | | | | |
| 12. I listen attentively to students when they talk and express my interest and appreciation in what they say. | | | | | | |
| 13. I show that what students say is important to me and should be important to others. | | | | | | |
| 14. I try not to get into the habit of needlessly repeating what I say. | | | | | | |

Adapted from J. W. Stewig, *Exploring Language with Children* (Charles E. Merrill, Columbus, 1974) 107-108.

## IN SUM

Listening is an active process. It requires practice and concentration. Since it is a process in which you spend a great deal of time, it's important to do it well. As one author suggests, "A failure to listen probably creates more interpersonal problems than any aspect of human behavior."[9] As a teacher, try to adhere to the following "Code for Listening" in order to avoid interpersonal problems and foster a supportive communication climate in your classroom.

## Code for Listening

As a teacher I shall:

1. be a good listener myself
2. use a classroom voice that is relaxed, unhurried, and nonthreatening
3. use sincere, varied, expressive facial expressions that will promote accurate listening
4. get everyone's attention before speaking
5. teach students that directions and instructions will be given only once

6.  not repeat a student's contributions, answers, or remarks but encourage students to listen to each other

7.  ask questions that require more than "yes," "no," or other short answers

8.  take time to listen to my pupils before and after school as well as in school

9.  create an emotional and physical atmosphere conducive to good listening

10. establish with my students the purpose for which they should listen to each activity

11. be well prepared for the material to be taught or the activity to be directed

12. vary my classroom program to include a variety of listening experiences such as sound films, discussions, individual and group reports, dramatic activities and demonstrations

13. teach my students the value and importance of good listening

14. build a program in which listening skills are consistently taught and practiced: for example, by interpreting unknown words through context, noting details, finding main and subordinate ideas, evaluating an expressed point of view in relation to facts or propaganda, and making valid inferences

15. teach my students to form desirable listening habits: for example, disregarding distractions and mannerisms of speakers, exercising mental curiosity about what is heard, and being courteous to speakers by looking for something interesting about speaker and subject.

## NOTES

1.  R. Rubin and C. Roberts, "A Comparative Examination and Analysis of Three Listening Tests," *Communication Education* 36 (1987): 142–153; T. Murray and J. Swartz, "Now Hear This . . .," *Teaching K–8* (Feb. 1989): 58–60; and D. Winn, "Developing Listening Skills as a Part of the Curriculum," *The Reading Teacher* (Nov. 1988): 144–149.

2.  L. Barker, *Listening Behavior* (Englewood Cliffs, NJ: Prentice Hall, 1971) 3.

3.  L. Steil, *Your Personal Listening Profile* (Minneapolis: Sperry Corporation, 1980) 4.

4.  K. Galvin, *Listening By Doing* (Lincolnwood, IL: National Textbook Co., 1985).

5.  W. A. Shrope, *Speaking and Listening: A Contemporary Approach* (New York: Harcourt Brace Jovanovich, 1979) 257.

6.  See, for example, V. DiSalvo, D. Larsen, and W. Seiler, "Communication Skills Needed by Persons in Business Organizations," *Communication Education* 25 (1976): 269; and M. Hanna, "Speech Communication Training Needs in the Business Community," *Central States Speech Journal* 29 (1978): 163–172.

7.  J. Littell and J. Littell, *The Language of Man*, Vol. I (Evanston, IL: McDougal Littell, 1972) 19.

8.  G. E. Frost, *Bless My Growing* (Minneapolis: Augsburg, 1974) 79.

9.  L. L. Barker, *Listening Behavior* (Englewood Cliffs, NJ: Prentice Hall, 1971) xi.

## SUGGESTIONS FOR FURTHER READING

Adler, M. *How to Speak; How to Listen.* New York: Macmillan, 1983.

Bassett, R., N. Whittington, and A. Staton-Spicer. "The Basics in Speaking and Listening for High School Graduates: What Should Be Assessed?" *Communication Education* 27 (1978): 293–303.

Bostrom, R. *Listening Behavior: Measurement and Application.* New York: Guilford Press, 1990.

Bostrom, R., and E. Waldhart. "Memory Models and the Measurement in Listening." *Communication Education* 37 (1988): 1–14.

Bozik, M. *Do You Hear What I Hear? Developing Student Listening Skills.* Des Moines, IA: Iowa Dept. of Education, 1988.

Bozik, M., and P. Carlin. *Listen! A Listening to Literature Program.* Littleton, MA: Sundance Publishing, 1989.

Brownwell, J., ed. *Multiple Perspectives: Proceedings of the Cornell Conference on Listening.* Ithaca, NY: Cornell University, 1988.

Choate, J., and T. Rakes. "The Structured Listening Activity: A Model for Improving Listening Comprehension." *The Reading Teacher* 41 (1987): 194–200.

Clark, A. J. "Communication Confidence and Listening Competence: An Investigation of the Relationships of Willingness to Communicate, Communication Apprehension, and Receiver Apprehension to Comprehension of Content and Emotional Meaning in Spoken Messages." *Communication Education* 38 (1989): 237–248.

Coakley, C., and A. Wolvin, eds. *Experiential Listening: Tools for Teachers and Trainers.* New Orleans, LA: Spectra, 1989.

Dalyrymple, H. "Theatre as a Listening Laboratory." *Communication Education* 36 (1987): 283–286.

Floyd, J. J. *Listening: A Practical Approach.* Glenview, IL: Scott Foresman, 1985.

Friedman, P. *Listening Processes: Attention, Understanding, Evaluation.* Washington, D.C.: National Education Association, 1986.

Funk, H. D., and D. Gary. "Guidelines for Developing Listening Skills." *The Reading Teacher* (May 1989): 660.

Goss, B. "Listening as Information Processing." *Communication Quarterly* 30 (Fall 1982): 304–307.

Gruber, K., and J. Gabeleen. "Sex Differences in Listening Comprehension." *Sex Roles: A Journal of Research* 5 (1979): 229–310.

Hirsch, R. *Listening: A Way to Process Information Aurally.* Scottsdale, AZ: Gorsuch Scarisbrick, 1979.

Hunsaker, R. *Understanding and Developing the Skills of Oral Communication Speaking and Listening.* 2nd ed. Englewood, CO: Morton Publishing, 1989.

Hyslop, N., and B. Tune. "Listening: Are We Teaching It and If So How?" *ERIC Digest* 3 (1988).

*The Journal of the International Listening Association* and the *ILA Listening Post* contain articles on all aspects of listening. Contact: Kittie Watson, Tulane University, New Orleans, LA 70118.

Overton, J., and D. Bock. "A Study of the Development, Validation, and Application of the Construit of Listening Reluctance." *Journal of the Illinois Speech and Theatre Association* 38 (1986): 31–42.

Roach, C., and N. Wyatt. *Successful Listening.* New York: Harper and Row, 1988.

Rhodes, S. "What the Communication Journals Tell Us About Teaching Listening." *The Central States Speech Journal* 36 (Spring/Summer 1985): 24–32.

Strothen, D. "On Listening." *Phi Delta Kappan* 68 (1987): 625–628.

Wolff, F., N. Marsnik, W. Tacey, and R. Nichols. *Perceptive Listening*. New York: Holt, Rinehart and Winston, 1983.

Wolvin, A. D. "The Listening Journal: An Instructional Strategy for a Listening Awareness Program." *Reading Horizons* (Winter 1977): 101–110.

Wolvin, A., and C. Coakley. *Listening*. Dubuque, IA: Wm. C. Brown, 1985.

# 4 NONVERBAL COMMUNICATION

## OBJECTIVES

After reading this chapter and completing the activities, you should be able to:

- Explain the importance of nonverbal communication in the classroom
- Explain the functions of nonverbal communication in the classroom
- Define the categories of nonverbal communication
- Provide examples of how each category affects classroom communication
- Discuss the impact of physical attractiveness on classroom communication
- Define kinesics
- Explain the significance of kinesic behavior in the classroom
- Define paralanguage
- Explain the significance of paralanguage in the classroom
- Discuss the relationship of teacher nonverbal behavior to teacher effectiveness
- Describe how to improve nonverbal communication

## INTRODUCTION

The following photographs were taken of actual classroom situations. Study the pictures. What messages do you get? What's being communicated? What nonverbal cues affect your perception? Compare your perceptions with the perceptions of others in your class.

Photos by James L. Shaffer

Some researchers indicate that 65 percent of the meaning we get from a given message is communicated nonverbally.[1] Nonverbal communication includes such areas as proxemics (the use of space), environmental factors, chronemics (the use of time), physical characteristics, artifacts, kinesics (body movement), touch, and paralanguage.

Nonverbal communication is important to the classroom teacher. A teacher's nonverbal behavior is integral to a student's attitude formation towards school.[2] Researchers[3] have shown that when teachers are trained how to use nonverbal communication in the classroom more effectively, student/teacher relationships improve. In addition, student cognitive and effective learning are improved.

An important axiom of communication is that one cannot not communicate.[4] Whenever we are perceived by another person, we communicate. Remember also that every communicative message has both a content and a relationship component. As we will see, nonverbal gestures, facial expressions, touch, and so on can affect the content message. In addition, the relationship aspect of a message is communicated primarily through nonverbal means. Thus, students will discern how you view your relationship with them by analyzing your nonverbal communication.

Perhaps the most famous study in nonverbal communication in the classroom is reported by Rosenthal and Jacobson's *Pygmalion in the Classroom*.[5] These researchers randomly labeled some elementary school children as high achievers and others as low achievers. This information was given to teachers. Students who were labeled as high achievers had raised their IQ scores significantly from the beginning of the school year to the end. Rosenthal and Jacobson suggest the role nonverbal communication may have played:

> *We may say that by what she [the teacher] said, by how and when she said it, her facial expressions, postures, and perhaps her touch, the teacher may have communicated to the children of the experimental group that she expected improved intellectual performance. Such communication . . . may have helped the child learn.*[6]

Rosenthal indicates that this finding is substantiated in research study after research study. In 1973 Rosenthal reported that of the 242 studies examining the "Pygmalion effect," 84 support it. Statistically, by chance alone, we would expect 12 (or about 5 percent) to support the effect.[7] A 1984 research review by Cooper and Tom indicates that these statistics still hold true.[8] Thus, the Pygmalion effect is more than just a chance happening. We'll return to the Pygmalion effect when we talk about teacher expectancy (see chapter 9).

Other researchers also indicate the importance of nonverbal communication in the classroom. Galloway argues that nonverbal communication often plays a more significant role in student learning than the formal teaching which takes place.[9] Much research suggests that teachers need to learn to use nonverbal behaviors in order to improve the quality of classroom communication.[10]

Doyle summarizes research on nonverbal communication in the classroom. According to Doyle, the data indicate:[11]

1.  Teachers use a relatively restricted number of nonverbal behaviors from the range of possible response options defined by category systems.
2.  A majority of teachers' nonverbal messages are used for controlling and directing purposes rather than for encouragement and supportiveness.
3.  Nonverbal interaction between teachers and students is generally characterized by formalism rather than intimacy.

Finally, recent research suggests that some students who have behavior problems may be suffering primarily from difficulties in interpreting nonverbal cues. Emory University psychologist Stephen Norwick found that students with behavioral problems could often process verbal information with little difficulty, but often misinterpreted nonverbal cues. For example, these students mistook a friendly gesture for a hostile one and then acted in ways that set off a series of negative events.[12]

As we analyze nonverbal communication in the classroom, it is important to remember that research in this area is somewhat limited. Proxemics, environmental factors, and kinesics have been extensively investigated within the classroom context. However, what we know concerning the other areas of nonverbal communication in the classroom—chronemics, physical attractiveness, artifacts, touch, and paralanguage—is derived primarily from investigations outside the classroom.

## FUNCTIONS OF NONVERBAL COMMUNICATION IN THE CLASSROOM

Nonverbal communication serves many functions in the classroom. As in any context, a nonverbal message can repeat, substitute for, complement, contradict, and regulate the verbal message. However, in the classroom context, nonverbal communication plays a significant role in several areas. These include self-presentation, identification of rules and expectations, feedback and reinforcement, liking and attitude, regulation of conversational flow, and classroom control. Let's briefly examine each of these.

### Self-Presentation

If you were asked to describe teaching, you would have little difficulty describing what a teacher does and how a teacher acts. How we define the job of teaching influences how we will present ourselves. For example, if you view teachers as authoritative information givers, your nonverbal cues will present this image. You will stand erect, speak in a commanding voice, and lecture from the front of the room. Students, too, present a particular image. They may nod their heads, take notes, and look very attentive. Your image of yourself, both as a teacher and a student, will affect your nonverbal behaviors in the classroom.

## Identification of Rules and Expectations

Although most teachers will verbally describe classroom rules to their students ("No late papers will be accepted. Class participation is expected. Misbehavior will not be tolerated."), most rules are communicated nonverbally. A gaze that connotes disapproval or the wagging finger tells you that your behavior is inappropriate, even though the teacher may never have verbally said so.

Similarly, expectations are communicated, in large part nonverbally. Rarely does a teacher say to you, "I expect you to do very well in this class." However, as we'll discuss in chapter 9, teachers' expectations for student achievement are most often communicated by such nonverbal cues as eye contact, seating arrangement, body orientation, and facial expressions.

## Feedback and Reinforcement

Even when a teacher fails to tell us, "Good job," we know how we are doing by her facial expressions, gestures, and body movements. A smile, an affirmative head nod, or a pat on the shoulder can all communicate approval. Similarly, a frown, quizzical look, or shake of the head can tell us we are not "on the right track."

Reinforcement, as we'll learn in chapter 8, has a powerful effect on a student's perception of self, school, and instructor. Smiles, frowns, eye contact, touch—all give students a message about how worthwhile they are. This is an example of how nonverbal messages tell us the most about the relationship level of a message. Most of us can remember teachers we didn't like or teachers we felt didn't like us. Obviously the teacher did not say, "I don't like you," but nonverbally we got the message.

## Liking and Affect

A teacher's nonverbal cues do more than communicate like or dislike of students. Generally we know, from a teacher's nonverbal cues, their attitude toward the subject they teach, the school system in general, and teaching in general. Immediacy behaviors (positive affect) are "nonlinguistic actions which send four simultaneous and complementary messages."[13] Immediacy behaviors (1) are approach behaviors, (2) signal availability for communication, (3) are typically multi-channeled, and (4) communicate interpersonal closeness and warmth.[14]

Research suggests that immediacy can be communicated in a variety of ways.[15] Varying voice pitch, loudness and tempo, smiling, leaning toward a person, face-to-face body position, decreased physical distance between teacher and student, arriving on time to class, removing physical barriers (such as standing or sitting behind a desk), gesturing, using overall body movements, and being relaxed and spending time with someone can all communicate immediacy.

Teachers who lecture from the same notes year after year, leave school immediately at the end of the day, are rarely seen at school functions such as athletic games or musical and theatrical events, and rarely interact with students outside the classroom may communicate not only a dislike of students, but a dislike of the educational environment generally.

Immediate teachers are viewed as approachable, friendly, open, and responsive to student needs.[16] In addition, immediate teachers are perceived as warm and relaxed. Nonimmediate teachers are perceived as cold, distant, and unfriendly.[17]

Richmond, McCroskey and Payne suggest three other positive effects of teacher immediacy:[18]

1.  Higher student affect for the subject matter and content
2.  Increased student/teacher and student/student interactions
3.  Increased chances of cognitive learning since students' attention spans are increased

A great deal of research has investigated the immediacy variable. In general, findings indicate that immediacy (vocal expressiveness, smiling, gestures, eye contact, relaxed body position, movement around the classroom, and, to some degree, touch) is significantly associated with students' perceptions of cognitive learning.[19]

In addition, immediacy behaviors relate to affect, not only for the subject matter, but for the teacher as well. Students like teachers with high immediacy more than those with low immediacy. Perhaps this is because teachers who have positive feelings about their students are more likely to be immediate, and in turn, students are more likely to respond reciprocally.[20]

## Regulation of Conversational Flow

Because of their power position in the classroom, teachers determine who talks, how often, how long, and when. As Andersen suggests:

*Nonverbally, instructors signal that it is a student's turn to talk by dropping their pitch, dropping gestures, relaxing and leaning back slightly, and ending a vocal phrase by looking directly at the student expected to respond. An in-structor can shorten student responses and acquire the speaking floor more quickly by nodding his or her head rapidly, opening his or her mouth as if to talk, inhaling, gesturing, leaning forward, and verbalizing during the first pause that is accompanied by eye contact.*[21]

Teachers can also use nonverbal cues to signal that it is not time to talk. Sometimes a particular student will want to answer every question. Instead of ignoring the student, the teacher might make eye contact while in the middle of an utterance. Eye contact timed in this way recognizes the student, but does not invite her to participate verbally. After the teacher finishes talking he can avoid eye contact with the overly verbal student and focus eye contact directly on another student.

## Classroom Control

Nonverbal communication can be used both to encourage desirable student behavior and control undesirable student behavior. Often nonverbal behavior is more effective than verbal behavior in controlling the classroom. None of us likes to be verbally reprimanded. Nonverbal behaviors used to control create less of the "me-against-you" attitude that often occurs with verbal reprimands. Suppose three or four students are talking together while you are lecturing. Increasing your eye contact with these students or moving in their direction may be enough to stop their talking. Such nonverbal movements are far less likely to disrupt other students who have been listening than, "Juan, Mary, Kim, please be quiet."

A major research focus in the communication literature is the power variable. This research is an effort to determine those strategies that teachers employ to gain student on-task compliance. Since the single best predictor of learning is simply "academic engagement time,"[22] the amount of active time spent on specific academic tasks consistently results in higher achievement gains.[23] Thus, the teacher uses her power to keep students working on their tasks. Power can be prosocial (based on reward, expert, and referent power) or it can be antisocial (based on coercive and legitimate power). The use of prosocial as opposed to antisocial messages to alter student behavior has been shown to increase perceptions of teacher immediacy, which lead to greater affective[24] and cognitive[25] learning. In addition, teachers' nonverbal behavior may play a major role in establishing and maintaining student cooperation in the classroom. Head nodding, smiling, and touching appear to operate as reinforcers of on-task behavior.[26] These teacher immediacy cues signal to students that on-task compliance is expected and valued.[27]

Researchers[28] have developed a typology of power strategies based on five bases of teacher power: coercive, reward, legitimate, expert, and referent power.

These researchers investigated the types of power alteration techniques teachers and students perceive that teachers use in effective classroom management. The result was a twenty-two item list of behavior alterations techniques and representative behavior alteration messages. (This line of power research will be discussed further in chapter 8).

In terms of classroom control, research indicates that college students' perception of the behavior alteration techniques used by their teachers is affected by their teachers' nonverbal immediacy orientation.[29] Students perceive that their more immediate teachers use primarily prosocial behavior alteration techniques and their nonimmediate teachers rely on antisocial behavior alteration techniques.[30] Students resist immediate teachers less. In other words, students are more willing to comply with teachers they like than those they dislike.[31] Immediate teachers who employed prosocial behavior alteration techniques were resisted less than immediate teachers who employed antisocial techniques. However, a nonimmediate teacher who employed prosocial techniques was resisted more than a nonimmediate teacher who used antisocial strategies. The researchers interpret this finding:

> *Students may perceive their more nonimmediate teachers' prosocial attempts to gain compliance as insincere. Claiming that "you'll find it a rewarding and meaningful experience," or that "it will help you later on in life," nonimmediate teachers may be perceived as communicating sarcasm or ridicule. Moreover, students may not assign reward-based power to the nonimmediate teacher. Given the negative affect associated with nonimmediacy, students may not believe that such teachers can deliver on promises of rewarding consequences.*[32]

Burroughs and his associates[33] examined the messages students communicate in order to resist teacher influence. These researchers found that students constructed significantly more resistance messages when the teacher was nonimmediate as opposed to when the teacher was immediate. Thus, immediacy seems to be related to both the messages teachers use to gain compliance and the amount of resistance they receive.

Often teachers want to increase student participation in their classrooms. Teachers need to do more than say, "I'd like us all to participate in this discussion." Their nonverbal behaviors such as eye contact, facial expressions, and gestures need to encourage participation. For example, smiling, gesturing, being vocally expressive, pausing to wait for student comments, and reducing spatial barriers can do much to encourage participation. One teacher I observed increased participation by doing three simple things: she had her students sit in a semicircle, she moved from behind her desk to sit in the semicircle with them, and she paused several seconds after asking a question so students could respond and participate.

## CATEGORIES OF NONVERBAL COMMUNICATION

Nonverbal communication can be categorized in several ways. In the next section, we'll examine the following categories of nonverbal communication: proxemics, spatial arrangements, environmental factors, chronemics, physical attractiveness, artifacts, kinesics, touch, and paralanguage.

### Proxemics

Proxemics is the study of how people use space. It includes territoriality and personal space. Territoriality is fixed space. You usually sit in the same place in the classroom, even if the seats aren't assigned. I have noticed this phenomenon in mass lectures of 300 students as well as in classrooms of 25 or 30 students.

Personal space has been compared to a bubble that surrounds us, which we carry with us wherever we go, and which we expand or contract depending on the situation. W H. Auden humorously discusses this "bubble" in the following poem.

> Some thirty inches from my nose
> The frontier of my Person goes,
> And all the untilled air between
> Is private pagus or demesne.
> Stranger, unless with bedroom eyes
> I beckon you to fraternize,
> Beware of rudely crossing it:
> I have no gun, but I can spit.[34]

If our personal space is invaded, we may not spit, but we usually become very uncomfortable, unless of course, we know the person well and he is special to us. For most encounters in the classroom, more distance is needed for students and teachers to be comfortable. Consider how you feel when a teacher stands over you while you're working at your desk. As teachers, we need to be careful of invading the personal space of our students.

### Spatial Arrangements

Think about the various classroom environments you have experienced and the effect these spatial arrangements had on the communication that occurred. Spatial arrangements (a form of territoriality) affect such communication factors as who talks to whom, when, where, for how long, and about what.

You may choose any of several different spatial arrangements for your classroom. The most common is the traditional row arrangement. The effect this arrangement has on communication is pictured in figure 4.1.[35] Notice that the percentage of participation is greater for students in the front and center rows. In a straight row arrangement, students most willing to communicate will tend to sit front and center. Those less willing to communicate will tend to sit further from the teacher and on the sides.

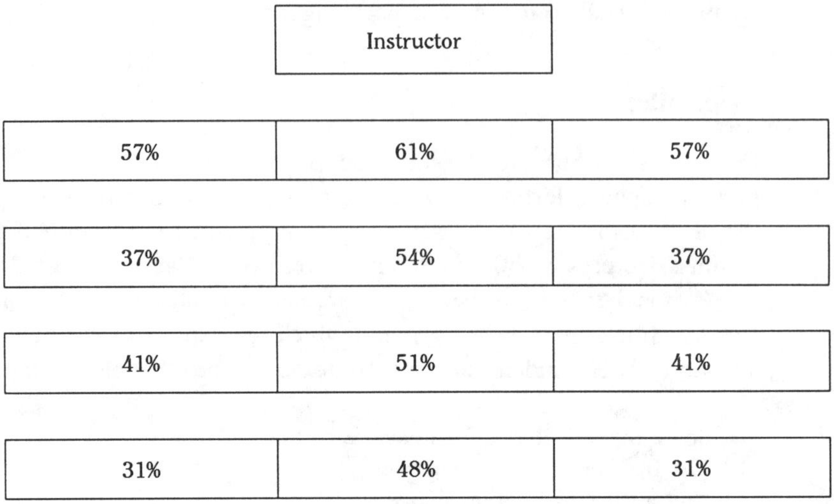

| | Instructor | |
|---|---|---|

| 57% | 61% | 57% |
|---|---|---|

| 37% | 54% | 37% |
|---|---|---|

| 41% | 51% | 41% |
|---|---|---|

| 31% | 48% | 31% |
|---|---|---|

*Figure 4.1* *The traditional classroom spatial arrangement: rows. Percentages indicate degree of participation in classroom.*

Two other common classroom arrangements are the horseshoe and the modular. The seats of the most active participation in each of these arrangements are designated in figures 4.2 and 4.3.[36]

Sommer, interested in comparing student participation in the row arrangement with other types of arrangements, studied four varieties of seating arrangements for one semester. The rooms selected were:

- two seminar rooms with horseshoe or open-square arrangements
- two laboratories with straight rows
- one windowless room with rows
- one room with rows, full of windows

Sommer concluded that

> although a higher proportion of people participated in the laboratory, there was a trend for greater absolute participation in the seminar rooms in terms of the larger total number of statements per class period. The implication is that a few people say more in a seminar arrangement, whereas participation

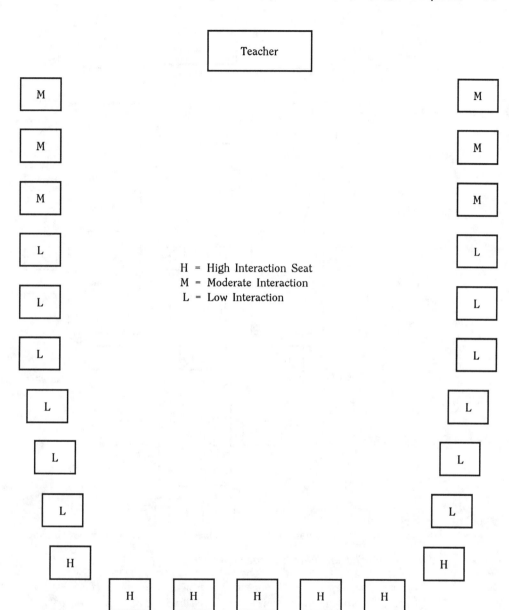

*Figure 4.2 The horseshoe arrangement.*

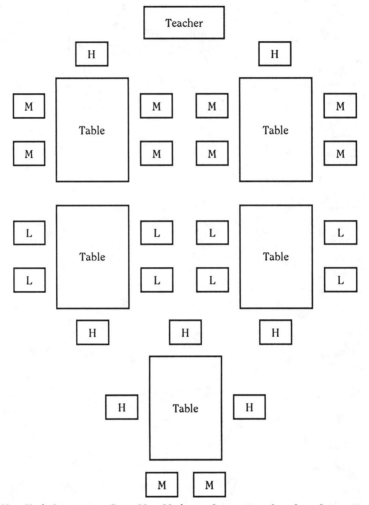

H = High Interaction Seat, M = Moderate Interaction, L = Low Interaction

***Figure 4.3*** *The modular arrangement*

*is more widespread with the straight row arrangement. There were no differences in participation between the open and windowless rooms.*[37]

Consider figure 4.4 on page 75. Psychologist Feitler and two fellow researchers showed this figure to 276 graduate and undergraduate students at Syracuse University's School of Education and asked the following questions.[38]

1. Which of the following classroom seating arrangements would you find the most and least comfortable if you were a student?

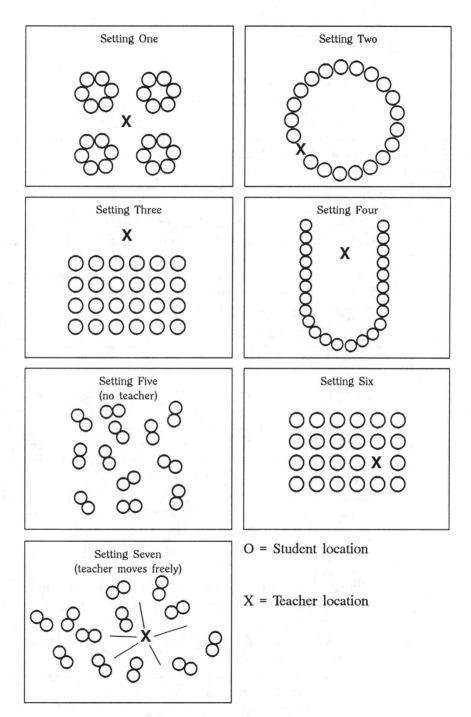

**Figure 4.4** *Feitler's spatial arrangement questionnaire.*

2. Which would you find the most and least comfortable if you were a teacher?

The results of the questions indicated that, whether the students thought of themselves as students or teachers, setting four was picked as most comfortable. Settings three and seven were also chosen as comfortable. Least comfortable for both teacher and student were settings one and six. The researchers interpreted these results as indicating the need for teacher control. Perhaps, however, the results can be explained by remembering that students and teachers have little experience with seating arrangements other than those in which the teacher has control.

McCroskey and McVetta[39] conducted research to answer the question, does the type of course being taught affect student preferences for classroom arrangements? By utilizing the traditional row, horseshoe, and modular arrangements, they found that students preferred the traditional arrangement over the horseshoe and modular arrangements for required courses and preferred horseshoe and modular arrangements over the traditional arrangement for elective courses.

### ACTIVITY 4.1

Now that you have considered different classroom arrangements, it's time to experiment with them. Try each arrangement as both teacher (with your class on varying days) and as student (possibly through the use of role-playing). Were your perceptions and conclusions about each arrangement accurate? You can get additional feedback from your students by copying figure 4.4 and asking them to state which are most and least comfortable for them. Compare their answers with yours. In your journal keep a record of each arrangement that you use in your teaching (or those you observe) and note how the arrangement may have affected the success of the lesson.

As a teacher, you need to be aware of how each of the three arrangements affect communication in the classroom. Your own experience as a student should tell you that the traditional row arrangement promotes teacher-student interaction. Very little communication occurs between students since the teacher dominates the classroom under this type of arrangement. The horseshoe arrangement increases student to student interaction. The modular arrangement promotes the most student to student interaction. Which arrangement you desire depends on many factors—the content you are teaching, the teaching style you utilize, how much you want your students to communicate, and so forth.

Some research suggests that a student's preference for a particular seat is determined by personality characteristics. Totusek and Totusek and Staton-Spicer[40] found that students who sit in seats of high participation (in the traditional arrangement) scored higher on measures of imagination than students who chose nonparticipation seats. Other research studies indicate that students who are apprehensive about communicating will choose seats of low participation.[41] Koneya, interested in whether certain types of students preferred certain areas of the classroom, found that low verbalizers avoid seats which promote communication more often than high verbalizers.[42]

Interestingly, occupancy of seats in high-participation areas affects, in a positive manner, not only how students view themselves, but also how they are perceived by their teacher and peers.[43] However, some sex and age differences are apparent: teachers regard males sitting in the rear and females sitting forward more positively in the early grades and less positively in the later grades.[44]

## ACTIVITY 4.2

Draw the seating arrangement in this class. How does this arrangement affect the communication taking place?

Where do you sit? What does this tell you about your own communication?

## Environmental Factors

Maslow and Mintz conducted a now classic study in which they compared the interaction of people in an ugly versus a beautiful room. They concluded that

> *the ugly room was variously described as producing monotony, fatigue, headaches, discomfort, sleep, irritability and hostility. The beautiful room, however, produced feelings of pleasure, comfort, enjoyment, importance, energy, and desire to continue in the activity.*[45]

Several studies have confirmed this finding in the classroom. Santrock[46] found that first and second graders worked longer in a room decorated with "happy" pictures than in a room decorated with "sad" or neutral pictures. Horowitz and Otto[47] compared the scholastic achievement of college students in a traditional classroom with that of students in a classroom with a great deal of color, comfortable seats, movable wall panels, and a complex lighting system. No difference in achievement was found. However, attendance in the experimental room was better, as was participation in class and group cohesion. In a similar study, Sommer and Olsen[48] remodeled a traditional classroom to create a "soft" classroom—one with cushioned benches, carpeting, and various decorative items.

The percentage of students voluntarily participating was greater in the soft class-room (79 percent) than in the traditional classroom (51 percent). In addition, the mean number of comments per student doubled (2.5 per student in the traditional classroom compared to 5 per student in the soft classroom).

Todd-Mancillas reviewed research demonstrating that color, lighting, and temperature all affect the classroom climate.[49] For example, warmer colors (yellows and pinks) are best for classrooms of younger children; cool colors (blues and blue-greens) are best for classrooms of older students. Summarizing previous color research, Malandro and Barker emphasize the effect of color:

> *One school was left unpainted, a second school was finished in the usual institutional color scheme of light buff walls and white ceilings, and the third was painted in accordance with the principles of color dynamics. In the third school the corridors were painted a cheerful yellow with gray doors; classrooms facing north were done in a pale rose; classrooms facing south depicted cooler shades of blue and green; front walls were darker than side walls; the art room was a neutral gray so as to avoid interfering with the colorful work that it contained; and green chalkboards were used to reduce glare. Over a two-year period, behavior in each school was observed. The results were clear; students in the third school showed greatest improvement on several variables measured—social habits, health, safety habits, and scholastic aptitude in language, arts, arithmetic, social studies, science, and music. Those in the unpainted school showed the least improvement in these areas and those in the traditional school fell somewhere in between.[50]*

Lighting can affect student/teacher communication. Poor lighting can lead to eye strain and fatigue, resulting in frustration and even hostility. Thompson suggests three guidelines for classroom lighting:

> *Maintain high levels of illumination. When students must expend energy just to see, they will have little left to understand what is being said. All areas of the room should be balanced in brightness. Factory and assembly-line workers have their work well illuminated. Industry has known for a long time that eye fatigue plays havoc with production schedules. To avoid sharp contrast, the visual field around the task should be only one-third as bright as the work area. No part of the visual field should be brighter than the immediate vicinity of the task. Avoid glare either from direct light sources or from reflecting surfaces.[51]*

Another environmental factor affecting classroom communication is temperature. If the classroom is too hot, learning may be affected since students become irritable and anxious to leave. If the room is too cold, it's difficult to concentrate on learning. The optimal classroom temperature appears to be 66°–72° in order to assure optimal student performance.[52]

The implications for teachers are obvious. If you value some of the behaviors and attitudes that environmental factors have been found to influence, then you should consider your classroom environment. Changes in classroom environment may lead to changes in classroom climate. Eventually, these changes may lead to changes in achievement.[53] At any rate, it's important for students to feel comfortable in the learning environment, and you can have a significant impact on how the environment is arranged. Keep in mind that any educational environment should:[54]

1. ensure a variety of stimuli
2. present a feeling of comfort and security
3. be adapted to the activity
4. allow for some privacy and individuality

## Chronemics

Chronemics is the study of people's use of time. Schools are organized temporally as well as spatially. Students often are admonished not to waste time, and classes are scheduled to meet at certain times and for specific lengths of time. The teacher's use of time in the classroom can greatly affect the communication that occurs. For example, the amount of time a teacher waits for a student to answer a question can affect interaction between teacher and student. Too often teachers fail to wait long enough for students to respond to questions—in fact, they seldom wait longer than five seconds! Silence certainly is not viewed as being golden in the classroom! Teachers seem to be afraid of silence and therefore answer their own questions or move rapidly from one student to another. This has a great impact on the communication interaction in the classroom.[55] Few students will be willing to interact in such an environment—only those who are highly verbal will respond. In addition, if students know the teacher will answer his own questions if they just wait long enough, the teacher will find himself doing just that!

Another area of chronemics involves the time spent on different subjects. The amount of time you spend on a given topic area communicates to students the importance of that area. How many times have you heard someone say, "I don't need to study that for the exam. The teacher spent hardly any time on it in class."

Time spent with individual students communicates our attitude toward them. Teacher expectancy research indicates that high expectancy students receive more teacher communication time than low expectancy students. For example, teachers talk to high expectation students more (praise more and have more academic interactions) and are more nonverbally active (head nods, smiles, supportive gestures).[56]

Time can affect students in a number of other ways as well. College professors often comment that students achieve better and participate more in their 10:00 A.M. classes or 2:00 P.M. classes than in their 8:00 A.M. or 4:00 P.M. classes. In addition, students may be either monochronic or polychronic; that is, they may work best when one activity, assignment, or project is scheduled at a time, or they may be able to engage in several activities at once. Students' "biological clocks" also affect their classroom performance. Morning-active students generally have higher academic achievement than those students who are most alert later in the day.[57] Your awareness of the ways in which students are affected by time can enable you to meet the individual needs of your students more effectively.[58]

Finally, students use time to communicate. Putting away pencils and packing up books signals to the instructor that the class period is nearly over.

## Physical Characteristics

Physical characteristics and artifacts (objects in contact with the interacting persons—perfume, jewelry, clothes, and so on) can also affect classroom communication and learning.

### *Physical Attractiveness*

As an eighth grader, I had an English teacher whose appearance completely prohibited learning. She was very attractive and quite well-endowed physically. She also wore very tight skirts and sweaters. From the very beginning of the year we learned little because we could not get beyond her appearance. Chaos reigned in that classroom all year! We were a very rowdy, uncooperative, defiant group of students. She had simply lost control of the classroom. As I look back, I'm sure she was quite knowledgeable in her subject area, and I'm not sure what, exactly, we thought of her. I do remember, however, that because of her manner, her dress, and her general appearance, she communicated something to us that made us sure we could get away with murder, and we did!

Chaikin's[59] research documents the effect a teacher's appearance can have on student's perceptions. Teachers who were rated more attractive were also rated as more competent and were more likely to motivate students than were teachers who were rated unattractive.

A recent study explored the impact of teachers' physical appearance and teaching philosophy on other people's perceptions of their competence. The attractive female authoritarian teacher was rated less negatively than other types of teachers.[60]

Singer [61] conducted research that examined attractiveness and its relationship to achievement. Singer found a positive relationship between attractiveness in freshman girls and high grades received from their male professors. Several researchers have found that teachers react more favorably to students they perceive as attractive than to those they perceive as unattractive.[62] Teachers also interact less with students perceived to be unattractive.[63]

Finally, body type can affect classroom communication. There are three general body types: (1) the ectomorph—tall and thin; (2) mesomorph—bony and muscular; and (3) endomorph—soft and round.

Much evidence suggests that your body type influences how others perceive you and communicate with you.[64] Ectomorphs are perceived to be anxious, tense, self-conscious, and reticent. Mesomorphs are perceived to be energetic, talkative, and dominant. Endomorphs are perceived to be jolly, warm, and complacent. What does all this have to do with you, the teacher? As I just indicated, physical attractiveness is important in the classroom. The standard for attractiveness seems to be the mesomorph, and students may interact with you on the basis of this image. Richmond, McCroskey and Payne summarize the effect of body type in the classroom:

> *Body type will determine how a person is perceived by others. The ectomorphic student will be perceived by the teacher as being high-strung, anxious, nervous, but probably competent. They might be perceived by their peers as being "nerdy." The endomorphic student might be perceived by the teacher as being slow, lazy, not too bright, but nice and funny. The mesomorphic student will be perceived as dependable, intelligent, competent, dominant, and appealing by the teacher. They are also often perceived as the ones who will do the best in athletics.*

> *Teachers who are ectomorphic will be perceived by students as being anxious, not composed, but perhaps intelligent. The endomorphic teacher will be perceived by students as being slow, lazy, underprepared, and not dynamic in the classroom. Lastly, the mesomorphic teacher will be perceived as credible, dependable, likeable, and competent, but possibly tough and dominant.[65]*

---

**ACTIVITY 4.3**                    **Physique - Temperament Stereotypes**

***Instructions***

Fill in each blank with a word from the suggested list following each statement. For any blank, three in each statement, you may select any word from the list of twelve immediately below. An exact word to fit you may not be in the list, but select the words that seem to fit most closely the way you are.

1.  I feel most of the time _____, _____, and _____.

| | | |
|---|---|---|
| calm | relaxed | complacent |
| anxious | confident | reticent |
| cheerful | tense | energetic |
| contented | impetuous | self-conscious |

2. When I study or work, I seem to be _____, _____, and _____.

| | | |
|---|---|---|
| efficient | sluggish | precise |
| enthusiastic | competitive | determined |
| reflective | leisurely | thoughtful |
| placid | meticulous | cooperative |

3. Socially, I am _____, _____, and _____.

| | | |
|---|---|---|
| outgoing | considerate | argumentative |
| affable | awkward | shy |
| tolerant | affected | talkative |
| gentle-tempered | soft-tempered | hot-tempered |

4. I am rather _____, _____, and _____.

| | | |
|---|---|---|
| active | forgiving | sympathetic |
| warm | courageous | serious |
| domineering | suspicious | soft-hearted |
| introspective | cool | enterprising |

5. Other people consider me rather _____, _____, and _____.

| | | |
|---|---|---|
| generous | optimistic | sensitive |
| adventurous | affectionate | kind |
| withdrawn | reckless | cautious |
| dominant | detached | dependent |

6. Underline one word out of the three in each of the following lines which most closely describes the way you are:

(a) assertive, relaxed, tense

(b) hot-tempered, cool, warm

(c) withdrawn, sociable, active

(d) dependent, dominant, detached

(e) enterprising, affable, anxious

(f) confident, tactful, kind

Now circle all the adjectives you have chosen in the tables below.

*Table 1*

| | |
|---|---|
| dependent | affected |
| calm | warm |
| relaxed | forgiving |
| complacent | sympathetic |
| contented | soft-hearted |
| sluggish | generous |
| placid | affectionate |
| leisurely | kind |
| cooperative | sociable |
| affable | soft-tempered |
| tolerant | |

*Table 2*

| | |
|---|---|
| dominant | talkative |
| cheerful | active |
| confident | domineering |
| energetic | courageous |
| impetuous | enterprising |
| efficient | adventurous |
| enthusiastic | reckless |
| competitive | assertive |
| determined | optimistic |
| outgoing | hot-tempered |
| argumentative | |

*Table 3*

| | |
|---|---|
| detached | awkward |
| tense | cool |
| anxious | suspicious |
| reticent | introspective |
| self-conscious | serious |
| meticulous | cautious |
| reflective | tactful |
| precise | sensitive |
| thoughtful | withdrawn |
| considerate | gentle-tempered |
| shy | |

Add up the number of adjectives you chose from each column. Suppose you have 7 adjectives in table 1 (endomorph personality characteristics), 12 from table 2 (mesomorph), and 2 from table 3 (ectomorph). Your score would be a 7/12/2. We would assume you are primarily mesomorphic with tendencies toward endomorphism.

J. B. Cortes and F. M. Gatti, "Physique and Self-Description of Temperament," *Journal of Consulting Psychology* 29 (1965): 434.

Two recent studies examine the relationship between adolescents' perception of their body type and depression. Depressed adolescents had poorer body images than their nondepressed peers. They viewed their bodies as less attractive and less competent. Gender differences in body image appeared among nondepressed adolescents, with boys more satisfied with their bodies than girls.[66] A negative body image also appears to be a good predictor of the persistence of adolescent girls' depression.[67]

In addition, body type has been found to affect academic competence and self-concept in early adolescence.[68]

### *Artifacts*

I was recently reminded of the impact of artifacts in the classroom. I always wear an ankle chain. Recently I entered a classroom on the first day of class wearing a business suit. One girl later told me she was "put off" by my clothing. It communicated a stiff, unyielding personality. But, she said, "I knew you would be human when I saw your ankle chain!"

An interesting study suggests the effects clothes can have in the classroom. High school boys who had much better achievement scores but who wore "unacceptable" clothing had lower grade point averages than those boys who wore clothing deemed "acceptable" by their peers.[69] Harrison[70] suggests that such attributes as grooming and hair style generally "signal the individual's concepts about beauty, his reference groups, his self-perceived or decided status. They indicate his definition of a communication situation. . . ."

In the classroom, researchers have examined student perceptions of "informally/casually dressed" and "formally dressed" teachers. "Formally dressed" teachers were perceived as more organized, more knowledgeable, and better prepared. Informally dressed teachers were perceived as more friendly, more sympathetic, fair, enthusiastic, and flexible.[71]

In recent studies a child's name has been shown to be a boost or a barrier to school success. Developmental psychology professor S. Gray Garwood of Tulane University asked teachers to list desirable and undesirable names. Garwood found sixth graders with those names and examined their achievement and self-concept scores. Students with desirable names had higher self-concept scores and, according to Garwood, had a better chance for higher achievement.[72]

In a similar study psychologists Herbert Harari and John McDavid gave a set of essays to eighty San Diego elementary school teachers. The teachers gave a higher grade to an essay written by David or Michael than to the same essay with the name Elmer or Herbert on it.[73]

## Kinesics

Kinesics is the study of body movement, gestures, facial expressions, eye contact, and so on. Ekman and Friesen[74] classified kinesic behavior into the following categories:

1. *Emblems* are nonverbal behaviors that have direct verbal translations. For example, "I don't know," may be communicated emblematically by a shrug of the shoulders and raised eyebrows.
2. *Illustrators* are nonverbal behaviors that are tied directly to speech. During a geography lesson a teacher might illustrate where a city is located by pointing to that city on a map.
3. *Affect displays* are facial expressions that communicate emotional states. Your frown may communicate displeasure with a student's answer. A confused expression or bored expression may communicate a certain emotional state in one of your students.
4. *Regulators* are nonverbal behaviors used to control and maintain verbal interactions. Rapid head nods may communicate, "Yes, I understand. Go ahead with the next portion of the lesson."
5. *Adapters* are nonverbal behaviors developed in childhood as adaptive behaviors to satisfy emotional or physical needs. Students, when they feel anxious or bored, may chew their pencils, bite their nails, click their pens, or tap their pencils on the desks. All of these are ways to adapt to their boredom or anxiety.

Willett and Smythe,[75] comparing the nonverbal behaviors of "effective" and "average" teachers, found that effective teachers used more motions than average teachers to facilitate student-to-instructor interaction, to focus student attention on key points, and to demonstrate and illustrate concepts to students. Seals and Kaufman[76] found that nonverbally active teachers elicit more positive perceptions from students than did inactive teachers.

In addition to influencing student attitudes, the teacher's kinesic behavior also influences student achievement. Rosenshine[77] reported that a teacher's use of kinesic behavior was positively related to student achievement. In other words, the more movement and gestures the teacher utilizes, the higher the achievement. Wycoff[78] found that, for secondary students, teacher movement resulted in better test scores on the material presented. However, elementary students exposed to more vigorous teacher movement scored lower on a comprehension test than did students learning from a less active instructor. Wycoff suggests that increased stimulus variation is attention catching for older students, but distracting for younger children.

Your kinesic behavior can communicate that you like or dislike your students. Mehrabian's[79] research indicates that liking, compared to disliking, is characterized by more forward lean, more pleasant facial expressions, and more openness of arms and body. An interesting study by Reece and Whitman[80] produced similar results. Using warm/cold labels rather than liking/disliking labels, these researchers found that people who were perceived as "warm" smiled, used direct eye contact, and tended to lean toward the other person. "Cold" persons did not smile, did not maintain direct eye contact, and slumped. Warmth cues, along with verbal reinforcers ("mm-hmm"), increased verbal output from the other person.

The warmth variable has been studied in the classroom for several years. The role of nonverbal behaviors in communicating warmth seems clear. Bayes[81] and Gafner[82] concluded that students do rely on the teacher's kinesic behavior to evaluate teacher warmth. Bayes examined the importance of teachers' smiles in contributing to perceived warmth. Keith and his colleagues also noted the importance of teachers' smiles on students' positive perceptions of their teachers.[83]

In addition to liking or disliking, kinesic behavior can communicate how much you trust your students. For example, when monitoring a test, do you walk around the room, watching what the students are doing, or do you sit at a desk and work, occasionally glancing up?

---

**ACTIVITY 4.5**                                                    **Teacher Walking Map**

The way a teacher moves about the classroom has a profound effect on the messages he conveys to students, on the ways in which he relates to students, and ultimately on the learning that occurs. His movement demonstrates how he feels about students; at the same time it has a determining effect on his relationships with students. For example, a teacher who always sits or stands behind a desk puts a physical barrier between himself and his students. If he remains behind the desk because he feels uncomfortable relating closely to students, the students will probably perceive him as being emotionally as well as physically distant. The students are not likely to attempt to relate more closely with him, so the emotional distance is thereby increased. Thus the very action of remaining behind a desk (which may not have been the result of a conscious choice on the part of the teacher) reinforces the original feeling that motivated the action. Even if the teacher is aware of the emotional distance between himself and his students, he is unlikely to bridge that distance until he realizes how his physical deportment is contributing to it.

Let's look at another example: If a generally active teacher who moves throughout the classroom consistently avoids one corner, it may be because a student in that corner makes the teacher uncomfortable. By avoiding that corner the teacher conveniently avoids the student, while at the same time creating even greater distance from that student. Until the teacher becomes aware of her pattern of movement, she is unlikely to confront and change her feelings of discomfort.

### Objectives

1.  To help you monitor your movement in a classroom
2.  To help you identify the possible effects of your classroom movement on students
3.  To assist you in making your physical movement contribute to your goals

### Directions

For a specified period of time (perhaps one period or one hour) a colleague observer can map on paper your movement about the classroom. The observer can use the following directions:

1.  Draw a map of the classroom, including the furniture arrangement.
2.  Chart with a pencil the teacher's location at the beginning of class, and follow his movement throughout the agreed-upon time period.
3.  Consecutively number spots at which the teacher stops.
4.  Draw concentric circles around spots where the teacher remains for significant time periods: one circle for every three minutes.

For example, a map of a traditional classroom with a teacher who spends most of his time in front might look something like the one shown on p. 88.

### Questions

1.  In which areas of your classroom did you spend most of your time?
2.  Did you neglect any area(s)?
3.  Did the students' activities determine your movements in any way?
4.  What effect did the seating arrangement have on your movements?
5.  What effect might your movement have had on students?
6.  Do you want to make any changes, based on the information you now have? Why or why not?

### Follow-up

A teacher's movement in the classroom can have a significant effect on the learning that occurs. It follows, then, that becoming aware of your movement, analyzing its possible effects, and planning for and carrying through movements that facilitate your goals should become part of your planning process. Your

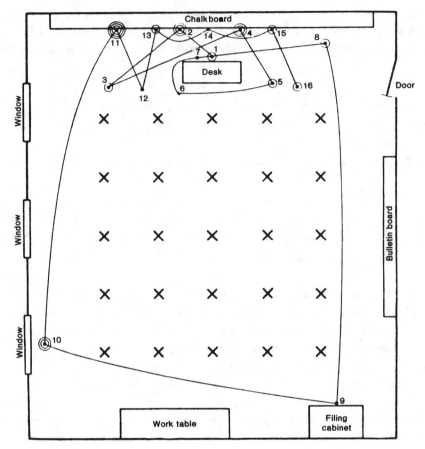

X = Student locations

lessons may determine some or all of your movements in the classroom. If you consistently include references to a map in your plans, or if you consistently use the chalkboard, your movements will be somewhat limited. If you wish to spend less time at the map or at the board, you could instead provide dittoed maps or other materials to distribute to students, thus freeing yourself to move in different ways. The lessons you plan should allow you as many options for movement as possible and should free, rather than restrict, your movement in the classroom.

Use the information that you gain by having your movement monitored and mapped to devise a plan of movement for a lesson you will use in the next few days. Be as specific in your plan as is appropriate for the lesson. Use the following questions to assist your planning:

1. Does the lesson itself dictate your movement in any way? For example, do you have to remain in one place in order to use audiovisual aids? Specify those elements of your lesson that require you to move in specific ways.
2. What effect might the movements you cited above have on the learning that occurs?
3. How else can you plan the lesson so that you can have greater choice of your movement in the classroom?

Following the lesson for which you planned your movement, evaluate for yourself afterward how your movements might have affected the learning that occurred.

---

### Eye Contact

One especially important area of kinesic behavior is eye contact. Eye contact signals that communication lines are open—that you're willing to communicate with another. Think about what you do when a teacher asks a question and you don't know the answer. You look down at your book, doodle, rearrange materials on your desk—anything to avoid looking at the teacher and thereby risking being called on!

In addition to this signaling function, eye contact may also be used to seek feedback, and/or convey information about relationships—for example, dominance and submission or liking and disliking. Exline[84] asked college students to indicate on a questionnaire how comfortable they were with varying amounts of eye contact from others. Students indicated they would be more comfortable with a person who, when speaking, listening, or sharing mutual silence, looked at them 50 percent of the time than one who looked at them 100 percent of the time. Thus, teachers who stare at students may create anxiety or perhaps even hostility.

Teachers who use moderate eye contact monitor and regulate their classrooms more easily. Have you ever received the "evil eye" from a teacher when you were being disruptive? Generally, when students feel teachers looking at them, they will stop being disruptive.

Although constant eye contact is not good, eye contact has been found to enhance comprehension.[85] In addition, direct eye contact usually communicates interest and attention, while lack of direct eye contact communicates disinterest and inattention.[86] The studies reviewed by Beebe[87] suggest that eye contact has a significant effect on student retention of information, attitudes toward the teacher, attention, and classroom participation.

### Facial Expression

A teacher can utilize facial expressions to manage interactions in the classroom (a "dirty look" may be enough to stop a student from whispering, for example), regulate communication, signal approval or disapproval, and reinforce or not reinforce. As teachers we need to consider what messages we are sending with our faces. Are we sometimes communicating messages we would rather not send? Learning to control our facial expressions may be a requirement of our profession. Sometimes we do not want to communicate what we're thinking. Increased sensitivity to and control over our display of emotions can improve the communication between teacher and students.

The teacher's facial expressions communicate much in the classroom. The teacher who smiles and has positive facial affect will be perceived as approachable and immediate. A teacher's dull facial expression may be perceived by students as disinterest in them and/or the subject matter.

In theory, a teacher should be able to use student facial expressions and gestures to determine student understanding of material. However, Jecker et al.[88] found that teachers, both novice and experienced, were not able to judge student understanding based on facial expressions and gestures alone. Sometimes we can "read" nonverbal kinesic cues wrong. Students are very adept at looking interested and awake when their minds are a million miles away!

## Touch

Touch is a "touchy" subject in our society. The following poem indicates how we Americans fear physical contact.

### We Fear the Physical

we fear
the
physical.

to touch,
perhaps
to hold . . .
to grasp,
enfold,
life over life,
arms around,
creature comfort,
flesh to flesh,
even
a hand held hard
at the right
moment.

we stay
separated
by what
has been driven
deep within
(slapped down
by frightened parents)
freedom
destroyed by
black-robed authorities

we sit alone
and hope someday
to have
the freedom to touch![89]

Touch can communicate many things—emotional support, tenderness, encouragement—and is an important aspect in most human relationships. Montagu, in his book *Touching: The Human Significance of Skin,* indicates the importance of touch in the development of healthy, happy individuals:

> *When affection and involvement are conveyed through touch, it is those meanings, as well as the security-giving satisfactions, with which touch will become associated. Inadequate tactile experience will result in a lack of such associations and a consequent inability to relate to others in many fundamental human ways.*[90]

Willes and Hoffman examined touch at the elementary and junior high school level.[91] The amount of touching between student and teacher declined steadily from kindergarten through sixth grade, but was still greater than most adults engage in. Junior high students engaged in about half as much touching as did students in the elementary grades. Most touching occurred between same-sex pairs.

As teachers we should be aware that touch in the elementary grades can be used as an effective means of communicating caring and understanding. Some research by Dr. L. J. Yarrow indicates that children who are touched often have higher IQs than those who don't receive a lot of touch. However, we must be aware that as students grow older, they equate touch with intimacy. Thus, although a teacher's touch is usually inappropriate with older students and will probably create a barrier to effective communication, remember that a pat on the shoulder or back may be appropriate at times and may be very much appreciated by a student.

## Paralanguage

The final nonverbal aspect we'll discuss is paralanguage. Paralanguage includes:

*Vocal qualifiers* — intensity (too loud, too soft), pitch height (too high, too low), and extent (drawl, clipping)
*Vocal qualities* — pitch, range, rhythm, articulation, resonance, tempo
*Vocal characterizers* — laughing, sobbing, whispering
*Vocal segregates* — "shh," "uh," "um," "uh-huh."

The combined effects of these four major components result in the unique sound that is your vocal signature.

Consider how important paralinguistic cues are to the overall image of the communicator. Have you ever talked to a blind date over the telephone and created an image of what the person looked like? Then, when you saw the person, how accurate had your fantasy been? Our voice helps shape the image others have of us.

Your paralinguistic cues can communicate your attitude. For example, if you say "Great job!" in an upbeat, somewhat loud, somewhat high pitch, you communicate your approval. If you say the same phrase in a lower, softer, sarcastic tone, you communicate your disapproval.

Your voice also communicates your feelings toward yourself or others. Generally, the more positive your feelings the faster the rate, louder the volume, and more varied the pitch will be.

Vocal cues can create the mood of a classroom. Obviously other nonverbal cues also contribute to the classroom's mood, but because teachers talk so often, paralinguistic cues no doubt carry quite a bit of weight! A harsh, threatening voice is much less conducive to learning than a pleasant, warm voice.

The effect of paralinguistic cues on comprehension is somewhat unclear. Some studies indicate that comprehension seems to be affected by vocal inflection combined with variation of voice quality, rate, and volume. [92] Perhaps variations in these qualities help maintain audience interest and this, in turn, increase comprehension. However, other researchers have found that vocal pitch variations did not improve comprehension.[93] Generally, research in paralanguage suggests that listeners judge the credibility of a speaker in accordance with the speaker's vocal behavior. Vocal inflection, for example, has been found to relate to a speaker's perceived effectiveness.[94] Similar results have been reported for good voice quality and articulation:

> *Thinness in female voices cued perception of increased immaturity on four levels: social, physical, emotional, and mental, while no significant traits were correlated to thinness in the male voice. Males with throaty voices were stereotyped as being older, more realistic, mature, sophisticated, and well adjusted; females with throatiness were perceived as being less intelligent, more masculine, lazier, more boorish, unemotional, ugly, sickly, careless, inartistic, naive, humble, neurotic, quiet, uninteresting, and apathetic.*[95]

It appears, then, that both the teacher's and students' paralanguage can affect perceptions of their personalities. These perceptions can, in turn, influence classroom communication patterns.

For example, students rate a monotone voice as the most objectional behavior of teachers. Students perceived the monotone voice as communicating boredom, noncaring, and nonimmediacy. As a result, students were less interested in the class, liked the class less, and learned less.[96]

## IMPROVING NONVERBAL COMMUNICATION

As stated in the introduction to this chapter, the impact of nonverbal cues on learning is not completely clear. Therefore, I cannot tell you the right nonverbal moves to make in the classroom. However, below is a nonverbal instrument used to record nonverbal behavior. The instrument was developed by two researchers, Love and Roderick,[97] after considerable observation of elementary and secondary teachers. Thus, these behaviors would seem to be some of the important nonverbal teaching practices. Studies using this instrument reveal two fairly consistent findings: (1) teachers who are nonverbally active are more effective (perceived as more interesting and informative), and (2) teachers can be trained to improve their nonverbal behavior.

## Love-Roderick Nonverbal Categories and Sample Teacher Behaviors

1.  *Accepts Student Behavior.* Smiles, affirmatively shakes head, pats on the back, winks, places hand on shoulder or head.
2.  *Praises Student Behavior.* Places index finger and thumb together, claps, raises eyebrows and smiles, nods head affirmatively and smiles.
3.  *Displays Student Ideas.* Writes comments on board, puts students' work on bulletin board, holds up papers, provides for nonverbal student demonstration.
4.  *Shows Interest in Student Behavior.* Establishes and maintains eye contact.
5.  *Moves to Facilitate Student-to-Student Interaction.* Physically moves into the position of group member, physically moves away from the group.
6.  *Gives Directions to Students.* Points with the hand, looks at specified area, employs predetermined signal (such as raising hands for students to stand up), reinforces numerical aspects by showing that number of fingers, extends arms forward and beckons with the hands, points to student for answers.
7.  *Shows Authority Toward Students.* Frowns, stares, raises eyebrows, taps foot, rolls book on desk, negatively shakes head, walks or looks away from the deviant, snaps fingers.
8.  *Focuses Students' Attention on Important Points.* Uses pointer, walks toward the person or object, taps on something, thrusts head forward, thrusts arm forward, employs a nonverbal movement with a verbal statement to give it emphasis.
9.  *Demonstrates and/or Illustrates.* Performs a physical skill, manipulates materials and media, illustrates a verbal statement with a nonverbal action.
10. *Ignores Student Behavior.* Lacks nonverbal response when one is ordinarily expected. (This is sometimes appropriate, particularly in classroom management.)

## IN SUM

The area of nonverbal communication is an important one for teachers. Our nonverbal communication affects students' perceptions of the classroom, which, in turn, affects how students view the educational environment, the people in it, and how much they desire to communicate.

A final comment about nonverbal communication—although I have isolated it from the verbal component of communication, such an isolation distorts the process of communication. Nonverbal communication can be used to reinforce, contradict, substitute for, accent, complement, or regulate the flow of verbal communication. Remember that the two systems—verbal and nonverbal—work together in the classroom.

## NOTES

1. R. L. Birdwhistell, *Kinesics and Context* (Philadelphia: U. of Pennsylvania P, 1970).

2. See research reviewed in A. Woolfolk and D. Brooks, "The Influence of Teachers' Perceptions and Performance," *The Elementary School Journal* 84 (March 1985): 513-528.

3. J. C. McCroskey, V. P. Richmond, T. G. Plax, and P. Kearney, "Power in the Classroom V: Behavior Alternation Techniques, Communication Training and Learning," *Communication Education* 34 (1985): 214-226.

4. An interesting article argues for a re-examination of this axiom: M. Motley, "On Whether One Can(not) Not Communicate: An Examination via Traditional Communication Postulates," *Western Journal of Speech Communication* 54 (1990): 1-20.

5. R. Rosenthal and L. Jacobson, *Pygmalion in the Classroom* (New York: Holt, Rinehart and Winston, 1968).

6. Rosenthal and Jacobson, 180.

7. R. Rosenthal, "The Pygmalion Effect Lives," *Psychology Today* (Sept. 1973): 56-63.

8. H. Cooper and D. Tom, "Teacher Expectation Research: A Review with Implications for Classroom Instruction," *The Elementary School Journal* 85 (1984): 77-89.

9. C. Galloway, "Teaching and Nonverbal Behavior," *Nonverbal Behavior: Applications and Cultural Implications*, ed. A. Wolgang (New York: Academic Press, 1979); E. Babad, F. Bernieri, and R. Rosenthal, "Nonverbal and Verbal Behavior of Preschool, Remedial, and Elementary School Teachers," *American Educational Research Journal* 24 (Fall 1987): 405-415.

10. See, for example, J. E. Brophy, "Classroom Organization and Management," *Elementary School Journal* 83 (1983): 265-286; J. Brophy, C. Evertson, L. Anderson, M. Baum, and J. Crawford, *"Student Characteristics and Teaching,"* (New York: Longman, 1981); J. Cook-Gumperz and J. J. Gumperz, "Communication Competence in Educational Perspective," *Communicating in the Classroom*, ed. C. Wilkinson (New York: Academic Press, 1982); H. Cooper and T. Good, *"Pygmalion Grows Up: Studies in the Expectation Communication Process,"* (New York: Longman, 1983); R. Rosenthal, ed., *Skill in Nonverbal Communication: Individual Differences* (Cambridge, MA: Oelgeschlager, Gunn, and Hain, 1979); and A. E. Woolfolk and D. M. Brooks, "Nonverbal Communication in Teaching," *Review of Research in Education*, ed. E. Gordon (Washington, D.C.: American Educational Research Association, 1983).

11. W. Doyle, "The Uses of Nonverbal Behaviors: Toward an Ecological Model of Classrooms," *Merrill Palmer Quarterly* 23 (1977): 181.

12. Quoted in Anne Jurmu Arnold, "What's New?" *Learning* (March 1983): 10.

13. P. Andersen and J. Andersen. "Nonverbal Intimacy in Instruction," *Communication in the Classroom*, ed. L. Barker (Englewood Cliffs, NJ: Prentice Hall, 1982) 100.

14. Andersen and Andersen, 98-120.

15. J. Andersen, "The Relationship between Teacher Immediacy and Teaching Effectiveness," *Communication Yearbook 3*, ed. D. Nimmo (New Brunswick, NJ: Transaction Books, 1979).

16. Andersen; J.C. McCroskey, et al., "Power in the Classroom V: Behavior Alteration Techniques, Communication Training and Learning," 214-226; V. P. Richmond, J. C. McCroskey, T. G. Plax, and P. Kearney, "Teacher Immediacy Training and Student Learning" Speech Communication Association Convention, Chicago, 1986.

17. See research reviewed in P. Kearney, T. Plax, V. Smith, and G. Sorensen, "Effects of Teacher Immediacy and Strategy Type on College Student Resistance," *Communication Education* 37 (1988): 54–67.

18. V. P. Richmond, J. C. McCroskey, and S. Payne, *Nonverbal Behavior in Interpersonal Relations* (Englewood Cliffs, NJ: Prentice Hall, 1987) 260.

19. J. Gorham, "The Relationship Between Verbal Teacher Immediacy Behaviors and Student Learning," *Communication Education* 37 (1988): 40–53; D. Kelly and J. Gorham, "Effects of Immediacy on Recall of Information," *Communication Education* 37 (July 1988): 198–207; V. Richmond, J. Gorham, and J. McCroskey, "The Relationship Between Selected Immediacy Behaviors and Cognitive Learning," *Communication Yearbook*, ed. M. McLaughlin (Beverly Hills, CA: Sage, 1987) 574–590.

20. T. Plax, P. Kearney, and T. Downs, "Communicating Control in the Classroom and Satisfaction with Teaching and Students," *Communication Education* 35 (1986): 379–388.

21. J. Andersen, "Instructor Nonverbal Communication: Listening to Our Silent Messages." *Communicating in College Classrooms*, ed. J. M. Civikly (San Francisco: Jossey-Bass, Inc., 1986) 46.

22. A. E. Woolfolk and L. McCune-Nicolich, *Educational Psychology for Teachers*, 2nd ed. (Englewood Cliffs, NJ: Prentice Hall, 1984).

23. See research reviewed in V. Richmond, J. McCroskey, P. Kearney, and T. Plax, "Power in the Classroom VII: Linking Behavior Alteration Techniques to Cognitive Learning," *Communication Education* 36 (1987): 1–12.

24. T. Plax, P. Kearney, J. McCroskey, and V. Richmond, "Power in the Classroom VI: Verbal Control Strategies, Nonverbal Immediacy and Affective Learning," *Communication Education* 35 (1986): 43–55.

25. Richmond, et al., *Power in the Classroom*, 1–12.

26. M. Nafpaktitis, G. R. Mayer, and T. Butterworth, "Natural Rates of Teacher Approval and Disapproval and Their Relation to Student Behavior in Intermediate School Classrooms," *Journal of Educational Psychology* 77 (1985): 362–367.

27. Kearney, *College Student Resistance*, 54–67.

28. P. Kearney, T. Plax, V. P. Richmond, and J. C. McCroskey, "Power in the Classroom III: Teacher Communication Techniques and Messages," *Communication Education* 34 (1985): 19–28; J. C. McCroskey, V. P. Richmond, T. G. Plax, and P. Kearney, "Power in the Classroom V: Behavior Alteration Techniques, Communication Training, and Learning," *Communication Education* 34 (1985): 214–226.

29. T. G. Plax, P. Kearney, T. M. Downs, and R. A. Stewart. "College Student Resistance toward Teachers' Use of Selective Control Strategies," *Communication Research Reports* 3 (1986): 20–27; Kearney, et al., "Effects of Teacher Immediacy"; R. A. Stewart, P. Kearney, and T. G. Plax, "Locus of Control a Mediator: A Study of College Students' Reactions to Teachers' Attempts to Gain Compliance," *Communication Yearbook 9*, ed. M. L. McLaughlin (Beverly Hills, CA: Sage, 1985) 691–704.

30. Plax, "Power in the Classroom VI," 43–55.

31. Kearney, et al., "Effects of Teacher Immediacy."

32. Kearney, et al., 64.

33. N. Burroughs, P. Kearney, and T. Plax, "Compliance-Resistance in the College Classroom," *Communication Education* 38 (1989): 214–229.

34. W. H. Auden, "Some Thirty Inches from My Nose," *Collected Poems* (New York: Random House, 1965) 25.

35. R. Sommer, *Personal Space: The Behavioral Basis of Design* (Englewood Cliffs, NJ: Prentice Hall, 1969) 118.

36. J. C. McCroskey and R. W. McVetta, "Classroom Seating Arrangements: Instructional Communication Theory ver-

sus Student Preferences," *Communication Education* 27 (March 1978): 101–102.

37. Sommer, *Personal Space*, 114.

38. F. C. Feitler, "Teacher's Desk," reprinted from K. Goodall, "Tie Line," *Psychology Today* 5 (September 1971): 12.

39. McCroskey and McVetta, "Classroom Seating Arrangements."

40. P. Totusek, "The Relationship between Classroom Seating Preference and Student Personality Characteristics" Speech Communication Association Convention, Minneapolis, Nov. 1978; P. Totusek and A. Q. Staton-Spicer, "Classroom Speaking Preference as a Function of Student Personality," *Journal of Experimental Education* 50 (Spring 1982): 159–163.

41. See, for example, McCroskey and McVetta, "Classroom Seating Arrangements."

42. M. Koneya, "Location and Interaction in Row and Column Seating Arrangements," *Environment and Behavior* 8 (1976): 265–282.

43. A. Schwebel and D. Charlin, "Physical Distancing in Teacher-Pupil Relationships," *Journal of Educational Psychology* 63 (1972): 543–550.

44. J. A. Daly and A. Suite, "Classroom Seating Choice and Teacher Perceptions of Students," *Journal of Experimental Education* 50 (Winter 1981–82): 64–69.

45. A. H. Maslow and N. L. Mintz, "Effects of Esthetic Surroundings: I. Initial Effects of Three Esthetic Conditions Upon Perceiving 'Energy' and 'Well-Being' in Faces," *Journal of Psychology* 41 (1956): 254–257.

46. J. W. Santrock, "Affect and Facilitative Self-Control: Influence of Ecological Setting, Cognition, and Social Agent," *Journal of Educational Psychology* 68 (1976): 529–535.

47. P. Horowitz and D. Otto, *The Teaching Effectiveness of an Alternative Teaching Facility* (Alberta, Canada: University of Alberta, 1973). (ERIC Document Reproduction Service No. ED 083 242).

48. R. Sommer and H. Olsen, "The Soft Classroom," *Environment and Behavior* (March 1980): 3–16.

49. W. Todd-Mancillas, "Classroom Environment and Nonverbal Behavior," *Communication in the Classroom*, ed. L. Barker (Englewood Cliffs, NJ: Prentice Hall, 1982) 77–97.

50. L. A. Malandro and L. Barker, *Nonverbal Communication* (Reading, MA: Addison-Wesley, 1983) 189–190.

51. J. J. Thompson, *Beyond Words: Nonverbal Communication in the Classroom* (New York: Citation Press, 1973) 81.

52. See research reviewed in Todd-Mancillas, "Classroom Environment," 84.

53. See, for example, W. Todd-Mancillas, "Classroom Environment," 77–97; L. Cahen, et al., *Class Size and Instruction* (New York: Longman, 1982); and D. Weldon, et al., "Crowding and Classroom Learning," *Journal of Experimental Education* 49 (Spring 1981): 160–176.

54. R. S. Feingold, "A Few Psychological Aspects to Consider in the Planning and Development of Gymnasiums." Unpublished manuscript as cited by L. Rosenfield, "Setting the Stage for Learning," *Theory into Practice* 16 (1977): 167–172.

55. See, for example, E. S. Grobsmith, *Nonverbal Modes of Learning: Dakota Sign Language and Gesture Communication* (Tucson, AZ: University of Arizona, 1973). (ERIC Document Reproduction Service No. ED 093160); G. J. Hammer, "Experimental Study of Prolonged Teacher Silence," *Social Science Record* 23 (1976): 32–34; J. V. Jensen, "Communicative Functions of Silence," A Review of *General Semantics* 30 (1973): 149–157; and A. F. Raymond, *An Analysis of Nonverbal Behaviors Exhibited by Two Groups of Science Student Teachers* (Norfolk, VA: Old Dominion University, 1973) (ERIC Document Reproduction Service No. FD 089 945).

56. See research reviewed in Cooper and Tom, "Teacher Expectation Research."

57. J. Biggers, "Body Rhythms, the School Day, and Academic Achievement," *Journal of Experimental Education* 49 (Fall 1980): 45–47; Hurt, et al., *Communica-*

tion in the Classroom (Reading, MA: Addison-Wesley, 1978).

58. R. Dunn, J. Beaudry, and A. Klavas, "Survey of Research on Learning Styles," *Educational Leadership* (March 1989): 50–58.

59. A. L. Chaikin, et al., "Students' Reactions to Teachers' Physical Attractiveness and Nonverbal Behavior: Two Exploratory Studies," *Psychology in the Schools* 15 (1978): 588–595.

60. S. Buck and D. Tiene, "The Impact of Physical Attractiveness, Gender, and Teaching Philosophy on Teacher Evaluations," *Journal of Educational Research* 82 (Jan/Feb 1989): 172–177.

61. J. E. Singer, "The Use of Manipulative Strategies: Machiavellianism and Attractiveness," *Sociometry* 27 (1964): 128–151.

62. J. Gibson, "Do Looks Help Children Make the Grade?" *Family Weekly* (June 27, 1982): 9; L. Schlossen and B. Algozzine, "Sex, Behavior, and Teacher Expectancies," *Journal of Experimental Education* 48 (Spring 1980): 231–236; research reviewed in Richmond, McCroskey, and Payne, *Nonverbal Behavior in Interpersonal Relations.*

63. See, for example, R. Algozzine, "What Teachers Perceive—Children Receive?" *Communication Quarterly* 24 (1976): 41–47; and M. Clifford and E. Webster, "The Effect of Physical Attractiveness on Teacher Expectation," *Sociology of Education* 46 (1973): 248–258.

64. For a good review of this literature, see Knapp, *Nonverbal Communication in Human Interaction* (New York: Holt, Rinehart and Winston, 1978); Richmond, McCroskey, and Payne, *Nonverbal Behavior in Interpersonal Relations.*

65. Richmond, McCroskey, and Payne, 244.

66. J. Rierdan, E. Koff, and M. Stubbs, "Gender, Depression and Body Image in Early Adolescence," *Journal of Early Adolescence* 8 (1988): 109–117.

67. J. Rierdan, E. Koff, and M. Stubbs, "A Longitudinal Analysis of Body Image as a Predictor of the Onset and Persistence of Adolescent Girls' Depression," *Journal of Early Adolescence* 9 (1989): 454–466.

68. R. Lerner, M. Delaney, L. Hess, J. Javonovic, and A. von Eye, "Early Adolescent Physical Attractiveness and Academic Competence," *Journal of Early Adolescence* 10 (Feb. 1990): 4–20; E. Koff, J. Rierdan, and M. Stubbs, "Gender, Body Image, and Self-Concept in Early Adolescence," *Journal of Early Adolescence* 10 (Feb. 1990): 37–55.

69. M. L. Knapp, *Nonverbal Communication in Human Interaction,* 131.

70. R. P. Harrison, *Beyond Words* (Englewood Cliffs, NJ: Prentice Hall, 1974) 115.

71. See research reviewed in Richmond, McCroskey, and Payne, *Nonverbal Behavior in Interpersonal Relations.*

72. Reported in *Learning* (March 1983): 8.

73. *Learning.*

74. P. Ekman and W. V. Friesen, "The Repertoire of Nonverbal Behavior: Categories, Origins, Usage, and Coding," *Semiotica* 1 (1969): 49–98.

75. T. H. Willett and M. J. Smythe, "A Descriptive Analysis of Nonverbal Behaviors of College Teachers," Speech Communication Association Convention, Washington, D.C., 1977.

76. J. M. Seals and P. A. Kaufman, "Effects of Nonverbal Behavior on Student Attitudes in the College Classroom," *Humanist Educator* 14 (1975) 51–55.

77. B. Rosenshine, "Objectively Measured Behavioral Predictors of Effectiveness in Explaining," American Education Research Association Convention, Chicago, 1968.

78. V. L. Wycoff, "The Effects of Stimulus Variation on Learning from Lecture," *Journal of Experimental Education* 41 (1973): 85–90.

79. A. Mehrabian, "Significance of Posture and Position in the Communication of Attitude and Status Relationships," *Psychological Bulletin* 71 (1969): 368.

80. M. Reece and R. Whitman, "Expressive Movements, Warmth, and Verbal Rein-

forcement," *Journal of Abnormal and Social Psychology* 64 (1962): 234-236.

81. M. A. Bayes, "An Investigation of the Behavioral Cues of Interpersonal Warmth," *Dissertation Abstracts International* 31 (1970): 2272 B.

82. G. Gafner, "Nonverbal Cues of Teacher Warmth as Perceived by Students," *Dissertation Abstracts International* 38 (1977): 212.

83. L. T. Keith, H. G. Tornatzky, and L. E. Pettigrew, "An Analysis of Verbal and Nonverbal Classroom Teaching Behaviors," *Journal of Experimental Education* 42 (1974): 30-38.

84. R. Exline, "Visual Interaction: The Glances of Power and Preference," *Nebraska Symposium on Motivation*, ed. J. K. Cole (Lincoln: U. of Nebraska P, 1971) 163-206.

85. S. Beebe, "Effects of Eye Contact, Posture, and Vocal Inflection upon Credibility and Comprehension," Speech Communication Association Convention, Minneapolis, Nov. 1978.

86. C. Galloway, "Nonverbal: The Language of Sensitivity," *Theory Into Practice* 10 (1971): 227-230.

87. S. Beebe, "The Role of Nonverbal Communication in Education: Research and Theoretical Perspectives," Speech Communication Association Convention, New York. 1980.

88. J. Jecker, N. Maccoby, M. Breitrose, and E. Rose, "Teacher Accuracy in Assessing Cognitive Visual Feedback from Students," *Journal of Applied Psychology* 48 (1964): 393-397.

89. B. Comear, *Fragments from an Unknown Gospel* (Boston: United Church Press, 1970) 46.

90. M. F. A. Montagu, *Touching: The Human Significance of the Skin* (New York: Columbia Press, 1971) 292.

91. F. N. Willes and G. E. Hoffman, "Development of Tactile Patterns in Relation to Age, Sex, and Race," *Developmental Psychology* 11 (1975): 866; F. N. Willis and D. L. Reeves, "Touch Interaction in Junior High Students in Relation to Sex and Race," *Developmental Psychology* 12 (1976): 91-92.

92. G. M. Glasgow, "A Semantic Index of Vocal Pitch," *Speech Monographs* 19 (1952): 64-68; C. Woolbert, "The Effects of Various Models of Public Reading," *Journal of Applied Psychology* (1920): 162-185.

93. C. E Diehl, R. C. White, and P. H. Satz, "Pitch Change and Comprehension," *Speech Monographs* (1961): 65-68; S. Beebe, "The Role of Nonverbal Communication in Education."

94. W. B. Pearce and F. Conklin, "Nonverbal Vocalic Communication and Perception of a Speaker," *Speech Monographs* 38 (1971): 235-242; P. J. Karr and M. Beatty, "Effects of Verbal-Vocal Message Discrepancy on Teacher Credibility," *Educational Research Quarterly* 4 (1979): 76-80.

95. D. W. Addington, "The Relationships of Selected Vocal Characteristics to Personality Perception," *Speech Monographs* 35 (1968): 499-502.

96. V. P. Richmond, J. S. Gorham, and J. C. McCrosky, "The Relationship between Selected Immediacy Behaviors and Cognitive Learning," *Communication Yearbook 10*, ed. M. L. McLaughlin (Beverly Hills, CA: Sage, 1986).

97. A. Love and J. Roderick, "Teacher Nonverbal Communication: The Development and Field Testing of an Awareness Unit," *Theory Into Practice* 10 (1971): 295-299.

## SUGGESTIONS FOR FURTHER READING

Andersen, P., J. Andersen, and S. Mayton. "The Development of Nonverbal Communication in the Classroom: Teachers' Perceptions of Students in Grades K-12." *Western Journal of Speech Communication* 49 (1985): 188-203.

Bourkr, S. "How Smaller Is Better: Some Relationships Between Class Size, Teaching Practices, and Student Achievement." *American Educational Research Journal* 23 (Winter 1986): 558-571.

Duran, R. L., and L. Kelly. "The Influence of Communicative Competence on Perceived Task, Social, and Physical Attraction." *Communication Quarterly* 36 (Winter 1988): 41-49.

Eakins, B., and R. G. Eakins. "Sex Differences in Nonverbal Communication." *Intercultural Communication: A Reader*, 5th ed. Ed. L. Samovar and R. Porter. Belmont, CA: Wadsworth, 1988, 292-310.

Fraser, B., and P. O'Brien. "Student and Teacher Perceptions of the Environment of Elementary School Classrooms." *The Elementary School Journal* 85 (May 1985): 567-580.

Gursky, D. "Schools with Style." *Teacher Magazine* (Jan. 1990): 46-51.

Hedges, L., and W. Stock. "The Effects of Class Size: An Examination of a Rival Hypothesis." *American Educational Research Journal* 20 (Spring 1983): 63-86.

Hickson, M. L., III and D. W. Stacks. *Nonverbal Communication: Studies and Applications.* Dubuque, IA: Wm. C. Brown, 1985.

Jones, M. Anway. "The Relationship Between Selected Simulated Vocal Cues and Students' Preferences Toward Female Instructors." SCA Convention. San Francisco, No. 1989.

Jones, S., and E. Yarbrough. "A Naturalistic Study of the Meaning of Touch." *Communication Monographs* 52 (1985): 19-56.

Katz, A. M., and V. T. Katz, eds. *Foundations of Nonverbal Communication: Readings, Exercises, and Commentary.* Carbondale and Edwardsville, IL: Southern Illinois, 1983.

Kearney, P., T. Plax, and N. Wendt-Wasco. "Teacher Immediacy for Affective Learning in Divergent College Classes." *Communication Quarterly* 33 (1985): 61-74.

Knapp, M. L. *Nonverbal Communication in Human Interaction*, 2nd ed. New York: Holt, Rinehart and Winston, 1978 and *Essentials of Nonverbal Communication*. New York: Holt, Rinehart and Winston, 1980.

Koch, R. "The Teacher and Nonverbal Communication." *Theory into Practice* 10 (1971): 231-242.

Leathers, D. G. *Successful Nonverbal Communication: Principles and Applications.* New York: Macmillan, 1986.

Lieberman, D. A., T. G. Rigo, and R. F. Campain. "Age Related Differences in Nonverbal Decoding Ability." *Communication Quarterly* 36 (Fall 1988): 290-297.

Morganstern, B. "Nonverbal Communication Classification System for Teaching Behaviors." *Communication Yearbook 2.* Ed. Brent Rubin. New Brunswick, NJ: Transaction Books, 1978. 473-486.

Remland, M. S., and T. S. Jones. "The Effects of Nonverbal Involvement and Communication Apprehension on State Anxiety, Interpersonal Attraction, and Speech Duration." *Communication Quarterly* 37 (Summer 1989): 170-183.

Shenkle, A. M. "Shaping the Classroom Landscape." *Learning* 88 (Sept. 1988): 61-64.

Spitzberg, B. and T. H. Hurt. "The Measurement of Interpersonal Skills in Instructional Contexts." *Communication Education* 36 (1987): 28-45.

Stewart, R. A., P. Kearney, and T. G. Plax. "Locus of Control a Mediator: A Study of College Students' Reactions to Teachers' Attempts to Gain Compliance." *Communication Yearbook 9*. Ed. M. L. McLaughlin. Beverly Hills, CA: Sage, 1985. 691–704.

Stohl, C. "Perceptions of Social Attractiveness and Communication Style: A Development Study of Preschool Children." *Communication Education* 30 (October 1981): 367–376.

Wiemann, M. O. and J. M. Wiemann. *Nonverbal Communication in the Elementary Classroom*. Urbana, IL: ERIC Clearinghouse on Reading and Communication Skills, 1975.

Wood, B. S. *Children and Communication: Verbal and Nonverbal Language Development*. 2nd ed. Englewood Cliffs, NJ: Prentice Hall, 1981.

# 5 SHARING INFORMATION

## OBJECTIVES

After reading this chapter and completing the activities, you should be able to:

- List the four factors to consider when choosing a teaching strategy
- Identify the variables that affect information processing in the classroom
- Designate four principles of information exchange and explain how they relate to lecturing
- Define learning style
- List advantages and disadvantages of the lecture method
- Designate when lecturing is an appropriate teaching strategy
- Identify communication barriers that often arise when lecturing
- Prepare a lecture using the five steps of lecture preparation
- Present a mini-lecture in a microteaching situation

## INTRODUCTION

A variety of teaching strategies exist from which teachers can choose—lecture, discussion, independent study, programmed learning, computer-assisted instruction, small-group instruction, peer instruction, etc. In any one day, a teacher may utilize several of these strategies. No one of these strategies has been found to be superior over any other.[1] How, then, can a teacher choose the "best" strategy for her students?

## CHOOSING A TEACHING STRATEGY

The choice of a teaching strategy is not an easy task. However, there are certain guidelines a teacher should follow. Four will be discussed here. Keep in mind that no one teaching method is inherently good or bad. However, given the guidelines presented here, you should be able to choose the appropriate strategy for your particular needs.

### The Teacher

The first consideration when determining which teaching strategy to use is the personality and expertise of you—the teacher. Anyone who has taught knows that he has more adaptability and skill in some approaches than in others. Some teachers feel most comfortable when lecturing, others feel quite capable of stimulating a class discussion. A teacher's ability to tolerate high levels of ambiguity, willingness to relinquish some of the control over the classroom, and the ability to tolerate low levels of organization and structure will influence a teacher's liking of the discussion method.

To a certain extent, you should use the approach with which you feel most comfortable. However, I would encourage you to experiment with a variety of teaching strategies. You might find you enjoy and do well in several approaches.

---

### ACTIVITY 5.1

You have completed several activities focusing on how you view yourself as a teacher. Reexamine your answers. With which teaching methods do you feel most comfortable? (If you have never taught, with which methods do you think you would feel most comfortable?) Explain your answer. Are you willing to try other teaching methods? Why or why not?

---

### Objective of the Lesson

A second important factor to consider is the objective of the lesson. If the objective is information acquisition, the lecture method would be one appropriate method. If the objective is to have students develop their critical thinking abilities, a discussion method would be more appropriate. It's imperative that you formulate objectives for each lesson and then utilize the teaching strategy that will best enable your students to meet those objectives.

## The Students

Students—their age, intelligence, motivational level, and previous learning of the subject matter—are an important consideration when choosing a particular teaching strategy. For example, the attention span of elementary school children is limited. Thus, the lecture method will not be as appropriate as some other teaching methods. Most researchers recommend only 10-20 minutes of lecturing for any age group. In addition, students who are below average in intelligence or educational experience may have difficulty learning via the lecture method. In contrast, students who are not highly motivated may benefit from the lecture method, since it affords them the structure they need in order to learn.[2]

---

### ACTIVITY 5.2

It's important for you to get to know your students. It's impossible for you to effectively teach students you don't know. The examples below suggest the types of questions you might ask your students on a questionnaire. The questions below are only suggestions. It's likely you'll want to add others depending on the age level of your students. Indicate to your students that all information is confidential and they may choose not to answer any questions they would rather not.

1. How old are you?
2. What is your father's occupation? Your mother's?
3. How many children are in your family?
4. Name a hobby or activity you enjoy.
5. What are your favorite academic subjects? Your least favorite?
6. Who are your best friends?
7. List three adjectives that describe you.
8. If you had one wish, what would it be?
9. What books, magazines, and newspapers do you read?
10. Do you have a job? If so, how many hours a week do you work? Describe your job.
11. In what extracurricular activities are you involved?
12. What is your major goal for this year?

---

## The Environment

Finally, the environment in which learning is to take place must be considered. The environment includes such variables as time, class size, and furniture arrangements. How much time will you have for the lesson itself? To adequately evaluate and handle students takes more instructional time with some teaching methods than with others. Class size is a factor to consider. For example, the larger the class, the more difficult it will be to use the discussion method. Some classrooms do not lend themselves to using small instructional groups. For example, if, in a straight row arrangement, chairs are bolted to the floor (as was the case in a classroom in which I taught), it's difficult to arrange furniture spatially in a manner conducive to small-group communication. Remember that the classroom is a system. All these factors—teacher, objectives, student, environment—interact to affect which teaching strategy is best for a particular lesson.

Keeping these general guidelines in mind, the next few chapters will examine specific teaching methods—the lecture, discussion, and the use of small groups. It's important to remember that these methods will be examined from a communication perspective. In other words, we'll be concerned with the communication interaction that occurs when each of these methods is utilized, as well as communication skills necessary in order to teach via each of these methods. The present chapter will be concerned with the lecture method. Although teachers of elementary school children will not use this method to the extent teachers of older students will, the principles discussed can be utilized for any information-sharing function in the classroom—giving directions, making explanations, conducting reviews.

Before we discuss the lecture method and other information-sharing functions in the classroom, we need to first examine how students process the information we share with them.

## PROCESSING INFORMATION

The language of the classroom and the language of instruction are largely verbal. Although the verbal learning process is obviously central to an understanding of classroom learning, psychologists have only recently begun to examine how students learn via verbal discourse. John Carroll[3] outlines four distinct problems in studying learning from meaningful verbal discourse.

1.  The problem of how the individual learns her language and how this learning makes it possible to learn from meaningful verbal discourse.
2.  The problem of how an individual understands sentences upon immediate presentation.
3.  The problem of how sentence comprehensions are retained.
4.  The problem of the relation between learning through language and learning by other means.

Until we have answers or solutions to these problems, Carroll suggests learning through verbal discourse will not be as effective as it could otherwise be.

Despite the lack of complete solutions to these problems, we still know certain things about how students learn from being told and what we as teachers can do to make that learning more effective. Students acquire and process information symbolically through language, their perceptions of you and the classroom situation, and their perceptions and communication with self. Several variables affect this symbolic interaction process in the classroom—sensory limitations, perception differences, emotional states, needs, values, and beliefs. We'll examine student variables, message variables, and some principles of information exchange teachers should consider when lecturing.

## Student Variables

All of us have *sensory limitations*. We may have a hearing or sight problem. However, even if we don't have an extreme problem, we all differ in how well we use our senses in the learning process. In addition, anytime we as teachers use a strategy that eliminates one or more of the senses used by students to receive messages, we are limiting their learning even further. Simply lecturing on how to dissect a frog is not nearly as effective as combining that lecture with student dissection of the frog.

Our perceptions greatly affect the way we communicate. We discussed this at great length in chapter 2. (This would be a good time to review that section of chapter 2.)

Our *emotional states* affect how well we are able to process information. It's extremely difficult to acquire and process any information when we are tired, depressed, anxious, or experiencing some kind of conflict or personal problem. The more supportive you can make the climate in your classroom, the less tense and anxious students will be and the easier it will be for them to acquire the information you present.

As Maslow has told us for years, when lower level needs (such as safety) are not met, students cannot fulfill higher level needs.[4] Maslow classified human needs into five hierarchical needs. An adaptation of his hierarchy for educational settings is shown in figure 5.1. For example, when I first started teaching, I taught in a school in which students came from very economically poor backgrounds. They were not very motivated. I remember one student in particular—Daryl. Daryl had given me nothing but trouble. I kept trying to persuade him that if he did well in school he could go to college and better himself. I was making an emotional appeal to Daryl's achievement need—a fairly high-level need on Maslow's hierarchy. One day it hit me why my appeals never worked.

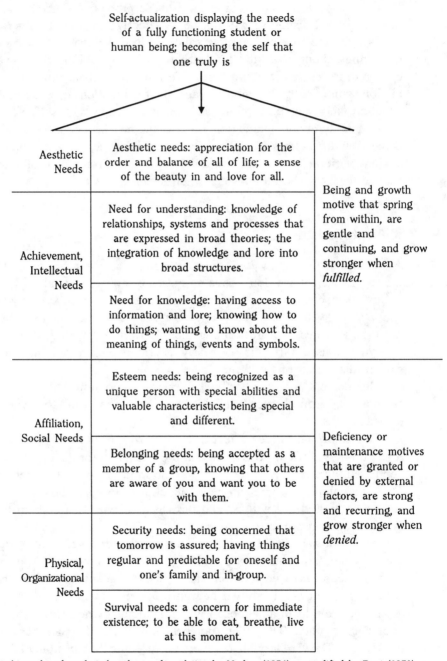

This hierarchy of needs is based on a formulation by Maslow (1954) as modified by Root (1970).

***Figure 5.1*** *A hierarchy of needs.*

From N. L. Gage and D. C. Berliner, *Educational Psychology* (Chicago: Rand McNally, 1974) 286.

Daryl had been absent for about a week. When he returned to school he came to see me. He had spent the week in jail. His father had been beating his mother and baby brother, so Daryl began to beat his father. The police were called and Daryl was arrested. Daryl couldn't be concerned with achievement needs. Any appeals I made to that need would never persuade Daryl to do anything. I had to make appeals on the level of needs that were most important to Daryl—security needs. Appealing to security needs, I told Daryl that if he did well in school, that might be one less thing his father could use as an excuse to get angry. If we're going to influence our students, we must meet them where they are. Appealing to the need that is not important to the student will never influence him.

Finally, a student's *attitudes and beliefs* can affect his information processing. How students feel about themselves can affect their information processing. How the student feels about you as a teacher can affect information processing. If a student does not like you or the topic covered, she will probably not respond well to the information you present.

Learning style examines how a learner learns and processes information.[5] According to Dunn, Dunn, and Price,[6] "learning style is the way in which responses are made because of individual psychological differences." Keefe defines learning style as "cognitive, affective, and physiological traits that serve as relatively stable indicators of how learners perceive, interact with and respond to the learning environment."[7] For example, Sinatra[8] reviewed a large body of research which indicates that the learning style of the gifted and talented can be described as independent, internally controlled, self-motivated, persistent, perceptually strong, task-committed, and nonconforming. These learners prefer learning through independent studies and projects rather than through lecture or discussion.

As Dunn and her associates[9] indicate, no learning style is better or worse than another. What is important, however, is the fact that the closer the match between each student's and the teacher's styles, the higher the grade point average. When students are permitted to learn difficult academic information or skills through their identified learning style preferences, students tend to achieve statistically higher test and aptitude scores than when instruction is dissonant with their preferences.

Teachers need to identify their students' learning styles. There are numerous commercially published instruments to measure one or many aspects of learning style (in the "Further Reading" section at the end of the chapter, several learning style tests are listed.). However, Cornett[10] suggests that even without formal instruments, it is possible to obtain assessment information from observations of students or discussing with students their own views by asking "How, when, where, and what do you learn best?" Another technique is to ask students to write or tell about a learning or study situation in which they were either productive or nonproductive and analyze the situation.

## ACTIVITY 5.3

Complete the Informal Learning Style Inventory[11] below.

### Informal Learning Style Inventory

*Directions*

1.  For the sections dealing with cognitive and affective styles, put an X on the line at a point where you think you fall with regard to the polar concepts expressed by the two words. For the section dealing with physical aspects of learning style, check your preferences and describe the environment in which you learn best.
2.  After completing the inventory draw a line connecting the X's. This, along with your preferences, will give you a rough profile of your learning and teaching style.

*Cognitive Style (concerned with processing, encoding, storage and retrieval of information)*

sequential . . . . . . . . . . . . . . . . . . . random

serial . . . . . . . . . . . . . . . . . . . simultaneous

focusing . . . . . . . . . . . . . . . . . . . scanning

separating . . . . . . . . . . . . . . . . . . . integrating

parts . . . . . . . . . . . . . . . . . . . whole

discriminate . . . . . . . . . . . . . . . . . . . generalize

sharpening . . . . . . . . . . . . . . . . . . . leveling

abstract . . . . . . . . . . . . . . . . . . . concrete

compartmentalization . . . . . . . . . . . . . . . differentiation

narrow categories . . . . . . . . . . . . . . . broad categories

analyze by describing . . . . . . . . . . . draw relationships based on functions and themes

reflective . . . . . . . . . . . . . . . . . . . impulsive

deductive . . . . . . . . . . . . . . . . . . . inductive

convergent . . . . . . . . . . . . . . . . . . . divergent

analytic . . . . . . . . . . . . . . . . . . . global

splitter . . . . . . . . . . . . . . . . . . . lumper

logical . . . . . . . . . . . . . . . . . . . metamorphic

words . . . . . . . . . . . . . . . . . . . images

time-oriented . . . . . . . . . . . . . . . . . . . nontemporal

digital . . . . . . . . . . . . . . . . . . . . . . . spatial
details and facts . . . . . . . . . . . . . . . . generalizations
careful . . . . . . . . . . . . . . . . . . . . . . quick
literal . . . . . . . . . . . . . . . . . . . . . . figurative
outline . . . . . . . . . . . . . . . . . . . . . summarize
surface approach . . . . . . . . . . . . . . . deep approach
memorize . . . . . . . . . . . . . . . . . . . . associate/understand
verbal communication . . . . . . . . . . . . nonverbal communication
implications . . . . . . . . . . . . . . . . . . analogies

### *Affective Style (concerned with attention, motivation and personality)*

objective . . . . . . . . . . . . . . . . . . . . subjective
practical . . . . . . . . . . . . . . . . . . . . theoretical
reality . . . . . . . . . . . . . . . . . . . . . . fantasy
subject-oriented . . . . . . . . . . . . . . . . people-oriented
realistic . . . . . . . . . . . . . . . . . . . . . imaginative
intellectual . . . . . . . . . . . . . . . . . . creative
close-minded . . . . . . . . . . . . . . . . . . open-minded
conformist . . . . . . . . . . . . . . . . . . . individualist
concentration . . . . . . . . . . . . . . . . . distraction
reserved . . . . . . . . . . . . . . . . . . . . . outgoing
thinker . . . . . . . . . . . . . . . . . . . . . intuiter
rigid . . . . . . . . . . . . . . . . . . . . . . . flexible
Groucho humor (puns, satire) . . . . . . . . . Harpo humor (slapstick)
competitive . . . . . . . . . . . . . . . . . . . cooperative
structured . . . . . . . . . . . . . . . . . . . . unstructured
intrinsically motivated . . . . . . . . . . . . . extrinsically motivated
persistent . . . . . . . . . . . . . . . . . . . . gives up easily
cautious . . . . . . . . . . . . . . . . . . . . . risk-taking
intolerant of ambiguity . . . . . . . . . . . . tolerant of ambiguity
internal locus of control . . . . . . . . . . . . external locus of control
leader . . . . . . . . . . . . . . . . . . . . . . follower
pessimistic . . . . . . . . . . . . . . . . . . . optimistic
future-oriented . . . . . . . . . . . . . . . . . present-oriented

does not like pressure . . . . . . . . . . . . . likes pressure

likes working alone . . . . . . . . . . . . . likes working in a group

### Physical Style (concerned with perceptual modes, energy level, time preferences and environment)

**Directions:** *Check your preferences*

| Receiving Information | | Expressing Yourself | |
|---|---|---|---|
| visual (reading and viewing) | _____ | visual (writing, drawing, etc.) | _____ |
| auditory (listening) | _____ | oral (speaking) | _____ |
| kinesthetic (feeling and doing) | _____ | kinesthetic (art, demonstrating, or showing) | _____ |
| smell | _____ | | |
| taste | _____ | | |

Describe the environment in which you learn best (lighting, furniture, room arrangement, noise level, time of day, etc.).

After completing this inventory, perhaps you will discover things about your learning and teaching style that you had not realized before. If your cognitive profile lies more to the left, then you probably are more left-brain oriented; if it lies to the right, then you are likely to be more right-brain oriented. If your affective profile lies to the left, you are probably more systematic, structured, and organized. If your affective profile is more to the right, you are probably more flexible, group-oriented, and creative. Perhaps you will discover a balance of right and left. What is important is to "know thyself." But remember, this is only a rough indicator!

## Message Variables

Message variables—both verbal and nonverbal—that increase attention will also increase the information processed. Organization of the message—the order in which points are presented—affects processing as well as recall. Points presented first or last in a lecture are better remembered and understood. Concrete language is better remembered and processed than ambiguous language. In addition, intense language facilitates information processing, since it increases, to a certain extent, the students' attention levels. Finally, a two-sided, rather than a one-sided message, creates greater retention and comprehension, since attention and perceptions are increased by the novelty and contrast produced by this message strategy.

## Principles of Information Exchange

In an attempt to make "learning from being told" easier for our students, the following principles of communication information exchange are recommended.

1. Create a *need to know* in your students. If you ask your instructor on the first day of class what will be expected—how many papers, texts, etc.—you'll listen to the answer. You feel a "need to know." Similarly, your students must have the same feeling if they are to listen to your lecture.

2. Make your information *relevant*. This may involve your relating the new information to already familiar information. If your instructor speaks to your class about persuasion theory, the information may not relate to your experience. If, on the other hand, your instructor relates the information about persuasion theory to advertising and explains how you are affected by persuasive techniques in advertising, you will be more interested in the information.

3. Information is more likely to be understood if it is *well organized, repeated, and has emotional impact.*

When presenting information, organization is very important. If you are describing a process, for example, you must begin "at the beginning" and follow through each step until you reach the end of the process. If you "skip around," your students will become confused and information will be lost.

Repetition is also important in retention of information. You should determine the four or five most important ideas in your lecture and utilize repetitions to "drive home" your point.

Think about this past week. What event "stands out" in your memory? Was it when you forgot your speech halfway through it? Perhaps it was a date, a class presentation, or an exam. No doubt it was an event filled with emotional impact. Information that contains such impact is more memorable than straight facts. In your lecturing you should make use of memorable examples, illustrations, and anecdotes to help insure your students' retention of your key ideas.

4. Retention and understanding are lessened if you *overload* your students with too much information. Most students can handle five to nine "bits" of information comfortably. Thus, only a few main points should be covered in a

single lecture. You can reduce information overload by chunking similar information together, previewing the information you'll present, using internal summaries, and narrowing your topic.

Teachers are often called upon to give information. No teacher escapes giving directions, specifying procedures, providing demonstrations, making assignments, and reviewing. Although we'll focus on the lecture as information sharing, remember that the suggestions made concerning the lecture relate to other forms of sharing information as well.

## THE LECTURE

> The robins sang and sang and sang,
> but teacher you went right on.
> The last bell sounded the end of the day,
> but teacher you went right on.
> The geranium on the window sill just died,
> but teacher you went right on.[12]

Too often, the above poem describes our students' reactions to our lecturing. However, this doesn't have to be the case. When you use the lecture method, it doesn't excuse you from having students involved during the lecture. Rhetorical questions, handouts to be completed as the lecture progresses, previewing the lesson, and continually referring to the reading assignment are all means of enhancing student involvement in the lecture. As you read about how to effectively construct and utilize a lecture, keep in mind that the lecture is a communicative event and the "give and take" of communicative messages is a continuous process.

Lecturing is, essentially, informative speaking. The major purpose of informative speaking is to secure clear understanding of the concepts you present. Before discussing the best method of constructing a lecture to help ensure that you create clear understanding, let's discuss the lecture method itself—it's limitations and appropriateness.

Following is a list of the advantages and disadvantages of the lecture method. Notice that the major advantage to lecturing is that vast amounts of information can be presented in a relatively expedient manner. The major idea permeating the disadvantages is that the communicative interaction between students and between student and teacher is quite limited.

### Advantages and Disadvantages to the Lecture Method

Lecturing is advantageous because:

1. It presents a human model.
2. It is inexpensive since the ratio of students to teacher is quite large.
3. It is flexible in that it can be adapted easily to a particular group of students, subject matter, etc.
4. It can cover vast amounts of information.
5. It provides for reinforcement.

   a. Teachers are rewarded by the attention they receive. As one instructor indicates:

   > *I enjoy the lecture method. It is the most dramatic way of presenting to the largest number of students a critical distillation of ideas and information on a subject in the shortest possible time. The bigger the class the better I perform intellectually. How else in teaching can you share with so many a lifetime of looking at and loving art? You stand on a stage in front of a screen on which the whole history of art is projected. You can be an explorer of African art, an interpreter of Greek sculptures, a spokesman for cathedral builders, an advocate of Leonardo, a political theorist for palace architects, an analyst of Picasso and philosopher of Sung painting. No other subject is as visually exciting in the classroom, and this is what keeps me turned on lecture after lecture, year after year. With that supporting cast and if he knew his lines, who wouldn't want to perform in front of a large audience?*[13]

   b. The humor, warmth, and enthusiasm bestowed on students by the effective lecturer can serve as reinforcement to them.

Lecturing is disadvantageous because:

1. Lectures are usually utilized when class size is fairly large. The size of the lecture class prohibits student-teacher interaction, as well as student-student interaction. Students often feel they are "just a number." This depersonalization may impair learning.
2. Since a large amount of information can be covered, students can become easily confused. If, as a lecturer, you don't pay close attention to nonverbal feedback from students, you won't know which material needs to be clarified.
3. It is difficult to probe deeply into material that is abstract or theoretical in nature.
4. It is difficult for students to maintain attention in such an inactive role for more than 15-20 minute intervals.
5. Lecture audiences are heterogeneous and it is therefore difficult to gear material to all audience members.

### When to Lecture

These advantages and disadvantages of the lecture method suggest when lecturing is appropriate and when other methods are perhaps more advantageous. The following list presents the conditions under which the lecture is appropriate and inappropriate.

Lecturing is appropriate[14] when:

1. The basic instructional purpose is to disseminate information.
2. The information is not available elsewhere.
3. The information must be organized and presented in a particular way.
4. It is necessary to arouse learner interest in a subject.
5. It is necessary to introduce an area of content or provide directions for learning tasks that will be developed via some other teaching method.

Lecturing is inappropriate when:

1. The basic instructional purpose involves forms of learning other than the acquisition of information.
2. The instructional objective involves higher cognitive levels, such as analysis, synthesis, and evaluation.
3. The learning task involves initiating or changing attitudes, values, beliefs, and behavior.
4. The information acquired must be remembered for a long period of time.
5. The information is complete, abstract, or detailed.
6. Learner participation is essential to the achievement of the instructional objective.

---

**ACTIVITY 5.4**

Analyze a lecture you recently presented or attended. Was the lecture method appropriate? Why or why not?

---

### Communication Barriers to Effective Lecturing

Even if you decide the lecture method is the most appropriate method for your particular objective, you must be aware of some general communication barriers to effective lecturing. Although there are several, the most common have been outlined by Hart:[15]

1. *There is too much or not enough information presented.* If you continually solicit feedback from your students, you'll be in a position to determine when "information overload" (and hence learner frustration) or when "information underload" (and hence learner boredom) exists. Erring in either direction brings about parallel but different educational problems.

2. *Information is presented too factually or too inferentially.* The "ideal" lecturer is probably neither a fact-spewing computer nor an inference-making guru—she is a scholar who extends knowledge by means of hard data or intelligently conceived hypotheses.

3. *Information is too concrete or too abstract.* Being the active, searching creatures they are, students will demand of a lecturer some capacity to satisfy both their "concrete" and "abstract" needs in some fashion. If you carefully mix-and-match your material, you should be able to satisfy both demands of students.

4. *Information is too general or too specific.* By carefully and consciously moving from the general, to the specific, and back again, you can introduce variety and can improve your students' chances of seeing the forest and the trees.

5. *Communication is feedback-poor or feedback-rich.* Because lecturing is, by nature, "a one-way information transmission system" you must often be quite creative in finding ways to assess the "learning potential" of your lecturing. Testing, of course, can and does tell what information is lost, but unfortunately it does not tell why it is lost. Better methods of getting at "whys" might be one or more of the following:

   a. *Selective feedback*—monitor the reaction of one or two "representative" members of the class and use these responses to bring about ongoing changes in your lecture.
   b. *Overt feedback*—many lecturers use the "if you don't understand something, sing out" technique. This is probably the most desirable type of feedback, but an instructor who uses such a technique had better mean it. Students won't tolerate being begged and then having their wrists slapped when the instructor is affronted by the feedback.
   c. *Delayed feedback*—setting up a "feedback committee" (who makes daily or weekly reports to the lecturer) is often a practical device. If the feedback group is representative of the class and insightful, they can be most helpful to you despite the delayed nature of their feedback.
   d. *Indirect feedback*—coaxing a fellow instructor to attend your lectures can often be helpful, since he is in a position to know what to look for. Obviously, "peer group" evaluations can sometimes be threatening but so too can bad teacher ratings!

e.  *Self feedback*—with the advent of audio- and video-taping equipment, the lecturer has a new ally. By reviewing your own lecture in such a fashion, many important insights can be derived if one makes a conscious effort to keep self-bias at a minimum. While any of these devices can provide you with helpful, corrective information, combining two or more of the techniques would create an even more ideal set of feedback circumstances. In addition, teachers need to monitor students' nonverbal feedback throughout the lecture. Too often teachers lecture, assuming they are being understood. Monitoring student nonverbal feedback and adjusting accordingly (clarifying, slowing down or speeding up the pace, providing an example) will add to the learning potential of the lecture.

6.  *Information is presented too rapidly or too slowly.* Most studies indicate that "normal conversational delivery" is best suited to covering most material with clarity and efficiency. Both excessively rapid and inordinately slow delivery of a lecture will decrease students' comprehension.

7.  *Information is presented too soon or too late.* Fortunately, the "too soon–too late" problems are easier to solve than most. With careful preparation of the lecture and with the knowledge of a few elementary communication principles, many such problems can be avoided. For example, by remembering that listeners find it easier to move from the simple to the complex, from the concrete to the abstract, or from the immediate to the futuristic, you can often avoid moving into material too quickly. Likewise, by knowing that listeners have a need for pattern, chronology, and completeness, you should be reminded that information must be "processed" or "wrapped-up" before students will be able to retain it.

8.  *Information is presented with too much or too little intensity.*

## PREPARING A LECTURE

Now that you understand the advantages, disadvantages, and appropriateness of the lecture method, it's time to begin constructing a lecture. Perhaps the most important consideration to keep in mind as you prepare your lecture is the learning objective(s) you want to accomplish. Everything you do in your lecture should relate to the objective(s). As you go through the preparation process, continually ask yourself, "How will this help me meet my learning objective?"

The steps in lecture preparation are five: (1) choose a topic, (2) narrow the topic, (3) gather supporting material, (4) organize the lecture, and (5) practice the lecture. We'll discuss each of these in detail.

## Choose a Topic

The first step in lecture preparation is to choose a topic. What information do you want your students to know? This step is fairly complex. In deciding what you want your students to know, several factors must be considered. First, you need to consider yourself. What do you know about the topic? Can you rely exclusively on your own knowledge or will you need to utilize the thoughts and/or research of others?

Your students must also be considered—their age and educational level are particularly important. Is the topic of real relevance to them? What knowledge do they already possess concerning the topic? What attitudes, past experiences, and unique characteristics do they have that would influence how the topic should be approached?

The classroom environment is another important factor. Are the physical environment and the psychological environment of the classroom conducive to covering the topic? Is there enough time? Will visual aids be necessary to create attention to and to clarify the topic?

---

### ACTIVITY 5.5

This activity is the first in a series. The remainder of the activities in this chapter will prepare you for the culminating activity—microteaching. Before progressing further, read Appendix A, which explains microteaching. When you are finished reading, choose a topic for a lecture. Analyze yourself, the student group to whom you will present the lecture, and the classroom environment in which the lecture will be given.

---

## Narrow the Topic

The next step in lecture preparation is to narrow your topic. You need to narrow your lecture topic until you have a simple sentence that states clearly and concisely what you wish to accomplish with your students (thesis statement). This funneling process is graphically illustrated in figure 5.2.

As you narrow your topic to a thesis statement remember that you must consider the same factors you considered when choosing your topic initially—yourself, your students, and the classroom environment. For example, you considered what you wanted your students to know in general about the topic. As you narrow the topic, you must ask yourself such questions as, what do I want my students to know specifically about this topic? Are they at an age level at which they can understand this particular aspect of the topic? What do they already know and

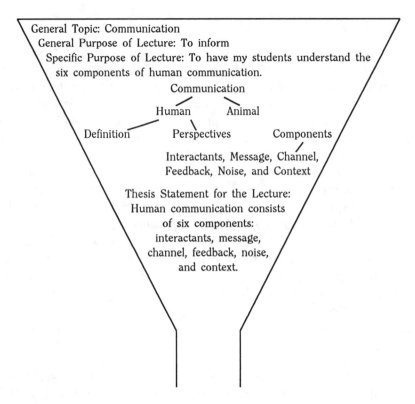

*Figure 5.2 The funneling process: Narrowing a lecture topic.*

how can I utilize this prior knowledge in my lecture? What material have I already taught them and how can I utilize this material in this lecture?

---

### ACTIVITY 5.6

Using the topic you chose in activity 5.5, narrow the topic to a thesis statement. You should plan for a fifteen-minute microteaching session. Thus, your thesis statement must be narrow enough so that you can adequately cover it in fifteen minutes.

---

### Gather Supporting Materials

The third step in lecture preparation is gathering supporting materials that will make the ideas you're presenting "come alive." Supporting materials can be verbal or nonverbal. They are the materials that provide proof and explanation of what you say.

As in every step of lecture preparation, you must consider yourself, your students, and the classroom environment when choosing supporting materials. (Remember the systems perspective!) What supporting materials do you have available already? For example, what personal experiences do you have that you can use as supporting material? Based on your past experiences with your students, what kinds of supporting material do they find particularly enjoyable and helpful? Finally, what constraints does the classroom environment place on you? Perhaps a limited budget prohibits the use of film, for example.

In addition to these considerations, you need to keep the basic purpose of the lecture—to create clear understanding—in the forefront. When choosing supporting materials, consider whether they help clarify your ideas and enhance student attention. Clarification devices are numerous. Table 5.1 presents a brief explanation of the most common types of verbal supporting material used for clarification.

A nonverbal form of supporting material is the visual aid. Visual aids can make your ideas more "concrete" by presenting a pictorial or graphic representation of the idea being explained. Visual aids can help maintain your student's attention also. However, these two purposes—clarification and maintaining attention—will be accomplished only if the visual aids you use are appropriate to the subject matter and the students. In addition, all visual aids should conform to the following standards.

1.  They should be large enough for all students—even those in the back of the lecture hall—to see. If you feel a need to ask your students, "Can you see this?" you know you've violated the first principle of the effective use of a visual aid!

2.  In addition to being large enough, visual aids that are simple rather than detailed, and utilize heavy, dark drawings or printing which can be easily seen should be used.

3.  Speak to your students, not to your visual aid. A mistake teachers often make, particularly when they use a blackboard, is to talk to the blackboard as they write or draw on it. This makes it difficult for students to hear you. In addition, you cannot "read" the feedback students send when your back is to them or when you are focusing on your aid rather than on them.

4.  Make sure you know why you are using the visual aid. It should be an integral part of the lecture. Don't use a visual aid unless there is a purpose for it.

5.  Do not pass the visual aid among your students. This is distracting. When students take time out to examine the aid, they break contact with what you are saying at that moment. If they don't take time to look at the aid, choosing to listen to you instead, the aid is useless.

6. Practice with the aid. Anything that can go wrong will go wrong! Be prepared for any eventuality. Most teachers have had the harrowing experience of planning a film that takes 45 minutes, only to arrive in class to find the projector doesn't work.

**Table 5.1** *Supporting materials: clarification devices.*

| Clarification Device | Function/Example |
|---|---|
| Example | Expository or descriptive passage used to make ideas, process, proposal, etc., clear. |
| a. Illustration | Detailed narrative example |
| 1. Hypothetical | Tells what *could* have happened |
| | An important concept in communication is self-fulfilling prophecies. If we define a situation as real, it becomes real in its consequences. Suppose you are a student in a mathematics class. You have taken other mathematics courses and have not done well. You define yourself as a poor student in this particular class. As a result of that definition, you rarely participate in class, you appear nervous, you cut class several times during the semester, and therefore miss content. As a result, you flunk the exam. The instructor calls you into her office and explains that you will have to do better if you want to pass the mathematics course. Your prophecy—that you're a poor student in math—has been fulfilled. |
| 2. Factual | Tells what *did* happen |
| | Rosenthal's work has shown that an expectation a teacher has for a child can lead to self-fulfilling prophecy in that child. Children were randomly labeled as "bloomers." Teachers were told which students were "bloomers" and which students were not. Eight months later, children who had been labeled "bloomers" did indeed bloom. They received higher test scores than students who were not designated as "bloomers." Teachers' expectations that students would do well led to self-fulfilling prophecies in the "bloomers." |
| b. Instance | An undetailed example—presents numerous examples of the same phenomenon. |
| | An important axiom of communication is that meanings are in people, not in words. How cold is cold? To some people, cold is 20 degrees above zero; to others it is 20 degrees below zero. How tall is tall? When you think of a large university, how many students do you envision? One writer tells us that the simple words, "I love you," can mean anything from, "I desire you sexually" to "I hate you." Think of such words as *democracy*, *cheap*, *dog*, and *happy*. Write down a brief definition of each. Now compare your "meaning" with the one of the person sitting next to you. How similar are they? |

*(Continued)*

| Clarification Device | Function/Example |
|---|---|
| Statistics | Using quantification in order to make a complex situation clear, to substantiate a claim, or make an abstract idea concrete.<br><br>Communication apprehension is a common problem. Research indicates that 1 out of every 5 students is highly apprehensive about communication, and another 20 percent are moderately apprehensive about communicating. |
| Testimony | Using the opinions or conclusions of others; can act as proof or add impressiveness to an idea.<br><br>Because meanings are in people, not in words, we should strive to make our words as explicit as possible. As Mark Twain so aptly indicated, "The difference between the right word and the almost right word is the difference between lightning and the lightning bug." |
| Definition | Presenting a meaning for a word—particularly important when the word is abstract or technical in nature.<br><br>Interpersonal communication is the process of establishing, maintaining, and terminating relationships. |
| Contrast | Pointing out the differences between two phenomenon, one of which is familiar to the students.<br><br>In contrast to the public speaking situation in which communication is very structured, interpersonal communication is a relatively unstructured communication context. In the public context, communication roles are very formalized. This is not true in the interpersonal realm. No one is designated as "speaker" and "receiver." Rather, both people are expected to assume those roles. |
| Comparison | Points out the similarities between something that is familiar to students and something that is not.<br><br>Communication, like life, is a process. It is ever-changing. Just as we cannot repeat part of our lives, neither can we repeat a communication event. Time has passed and so, even if we say the same words, they are not really the "same." Likewise, communication, like life, is irreversible. |
| Restatement/ Repetition | Restatement is the reiteration of an idea in different words; repetition, in the same words. Both restatement and repetition are used to "drive home" an idea.<br><br>Let me remind you. We communicate—not by what we are, but by what listeners understand. We communicate—not by what we intend to say, but by what listeners see, hear, and are willing to accept. We communicate—not by what we say, but by what listeners hear.* |

Adapted from A. Monroe and D. Ehninger, *Principles of Speech Communication*, 7th ed. (Glenview, IL: Scott, Foresman, 1975) 110–120.
*From Waldo W. Braden, "Beyond the Campus Gate," in *Principles of Speech Communication*, 7th ed. by A. Monroe and D. Ehninger (Glenview, IL: Scott, Foresman, 1975) 121.

**ACTIVITY 5.7**

Examine your thesis statement from Activity 5.6. What supporting materials will you use to develop this thesis statement? Describe them.

## Organize the Lecture

Most teachers agree that an organized lecture is better than an unorganized lecture. As Buxton tells us, ". . . the goal of lecturing is, after all, communication, and it is likely to be more effective if there is an evident order or sequence."[16]

In her review of research on direct instruction, Anderson[17] reports that several studies indicate the importance of organization to an effective lesson. Brophy and Good summarize principles for lesson organization:

> *Achievement is maximized when teachers not only actively present material, but structure it by beginning with overviews, advance organizers, or review of objectives; outlining the content and signaling transitions between lesson parts; calling attention to main ideas; summarizing subparts of the lesson as it proceeds; and reviewing main ideas at the end. Organizing concepts and analogies helps learners link the new to the already familiar. Overviews and outlines help them to develop learning sets to use: Rule-example-rule patterns and internal summaries tie specific information items to integrative concepts. Summary reviews integrate and reinforce the learning of major points.*[18]

A lecture has a general organization of introduction, body, and conclusion. The body can be organized according to several patterns. We'll discuss these in detail later. First, however, let's examine purposes and types of introductions and conclusions.

The introduction of your lecture should accomplish the following three purposes.

1. Establish student-teacher rapport. One of the most important variables in the teaching-learning process is the relationship between a teacher and his students. Students feel better about themselves and the learning situation when they feel their relationship with their instructor is a positive one.[19] Students will be more willing to listen if you establish rapport in your introduction.

2. Gain student attention. If students are not attending to what's being said, they cannot learn it. Thus, the introduction must "grab" them and make them want to listen to the rest of the lecture.

3.  "Set the scene." The introduction should preview what you'll cover in your lecture. If you have three main points, enumerate each of those for students. Indicate to them what your objectives are—what they will be expected to know from having heard the lecture. In addition, students should know why what you have to say is important—why they need to know the content you'll cover.

Several different types of introductions can accomplish these three purposes. You might use a quotation, anecdote, a series of rhetorical questions, examples, startling statement of fact, or opinion. Whichever method you choose, make sure it is relevant to your students and the lecture material.

The conclusion to the lecture should accomplish two purposes.

1.  *Post-organize.* Too often we confuse coverage of content with learning. Student exposure to the subject and student learning of the subject are not synonymous. Students need to be reminded of what it was they were to learn from the lecture. This is easily done by summarizing your main points.
2.  *Provide a sense of closure.* Avoid false endings. It is frustrating to students to feel that you're finished and then have you add "just one more point."

In addition to a summary, you might also want to conclude your lecture with a quotation, an example, or any of the methods of introduction discussed earlier. One good technique is to refer back to your introduction. This helps tie your lecture together, making it a complete package. Suppose you began a lecture on perception by showing the transparency of the young-old woman (p. 30 of chapter 2) and asking students, "How old is the woman shown here?" You then explain the process of perception, why we don't all perceive people and events identically, techniques to make us more accurate perceivers, etc. In the conclusion to the lecture you might show the transparency again as you summarize the major points: *We began this lecture with this picture. You now know the process you went through in perceiving the woman (enumerate them), why we didn't all agree on her age (enumerate those reasons), and what you can do to eliminate problems in perception (enumerate those).* The main points of the body of your lecture can be arranged according to several patterns. The most often used organizational patterns are presented in table 5.2. Examples of each are also provided.

The important thing to remember about organizing the body of your lecture is that it should relate to the central idea of the lecture and the instructional objective(s).

**ACTIVITY 5.8**

Organize your lectures choosing any of the organizational patterns we discussed, then outline your lecture. Your outline should follow the form below.

Thesis statement:
Organizational pattern chosen for the body of the lecture:

Why did you choose this pattern?

Outline your lecture in correct outline form.

*Table 5.2*  *Organizational patterns for the body of the lecture.*

| Type | Definition | Example |
|------|------------|---------|
| Chronological | A time sequence | In preparing a lecture, five sequential steps must be followed: choose a topic, narrow the topic, gather supporting materials, organize the lecture, practice the lecture. |
| Spatial | Space relationships— moving systematically from east-to-west, front-to-back, center-to-outside, etc. | Proxemic behavior differs across cultures. A "comfortable" distance between people as they converse differs. We'll examine this phenomena in the U.S. and Latin America. We'll then "fly across the ocean" and examine conversational distances of Europeans and Southern Europeans. Finally, we'll examine the proxemic behavior of Asians and Arabs. |
| Causal | Enumerating causes and moving to effects or enumerating effects and moving to causes. | We all structure our own reality since we all perceive differently. Our perceptions differ because of differing environments, differing stimuli, differing sensory receptors, and differing internal states. |
| Problem- Solution | Describe problem and present a solution | Researchers tell us that one of the major problems for people in the 1990s is the developing and maintaining of warm, personal relationships. The only way for us to solve this problem is to learn how to communicate effectively. |

*(Continued)*

| Type | Definition | Example |
|------|-----------|---------|
| Topical | The topic provides its own organizational structure. | Human communication consists of six components: Interactants, Message, Channel, Feedback, Noise, and Context. |

## Deliver the Lecture

You're now ready to present your lecture. As I indicated earlier, a teacher's delivery can have a great impact on students' reactions to a lecture. If you are enthusiastic about your lecture material, that enthusiasm will come through in your delivery. An animated, enthusiastic delivery can greatly affect your students' desire to listen to you and, thus, enhances their learning.

Most classroom lectures are delivered extemporaneously, i.e., using brief notes so that you can maintain eye contact and a sense of connection with your students. This type of delivery is particularly effective for the lecture because it leaves you free to change your delivery in response to your students' reactions. You can rephrase and repeat ideas as necessary. In addition, your tone will be more conversational, since you must think about your ideas as you phrase them.

Effective delivery takes careful planning and practice. Below are some principles that should be useful to you.

1.  *Think—really think—about what you're saying.* Speak ideas rather than simply reciting words.

2.  *Communicate.* Think of your lecture as a dialogue, not a soliloquy. Talk with your students, not at them. This involves being direct and conversational and looking at your students. Remember that they are not empty chairs, but are alive. Don't just look at them—really see them and relate to them.

3.  *Support and reinforce your ideas with your body, face, and voice.* Vocal aspects of which you should be aware are pitch, intensity, rate, and quality. Pitch is the highness or lowness of your voice. Studies indicate that a variety in pitch is more effective for speaking than is a monotone of pitch. Your own experience supports this idea. A teacher who speaks in a monotone soon begins to make us weary. In addition, such monotone diminishes student comprehension and retention of what is said. To be an effective lecturer, then, you'll need a variety in pitch. Remember, however, that the variety in your pitch should be meaningful—should emphasize the thoughts you are communicating.

Vocal intensity refers to the loudness of your voice. A voice that is too loud or too soft is distracting. You should use loudness, just as you use pitch, to emphasize important thoughts. Remember too that a decrease in loudness can be just as effective for emphasis as can an increase in loudness. The important point here is that variety in intensity is important and you should strive for such variety.

Most beginning lecturers speak too fast. Their speech rate—the timing and pacing of their vocal delivery—is seldom varied. One way to vary the rate of your speech is through the use of the pause. Pauses "punctuate" a speaker's thoughts just as commas, periods, and semicolons punctuate written discourse.

Oral punctuation—the pause—will help students accurately interpret the messages you send. Pauses also allow students time to reflect on what they have heard and how the previous statements made relate one to another. Finally, pauses provide emphasis that will aid in student retention as well as comprehension.

As a lecturer, don't be afraid to use the pause as a means of providing yourself time to "gather your thoughts." If you need to reflect on "where you are," do so. Remember that pauses seem much longer to you than they do to your students. Don't feel a need to fill your pauses with "uhs" or "ahs." Such vocalized pauses are very distracting.

Voice quality is the special sound of your voice. Obviously, a pleasant voice quality is more effective than a nasal, shrill, hoarse, or breathy quality. One way to make your voice quality pleasant is through sharp, precise articulation. A lecturer who mumbles or has a "mushy" quality is difficult to understand. Since your goal as a lecturer is to present information clearly, articulation problems such as those mentioned above must be avoided.

Slovenly pronunciation, like slovenly articulation, must be avoided. If your pronunciation is not clear or correct, students may misunderstand you—again cutting down on their comprehension.

In addition to vocal factors in delivery, you should also be aware of the visual factors of effective delivery. Your interest in your topic can be communicated by your posture, gestures, and facial expressions. Stand erect, poised, and relaxed. You'll look better and feel better. In addition, it is easier to move from that position in order to emphasize ideas or signal variations in thought.

Gestures should flow from your thoughts. Don't force them. Most of us use gestures naturally in our conversations. Patterned or mechanical gestures distract, rather than complement what you're saying. The key here is to be natural.

Facial expressions also communicate much about your interest in the topic presented. A "deadpan" expression does not enhance your presentation. As I've suggested before, look at your audience. Eye contact and animated facial expressions are very important for generating interest and enthusiasm in your students. If you fail to look at your students, they no doubt will suspect you are unconcerned or ill-at-ease. If you don't have visual contact with your students, there is no way you can adjust to their feedback.

4. *Adapt to your students.* Watch for cues indicating that you need to change some aspect of your delivery—pace, volume, pitch, gestures, etc.

An interesting study examined the way in which students signal a lack of comprehension. In lecture classes students often ignored the problem of lack of comprehension. In fact, ignoring was found to be more prevalent in the lecture than in discussion or small group formats. Indicating confusion (with either a quizzical look or some short expression such as "Huh?") and asking for elaboration were used less in the lecture than in the other two formats.[20]

5. *Be enthusiastic.*

6. Those of you who are beginning teachers should *practice your delivery.* Practice "on your feet" and aloud. If possible, you should practice in the room in which you'll actually present the lecture. You may practice before a mirror in order to get an idea of the visual image you present or you may want to get some friends to listen to you. The advantage to the latter is that they can comment on how they view you. You might videotape your lecture. Or, if videotaping is not possible, at least audiotape your lecture.

## Maintaining Attention

Perhaps your most difficult task as a lecturer is to maintain the attention of your students. If students don't attend to what is being presented in the lecture, they cannot learn it. Several factors can help you to hold the attention of your audience. We'll examine seven of the most common factors. If you are to maintain attention, you must make your lecture topic and supporting materials relevant. When I outlined principles of information exchange, I mentioned the fact that you need to "create a need to know" in your students. One of the best ways to create a need to know is to *make your information relevant.* Two factors will aid you in making information relevant: proximity and reality. Elements that are close to students in time and/or space are more relevant than elements that are far removed from their experience. Whenever possible, make use of incidents that occur at your school or in your community. Use examples that are recent. Rather than talking in general abstract terms, refer to the immediate, the concrete, and the actual. For example, if you are lecturing on the strategies used by politicians in their campaigns, use examples from local campaigns or from well-known national figures rather than using hypothetical or historical examples.

It's long been known that active learning is more effective than passive learning.[21] One means of involving students is to *insert questions into the lecture.* Berliner[22] noted that questions can serve the following functions in a lecture:

1. *Emphasis.* You can call special attention to important points by asking a question.

2. *Practice.* A response to a question enables the student to practice her newly acquired knowledge. The old adage, practice makes perfect, seems to be borne out in educational research.

3. *Self-Awareness.* Students can be made aware that they do not understand the material. Often students are robotlike in a lecture—sitting quietly and taking notes. They often do not realize they didn't comprehend the material until they study it later. Questions can stimulate their thinking while they're in the lecture, when it's still possible to get clarification from the instructor.

4. *Diversion.* Much like a coffee break at work, questions inserted into a lecture can represent a form of stimulus variation. As we'll discuss later, stimulus variation can be an aid to attention and, thus, to learning.

5. *Review.* Questions scattered throughout the lecture could require students to review previous material presented in the lecture in order to answer the question. If questions are structured so that such a review is necessary, students are exposed to the lecture material more than just once. This increased exposure should enhance learning.

In addition to inserting questions into the lecture, attention can be enhanced by *your enthusiasm and activity during the lecture.* If you are excited about lecturing, you can generate excitement in your students. Don't lecture because you have to say something, lecture because you have something to say! Rosenshine[23] reviewed five correlational studies in which ratings of enthusiasm by the instructor were correlated with student achievement. Significant correlations ranged from .37 to .56. Other researchers[24] have found similar results—that students learn more from lectures delivered dynamically and enthusiastically.

Rosenshine[25] found that *variety in movement and gesturing* by a lecturer correlated positively with student achievement. This may be because activity generates enthusiasm. At any rate, if you're to be effective as a lecturer, research indicates you need to use a variety of vocal and facial expressions, gestures, and movement in your delivery.

A third major means of maintaining attention is a *combination of the familiar and the novel.* As Monroe and Ehninger suggest, "In a spoken message, the familiar holds attention primarily when the speaker introduces it in connection with something unfamiliar or when some fresh or unknown aspect of it is pointed out."[26] Familiarity, in the extreme, may breed contempt, but it is necessary to a certain degree. New material needs to be related to something familiar if learning is to occur.

Things that are new or unusual "catch our eye." We're all interested in new experiences, new ideas, new products. The unusual is also attention getting. As John B. Bogart tells us, when a dog bites a man that is not news, but when a man bites a dog that is news!

*Suspense and conflict* can create interest and maintain attention. When the outcome of an event is uncertain, the uncertainty increases our attention. Soap operas always end each day with a conflict situation or a suspenseful event. However, we can get bored with soap operas when the conflict is never resolved or the suspense unending. So too will students "give up" listening if you make the information too mysterious or if there seems little hope of resolving the conflict.

*Fresh, sparkling, appropriate humor* is excellent as an attention-maintaining device. Humor can help students enjoy their learning experience by providing a change of pace, relieving tensions, or promoting good student-teacher relationships. Remember that to be effective, humor must be brief, fresh, relevant, and in good taste.[27]

The saying, "variety is the spice of life," may be trite, but, in the case of lecturing, it's true. A monotonous sentence structure, cliches, lack of movement, or the constant use of a single communication channel soon bore students. Whatever you as a lecturer can change fairly often without creating distractions from the subject matter will no doubt help students maintain their attention.

---

**ACTIVITY 5.9**

Present your lecture. Have your "students" evaluate you. A suggested evaluation form is included here. Also, analyze yourself using the form:

### *Lecture Evaluation Form*

Lecturer's Name _____

Topic _____

Please mark an "x" in the space that best represents your evaluation of the lecture.

|  | Poor | Adequate | Good | Excellent |
|---|---|---|---|---|
| *Enthusiasm* | | | | |
| Speaks expressively or emphatically | _____ | _____ | _____ | _____ |
| Moves about while lecturing | _____ | _____ | _____ | _____ |
| Gestures with hands and arms | _____ | _____ | _____ | _____ |
| Shows facial expressions | _____ | _____ | _____ | _____ |
| Uses humor | _____ | _____ | _____ | _____ |
| Reads lecture verbatim from notes | _____ | _____ | _____ | _____ |
| *Clarity* | | | | |
| Uses concrete examples of concepts | _____ | _____ | _____ | _____ |
| Gives multiple examples | _____ | _____ | _____ | _____ |
| Points out practical applications | _____ | _____ | _____ | _____ |

| | Poor | Adequate | Good | Excellent |
|---|---|---|---|---|
| Stresses important points | _____ | _____ | _____ | _____ |
| Repeats difficult ideas | _____ | _____ | _____ | _____ |
| *Interaction* | | | | |
| Addresses students by name | _____ | _____ | _____ | _____ |
| Encourages questions and comments | _____ | _____ | _____ | _____ |
| Talks with students after class | _____ | _____ | _____ | _____ |
| Praises students for good ideas | _____ | _____ | _____ | _____ |
| Asks questions of class | _____ | _____ | _____ | _____ |
| *Task Orientation* | | | | |
| Advises students regarding exams | _____ | _____ | _____ | _____ |
| Provides sample exam questions | _____ | _____ | _____ | _____ |
| Proceeds at rapid pace | _____ | _____ | _____ | _____ |
| Digresses from theme of lecture | _____ | _____ | _____ | _____ |
| States course objectives | _____ | _____ | _____ | _____ |
| *Rapport* | | | | |
| Friendly, easy to talk to | _____ | _____ | _____ | _____ |
| Shows concern for student progress | _____ | _____ | _____ | _____ |
| Offers to help students with problems | _____ | _____ | _____ | _____ |
| Tolerant of other viewpoints | _____ | _____ | _____ | _____ |
| *Organization* | | | | |
| Puts outline of lecture on board | _____ | _____ | _____ | _____ |
| Uses headings and subheadings | _____ | _____ | _____ | _____ |
| Gives preliminary overview of lecture | _____ | _____ | _____ | _____ |
| Signals transition to new topic | _____ | _____ | _____ | _____ |
| Explains how each topic fits in | _____ | _____ | _____ | _____ |
| Suggestions for improving the lecture | _____ | _____ | _____ | _____ |

Adapted from H. Murray, "Classroom Teaching Behaviors Related to College Teaching Effectiveness," *Using Research to Improve Teaching.* Ed. J. Donald and A. Sullivan (San Francisco: Jossey-Bass, 1985) 25.

## IN SUM

Lecturing has been described as "the process whereby the notes of the professor become the notes of the student without going through the minds of either."[28] If you go through the steps of lecture preparation discussed in this chapter—choose a topic, narrow the topic, gather supporting materials, organize the lecture, and practice the lecture—you should be able to make your lecture a communicative transaction with your students. Not only will your notes go through your mind, but through your students' minds as well!

## NOTES

1. R. Dubin and T. Traveggia, *The Teaching-Learning Paradox* (Eugene, OR: U of Oregon, 1968) 35.
2. N. L. Gage and D. C. Berliner, *Educational Psychology* (Chicago: Rand McNally, 1975) 469.
3. J. Carroll, "On Learning from Being Told," *Educational Psychologist* (March 1968): 324–338.
4. From A. H. Maslow, *Motivation and Personality* (New York: Harper and Row, 1954).
5. R. Sinatra, *Visual Literacy Connections to Thinking, Reading and Writing* (Springfield, IL: Charles Thomas, 1986).
6. R. Dunn, K. Dunn, and G. Price, "Identifying Individual Learning Styles," *Student Learning Styles: Diagnosing and Prescribing Programs*, ed. O. Kiernan (Reston, VA: National Association of Secondary School Principals, 1979) 53.
7. J. Keefe, "Assessing Student Learning Styles: An Overview," *Student Learning Styles and Brain Behavior*, ed. J. Keefe (Reston, VA: National Secondary School Principals, 1982) 44.
8. R. Sinatra, *Visual Literacy*.
9. R. Dunn, J. Beaudry, and A. Klavas, "A Survey of Research on Learning Styles," *Educational Leadership* (March 1989): 50–58.
10. C. Cornett, *What You Should Know about Teaching and Learning Styles*, (Bloomington, IN: Phi Delta Kappa Educational Foundation, 1983).
11. Cornett, 15–18.
12. A. Cullum, *The Geranium on the Window Sill Just Died but Teacher You Went Right On* (New York: Quist Press, 1971) 56.
13. A. Elsen, "The Pleasures of Teaching," *The Study of Education at Stanford: Report to the University. VIII. Teaching, Research, and the Faculty* (Stanford; CA: Stanford U, 1969) 21.
14. Adapted from C. Verner and G. Dickinson, "The Lecture: An Analysis and Review of Research," *Adult Education* 17 (1967): 94.
15. R. P. Hart, "Lecturing as Communication: Problems and Potentialities" (W. Lafayette, Indiana: Purdue Research Foundation, 1973), 10–14.
16. C. E. Buxton, *College Teaching: A Psychologist's View* (New York: Harcourt Brace, 1956) 500.
17. I. Anderson, "Classroom Instruction," *Knowledge Base for the Beginning Teacher*, ed. M. Reynolds (New York: Pergamon, 1989).
18. J. Brophy and T. Good, "Teacher Behavior and Student Achievement," *Handbook of Research on Teaching*, ed. M. C. Wittock (New York: Macmillan, 1986) 362.
19. For a review of research in this area, see Pamela Cooper Leth, "Self-Concept and Interpersonal Response in the Classroom: An Exploratory Study" (Ph.D. diss., Purdue University, 1977); and Jean Civikly, "Self-Concept, Significant Others, and Classroom Communication," *Communication in the Classroom: Contemporary Theory and Practice*, ed. L. L. Barker (Englewood Cliffs, NJ: Prentice Hall, 1981): 146–168.
20. W. Kendrick and A. L. Darling, "Problems of Understanding in Classrooms: Students' Use of Clarifying Tactics," *Communication Education* 39 (1990): 15–29.
21. See, for example, A. Davis, L. Alexander, and S. Yelon, *Learning the System Design* (New York: McGraw-Hill, 1974); and M. Dunkin and B. Biddle, *The Study of Teaching* (New York: Holt, Rinehart and Winston, 1974).
22. D. C. Berliner, "The Effects of Test-like Events and Note-Taking on Learning from Lecture Instruction" (Ph.D. diss., Stanford U, 1968).
23. B. Rosenshine, *Teaching Behaviors and Student Achievement* (London: National Foundation for Educational Research in England and Wales, 1971).

24. See, for example, W. D. Coats and U. Smidchens, "Audience Recall as a Function of Speaker Dynamism," *Journal of Educational Research* 57 (1966): 189–191, and J. E. Ware, Jr., "The Doctor Fox Effect: An Experimental Study of the Effectiveness of Lecture Presentations and the Validity of Student Ratings" (Ph.D. diss., Southern Illinois U, 1974).

25. B. Rosenshine, "Objectively Measured Behavioral Predictors of Effectiveness in Explaining," *Research into Classroom Processes*, ed. I. D. Westburg and A. A. Ballack (New York: Teacher's College Press, 1971) 51–98.

26. D. Ehninger, B. Gronbeck, and A. Monroe, *Principles of Speech Communication* 9th ed. (Glenview, IL: Scott Foresman, 1984) 39.

27. J. Civikly, "Humor and the Enjoyment of College Teaching" *Communicating in College Classrooms*, ed. J. Civikly (San Francisco: Jossey-Bass, 1986) 61–70.

28. E. J. Walker and W. J. McKeachie, *Some Thoughts about Teaching the Beginning Course in Psychology* (Belmont, CA: Brooks/Cole, 1967) 13–14.

## SUGGESTIONS FOR FURTHER READING

Anderson, J. "Cognitive Styles and Multicultural Populations." *Journal of Teacher Education* 39 (1988): 2–7.

Armour-Thomas, E. "The Application of Teacher Cognition in the Classroom: A New Teaching Competency." *Journal of Research and Development in Education* 22 (Spring 1989): 29–35.

Bauer, E. "Learning Style and the Learning Disabled." *The Clearing House* (Jan. 1989): 206–207.

Broadwell, S. "It's So Technical I Have to Lecture." *Training* (March 1989): 444.

Buchanan, E. "An Analysis of Student Expectations Regarding Concepts of Teaching Format." *ERIC ED 280 351* (Jan. 1986): 13.

Canfield, A., and J. Canfield, "Learning Styles Inventory." *Humanics Media* Liberty Drawer 79770, Ann Arbor, MI 48107 (1976).

Cashin, W. E. "Improving Lectures." *Idea Paper No. 14, ERIC ED 267 721*, Manhattan, KS (Sept. 1985): 5.

Cooper, P., and K. Galvin. "What Do We Know about Research in Teacher Training in Instructional Strategies?" *Central States Speech Journal* 36 (Fall 1985): 186–192.

Cruickshank, D. "Applying Research on Teacher Clarity." *Journal of Education* 35 (March/April 1985): 44–47.

Darling, A. "Signalling Non-Comprehensions in the Classroom: Toward a Descriptive Typology." *Communication Education* 38 (1989): 34–45.

Duffy, G. G., L. R. Roehler, M. S. Melmoth, and L. G. Vaurus. "Conceptualizing Instructional Explanation." *Teaching and Teacher Education* 2 (1986): 197–214.

Duffy, G. G., L. R. Roehler, and G. Rackliffe. "How Teacher's Instructional Talk Influences Students' Understanding of Lesson Content." *The Elementary School Journal* 87 (1986): 3–16.

Dunn, R., K. Dunn, and G. Price. *Learning Style Inventory, 1975, 1978, 1985.* Available from Price Systems, Box 3067, Lawrence, KS 66046-0067.

Frank, B. "Effect of Field Independence on Study Technique on Learning from a Lecture." *American Educational Research Journal* 21 (Fall 1984): 669-678.

Frederick, P. J. "The Lively Lecture—8 Variations." *College Teaching* 34 (1986): 43-50.

Gleason, M. "Ten Best on Learning: A Bibliography of Essential Sources for Instructors." *College Teaching* 33 (1985): 8-10.

Gregorc, A. *Transaction Ability Inventory.* Department of Secondary Education, U of Connecticut, Box U-33, Storrs, CT 06268.

Gunter, M. A., and P. Hotchkiss. "Yuk! Peanut Butter Again: Avoiding Instructional Monotony." *Action in Teacher Education: Journal of the Association of Teacher Educators* 7 (Fall 1985): 31-36.

Hines, C., D. Cruickshank, and J. Kennedy. "Teacher Clarity and Its Relationship to Student Achievement and Satisfaction." *American Educational Research Journal* 22 (Spring 1985): 87-99.

Kallison, J. "Effects of Lesson Organization on Achievement." *American Educational Research Journal* 23 (Summer 1986): 337-347.

Kardash, C., L. Cukowski, and L. Bentmann. "Effects of Cognitive Style and Immediate Testing on Learning from a Lecture." *Journal of Educational Research* 81 (July/Aug. 1988): 360-365.

Kolb, D. "Learning Style Inventory" in "Disciplinary Inquiry Norms and Student Learning Styles: Diverse Pathways for Growth." *The Modern American College.* Ed. A. Chickering. San Francisco: Jossey-Bass, 1981.

*Learning Styles Network Newsletter.* New York: National Association of Secondary School Principals and St. John's U.

"Lecturing Tips for Large Classes." *The Teaching Professor* (April 1988): 1-2.

Leinhardt, G., and R. Putnam. "The Skill of Learning from Classroom Lessons." *American Educational Research Journal* 24 (Winter 1987): 557-587.

Lowman, Joseph. *Mastering the Techniques of Teaching.* San Francisco: Jossey-Bass Higher Education Series, 1984.

Myers, I., and K. Briggs. *Myers-Briggs Type Indicator.* Palo Alto, CA: Consulting Psychologists Press, Inc., 1976.

"Organization: Communicating the Structure." *The Teaching Professor* 2 (Sept. 1988): 1-2.

Osterman, D., M. Christensen, B. Coffey. *The Feedback Lecture. Idea Paper #13.* Center for Faculty Evaluation and Development. Manhattan, KS: Kansas State U, Jan. 1985.

Penner, J. G. *Why Many College Teachers Cannot Lecture: How to Avoid Communication Breakdown in the Classroom.* Springfield, IL: Charles C. Thomas, 1984.

Pettigrew, F., and C. Buell. "Preservice and Experienced Teachers' Ability to Diagnose Learning Styles." *Journal of Educational Research* 82 (Jan./Feb. 1989): 187-191.

Shenkle, A. "Teaching Style: Connecting with Your Students." *Learning* 89 (Feb. 1989): 79-82.

Simbo, F. K. "The Effects of Notetaking Approaches on Student Achievement in Secondary School Geography." *Journal of Educational Research* 81 (July/Aug. 1988): 377-381.

Sistek, V. "How Much Do Our Students Learn by Attending Lectures?" *ERIC ED 271 079* (1986): 10.

Stasz, C. "Lecturing is Not Dead—A Nature Hike Through Effective Teaching." *The Teaching Professor* (Aug. 1988): 3-4.

Svinicki, M. "How to Pace Your Lectures." *The Teaching Professor* 3 (Nov. 1989): 1-2.

Warner, D. "Using Cognitive Discrimination Training to Develop Classroom Knowledge." *Journal of Teacher Education* (May/June 1985): 55-60.

Weaver, R. L., II, and H. W. Cotrell. "Lecturing: Essential Communication Strategies." *Teaching Large Classes Well*. Ed. M. Gleason Weimer. *New Directions for Teaching and Learning*, no. 32. San Francisco: Jossey-Bass, Winter 1987.

Woods, J. D. "Lecturing: Linking Purpose and Organization." *Improving College and University Teaching* 31 (1983): 61–64.

# 6 LEADING CLASSROOM DISCUSSIONS

## OBJECTIVES

After reading this chapter and completing the activities, you should be able to:

- List the advantages and disadvantages of the discussion method of instruction
- Diagram and explain the experiential learning process
- Compare and contrast the discussion and lecture methods in terms of their characteristics
- Outline the steps in discussion preparation
- Define critical thinking
- Write a question for each level of Bloom's taxonomy
- Designate ways to improve your questioning behavior
- Given various situations, respond appropriately in terms of Johnson's categories
- Differentiate between supportive and defensive communication climates
- List ways to create a supportive climate in your classroom
- Microteach a lesson using the discussion method

## INTRODUCTION

*Most teachers would like to engage their classes in discussions which involve many pupils, and yet so often classrooms are dominated by the talk of*

*the teacher and a few verbal youngsters who perhaps have learned to re-*
*spond in ways which teachers approve, or who are not easily daunted, or*
*who have strong drives to participate and be recognized. A teacher must*
*learn to recognize and avoid subtle rejections which discourage pupil talk.*[1]

Perhaps one of the most difficult teaching methods to master is the discussion method. As teachers, most of us would like our pupils to participate more, ask more thoughtful questions, or engage in critical thinking more often. Students can do all these things, but as teachers we need to provide them the opportunity to do so. The discussion method provides such an opportunity.

## WHEN TO USE THE DISCUSSION METHOD

As is the case with any teaching method, there are times when the discussion method will be appropriate, other times when it will not be. Some of the first considerations in determining the discussion method's appropriateness are those listed in the previous chapter—the parts of the system: you, the teacher; your students; and the educational environment. In addition to these considerations, McKeachie suggests that the discussion method is appropriate when the teacher is striving to:

1. Use the resources of members of the group
2. Give students opportunities to work out ways to apply these principles
3. Get prompt feedback on how well his teaching objectives are being reached
4. Help students learn to think in terms of the subject matter by giving them practice in thinking
5. Help students learn to evaluate the logic of, and evidence for, their own and others' positions
6. Increase students' awareness of class readings and lectures, and to help them formulate problems that require them to seek information from the readings and lectures
7. Gain students' acceptance of information or theories counter to their folklore or previous beliefs[2]

## ADVANTAGES AND DISADVANTAGES OF THE DISCUSSION METHOD

The discussion method, like all teaching methods, has advantages and disadvantages. These are listed below. When choosing the discussion method, it's important to consider these advantages and disadvantages and their relationship to your particular teaching objectives. Advantages of the discussion method:

1.  Two heads are better than one—more ideas, resources, and feedback are generated
2.  It provides students practice in expressing themselves clearly and accurately
3.  It helps students gain skill in defending and supporting their views
4.  Discussions expose students to a variety of ideas, beliefs, and information different from their own
5.  There are motivational effects—students enjoy the activity and feedback discussion provides

Disadvantages of the discussion method:

1.  It takes considerable time
2.  Successful discussion requires that teachers and students possess discussion skills

## ACTIVITY 6.1

Consider your teaching field. Considering the advantages, disadvantages, and appropriateness of the discussion method, list three topics for which the discussion method would be appropriate and explain why.

## CHARACTERISTICS OF THE DISCUSSION METHOD

The discussion method is characterized by (1) experiential learning, (2) an emphasis on students, (3) a focus on higher levels of learning, and (4) use of questions. Let's examine each of these.

### Experiential Learning

One of the major characteristics of the discussion method of teaching is that it is based on experiential learning. The underlying assumption of experiential learning is that we learn best when we are actively involved in the learning process—when we "discover" knowledge through active participation.[3] Johnson and Johnson diagram the experiential learning process as shown in figure 6.1.[4]

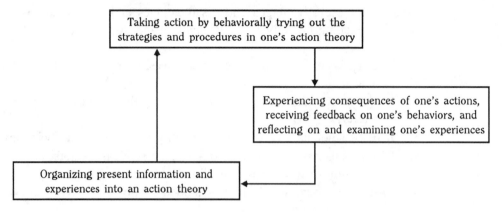

*Figure 6.1  The experiential learning cycle.*

Using the discussion method, a student's concrete, personal experiences are followed by observation, reflection, and examination of these experiences. This process leads to the formulation of abstract concepts and generalizations, which, in turn, leads to hypotheses to be discussed and tested in future experiences. This four-step process occurs in the discussion as a whole, as well as in each individual student's mind.

---

### ACTIVITY 6.2

Read the following case study.[5] In a small group, discuss how the cycle of experiential learning is exemplified.

"You've all had time to finish the story assigned for today," said Ms. Garber to one of her fourth grade reading groups, "so let's take some time to discuss it."

"I wish I was Whitey and lived on a ranch. He was lucky."

"Yeah. He was a real cowboy, and he was only the same age as us."

"What do you mean by 'real' cowboy?" asked Ms. Garber.

"Well, he had his own horse, and he wore cowboy clothes."

"And he worked like the cowboys do. He roped cattle and he rode around the ranch."

"He didn't rope cattle like at a roundup. All he did was use his rope to pull a calf out of the mud."

"Do you think that would be part of the job of a cowboy?" Ms. Garber inquired.

"Sure."

"I saw a show on TV where the rustlers got the cattle. But they didn't take the meat like in this story and leave the hides. They took the cattle with them."

"Yeah, I saw a show like that. The bad guys were rustlers."

"How did the rustlers look in this story?" asked Ms. Garber.

"Well, they were just ordinary. They didn't look like bad guys."

"Would you read the part of the story that tells about that, Sandy?" Ms. Garber requested.

Sandy found the place and read, "They didn't look like the bad men Whitey had imagined. They weren't wearing guns, and they didn't talk big to the sheriff. They wore overalls, like homesteaders. One even had on a straw hat and plow shoes. Whitey was mighty disgusted with them."[6]

"Why was Whitey disgusted with them?" was the next question.

"Because they looked like ordinary people instead of like bad men."

"Why would that matter?" pursued Ms. Garber.

"Well, it would have been more fun for Whitey if they looked like the bad guys we see on TV. He probably read some stories about rustlers and then he was disappointed."

"So it might have been more exciting to him if the rustlers had guns in their holsters and if they sounded tough. Probably most thieves just look like ordinary people, though," commented Ms. Garber. "How can you figure out how much reward money Whitey received for his part in catching the rustlers?"

"You have to divide six into fifty, because there was fifty dollars and it had to be shared by six people."

"How much did that amount to, then?"

"About eight dollars and something—so Whitey couldn't buy a saddle."

"I've got eight dollars saved up for a bike."

"Where did you get the money to save?" asked Ms. Garber.

"Well, I get a quarter for an allowance, and if I do some extra things for my mother sometimes I get paid."

"This summer we sold lemonade and we made some money. But we spent it."

"Do you think Whitey's uncle might give him any more calves of his own, so that he could try again to earn some money?" inquired Ms. Garber.

"He doesn't need the money anymore. Because the cattlemen gave him a saddle."

"Yeah, but the story said he had old boots and an old hat, so he could still have things to buy."

"Or he could save up to buy his own ranch when he's grown up."

"Why do you think," Ms. Garber went on, "that Whitey's uncle said not to bother the rustlers on the way into the range?"

"Well, they had to catch them with the meat—otherwise they couldn't really prove that they were the thieves."

"Yeah,—they had to catch them with the goods."

"What does that mean—the 'goods'?" Ms. Garber asked.

"The things you steal are the goods."

"What do you think the sheriff meant when he said, "We'll put these men to soak in the cooler for a spell?" asked Ms. Garber.

"The cooler's the jail. He was going to put them in jail."

"What's the reason for having jails?" was Ms. Garber's next question.

"If you do something bad you can go to jail. Like these rustlers took cattle that wasn't theirs, so they had to be locked up."

"You have to have a jail to keep the bad people away from the other people."

"I know somebody who went to jail. A man on our street took some money from the place where he worked, so they sent him to jail."

"All right. That's all the time we have today," said Ms. Garber.

"For your seat work tomorrow I'm going to assign you to groups so that you can make up a script for a TV show about a cowboy or cowgirl on a ranch. For homework tonight you can think of ideas for your script. Now let's quietly take our chairs back to our places."

## Emphasis on Students

The second characteristic of the discussion method, and one which flows directly from the experiential learning characteristic, is the emphasis on students. Students are the focus of this method. It is their experiences that serve as the basis for the discussion. Although you—the teacher—must have a specific goal in mind and a general framework for reaching the goal, student input determines the specific framework the discussion takes.

## Focus on Higher Levels of Learning

The third characteristic of the discussion method is the focus on higher levels of thinking. One way to do this is to use Bloom's Taxonomy of Cognitive Educational Objectives.[7] These objectives correspond to levels of thinking (table 6.1).

Note that the taxonomy is hierarchical. Knowledge is the lowest level of learning; evaluation, the highest. Note also that in order to be able to analyze, the student must know the material, comprehend it, and apply it. Thus, the ability to perform at a given level necessitates the mastery of the levels preceding it.

The discussion method focuses on the higher levels of learning. It provides students the opportunity to analyze, synthesize, and evaluate the material and ideas.

## Focus on Critical Thinking

Much has been written recently about the importance of teaching critical thinking skills. One can hardly pick up an education-related journal or magazine without

***Table 6.1*** *Major categories of Bloom's Cognitive Domain of the Taxonomy of Educational Objectives.*

---

1. *Knowledge*—the ability to recall previously learned material
2. *Comprehension*—the ability to grasp the meaning of material; the ability to translate material from one form to another (for example, words to numbers), explain and summarize material, and predict effects or consequences
3. *Application*—the ability to use learned material in new situations
4. *Analysis*—the ability to break down material into its component parts; includes identifying the parts, analyzing the relationship between the parts, and recognizing the organizational principles involved
5. *Synthesis*—the ability to put parts together to form a new whole (writing a theme, creating a speech, etc.)
6. *Evaluation*—the ability to judge the value of material based on definite criteria

---

coming across an article on the topic. A growing consensus is that although "the basics" are extremely necessary, students must also be competent thinkers.[8] Too often testing and accountability drive the educational system so that the main message communicated to students is that they should provide "the right answer." Paul contends that the right answer should not be the end product of education, but rather that an inquiring mind should be:

> *A passionate drive for clarity, accuracy, and fair-mindedness, a fervor for getting to the bottom of things, to the deepest root issues, for listening sympathetically to opposite points of view, a compelling drive to seek out evidence, an intense aversion to contradiction, sloppy thinking, inconsistent application of standards, a devotion to truth as against self-interest—these are essential components of the rational person.*[9]

Certainly the concept of critical thinking is not new. In fact, it dates back to Socrates. Critical thinking can be defined as "reasonable reflective thinking that is focused on deciding what to believe or do."[10] Critical thinkers try to be aware of their own biases, be objective, and be logical.

In reviewing literature in the area of critical thinking, it's apparent that developing critical thinking skills involves consideration of three areas: instructional design, a focus on learning by doing, and strategic teaching.

Osborne and Freyberg[11] summarized the research on the characteristics of instruction that fosters thinking. In order to foster critical thinking, instruction should be designed in a series of phases. Phase one is a preliminary phase in which the teacher and students identify students' existing ideas. This might be done through a series of questions or perhaps a diagnostic test. For example, when I teach a unit on how to critique speeches, I begin by asking, "What criteria should be used to critique a speech?" The second phase is a focusing phase in which students and teachers clarify the students' initial ideas. This phase usually takes place in a discussion after students record their initial ideas. In the case of the critique unit, the students and I discuss each criteria to make sure we understand what each one entails. The third phase involves an activity or situation that challenges the students' initial ideas. I might ask a series of "What if . . ." questions to stimulate student thinking about the consequences of the criteria used. Finally, there is an application phase, when students have the opportunity to practice using the new material in a variety of contexts. At this point in the critique unit, students view video-taped speeches, critique them, and then discuss their critiques.

When we wish to focus on teaching critical thinking, we must also focus on learning by doing. More time must be spent on having students actively use knowledge to solve problems and less time simply reading about them.

Jones and her associates call for "strategic teaching."[12] This concept calls attention to the role of the teacher as a strategist, making decisions about the what, when, and how of teaching and learning. *What* decisions involve decisions about the substance of instruction—the content, skills, and strategies. *When* decisions involve making decisions about the conditions under which it is appropriate to apply a given strategy or skill and about teaching students this information. The *how* refers to making decisions about the particular procedures needed to implement a given strategy or skill and about teaching those procedures to students. This concept of strategic teaching focuses primarily on the teacher as a model and mediator. As a model, the strategic teacher demonstrates how to think through a given task, how to apply the strategies, and "what to do when you don't know what to do." As a mediator, the strategic teacher intercedes between the students and the learning environment to help students learn and grow, anticipates problems in learning and plans solutions to solve them, and guides and coaches students through the initial phases of learning to independent learning.

One of the key ideas here is the idea of coaching. The effective coach:[13]

1.  Needs to monitor and regulate student attempts at problem solving so students don't go too far toward the wrong solution, yet have the opportunity to experience the complex processes and emotions of real problem solving.

2.  Helps students reflect on the processes used while solving problems and contrast their approaches with those used by others. Often this involves having students think aloud as they work or discuss later the process they engaged in to solve the problem.

3.  Uses problem solving activities/exercises for assessment. For example, many teachers begin a lesson with an activity to determine what students already

know. For example, when I teach students how to coach forensic events, I begin the class with a diagnostic activity. Students are given a list of forensic events and asked to describe them. In this way, the students and I learn what it is they need to learn and what they already know about forensic events.

4.   Uses problem-solving exercises/activities to create "teachable moments." Students need to be given opportunities to contrast their initial ideas and strategies with other possibilities or alternatives. Students need to "see" how new knowledge affects their own perception and comprehension—how it relates to a variety of situations. Studies indicate that when information is introduced in a problem-solving context, it is more likely to be used in new contexts rather than remain inert.[14]

5.   Carefully choose problem-solving experiences that help students develop component skills in the context of attempting to achieve overall meaningful goals. For example, using problem-solving activities that use students' everyday knowledge and help them discover and correct their misperceptions will help students see how the knowledge they learn is integrative.

6.   Does not have to be a teacher. Coaches can be other students in the classroom. Using other students as coaches works well when a supportive classroom climate has been fostered, since in such a classroom, cooperative learning is also fostered. In an increasingly complex society, skills of cooperative learning are becoming essential to individual and national success. (Cooperative learning will be discussed further in chapter 7.)

## Use of Questions

Finally, the discussion method involves the utilization of a questioning strategy. You must have carefully sequenced questions in order to organize the discussion. In addition, you must be flexible and adapt your questioning strategy to the needs of the students as the discussion evolves. Student responses must be integrated into the discussion and student questions should be elicited. Sound difficult? It is! Because questioning and response skills are perhaps the most difficult to master, a great deal of time will be spent discussing these later in this chapter.

Even though it is possible to identify a general structure for all discussions, there are different types of discussions. Hyman[15] discusses five types.

1.   *Explaining:* analyzes the causes, reasons, procedures, or methods for what has occurred. For example, (1) "Why have terrorist activities increased in the past 20 years?" (2) "How did Japan become an electronic giant since 1945?"

2.  *Problem solving:* seeks to answer a conflict or problem facing the group or the larger community outside the classroom. For example, (1) "How can we decrease sexism—male and female sexism—in our school?" (2) "How can the federal government win its battle against illegal drugs?"

3.  *Debriefing:* reflects on the facts, meaning, and implications of a shared activity such as a trip to the Statue of Liberty, a view of the play or film *Death of a Salesman*, participation in a mock 4-H convention, or hearing a guest speaker from NASA on "Space Travel in the Next Century." For example, "Let's now discuss our trip to the Statue of Liberty. What did we see and then what does it all mean?"

4.  *Predicting:* predicts the probable consequences of a given situation, condition, or policy. For example, (1) "If the greenhouse effect on our planet continues, what will happen to the plant and animal life, as we know it today?" (2) "What are the implications for humankind now that twentieth-century medicine has increased the average length of life to about 65 years?"

5.  *Policy deciding:* sets policy on how the group should act or recommends policy for the larger community outside the classroom. For example, (1) "Should we *as a class* participate in our town's protest parade next Tuesday against the state government building a dam here on Silver Creek?" (2) "Should the United States government ban cigarette smoking in the entire country?"

## PLANNING THE DISCUSSION

A discussion, like a lecture, should have an introduction, a body, and a conclusion. We'll examine the introduction and the conclusion first, and then spend a great deal of time examining the body of a discussion.

### The Introduction

The introduction to the discussion should create attention in the students. It should motivate them to want to discuss the topic or idea. In addition, it should clarify the purpose of the discussion. In other words, it should preview the main points to be covered. Also, it should create a "need to know" in students by explaining the importance and relevance of the topic to them.

### The Conclusion

The main purpose of the conclusion is to tie the entire discussion together. Often students leave a discussion session saying things like, "That was interesting, but

I'm not exactly sure what I was supposed to get out of it." As a teacher, you need to summarize the major ideas developed in the discussion. You might also preview how the knowledge learned will relate to topics to be discussed in upcoming lessons.

---

**ACTIVITY 6.3**

Choose a discussion topic and prepare an introduction for a discussion. Also, prepare a conclusion.

---

## The Body

Planning the body of the discussion is somewhat different from planning the body of a lecture. The emphasis for the teacher is not, "What am I going to say?" but rather, "What questions can I ask that will enable my students to meet the objectives?" Thus, although the body of the discussion may follow one of the general organizational patterns discussed in chapter 5, the pattern will be developed by your (and your students') use of questions and responses rather than by your explanations, examples, etc. In other words, you and students share the development of the body of the discussion.

Your major problem in planning your discussion will be developing a sequence of questions. Before we discuss sequencing, however, we need to examine teacher questioning behavior in general.

## The Importance of Questions

You may be asking yourself, "What's so important about questions?" Questioning is, perhaps, the most influential single teaching act because teacher questions determine:

1. Which mental processes students engage in (we'll return to this later)
2. Which points of a topic students can explore
3. Which modes of thought students learn

Research indicates that ⅔ to ⅘ of the average school day is taken up with questioning—primarily teacher questions. This has been true since 1912. In fact, an average of less than one question per class period was initiated by students.[16] We not only know that a lot of questions are asked during the school day, but we also know the pattern of interaction these questions elicit. Researchers[17] describe the basic interaction pattern as:

Solicitation (SOL) by the teacher
Response (RES) by the student
Reaction (REA) by the teacher

In other words, the teacher asks a question (46.6 percent of all teacher "moves" in the classroom are solicitations), the student answers the question, and the teacher reacts to the student's answer.

The basic philosophy that will be developed in this chapter is that we need to share, or perhaps even reverse this SOL–RES–REA cycle in discussion. We need to do this because:

1. Students can't learn to be good communicators without communicating. If we "buy" the idea that every teacher is a teacher of communication, then all of us, regardless of our teaching area, need to encourage student communication.

2. Communication is a process, and we deny this tenet of communication if we fail to make teaching a process or if we don't encourage student participation in the learning process.

3. If we want students to be more than mere receptacles of knowledge, we must make them a part of the learning process. One way to do this is to encourage students to question themselves and others. The teacher's use of questions in the classroom can encourage students to be critical questioners.

As Joseph Green suggests, "'What's in a question?' you ask. Everything. It is a way of evoking stimulating responses or stultifying inquiry. It is, in essence, the very core of teaching."

Since meaning is derived from social interaction, it seems reasonable that students need to be active in the interaction process. The more active students are in the process, through questioning and discussion, the clearer their meanings can be. Students need the opportunity to clarify the meaning of concepts and relationships in the classroom in order to be effective learners. Your questions and your encouragement of student questions can provide that opportunity.

### Requiring Different Thinking Levels

When we vary question levels, probe, rephrase, prompt, wait for student responses, ask process questions ("How did you get that answer?"), and stress student's understanding of meaning, we promote critical thinking. We challenge students to think, not just "parrot back" to us what we've taught or what they've read in the textbook.

Most educators agree that questioning skills are very important, but teachers in training receive very little instruction in either the theory or the art of question asking. For example, treatment of this skill in speech communication methods textbooks ranges from complete neglect to one or two pages.[18] So, where do we begin? The best place is to return to Bloom's Taxonomy. Your questions, depending on how they are asked, can require different levels of thinking. Table 6.2 indicates the categories, examples, and typical question terms for each category.[19]

*Table 6.2* *Categories of cognitive skills you can require of your students with your in-discussion questions (based on Bloom's Taxonomy of Cognitive Objectives).*

| Category | Key Word | Typical Question Terms |
|---|---|---|
| A. **Knowledge:** Questions that required simple recall of previously learned material.<br><br>Example: What are the components of Berlo's communication model? | Remember | 1. Name<br>2. List; Tell<br>3. Define<br>4. Who? When? What?<br>5. Yes or No Questions: "Was . . .?" "Is . . .?"<br>6. How many? How much?<br>7. Describe, label, match, select |
| B. **Comprehension:** Questions that require students to restate or reorganize material in a rather literal manner to show that they understand the essential meaning.<br><br>Example: Explain Berlo's model in your own words. | Understand | 1. Give an example<br>2. What is the author's most important idea?<br>3. What will the consequences probably be?<br>4. What caused this?<br>5. Compare. (What things are the same?)<br>6. Contrast. (What things are different?)<br>7. Paraphrase, rephrase, translate, summarize, defend |
| C. **Application:** Questions that require students to use previously learned material to solve problems in new situations.<br><br>Example: A Democrat and a Republican are discussing foreign policy. Where in Berlo's model of communication would you predict their communication will break down? | Solve the problem | 1. Solve<br>2. Apply the principle (concept) to<br>3. Compute, prepare, produce, relate, modify, classify |

*(Continued)*

***Table 6.2*** *Categories of cognitive skills you can require of your students with your in-discussion questions (based on Bloom's Taxonomy of Cognitive Objectives). (Continued)*

| Category | Key Word | Typical Question Terms |
|---|---|---|
| D. **Analysis:** Questions that require the student to break an idea into its component parts for logical analysis.<br><br>Example: Here are four models of the communication process. How are the components of these models similar? How do they differ? | Logical Order | 1. What reasons does the author give for his conclusions?<br>2. What does the author seem to believe?<br>3. What words indicate bias or emotion?<br>4. Does the evidence given support the conclusion?<br>5. Break down, differentiate, distinguish |
| E. **Synthesis:** Questions that require the student to combine her ideas into a statement, plan, product, etc., that is new for her.<br><br>Example: Diagram your own model of communication. | Create | 1. Develop a model . . .<br>2. Combine those parts . . .<br>3. Write a speech . . .<br>4. Create, combine, design, diagram, document, propose, write |
| F. **Evaluation:** Questions that require the student to judge something based on some criteria.<br><br>Example: Which of the three models presented in class did you think depicts the communication process most accurately? | Judge | 1. Evaluate that idea in terms of . . .<br>2. For what reasons do you favor . . .?<br>3. Appraise, criticize, justify, assess |

## ACTIVITY 6.4

Tape a classroom discussion (at least 15 minutes) in which you are involved. Classify the questions asked according to:

1. Student initiated or teacher initiated
2. Level on Bloom's Taxonomy

What do your "findings" tell you about classroom discussion?

*I started the discussion with the question, "What do teachers want from children in school?" After some initial hesitation, the group responded that teachers want children to learn, to do well, to get good grades, and to go on to college. The children were repeating all the cliche answers that they had heard from their parents and their teachers for so long. As I stated my questions more clearly, however, asking what the teachers want from children every day, they said that the teachers want answers. In response to, "Answers to what?" the children said answers, both oral and written, to all kinds of questions that teachers pose. Because I was pursuing a particular course, I asked the children to discuss the kinds of answers teachers wanted. Did the teachers want any particular kind of answer? After a few hesitations and a few false starts, one of the children answered, "Yes, what the teacher wants is right answers." When I followed with, "Do you mean that the questions asked are questions that can be answered by a right answer?" there was general agreement that they were. I then asked them, "Can teachers ask questions that do not have right and wrong answers but that still can have important answers?" This question threw the students completely off balance and they were unable to recover for the rest of the discussion. Despite much talk, no satisfactory response emerged. Because I was in a teaching situation and because we were in school, the students' orientation was almost totally to right and wrong answers. One boy, however, said, "Do you mean questions we give our opinions on?" When I asked him to continue, he said, "Well, do teachers ever ask questions that call for the opinions of the students in the class?" He thought for a while, and the others thought for a while, and they decided that what they thought—their opinions, their ideas, their judgments, and their observations—was rarely asked for in class.[20]*

As indicated in the previous example, research findings consistently indicate that most teacher questions occur on the knowledge (recall) level. Gall[21] found that 60 percent of questions asked by teachers were recall level, 20 percent were procedural, and only 20 percent required students to think at higher levels of Bloom's Taxonomy. In a more recent study, Gall[22] found that 80 percent of the questions asked in classrooms required students to do something other than think. Hargie,[23] in a recent review of research related to questioning behaviors, reported similar results. If one of our goals as teachers is to help students develop their cognitive abilities, we need to ask them questions that require higher level cognitive processes than mere recall. In addition, higher order questions require more student talk to answer them, so student participation increases. This is the first step in changing the typical SOL–RES–REA cycle of classroom communication. Finally, we need to ask higher order questions because questions affect achievement. Deethardt and Redfield and Rousseau[24] cite research indicating that a teacher's asking of higher order questions has been linked to greater student achievement.

Good and his colleagues[25] found that higher achievers asked significantly more substantive than procedural questions and that this pattern was reversed for low achievers.

Remember that there's nothing inherently wrong with lower level questions. In fact, we need them in the sequence of our questions. Notice the questioning sequence in the following example and the role of lower level questions in creating the sequence.[26]

*Knowledge:* When was *Lyrical Ballads* published?

*Comprehension:* Compare a poem by Wordsworth with one by Coleridge. What differences to you find? Similarities?

*Application:* Does this particular poem show the characteristics of poetry as indicated by Wordsworth and Coleridge in the "Preface" to *Lyrical Ballads*? If so, how? If not, what are the differences?

*Analysis:* What would some journalists and writers of the nineteenth century attack in *Lyrical Ballads*?

*Synthesis:* From studying Wordsworth's poetry, what conclusions can you make about his beliefs?

*Evaluation:* Do you feel that the concepts of romanticism as expressed by Wordsworth and Coleridge are still affecting our modern literature? Explain.

---

**ACTIVITY 6.5**

Using your topic from activity 6.3, develop the body of your discussion by preparing a sequence of questions. Begin with the knowledge level and progress to the evaluation level.

---

Although the taxonomy is helpful in determining the level of cognitive process you are requiring of your students, it is not without limitations. Several important types of questions are omitted. For example, the taxonomy does not include questions that cue students on an initially weak response, i.e., the probing question. Questions such as, "Why?" "Could you elaborate?" "Can you think of any other examples?" "Doesn't that contradict what you said previously?" are all examples of probing questions.

Probing questions are important. Shepardson,[27] analyzing teacher-directed discussions in elementary classrooms, found a significant positive relationship between the frequency of teacher probing questions and the amount of student oral participation. Rosenshine,[28] in a review of relevant research studies, reported that a positive relationship existed between a teacher's probing and pupil achievement.

Also missing from the taxonomy are questions that create a discussion atmosphere. For example, a question like "Johnny, do you agree with _____?" encourages students to question one another—an idea we'll return to later in this chapter.

Strict adherence to the taxonomy may stagnate our inquiry into the questioning process. Researchers have investigated the questions teachers ask, but they have not identified the types teachers should ask in differing teaching situations and subjects. The point is this: use the taxonomy to examine your questioning behavior, but don't become a slave to it. Realize both its advantages and limitations.

### Improving Classroom Questions

#### Let It Live

Never kill a question;
it is a fragile thing.
A good question deserves to live.
One doesn't so much answer it as converse with it,
or, better yet, one lives with it.
Great questions are the permanent
and blessed guests of the mind.
But the greatest questions of all
are those which build bridges to the heart,
addressing the whole person

No answer should be designed to kill the question.
When one is too dogmatic, or too sure,
one shows disrespect for truth
and the question which points toward it.
Beyond my answer there is always more,
more light waiting to break in,
and waves of inexhaustible meaning
ready to break against wisdom's widening shore.
Wherever there is a question, let it live![29]

Your success in the discussion method of teaching will depend greatly on your ability to let questions "live." Listed below are several guidelines to help you develop and improve your questioning skills:

1. *Have a commitment to questions.* Developing questioning skills is difficult. In order to really master the art, you have to be willing to take the time and effort required.
2. *Have a clear purpose.* Why are you asking the question? What's the response you want? Pupils demonstrate increased achievement when clear-cut goals are communicated.[30]

3. *Phrase questions clearly.* If "the major point about the formulation of a question is that it defines the kind of answer possible and it affects several characteristics of the eventual answer given,"[31] then it behooves the teacher to phrase his questions clearly. If students are unfamiliar with the words in the question, they cannot answer it even if they know the information being requested. In addition, teachers should ask only one question at a time. When teachers ask several questions in succession without waiting for a student response, student learning is negatively affected.[32]

4. *Write out a sequence of "major" questions.* Begin with knowledge level questions and progress to evaluation level questions. This practice will help you keep the class progressing systematically toward your objective.

5. *Know your subject matter* so well that you can direct your energies to the observation and direction of students' mental processes rather than having to focus on your notes.

6. *Keep all students on-task.* Since only one student is answering a question at a given moment, there is the chance that other students may get off-task. Off-task behavior is associated with decrements in learning.[33] One option that is useful in keeping students on-task is the "overhead technique": ask a question, pause, recognize or call on a student. Some researchers suggest that this technique increases the chances that all students will be considering the answer, since no one knows who will be asked to respond.[34]

7. *Don't answer your own questions.* If students learn you'll answer your questions if they just wait long enough, they'll "wait you out." Wait for students to answer. Silence seems very frustrating to teachers, yet it is not only desirable, but necessary:

There will be some silence in any class,
Sometimes it may be just dead silence
with nothing happening.
This is a terrifying thing;
one can only ask the spirit to brood over it,
creating again,
repeating the first miracle,
turning nothing into something.

But there are other silences,
the silence of reflection,
of confession, or reaffirmation,
or, the silence of recognition,
affection, opposition,

or even the silence of struggle
and decision. . . .[35]

8.  *Respond to student answers positively and constructively:*
    a.  Distribute questions so that all, including nonvolunteers, are included. A recent study by Wood and Wood[36] found that the teacher exerts considerable control over classroom discussion through her questions. Wilen[37] argues that, as a result, students' freedom to participate is stifled because they have become dependent on the teacher. Thus, encouraging student-student interaction by involving a balance of volunteering and nonvolunteering students forces the focus to shift from the teacher to the students. In this way, the discussion process contributes to students' "ownership" of their learning.
    b.  Build on contributions. Use student responses to build other questions and draw out further information: "Good point. How do you think that relates to our discussion of theme earlier today?"
    c.  Reflect questions directed to you back to the class—"That's an interesting question. Can anyone help us out?" or "I'm not sure. Does anyone have an idea?"
    d.  Don't stifle interaction by criticizing or ignoring responses, or by interrupting a student's answer. None of us likes to communicate under such circumstances.
    e.  Praise the student's answer if it is of sufficient quality. However, remember that praise is effective only if it is specific and credible.[38]
    f.  Reexplain the information or skills about which the student is uncertain.[39]
    g.  Ask probing questions to provide a hint or clue that will assist the student in strengthening his initial response.[40]
9.  *Set students in a semicircle*. Remember our discussion of seating arrangements in chapter 4. The semicircle or horseshoe (U-shaped) arrangement encourages participation.
10. *Practice*. Microteaching sessions and observing your own questioning techniques, as well as the questioning techniques of others, can help you increase your own skills.

Two additional guidelines are (1) allow time for students to answer and (2) encourage students to comment on the answers of other classmates as well as to ask one another questions. Because these two guidelines have been shown to improve discussions in several ways, each will be examined more closely.

### Wait Time

Wait-time is the amount of time the teacher waits for a response after asking a question. Frequently, teachers have a pattern of rapid fire questioning. Hoetker[41] found an average of five questions per minute in junior high English classes. In one research study,[42] third grade teachers asked a question every 43 seconds in their reading groups. Generally, teachers wait no more than 1 second for a student response and after the student does respond, teachers begin their reaction or pose the next question in less than one second. When students are asked a question, they must go through a series of steps before responding. They must attend to the question, decipher its meaning, generate a covert response, and generate an overt response. To expect students to do this in 1 to 3 seconds is unrealistic!

Wait time is of two types:[43]

*Wait time 1:* How long do you think you wait after you ask a question for students to begin an answer?

*Wait time 2:* After students give you an answer, how long do you wait for further explanation or elaboration?

Rowe[44] reports that if teachers increase the average length of wait time after asking a question and after hearing a student response the changes in student use of language and logic, as well as student and teacher attitudes and expectations, are pronounced.

Increased wait time increases student responses, speculative thinking, number of questions asked by students, student-student interactions, variety of students volunteering in discussions, student confidence, and achievement. In addition, disciplinary problems and failure on the part of students to respond decrease. Perhaps most interesting is the effect on certain students, particularly minority students. When wait time increased, these students did more task relevant talking and took a more active part in discussions.

Increased wait time also has an effect on teachers. When teachers increase their wait times, the level of their questions is more cognitively advanced and greater continuity in the development of ideas exists.

In a study of mathematics and language arts classes,[45] an increase in wait time was associated with increases in the average length of student responses, the proportion of teacher soliciting, the proportion of teacher structuring and the proportion of probing after a student response. Changes in the types of teacher questions were observed also. In mathematics there was an increase in the proportion of questions requiring application of concepts, and in language arts there was an increase in the proportion of questions requiring student comprehension.

Rowe[46] lists several responses that can interfere with wait time as well as communicate unwanted messages to students:

1.  *"Think!"* Too often we rush into a statement such as this before three seconds has elapsed. This probably communicates our exasperation and is of very little help to students.
2.  *Mimicry*—Often teachers repeat some or all of a student's answers. Often the repetition begins before the desirable Wait Time 2. The implicit message in this is that there is no payoff for listening to each other or trying to evaluate what they say since the tone of the teacher will tell which answers are acceptable and which are not.
3.  *"Yes . . . but . . . and . . . though"* constructions. When we respond with these constructions, students feel as if the discussion is "going nowhere." These constructions signal that the speaker does not receive and explore the new ideas but rather is more concerned with countering them.
4.  *"Isn't it?"* and *"Right?"* These responses produce compliance, at least on the surface.
5.  *"Don't you think that . . . ?"* This phrase sounds, at first hearing, like a question. However, such a construction makes it very difficult to disagree since the implicit answer is "yes."

### Student-Student Interaction

Johnson and Johnson[47] review research which suggests that when students interact with one another in a cooperative way, achievement increases, student attitudes toward learning and teachers are more positive, and self-esteem and motivation increase. Discussion which encourages students to work together to solve problems and to talk through ideas fosters positive results.

If you follow the previous guidelines, two phenomenon will occur in your classroom.

1.  Student participation will increase. You'll foster a positive attitude toward discussion.
2.  Students will become questioning beings. Postman and Weingartner suggest, "Children enter school as question marks and leave as periods."[48] They'll remain question marks in an atmosphere that fosters their curiosity and creativity—in a classroom in which questions are encouraged.

One teacher describes the effect of using guidelines such as those presented here:

> *"Since I changed my method of questioning, I've found that my students have changed their attitudes toward learning. This change, very subtle at first, is now quite startling. Students pay attention. They listen to each other and give answers that show they're thinking about what they're going to*

*say. The quality of their questions has also improved. They seem to have a better understanding of concepts and are showing improvement on tests and written work."*

*"Since I have become used to this new style, the amount of material I cover seems to be about the same now as it was in the past, although I must admit that when I was learning to use good questioning techniques, the process did take longer."*[49]

Perhaps the determinant of commitment to the discussion method is your self-concept as a teacher. You must feel comfortable enough to relinquish your control as "the teacher" and become a learning facilitator. When you encourage students to question you, themselves, and other students, everyone becomes a "teacher." If you are a person who has a low tolerance for ambiguity and a high need for control, the discussion method is probably not for you.

---

**ACTIVITY 6.6**

Examine the questions below. Answer them and discuss your answers with a small group of your classmates.

*Am I a thinking teacher?*

1. When students pose unusual or divergent questions, how often do I ask, "What made you think of that?"
2. Do students automatically accept whatever the text says as the right answer, or do they feel free to question it?
3. When a decision has to be made between involving the class in a discussion of an intriguing, topic-related idea brought up by a student or moving on to "cover" content, how often do I choose the former?
4. Do I frequently encourage students to seek alternative answers?
5. How often do students give reasons for making statements?
6. Do I use subject matter as a source from which students generate their own questions or problems? Do we then seriously consider those questions?
7. Can most of the questions I pose during class be answered with short replies or do they elicit longer responses?
8. How often do students spontaneously engage in critiquing each other's thinking?
9. How often do the students relate subject matter to experiences in other subjects or in their personal lives?
10. Do I stress how to think rather than what to think?

11.  How often do students set objectives for their own learning?
12.  How often do students collaborate to solve subject matter questions?
13.  Is one focus in my classroom trying to understand how and why people mentioned in texts created ideas, solutions, experiments, rules, and principles?
14.  How often do students actively listen to each other?

Adapted from Ruth Duskin Feldman, "What Are Thinking Skills?" *Instructor* (April 1986): 36.

## Response Styles

Your response to students' questions and answers are just as important as the questions you ask. Response styles are a major determinant of the climate that pervades your classroom.

David Johnson, in his text *Reaching Out*,[50] suggests five possible response styles.

1.  *Advising and Evaluating (E):* A response that indicates the receiver has made a judgment of relative goodness, appropriateness, effectiveness, or rightness of the sender's problem. The receiver has in some way implied what the sender might or ought to do.
2.  *Analyzing and Interpreting (I):* A response that indicates the receiver's intent to teach, to tell the sender what his problem means, how the sender really feels about the situation. The receiver has either obviously or subtly implied what the person with the problem might or ought to think.
3.  *Reassuring and Supporting (S):* A response that indicates the receiver's intent is to reassure, be sympathetic, to reduce the sender's intensity of feeling. The receiver has in some way implied that the sender need not feel as he does.
4.  *Questioning and Probing (P):* A response that indicates the receiver's intent is to seek further information, provoke further discussion along a certain line, or question the sender. The receiver has in some way implied that the sender ought or might profitably develop or discuss a point further.
5.  *Paraphrasing and Understanding (U):* A response that indicates the receiver's intent is to respond only to ask the sender whether the receiver correctly understands what the sender is saying, how the sender feels about the problem, and how the sender sees the problem.

**ACTIVITY 6.7** [51]

Read the following. Label the responses as understanding, interpretive, evaluative, supportive, or probing. Check your answers with the key at the end of this chapter.

Frank: *"I just never seem to have any money. I have a good-paying job, but it seems as soon as I get my paycheck, it's gone. Then I have to scrimp and save the rest of the month. Now my car needs a new engine and I don't know where I'm going to get the money to pay for it."*

a.   Tell me more about how you manage your money. Have you tried budgeting? What are your major expenses?

b.   You're feeling depressed on account of your chronic lack of money and your unsureness of how you are going to pay for your needed car repairs.

c.   You may be wasting money on nonessentials. I think if you tried keeping a budget, you would be able to manage much better.

d.   I'm sure the money for your new car engine will turn up. Don't worry. You have always managed in the past.

e.   Depression such as you are experiencing often comes from a feeling of being helpless to solve your problems. Once you feel that you have some control over your financial problems, you'll feel better.

Carl Rogers[52] observed individuals in all types of settings and found that:

1.   Evaluating responses were used most frequently
2.   Interpreting was next
3.   The third most frequent type of response was supporting
4.   Probing response was fourth
5.   The least frequent response was understanding
6.   If a person uses a category as much as 40 percent of the time, she is always seen as responding that way.

The categories per se are neither good nor bad. It's the overuse or underuse of the categories that should be avoided. Each type of response is appropriate in certain situations and with certain students.

Teachers, because of their job of evaluating students, no doubt overuse the evaluative response to a large extent. Gibb tells us that evaluative responses make people feel defensive, primarily because evaluative responses threaten a person's self-concept. When we are threatened, we tend to defend ourselves. After an eight-year study, Gibb delineated two communication climates—defensive and supportive. Six paired categories of behaviors were also delineated. Table 6.3 lists Gibb's definitions of those paired behaviors.[53]

**Table 6.3** *Defensive vs. supportive communication climates.*

| Defensive Climates | Supportive Climates |
| --- | --- |
| 1. **Evaluation.** To pass judgment on another; to blame or praise; to make moral assessments of another; to question his standards, values, and motives and the affect loadings of his communication. | 1. **Description.** Nonjudgmental; to ask questions that are perceived as genuine requests for information; to present "feelings, events, perceptions, or processes that do not ask or imply that the receiver change behavior or attitude."<br><br>    If we use "you" language—"You are not doing your best." we are evaluating. If we use "I" language—"When you don't do as well as I think you can, I get frustrated"—we are describing. |
| 2. **Control.** To try to do something to another; to attempt to change an attitude or the behavior of another—to try to restrict her field of activity; "implicit in all attempts to alter another person is the assumption of the change agent that the person to be altered is inadequate." | 2. **Problem Orientation.** The antithesis of persuasion; to communicate "a desire to collaborate in defining a mutual problem and in seeking its solution" (thus tending to create the same problem orientation in the other); to imply that he has no preconceived solution, attitude, or method to impose upon the other; to allow "the receiver to set his own goals, make his own decisions, and evaluate his own progress—or to share with the sender in doing so."<br><br>    Control is an "I know what's best for you" attitude. Problem orientation is "We have a problem. What can we do to solve it?" attitude. |
| 3. **Strategy.** To manipulate others; to use tricks to "involve" another, to make her think she was making her own decisions, and to make her feel that the speaker had genuine interest in her; to engage in a stratagem involving ambiguous and multiple motivation. | 3. **Spontaneity.** To express guilelessness; natural simplicity; freedom of deception; having a "clear id"; having unhidden uncomplicated motives; straightforwardness and honesty.<br><br>    Whenever we try to trick or manipulate another person into doing what we want, we are using a strategy. Spontaneity is expressing ourselves honestly. How many of us wish for a simple, honest, "I just didn't get the paper done" instead of the "My dog ate the paper" excuse! |
| 4. **Neutrality.** To express lack of concern for the welfare of another; "the clinical, detached, person-is-an-object-of-study attitude." | 4. **Empathy.** To express respect for the worth of the listener; to identify with his problems, share his feelings, and accept his emotional values at face value. |

*(Continued)*

**Table 6.3** *Defensive vs. supportive communication climates. (Continued)*

| Defensive Climates | Supportive Climates |
| --- | --- |
| | **4. Empathy.** *(Continued)*<br>    Students feel defensive when they perceive our neutrality—"She doesn't really care about me. I'm just another student to her." Being empathetic—putting ourselves in another's shoes—can communicate to students that we care about them personally. Remember, being empathetic doesn't mean we agree with the student's feelings—just that we respect those feelings. |
| **5. Superiority.** To communicate the attitude that one is "superior in position, power, wealth, intellectual ability, physical characteristics, other ways" to another; to tend to arouse feelings of inadequacy in the other; to impress the other that the speaker "is not willing to enter a shared problem-solving relationship, that he probably does not desire feedback, that he does not require help, and/or that he will be likely to try to reduce the power, the status, or the worth of the receiver." | **5. Equality.** To be willing to enter into participative planning with mutual trust and respect; to attach little importance to differences in talent, ability, worth, appearance, status, and power.<br>    We have all had teachers who constantly remind us that they are the teacher—the superior intellectual being in the classroom. Remember how thrilled you were when the teacher made a mistake? A teacher who believes in equality communicates that everyone has value—regardless of their intellectual capabilities. In addition, such a teacher communicates that everyone makes mistakes and that everyone—teacher and students—can learn from one another. |
| **6. Certainty.** To appear dogmatic; "to seem to know the answers, to require no additional data;" and to regard self as teacher rather than as co-worker; to manifest inferiority by needing to be right, wanting to win an argument rather than solve a problem, seeing one's ideas as truths to be defended. | **6. Provisionalism.** To be willing to experiment with one's own behavior attitudes, and ideas; to investigate issues rather than taking sides on them, to problem solve rather than debate, to communicate that the other person may have some control over the shared quest or the investigation of ideas. "If a person is genuinely searching for information and data, he does not resent help or company along the way."<br>    We have all known people who are always right—who believe they have a corner on ultimate truth. Generally we expend a great deal of energy trying to prove these people wrong. In provisionalism, although the person may have a strong opinion, she is willing to acknowledge another's viewpoint. |

Most students feel defensive. Our educational environments have fostered this defensiveness through the different status and roles in classrooms and the use of grades. Students often feel controlled by the teacher who is in a superior, "always right" position. They also feel strategies are used to manipulate them and that teachers are often neutral to their problems. Rosenfeld examined coping mechanisms used by students when they felt defensive. Rosenfeld summarizes his findings:

> *In disliked classes, characteristic coping mechanisms are "daydreaming" and "resisting the teacher's influence." In general, the coping mechanisms used by students in disliked classes fall into two categories: active and passive. "Resisting the teacher's influence," "retaliating against the teacher," and "forming alliances against the teacher" are active strategies for coping with a hostile environment, whereas "not doing what the teacher asks," "hiding feelings," and "daydreaming," are passive strategies for accomplishing the same end.* [54]

Your response style should attempt to eliminate defensive feelings in students. An understanding response style, for example, will help students feel that you are concerned with helping them solve problems and are concerned about them. No doubt an understanding response will also create a climate of provisionalism, equality, and spontaneity.

The point is this—strive to create a supportive communication climate by using the appropriate response style for the students and the situation. Students will be more willing to participate in discussions when they feel supported rather than threatened.

## ACTIVITY 6.8

Here are some common situations in the educational environment. Write a response for each category. Then indicate whether that response would create supportiveness or defensiveness in the person.

*Teacher to another teacher:* "My 10:30 class is so stupid! I don't know what to do with them! They refuse to learn anything!"

|  | Supportive | Defensive |
|---|---|---|
| Evaluating response: |  |  |
| Interpreting response: |  |  |
| Supporting response: |  |  |
| Probing response: |  |  |
| Understanding response: |  |  |

*Third grader coming in from recess, to teacher:* "They won't let me play in the game!"

|  | Supportive | Defensive |
|---|---|---|
| Evaluating response: |  |  |
| Interpreting response: |  |  |
| Supporting response: |  |  |
| Probing response: |  |  |
| Understanding response: |  |  |

*Parents to teacher:* "We've helped Johnny with his math at home. You said if we did that, his grades would improve. They haven't."

|  | Supportive | Defensive |
|---|---|---|
| Evaluating response: |  |  |
| Interpreting response: |  |  |
| Supporting response: |  |  |
| Probing response: |  |  |
| Understanding response: |  |  |

*Student to teacher:* "I was here yesterday for our appointment and you weren't here. That's the second time you've failed to 'show up.' Don't you want to help me?"

|  | Supportive | Defensive |
|---|---|---|
| Evaluating response: |  |  |
| Interpreting response: |  |  |
| Supporting response: |  |  |
| Probing response: |  |  |
| Understanding response: |  |  |

*Student to teacher:* "This grade is unfair. I really worked hard. Mary didn't work nearly as hard as I did, and she got a better grade."

|  | Supportive | Defensive |
|---|---|---|
| Evaluating response: |  |  |
| Interpreting response: |  |  |
| Supporting response: |  |  |
| Probing response: |  |  |
| Understanding response: |  |  |

*Teacher to teacher:* "I see on your class list you have Larry Brewer this semester. Good luck! He's the biggest troublemaker in school!"

| | Supportive | Defensive |
|---|---|---|
| Evaluating response: | | |
| Interpreting response: | | |
| Supporting response: | | |
| Probing response: | | |
| Understanding response: | | |

*Eleventh-grade girl to teacher:* "I think I'd like to quit school. I'm flunking my courses and it seems like the harder I try, the worse I do."

| | Supportive | Defensive |
|---|---|---|
| Evaluating response: | | |
| Interpreting response: | | |
| Supporting response: | | |
| Probing response: | | |
| Understanding response: | | |

*Tenth grader to teacher:* "I hate to go home after school. My parents fight all the time and I can't stand my sister. It's miserable at home."

| | Supportive | Defensive |
|---|---|---|
| Evaluating response: | | |
| Interpreting response: | | |
| Supporting response: | | |
| Probing response: | | |
| Understanding response: | | |

No doubt you're thinking, "This all sounds fine. Response styles should create supportive climates. But what, exactly, can I do to create a responsive, supportive climate in my classroom?" Listed below are several pragmatic suggestions to help you respond appropriately to your students and thus encourage their participation.[55]

1. *Accept and develop students' ideas.* Demonstrate verbally and nonverbally that you are receiving the message. Ask the student or ask other students to expand or clarify the idea presented.

2. *Accept and develop students' feelings.* Feelings are real. Demonstrate verbally and nonverbally that you are receiving the message and that you are interested in it. Make sure you understand what they're saying and ask any questions necessary to assist them in communicating their specific feelings. Too often we as teachers are concerned with the students' ideas, but not with the student:

To learn is to live,
to be,
to grow
in the light of new knowledge.

Why do we fragment,
dissect, destroy
the learner
in the learning?[56]

Gauge when to pursue students' feelings and when to take no action. Here, you as the professional must make the decision based on your knowledge of the student.

3. *Praise rather than criticize.* It is so easy to be critical and the results are so obvious. You accomplish much more by enhancing the student's self-concept than by destroying it with criticism. When students are not succeeding, it is time you reevaluated your objectives in terms of the pupil and the methods, strategies, and activities you have provided. It is time to be critical of your program rather than of the students.

4. *Encourage.* When you encourage, you are demonstrating your belief in the student and her ability. Nothing is achieved when you abruptly tell a student that she couldn't possibly succeed in a task.

5. *Insure a level of success for the students.* Students will succeed in our classrooms if we provided opportunities for success. This initial success will spur them on. Stop focusing on the syllabus, the sacred text, the test in your files; focus on the student; make the match so that some measure of success will ensue.

6. *Listen.* How many times do you and I listen and not hear? Listening to our students provides us with a wealth of information not found in the permanent records. By really "tuning in" on our students, we obtain the vital data that will enable us to instruct them as individuals.

### *HELP*

"HELP!"
she screamed
and
i thought she
said
"hello!"
so i said
"hi . . . how are you?
she told me
how it was for
her
and all i heard
was . . . "fine."

she whispered
"i'm going under,
please pull me up!"
and i listened
to the voice
but never
heard the words
or saw the truth within
her eyes
(her soul screaming).
now i know
better
now that
it is much
too late.[57]

7. *Allow for pupil talk.* Don't talk most of the time. From my own experience, I have found this is a most difficult task to accomplish. When you have grown accustomed to information giving, the initial frustrations in monitoring yourself and reducing the amount of teacher-talk are great. Redirecting questions to students, rather than simply answering questions directed toward you, can increase pupil talk.

8. *Abide by the rules of effective feedback.* Effective feedback is specific rather than general. Telling a student, "Your organization was ineffective," does little to help the student. What, specifically, was ineffective and what can be done to eliminate the problem? Effective feedback is well-timed. In general, the more immediate the feedback the better. However, there are situations in which feedback should be delayed; for example, if the student is not ready to listen to the feedback. Effective feedback focuses on the behavior, not the individual. There is a difference between saying, "You're stupid," and "I think you'll need more support for that idea before I can accept it."

9. *Metacommunicate.* Communicate about your communication. Make sure that you and the student both understand what's being said. Verify what you hear, i.e., "If I understand you correctly, you're suggesting that. . . ."

10. *Accept pupil mistakes.* If you are to create a climate where pupils are to be themselves and are accepted as human beings, then mistakes must be received as a valuable part of learning. Accept the mistakes without reprimand, but focus on why the student made the mistake. For example, you might say something like, "OK, Jamie, let's think about this. Let's examine what you said in relation to what you read in the text and see why your answer is incorrect."

11. *Don't seek instant closure.* Since one of our major goals is the development of process, provide students with time to process information. Don't anticipate instant responses to a problem. Pause—give students time to process the content, to formulate complete responses.

12. *Be authentic.* So many of us wear our professional role of teacher well. We erect our wall and hold our pupils at a safe distance. We are excellent actors and actresses; our performances are superb. At 3:30 or 4:00 we return to our real selves. We are doing our pupils a major disservice. The time to be real, to be ourselves, to demonstrate our wholeness and individuality is in the classroom. Our students should know us and view us as total individuals, with thoughts, feelings, values, and beliefs which may not coincide with theirs but which are there nonetheless. Our relationships should be honest, not based on the role-functions of the teacher as stated in X manual. We have to break down the artificial barriers we have created.

13.   *Use a variety of responses.* Beginning teachers often ask, "What do I do if no one answers my question or if the answer given is wrong?" Too often beginning teachers give a one word response such as "Good" or "Right" if a student's answer is correct. To stimulate questions, it's important to use a variety of response techniques. The list below suggests a variety of responses for various situations.

A.   When the student's answer is correct

   1.   Praise the student
   2.   Restate the correct response as given by the student
   3.   Modify the answer if necessary while maintaining the student's original idea
   4.   Apply the student's answer to some situation
   5.   Compare the student's response to something in the text, something already discussed or some concurrent similar event
   6.   Summarize the response to draw a conclusion or to make a point
   7.   Call on another student to agree, disagree, or build on the original answer

B.   When the student's answer is incorrect

   1.   Support the student's answer while saying the response is incorrect "Good try, John, but that's not the correct answer."
   2.   Rephrase the question
   3.   Provide additional information for the student's use
   4.   Probe the student's response for a route to the correct answer

C.   When the student's response is "I don't know"

   1.   Urge the student to try to answer
   2.   Restate the question
   3.   Rephrase the question
   4.   Redirect the question to another student
   5.   Ask the student what part of the question is unclear or if he can answer part of the question.

**ACTIVITY 6.9**

Microteach your lesson. Videotape it. Evaluate your lesson.

   I.  Introduction to the lesson:
       A.  Attention gaining strategy was
           Successful _____ _____ _____ _____ _____ Unsuccessful
       B.  Motivating strategy was
           Successful _____ _____ _____ _____ _____ Unsuccessful
       C.  Preview was
           Successful _____ _____ _____ _____ _____ Unsuccessful
       Comments:

  II.  Questioning strategy
       A.  Most questions were asked on the _____ level.
       B.  Any probing questions asked?
       C.  Did students ask questions of me? Of one another?
       Comments:
           Generally, my questioning behavior was
           Effective _____ _____ _____ _____ _____ Ineffective

 III.  Response style:
       A.  What did I do to create a supportive, responsive climate?
       B.  Which of Johnson's categories were used most often? Least often?
           What does this information suggest?
       Comments:
           Generally, my response style was
           Effective _____ _____ _____ _____ _____ Ineffective

  IV.  Conclusion
       A.  Summary was
           Successful _____ _____ _____ _____ _____ Unsuccessful
       Comments:

   V.  General Reactions
       A.  How did you feel about yourself during the microteaching?
       B.  What did you like about the experience?
       C.  What did you dislike about the experience?
       D.  How did your "students" react to you?
       E.  What were your greatest strengths?
       F.  What were your greatest weaknesses?
       G.  What have you learned about your teaching via the discussion method?

## IN SUM

In this chapter we have examined the discussion method of teaching. We have stressed not only the mechanics of this method, but the attitude toward teaching necessary to utilize this method effectively. Gerhard Frost summarizes that attitude:

### Deliver Us!

From classrooms
that creak and squeak
rule-ridden and constrictive
defensive and rigid,
reflecting the neuroses
of adults
rather than the needs

of children;
from prison-houses
of artificiality and anxiety,
where nothing breathes,
Good Lord,
deliver us![58]

### Key to Activity 6.7

A.  Probing
B.  Interpreting
C.  Evaluating
D.  Supporting
E.  Understanding

## NOTES

1. E. Amidon and E. Hunter, *Improving Teaching: The Analysis of Classroom Verbal Interaction* (New York: Holt, Rinehart and Winston, 1967) 103.

2. W. McKeachie, *Teaching Tips* (Lexington, MA: D.C. Heath, 1969) 37.

3. See, for example, A. Davis, L. Alexander, and S. Yelon, *Learning System Design* (New York: McGraw-Hill, 1974); and G. Stanford and A. Roark, *Human Interaction in Education* (Boston: Allyn and Bacon, 1975).

4. D. Johnson and E. Johnson, *Joining Together: Group Theory and Group Skills*, 3rd ed. (Englewood Cliffs, NJ: Prentice Hall, 1987) 18.

5. Amidon and Hunter, *Improving Teaching*, 114–116.

6. "Whitey Steers Ahead," *Above the Clouds: Winston Basic Readers* (New York: Holt, Rinehart and Winston, 1962) 196.

7. B. S. Bloom et al., *Taxonomy of Educational Objectives: Cognitive Domain* (New York: David McKay Co., 1956).

8. See research reviewed in R. Marzaano, R. Brandt, C. Hughes, B. Jones, B. Presseisen, S. Rankin, and C. Suhor, *Dimensions of Thinking: A Framework for Curriculum and Instruction* (Alexandria, VA: Association for Supervision and Curriculum Development, 1988).

9. R. W. Paul, Program for the Fourth International Conference on Critical Thinking and Educational Reform, (Rohnert Park, CA: Sonoma State Univ. Center for Critical Thinking and Moral Critique, 1986) 1.

10. R. Ennis, "Goals for a Critical Thinking Curriculum," *Developing Minds: A Resource Book for Teaching Thinking*, ed. A. Costa (Alexandria, VA: Association for Supervision and Curriculum Development, 1985) 54.

11. R. Osborne and P. Freyberg, *Learning in Science: The Implications of Children's Science* (Portsmouth, NH: Heinemann, 1985).

12. B. Jones, A. Palincsar, D. Ogle, and E. Carr, *Strategic Teaching and Learning: Cognitive Instruction in the Content Areas* (Elmhurst, IL: North Central Regional Education Laboratory, 1989).

13. J. Bransford and N. Vye, "A Perspective on Cognitive Research and Its Implications for Instruction," *Toward the Thinking Curriculum: Current Cognitive Research*, ed. L. Resnick and L. Klopfer (Association for Supervision and Curriculum Development, 1989).

14. See, for example, L. Adams, J. Kasserman, A. Yearwood, G. Perfetto, J. Bransford, and J. Franks, "The Effects of Fact versus Problem-Oriented Acquisition," *Memory and Cognition* 16 (1988): 167-175.

15. R. Hyman, "Discussion Strategies and Tactics," *Questions, Questioning Techniques, and Effective Teaching*, ed. W. Wilen (Washington, D.C.: National Education Association, 1987) 138-139.

16. M. Gall, "Synthesis of Research on Teachers' Questioning," *Educational Leadership* (Nov. 1984): 40-47.

17. A. Bellack et al., *The Language of the Classroom* (New York: Teachers College, 1961).

18. J. F. Deethardt, "The Use of Questions in the Speech-Communication Classroom" *Speech Teacher* 23 (1974): 15-20.

19. Adapted from A. Clegg, Jr., et al., "Teacher Strategies of Questioning for Elicited Selected Cognitive Student Responses," American Educational Research Association Annual Meeting, Los Angeles, Feb. 1969. 8-9.

20. W. Glasser, *Schools without Failure* (New York: Harper and Row, 1969) 51.

21. M. Gall, "The Use of Questions in Teaching," *Review of Educational Research* 40 (1970): 707-721; Gall, "Synthesis of Research."

22. Gall, "Synthesis of Research", 40-47.

23. O. Hargie, "The Importance of Teacher Questions in the Classroom," *Educational Research* 20 (1978): 99-102.

24. J. F. Deethardt, "The Use of Questions," 15-20; D. Redfield and E. Rousseau, "A Meta-Analysis of Experimental Research on Teacher Questioning Behavior," *Review of Educational Research* 51 (Summer 1981): 237-246.

25. T. Good, R. Stavings, K. Harel, and H. Emerson, "Student Passivity: A Study of Question Asking in K-12 Classrooms," *Sociology of Education* 60 (1989): 181-199.

26. C. Duke, "Questions Teachers Ask: By-Pass or Through-Ways?" *The Clearing House* 45 (April 1971): 468-472.

27. R. Shepardson, "An Analysis of Teacher Questioning and Response Behaviors, and Their Influence on Student Participation during Classroom Discussions," *Dissertation Abstracts International* 33 (1973): 5016A.

28. B. Rosenshine, *Teaching Behaviors and Student Achievement* (Slough, Great Britain: NFER, 1971).

29. G. E. Frost, *Bless My Growing* (Minneapolis: Augsburg Publishing House, 1974) 31.

30. D. P. Ausbel, "The Use of Advanced Organizers in the Learning and Retention of Meaningful Material," *Journal of Educational Psychology* 51 (1960): 267-272; Gall, "Synthesis of Research."

31. J. Dillon, "Questioning," *Handbook of Communication Skills*, ed. O. Hargie (London: Croom Helm, 1986): 107.

32. M. Gall and T. Rhody, "Review of Research on Questioning Techniques," *Questions, Questioning Techniques, and Effective Teaching*, ed. W. Wilen (Washington, D. C.: NEA, 1987) 23-48.

33. D. C. Berliner and C. W. Fisher, *Perspectives on Instructional Time* (New York: Longman, 1985).

34. G. McKenzie, "Effects of Questions and Test-Like Events on Achievement and On-Task Behavior in a Classroom Concept Learning Presentation," *Journal of Educational Research* 72 (1979): 348–351.

35. Frost, *Bless My Growing*, 72.

36. D. Wood and H. Wood, "Questioning and Student Initiative," *Questioning and Discussion: A Multidisciplinary Study*, ed. J. Dillon (Norwood, NJ: Ablex, 1987).

37. W. Wilen, "Effective Questions and Questioning: A Classroom Application," *Questions, Questioning Techniques, and Effective Teaching*, ed. W. Wilen (Washington, D.C.: NEA, 1987) 107–134.

38. J. Brophy, "Teacher Praise: A Functional Analysis," *Review of Educational Research* 51 (1981): 5–32.

39. B. Rosenshine, "Synthesis of Research on Explicit Teaching," *Educational Leadership* 43 (1986): 60–69.

40. Gall and Rhody, "Review of Research."

41. J. Hoetker, "Teacher Questioning Behavior in Nine Junior High School English Classes," *Research in the Teaching of English* 2 (1986): 99–106.

42. L. Gambrell, "The Occurrence of Think-Time During Reading Comprehension," *Journal of Educational Research* 77 (1983): 77–80.

43. M. Rowe, "Using Wait Time to Stimulate Inquiry," *Questions, Questioning Techniques, and Effective Teaching*, ed. W. Wilen, (Washington, D. C.: NEA, 1987) 95–106.

44. M. Rowe, "Wait Time: Slowing Down May Be a Way of Speeding Up!" *Journal of Teacher Education* (Jan./Feb. 1986): 43–48.

45. K. Tobin, "Effects of Teacher Wait Time on Discourse Characteristics in Mathematics and Language Arts Classes," *American Educational Research Journal* 23 (Summer 1986): 191–200.

46. Rowe, "Using Wait Time."

47. R. Johnson and D. Johnson, "Student-Student Interaction: Ignored But Powerful," *Journal of Teacher Education* (July/Aug. 1985): 22–26.

48. N. Postman and G. Weingartner, *Teaching as a Subversive Activity* (New York: Dell, 1969) 60.

49. Mentor teacher and principal Dave Schumaker of Santa Cruz, California as quoted in Ruth Duskin Feldman, "What Are Thinking Skills," *Instructor* (April 1986): 37.

50. D. W. Johnson, *Reaching Out*, 4th ed. (Englewood Cliffs, NJ: Prentice Hall, 1990) 189–194.

51. Johnson, 187–188.

52. Johnson, 198.

53. Adapted from J. Gibb, "Defensive Communication," *Journal of Communication* 11 (1961): 142–148.

54. L. B. Rosenfeld, "Communication Climate and Coping Mechanisms in the College Classroom," *Communication Education* 32 (1983): 173.

55. Adapted from M. Gerhard, *Effective Teaching Strategies with the Behavioral Outcomes Approach* (West Nyack, NY: Parker, 1971).

56. Frost, *Bless My Growing*, 86.

57. B. Comear, *Fragments from an Unknown Gospel* (Boston: United Church, 1970) 14.

58. Frost, *Bless My Growing*, 71.

## SUGGESTIONS FOR FURTHER READING

Barell, J. "You Ask the Wrong Questions." *Educational Leadership* 43 (May 1985): 18–23.

"Building Better Thinkers: A Blueprint for Instruction." *Learning 90* 18 (Feb. 1990): 40–56.

Clarke, J. "Designing Discussions as Group Inquiry." *College Teaching* (Fall 1988): 140–143.

Dantonio, M., and L. Paradise. "Teacher Question-Answer Strategy and the Cognitive Correspondence Between Teacher Questions and Learner Responses." *Journal of Research and Development in Education* 21 (Spring 1988) 71.

Dillon, J. T. "The Classification of Research Questions." *Review of Educational Research* 54 (Fall 1984): 327–362.

———. "The Multidisciplinary World of Questioning." *Questions, Questioning Techniques, and Effective Teaching.* Ed. W. Wilen. Washington, D.C.: National Education Association, 1987. 49–66.

———. "Questioning in Science." *Questions and Questioning: An Interdisciplinary Reader.* Ed. M. Meyer. Berlin: De Gruyter, 1987.

———. *Questioning and Teaching: A Manual of Practice.* New York: Methuen, 1987.

———. "Research on Questioning and Discussion." *Educational Leadership* 42 (November 1984): 50–56.

———. "Student Questions and Individual Learning." *Educational Theory* 36 (Fall 1986): 333–341.

———. "Using Questions to Foil Discussion." *Teaching and Teacher Education* 1 (1985): 109–121.

Ennis, R. "Is Answering Questions Teaching?" *Educational Theory* 36 (1986): 343–347.

Feezel, J. "Teacher Questions as Students Hear Them." *Teacher Talk* 7 (Spring 1989): Northwestern U. School of Speech.

Galvin, K. "Building an Interactive Learning Community: The TA Challenge." Second National Conference on the Training and Employment of Graduate Teaching Assistants. Seattle, Nov. 1989.

———. "Classroom Roles of the Teacher." *Teaching Communication: Theory, Research and Methods.* Ed. J. Daly, G. Friedrich, and A. Vangelisti. Hillsdale, NJ: Erlbaum (in press).

Gersten, R., M. Gall, D. Grace, D. Erickson, and S. Stieber. "Instructional Correlates of Achievement Gains in Algebra Classes for Low-Performing High School Students." Annual Meeting of American Educational Research Association. Washington, D.C., April 1987.

Golub, J., and L. Reid. "Activities for an 'Interactive' Classroom." *English Journal* 78 (April 1989): 43–48.

Harms, T., R. Woolever, and R. Brice. "A Questioning Strategies Training Sequence: Documenting the Effect of a New Approach to an Old Practice." *Journal of Teacher Education* 30 (Sept./Oct. 1989): 40–43.

Hatch, D., and C. Farris. "Helping TAs Use Active Learning Strategies." *Teaching Assistant Training in the 1990s.* Ed. J. Nyquist, R. Abbott, and D. Wulff. San Francisco: Jossey-Bass, 1989. 89–99.

Johnson, D., R. Johnson, P. Roy, and E. Holubec. *Circles of Learning: Cooperation in the Classroom.* Alexandria, VA: Association for Supervision and Curriculum Development, 1984.

Kulik, J., and C. Kulik. "Timing of Feedback and Verbal Learning." *Review of Educational Research* 58 (Spring 1988): 79–97.

Kurfill, J. "Critical Thinking: Theory, Research, Practice and Possibilities." *ASHE-ERIC Higher Education Report* 2, 1988.

McKenzie, G., and M. Henry. "Effects of Test-Like Events on On-Task Behavior, Test Anxiety, and Achievement in a Classroom Concept Learning Presentation." *Journal of Educational Research* 72 (1979): 370–374.

O'Keefe, V. "Affecting Critical Thinking Through Speech." *ERIC Clearinghouse on Reading and Communication Skills and the SCA*. Urbana, IL, 1986.

Passe, J. "Phil Donahue: An Excellent Model for Leading a Discussion." *Journal of Teacher Education* 35 (Jan./Feb. 1985): 43–48.

Raphael, T., and P. D. Pearson. "Increasing Students' Awareness of Sources of Information for Answering Questions." *American Educational Research Journal* 22 (Summer 1985): 217–236.

Rogers, R., and J. Reiff. "Developing Computer-Based Interactive Video Simulations on Questioning Strategies." *Action in Teacher Education* 11 (Fall 1989): 33–36.

Rubin, L. "The Thinking Teacher: Cultivating Pedagogical Intelligence." *Journal of Teacher Education* (Nov./Dec. 1989): 31–37.

Schuck, R. "An Empirical Analysis of the Power of Set Induction and Systematic Questioning as Instructional Strategies." *Journal of Teacher Education* (March/April 1985): 38–43.

Singer, M. "Mental Processes of Question Answering." *The Psychology of Questions*. Ed. A. Graessner and J. Black. Hillsdale, NJ: Erlbaum, 1986.

Smith, B. M., J. B. Schumaker, J. Schaeffer, and J. A. Sherman. "Increasing Participation and Improving the Quality of Discussions in Seventh-Grade Social Studies Classes." *Journal of Applied Behavior Analysis* 15 (Spring 1982): 97–110.

Stahl, S., and C. Clark. "The Effects of Participatory Expectations in Classroom Discussion on the Learning of Science Vocabulary." *American Educational Research Journal* 24 (1987): 541–555.

Talmage, H., E. Pascarella, and S. Lord. "The Influence of Cooperative Learning Strategies on Teacher Practices, Student Perceptions of the Learning Environment, and Academic Achievement." *American Educational Research Journal* 21 (Spring 1984): 163–180.

Watson, E. "How to Ask Better Questions." *Learning 88* (Sept. 1988): 94.

Welty, W. "Discussion Method Teaching." *Change* (July/Aug. 1989): 41–49.

# 7  SMALL GROUP COMMUNICATION

## OBJECTIVES

After reading this chapter and completing the activities, you should be able to:

- Explain the small group process utilizing Rosenfeld's model
- Analyze your behavior in small groups
- Improve your small group communication skills
- Evaluate small group communication

## INTRODUCTION

> *No man is an Island, intire of itselfe; every man is a peece of the continent, a part of the main: if a Clod bee washed away by the Sea, Europe is the lesse, as well as if a Promontorie were, as well as if a Mannor of thy friends or of thine owne were; any man's death diminishes me, because I am involved in Mankinds: And therefore never send to know for whom the bell tolls; It tolls for thee.*
>
> *John Donne*

Much of our lives is spent in groups—family, peer, and professional groups. We are socialized and obtain our identity through our communication within groups. Much of what we learn about ourselves is learned through interaction in groups. We see our image of self mirrored by others in the small groups to which we belong. In addition, we use language to rehearse and adapt to problems. Because of the pervasiveness of groups in our life, it's important that teachers provide their students with experience in small group communication. The more opportunities we provide students to "try out" behavior in small groups and to internalize the mirrored reactions of others to these behaviors, the more effective communicators our students can be.

This chapter will examine the characteristics, advantages, and disadvantages of small groups within the educational environment. In addition, several variables relating to small group communication will be discussed.

## ADVANTAGES AND DISADVANTAGES OF SMALL INSTRUCTIONAL GROUPS

The advantages and disadvantages to the small group teaching method are similar to those of the discussion method. These are listed below. When considering the small group as a teaching method, keep these advantages and disadvantages in mind. Consider your students and your objectives, making sure that the method is appropriate to these.

Advantages of the small group method:

1. Enhances student motivation and fosters positive attitudes toward the subject matter: Students enjoy working together in small groups
2. Develops student's problem-solving and decision-making skills
3. Enables a student to share her ideas with other students for critiquing and comparison

Disadvantages of the small group method:

1. Time consuming
2. Students need an understanding of small group communication processes

## DEFINITION OF A SMALL GROUP

Numerous definitions of "small group" exist. Most of these definitions stress the interactional nature of small groups: a number of persons who communicate with one another often over a span of time and who are few enough so that each person is able to communicate with all others not second hand, but face to face.[1]

After reviewing theories of small group communication, Rosenfeld developed a general model of the small group process, which presents the relationship among the basic components of a small group.[2] This model is presented in figure 7.1.

According to the model, small group processes occur across time and also change across time. Thus, small group processes are dynamic, and the relation-

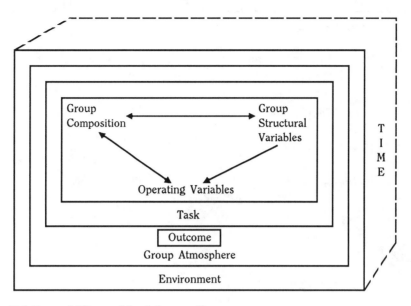

***Figure 7.1*** *Rosenfeld's model of the small group process.*

ships among the components are constantly changing. Group composition consists of the members in the group—their attitudes, personalities, self-concepts, needs, and perceptions. Included also are group interaction variables, such as size and compatibility. Group structural variables are communication and attraction networks in the group. Operating variables are the roles, norms, and operating procedures of the group. The group—composition, structural, and operating variables—exists within a framework consisting of four variables—task, outcomes, group atmosphere, and environment. The task is the primary purpose of the group, the reason for the group's existence. The outcome is what the group accomplishes (quality, quantity, appropriateness, and efficiency of outcomes) and the group's satisfaction with the outcomes. This outcome, regardless of whether it's positive or negative, affects subsequent group interactions. Group atmosphere is the emotional climate of the group. The environment is both physical and social. It places limitations on the group that can either facilitate or hamper task accomplishment.

Note that Rosenfeld takes a systems perspective to examining groups. The model indicates that each component interacts with every other component. In addition, the perceptions and meanings of group members are considered important to the functioning of the group.

I'll use this model as the basis for discussing small groups in the classroom. Although I'll discuss each component separately, keep in mind that these components interact, thus affecting each other.

**ACTIVITY 7.1**

Your instructor will place you into groups of five members. As a group, analyze your classroom in terms of Rosenfeld's model.

*Group composition:*

*Structural variables:*

*Operating variables:*

*Task:*

*Outcome:*

*Group atmosphere:*

*Environment:*

## GROUP COMPOSITION

Groups consist of persons. Each person entering the group brings with him a variety of attitudes, capabilities, and personality variables. All these enter into the group's system and affect the group's ability to work together to complete the task. McGrath and Altman summarized the research examining group composition and concluded that "a consistent positive relationship exists between the capabilities and skills of group members and their performance."[3] In terms of the classroom environment, it would be helpful if the teacher could "match" students' individual characteristics when forming small groups. Khan and Weiss suggest that "a group in which an individual's social, emotional, and personality needs are met will seem to facilitate and encourage effective learning."[4] Obviously, this is not possible to the extent that it is probably needed. However, the teacher does know her students and can use this knowledge when forming small instructional groups to insure some compatibility among members.

Size is a factor in group composition. The larger the group, the less feedback each group member can perceive. Remember when I discussed the complexity of communication. When two people communicate, there are really six. Imagine the complexity when several people interact in a small group! Each person cannot be attuned to all the feedback bombarding him. As the size of a group increases, interpersonal relationships increase geometrically. A three-member group has three basic interpersonal relationships; a group of five members has ten such relationships; a group of ten has forty-five basic interpersonal relationships.[5] Slater [6] found that group members were most satisfied when groups consisted of five members. Members of larger groups reported that their groups were disorderly; members of smaller groups worried about alienating others.

## GROUP STRUCTURAL VARIABLES

### Networks

Patterns of communication flow—communication networks—can affect both the satisfaction and performance of group members. Leavitt[7] investigated the effects of four physical structures on communication within five-member groups. The communication networks are pictured in figure 7.2 with arrows indicating the direction of communication flow.

Leavitt reported that the wheel and Y networks (centralized; messages flowing through a central member) were more efficient in solving simple problems, but the members were more dissatisfied than in the other two networks. Although the circle network was the most inefficient in terms of time, the members were the most satisfied. (It is important to note that centralized networks are efficient when the task is relatively simple, while decentralized networks are more efficient when the task is more complex.) What does Leavitt's research tell us about small groups in the classroom? Centralized networks create feelings of being peripheral, or unimportant. These feelings in turn lead to a reduction in communication. In decentralized networks, like the circle, communication flows equally. In class-

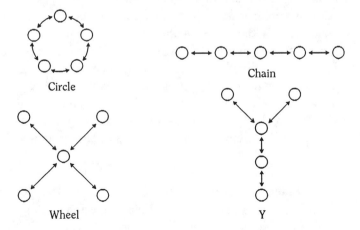

*Figure 7.2 Different types of communication networks.*

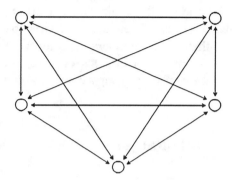

***Figure 7.3*** *An all-channel network.*

rooms where different people are central to the discussion at different times and where issues are discussed by everyone, greater feelings of involvement and satisfaction and, thus, a steadier flow of communication will occur. Thus teachers need to arrange the physical structures in their classrooms so that an all-channel network is possible (figure 7.3).

## Attraction

Attraction—the liking of group members for one another—is another structural variable that can affect the group members' satisfaction and performance. Several factors affect our liking for others—proximity, rewards, trust, and supportiveness. One of the major factors is homophily, or our perception of the degree of similarity between us and the other person. The greater the degree of perceived homophily between two people, the greater the likelihood of attraction and the more effective the communication will be.

One means a teacher has of examining the attraction networks in her class is sociometry—"the study of the patterns of interrelations between people, and the process of their measurement in respect to membership in the group."[8] A sociometric questionnaire indicates to the teacher the degree to which individuals are accepted or rejected by the group, as well as the reasons for that acceptance or rejection. Such information can help the teacher determine if the group should continue to work together or if some changes in group membership are necessary.

Rosenfeld[9] outlines five general rules to ensure an adequate sociometric questionnaire:

1. Select situations which provide a real opportunity for interaction. Information derived from an artificial situation or one which is structured to minimize interaction will be meaningless. Asking an individual to select some-

one he would prefer to be with in a therapy group, where interaction would necessarily be great, is more meaningful than asking him to select someone to type his term paper, where there may be no interaction at all.

2.  Select situations where there are a variety of possible types of interaction. Individual preferences differ according to the circumstances in which individuals are placed. Selecting someone to be part of a crowd, as many parties turn out to be, is easier and certainly less crucial than selecting someone to form a dyad (pair), as on a date. But information concerning both is necessary to understand the individual's preferences. Along with varieties in levels of interaction (certainly the level of individual interaction at a party is different than on a date), variety in the types of interaction should be given. Both work and social relationships should be sampled on the questionnaire, as well as levels of interaction for each. Asking someone with whom she prefers to work on a problem may result in a different answer than asking her to select someone with whom she can discuss a new idea; although both situations ostensibly relate, they differ in level and type of interaction. A full analysis of the interrelationships in a group requires responses to different types of situations.

3.  Require a limited number of responses to questions. It is often difficult for individuals to provide more than three responses to any given question. As the number of responses required increases, the quality of the distinctions made decreases proportionately.

4.  State questions in the conditional ("should" or "would") tense. It is difficult for individuals to accept and reject others. Accepting one individual implies the rejection of others. To help ease the tension that this might create, questions should be stated in the conditional tense. Under this condition, individuals are more likely to be honest, and honesty is crucial if the analysis is to be meaningful and accurate.

5.  Avoid negative questions such as "With whom would you *not* want to sit?" As already mentioned, people do not like to make negative judgments of others. Negative questions are likely to make respondents uneasy, which in turn might make them respond less than honestly. Negative questions may also cause some resentment;  often they are not even responded to.

---

### ACTIVITY 7.2

In your group of five members, develop a sociometric questionnaire. Administer the questionnaire to another group in your class.

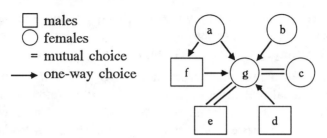

*Figure 7.4 The star sociogram.*

After the questionnaire is administered, the results must be tabulated. Perhaps the easiest way to tabulate results is via a sociogram. A sociogram is a diagram depicting the interrelationships in a group. The star sociogram is one type of sociogram that is fairly popular. A star diagram is depicted below in figure 7.4.

The sociogram presented in figure 7.4 indicates that two reciprocal relationships exist in the group—g and e; g and c. The sociometric questionnaire and resulting sociogram can provide you with information on the nature of relationships within the group, the basis of these relationships, and whether the relationships are reciprocal. In addition, the nature of the communication network can be predicted.

---

**ACTIVITY 7.3**

Tabulate the results of the questionnaire you administered in Activity 7.2. Before making a star sociogram, complete a two-fold table.[10] Assume your questionnaire consisted of four questions:

1. Whom would you choose as a teacher?
2. Whom would you choose to work with in solving a problem?
3. Whom would you choose to ask for help on a personal problem?
4. Whom would you choose as most intelligent?

|  |  | Person Selected | | | | |
|---|---|---|---|---|---|---|
|  |  | Jeff | Jane | Mary | John | Mark |
|  | Jeff |  |  | 3 |  |  |
|  | Jane |  |  |  |  |  |
| Person Selecting | Mary |  | 4 |  |  |  |
|  | John |  |  |  |  | 2 |
|  | Mark | 1 |  |  |  |  |

The two-fold table indicates that Mark chose Jeff as a teacher (question 1); Mary chose Jane as the most intelligent (question 4); and John chose Mark to work with in solving a problem (question 2).

Person Selected

| | | | | |
|---|---|---|---|---|
| | | | | |
| | | | | |
| | | | | |

Person Selecting

### *Draw a Star Sociogram*

What do the two-fold table and the star sociogram tell you about the attraction network in the group you studied?

What does this information tell you about the communication networks of the group? About members' effectiveness in working together?

## OPERATING VARIABLES

Operating variables consist of the roles enacted and the norms developed as the group develops. Before discussing roles and norms, the phases of development of task groups—the type of most small instructional groups—will be discussed.

### Group Development

Although there are several theories of group development,[11] Fisher's[12] theory of group development will be used because it focuses on verbal interaction. Four phases, each with a characteristic interaction pattern, emerged from Fisher's analysis of ten groups.

*The orientation phase* was primarily concerned with social interaction—with "getting acquainted, clarifying and tentatively expressing attitudes."[13] There's a great deal of agreement during this phase as people work toward interpersonal understanding of one another. Opinions are expressed in tentative and qualified terms.

*The conflict phase* is filled with dissent and dispute. Statements are less ambiguous than in the orientation stage. Polarization occurs as coalitions advocating similar views appear.

*Emergence* is characterized by cooperation. People become less polarized. Favorable comments are followed by more favorable comments, until a group decision emerges. Unfavorable comments become more ambiguous.

In the *reinforcement phase,* dissent is almost nonexistent. The group is concerned with affirming its unity as each member reinforces the decision. The ambiguity so prevalent in phase three tends to disappear. This is the "pat ourselves on the back" phase.

These four stages have been referred to as forming, storming, norming, and performing.

Any small task group will progress through these stages. It's important for you to be aware of these phases so you can gauge how groups in the classroom are progressing toward task completion. In addition, an awareness of these phases indicates that you should not be concerned when conflicts arise within groups. We'll return to the conflict phase when the group atmosphere component is discussed.

## Roles

Shakespeare once wrote

> All the world's a stage;
> And all the men and women
> merely players;
> They all have their exits,
> and their entrances;
> And one man in his time
> plays many parts.

The parts we play in small groups are termed roles. More precisely, a role is the "pattern of behavior which characterizes an individual's place in a group."[14] Several systems for examining roles in a group have been formulated.[15] One of the most useful role analyses is presented by Bales.[16] His Interaction Process Analysis focuses on communication. The underlying assumption is that people act and react in group communication. One person makes a comment; another person responds. These interactions can be categorized into twelve roles. These roles, in turn, can be broken down into task roles (those communication behaviors facilitating the group's completion of the task) and socioemotional roles (those communication behaviors relating to the interpersonal relations in the group). Figure 7.5 illustrates these categories.[17]

The communication behavior types are paired according to typical comment response expectations. Each pair implies a problem area for groups (a–f). The approximate percentage of comments within each category is given in parentheses. Categories one and four (1–3 and 10–12) are concerned with the socioemotional roles, while categories two and three (4–9) constitute task roles.

A key role in the small group is the leadership role. The question of what makes an effective leader has plagued researchers and theorists. Several theories of leadership have been posited: trait theory (a good leader is born, not made),

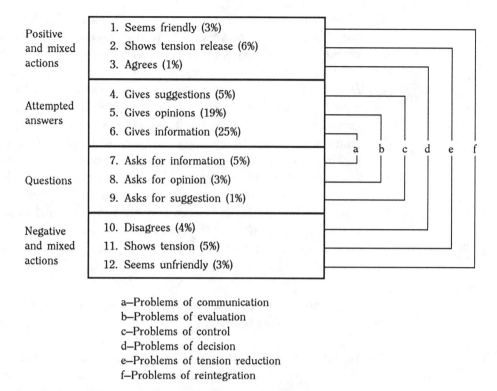

| Positive and mixed actions | 1. Seems friendly (3%) |
| | 2. Shows tension release (6%) |
| | 3. Agrees (1%) |
| Attempted answers | 4. Gives suggestions (5%) |
| | 5. Gives opinions (19%) |
| | 6. Gives information (25%) |
| Questions | 7. Asks for information (5%) |
| | 8. Asks for opinion (3%) |
| | 9. Asks for suggestion (1%) |
| Negative and mixed actions | 10. Disagrees (4%) |
| | 11. Shows tension (5%) |
| | 12. Seems unfriendly (3%) |

a—Problems of communication
b—Problems of evaluation
c—Problems of control
d—Problems of decision
e—Problems of tension reduction
f—Problems of reintegration

*Figure 7.5* *Bales's twelve small-group communication roles.*

circumstances theory (a person may be a good leader in some circumstances, but not in others), function theory (leadership consists of certain functions that groups must have performed; these functions are behaviors that can be learned by anyone), leadership styles (autocratic, democratic, laissez-faire), and contingency theory (a leader's effectiveness is contingent or dependent upon the combination of her behavior and the situation).

The functional view of leadership is particularly viable for classroom groups. This approach to leadership focuses on the communicative behaviors of individual members and their relative contribution to the group's process. In other words, leadership does not need to be thought of in terms of a certain individual. Rather, it can be considered a function to be performed. Fisher and Ellis[18] suggest that a leader must function in three areas—group procedures, task requirements, and social needs—and provide a list of some function in each area.

A.  Group Procedures: All groups must be guided through their tasks in an orderly manner. Every type of group establishes procedures for accomplishing goals.

1. *Plan an Agenda.* An agenda is a list of topics to be discussed during the group's meeting. The leader should either prepare an agenda before the group meets or direct the group before the meeting actually begins to agree on what it will talk about.

2. *Handle Routine "Housekeeping" Matters.* These are tasks that typically must be completed before the group begins considering the central issues of the meeting. The tasks could be such things as taking roll, calling the meeting to order, distributing handouts, or making any necessary announcements or modifications to the agenda.

3. *Prepare for the Next Meeting.* Group members need to be informed about such things as the meeting's location, date, and time. The leader should make sure that the physical conditions are appropriate; that is, the room is of sufficient size; there are enough chairs, and any equipment (e.g., projectors and slides) is available and operating.

B. Task Requirements: Leadership behaviors that help the group achieve its goals are task-oriented behaviors.

1. *Initiate a Structure.* Effective leaders organize and direct things so that the group makes progress toward its goals. The leader suggests ways of doing things and proposes tasks and goals for the group.

2. *See Information.* Functional behaviors in this area include requesting facts, asking questions, and getting clarification on unclear points of information.

3. *Give Information.* Very simply, leaders offer facts and information relevant to the group's concerns.

4. *Offer Informed Opinions.* Leaders seek information so that they can offer informed opinions; it is counterproductive to confuse the members with ambiguous or indefensible opinions. Leaders also offer their informed opinions at the right time, neither stating them too soon nor remaining silent too long.

5. *Clarify and Elaborate.* Reducing ambiguity and clarifying ideas by asking questions and making statements are important leadership functions. A good leader can recognize when the members are confused or unclear about an idea because it has been expressed in abstract language. The leader should also be capable of relating one idea to another and of seeing the big picture. Because group members are often preoccupied with their own ideas, it is up to the leader to clarify the connections between ideas so that the members understand the ideas' implications.

6. *Summarize the Group's Main Points and State Its Consensus.* Group members usually express many opinions and ideas during the course of a discussion. Some of these are carefully thought out, but others are rather haphazard and superficial. In either case, it is important that they be summarized. A leadership function has been performed when someone restates the main points in clear language and summarizes the members' various arguments. A truly skillful and balanced summary will include all the main points and arguments.

C. Social Needs: A leader who attends to social needs is concerned with promoting a harmonious and pleasant social environment in the group; this requires the leader to be sensitive to the group's individual members and their interpersonal relationships.

1. *Express Feelings.* This is very difficult in most work groups. Nevertheless, there are times when it is important. A leader should not force group members into a soul-searching session but can call attention to feelings that are bothering people. A leader can provide support for a group member who has been personally attacked and can reinforce a less confident member. A leader who freely expresses feelings and shows concern for the feelings of others will establish a friendly and productive work environment. And the best way to stimulate others to talk about their feelings is to do it yourself. So if as a leader you say what is on your mind, others will likely follow.

2. *Facilitate Involvement and Communication.* Almost all groups have members who do not participate or are not very involved in group life. Leaders must work to keep everyone participating; otherwise, the group loses valuable input. There are a number of ways to stimulate communication and involvement, but the following three are the most common and effective:

   a. *Make sure you reinforce any attempts to participate by shy or reluctant members.* Verbal reinforcements are simple and effective, such as saying, "Good idea, I hadn't thought of that."

   b. *Directly engage people in communication.* A leader might find it necessary simply to remind group members that they have an obligation to participate, telling them directly that the quality of the discussion depends on their participation. Also, a leader can address questions directly to individuals; this will pull a person into the interaction, and then if the person's contributions can be reinforced, there will be even stronger incentives to continue participation. Giving assignments is another way to encourage involvement in the group. At the close of a meeting or work session, a leader should give directions for the next time, and group members who are responsible for some type of work and must come prepared to report will naturally be involved in the interaction.

c. *Increase the chances for participation.* Sometimes groups are so large that people find it difficult to "jump in"; the leader might consider dividing the group into small clusters to give everyone an equal chance to participate. There is also the problem of the overpowering member or subset of members who dominate the discussion. A leader should not allow one member to dominate the discussion. Finally, the leader can use the structural arrangement of the group to an advantage. Place a group member in a central position (such as in the middle of a network or at the head of a table), and this will increase the frequency of the member's participation.

3. *Harmonize.* Harmonizing is getting the members to cooperate and creating a supportive climate in the group. The skilled harmonizer knows the difference between (1) a healthy and valuable exchange of ideas, which may include honest disagreement, and (2) nasty arguments that interfere with the group's productivity and are based on individual egos and ambitions. A leader can always simply restate opposing positions, ask the members to clarify their views, and then try to find compromises.

Students learn best when they are actively involved in the learning process.[19] Thus, all group members need to contribute, to feel a part of the group if learning is to be effective. Each individual in the group should play several roles at different points in time. What role a student takes in a group depends on such factors as the demands of the situation (time, place, group membership) and the student's personality.

---

### ACTIVITY 7.4

Think about the group in this classroom. In terms of the activities (7.1–7.3) your group has completed, answer the following questions.

1. What task roles did you assume? Under what conditions did you assume them? How successful were you in aiding the group in completing its task?

2.  What socioemotional roles did you assume? Under what conditions did you assume them? How successful were you in these socioemotional roles?

3.  Discuss your answers to questions 1 and 2 with your group members. Did they perceive you in a similar manner? If not, why not?

## Norms

Think about this class. What are some rules of this class that you are expected to follow? Your teacher is expected to follow? In small group communication, these rules are termed norms. Norms are rules adopted by group members. They influence perceptions, cognitions, evaluations, and behaviors of group members. By following norms, we don't have to rethink each situation. We know what is expected and we simply "follow the rules."

A colleague of mine asked me to lecture to his class of 160 students while he was absent. As I progressed through the lecture, I kept asking questions of the students. No one answered. I employed all the correct questioning strategies. Still no one answered. Finally, I asked, "Are you used to being asked questions during lecture?" One student replied, "Dr. Cooper, it's your job to lecture. It's our job to listen. We're not supposed to have to answer questions during lecture." I had violated a norm of that classroom! This example demonstrates another fact about norms—they are rules that are not to be violated. When a group member violates norms, that group member is "set straight" in one way or another.

All groups have norms. They may be explicit or implicit, formal or informal. Johnson[20] sets forth seven guidelines for the establishment and support of group norms:

1.  For members to accept group norms, they must recognize that they exist, see that the other members accept and follow them, and feel some internal commitment to them.

2.  Members will accept and internalize norms to the extent that they see them as helping accomplish the goals and tasks to which they are committed. It is helpful, therefore, for a group to clarify how conformity to a norm will help goal accomplishment.

3.  Members will accept and internalize norms for which they feel a sense of ownership. Generally, members will support and accept norms that they have helped set up.

4.  Group members should enforce the norms immediately after a violation. Enforcement should also be as consistent as possible.

5.  Appropriate models and examples for conforming to the group norms should be present. Members should have the chance to practice the desired behaviors.

6. Cultural norms that help in goal accomplishment and group maintenance and growth should be imported into the group.
7. Because norms exist only to help group effectiveness, they should be flexible so that at any time more appropriate norms can be substituted.

---

**ACTIVITY 7.5**

Write down as many formal and informal norms for this class as you can. For example, do you call your teacher by first name or title and last name.

Divide into your small group. Share your responses with your group members. Record all responses.

Return to your class. Pool your responses. What are the common norms? Which are conducive to classroom learning? Why? Which norms should be eliminated? Why?

---

## TASK

### Defining the Task

The real key to effective use of small instructional groups in the classroom is the planning and organizing of the task. Simply telling students to "get together and solve this problem," or "work in groups to complete the assignment," or "get together in small groups and discuss Ethan Frome," will make their learning experience frustrating at best! You must take considerable time to "set the scene." Any unfamiliar terms or concepts should be defined and clarified. The goal of the small group task, as well as the time allotted for them to complete the task, should be clear to students. When groups have completed the task, you must process the experience, that is, answer the question students always ask: What were we supposed to get out of this? The class as a whole should discuss the major themes and subtopics their individual groups discussed. This material should be related to previous topics and readings, and implications of the new material for students should be identified.

Brophy[21] reviewed literature describing teacher communications about tasks that help to create a classroom environment in which tasks may be perceived as valuable and offered suggestions for motivating students to learn that include modeling outside learning (e.g., reporting on learning through newspapers), communicating the assumption that students are eager learners who recognize the value of learning; minimizing performance anxiety; inducing curiosity or dissonance about the topic; making abstract content more personal, concrete, or familiar; and modeling task-related thinking and problem solving.

Several tasks are available for small instructional groups to complete. The main types of small group tasks will be discussed briefly.

### Problem-Solving Tasks

A variety of discussion groups in which students make a decision or solve a problem can be utilized in your classroom. For example, you might divide your math class into "families." Each family is provided a monthly income and a list of fixed expenses such as lodging, car payment, department store credit charges, and so on. Each family must determine how the remainder of their monthly income is to be spent—how much should be budgeted for recreation, food, clothing, and so forth.

Before attempting to solve a problem, either real or hypothetical, students should be familiar with problem-solving patterns. For example, students could be taught the pattern of problem solving outlined below:

1. Identify the problem—its limits and specific nature.
2. Analyze the problem—its causes and consequences.
3. Set up standards for possible solutions. What criteria would a good, workable solution have to meet?
4. Suggest possible solutions.
5. Choose the best solution. Which one of the solutions suggested in step 4 meet the most criteria outlined in step 3?

Groups can be exposed to real-life situations through print or media case studies. Students are asked to analyze the situations presented. Cases can be brief, taking only one class period to analyze, or quite lengthy, requiring several class periods to analyze. Students are requested to come to an agreement on a decision concerning the case study. This agreement can be reached in several ways—majority vote, minority vote, consensus, compromise, or an expert's decision.

Majority vote assumes that although 51 percent of the group members agree on the decision, dissenting (minority) views have been heard. Minority vote can occur when a subgroup determines the decision. Perhaps the entire group has difficulty meeting, and so members agree to abide by the decision of those members who do meet. The main problem here is that the total group may not really be committed to the decision, and conflicts remain unresolved. Decision by consensus occurs when all group members support the decision. Every student must feel he has had a chance to influence the decision. Although this type of decision making requires the most time, it has the strongest commitment of group members. Decision by compromise occurs when group members cannot agree on a decision. This is an "average" decision, in that a middle-of-the road decision is made. Commitment by all group members is rarely possible, and the quality of the decision is less than in other forms of decision making. Sometimes a group will view one member as an "expert" on the problem and will designate the expert to make the decision.

A final type of discussion task for a small instructional group is an assigned topic. Groups are presented with a topic to discuss, rather than a case study. The topic might be a follow-up to a lecture you presented. The members' combined experience, research, and understanding are used to stimulate interest, develop further understanding of the topic, and expose group members to a variety of viewpoints.

### Role-Play Tasks

Small groups may be used in role play situations as a means of learning to solve problems and relate to others. Group members are presented with a situation and asked to assume roles and act out the situation. Observations are made by other class members. These observations are then compared to the reactions and observations of the role players.

Role play has several advantages outlined by Callahan and Clark. Role plays

> permit students to use information in the light of the particular perceptions of the role being played. They make it possible to examine concepts and ideas from different viewpoints expressed in the role playing. They help promote understanding and deepen insights through the necessity of thinking as the character being portrayed. They can provide opportunity for greater understanding by having students act out roles and positions different from those they would tend to favor and approve. Such reversal of roles helps to deepen the awareness of the complex, controversial nature of much knowledge and of many issues.[22]

### Research Tasks

Students can be divided into small groups and asked to research a topic area. Research groups enable students to develop research skills and critical thinking. For example, a social studies teacher might want students to study Mexico. Small research groups could be formed, one to research customs, one to research the history of Mexico, one to research the geography, one to research Mexican–U.S. relations, etc. Each group could then report its findings to the class.

### Games/Simulation Tasks

You might present your class with a simulation, a game, or a simulation-game task that could utilize several small groups. A simulation models reality, while a game is an activity in which participants agree to abide by a set of rules. A simulation game, then, is an activity that models reality and the participants agree to "follow the rules." A simulation game often portrays adult society. Thus, students are encouraged to make responsible decisions in complex situations they may well come across in later life. If your goal as an educator is to prepare students for life in society, simulation games may be one of the most effective means of accomplishing your goal.

---

**ACTIVITY 7.6** [23]                                                                 Negotiations

"Play" the following simulation game. (Created by Bill Wallace, Kellogg Community College, Battle Creek, Michigan.)

### Objectives

1. To provide activities within the classroom that permit students to become aware of and sensitive to the problems inherent in reaching compromise and consensus through negotiations.
2. To place students in negotiation situations so that they may develop and improve their skills for future implementation of this technique.

### Directions

Glitz Company, famous for its production of the Glitz Gadget, has announced a stalemate in current contract negotiations. Unless a settlement is reached by 6:00 P.M. next Wednesday, a nationwide strike will take place. The task of the participants is to achieve an agreement in two days of classroom time (plus time used for outside research and consultation). Rules and regulations for conduct follow:

1. Each negotiating "group" will consist of two members representing management, two members representing labor, and an outside observer.
2. The observer will not participate in the negotiations, but will take notes so that he can discuss the following communication concepts during the debriefing period: trust, cooperation and competition, feedback, perception, conflict resolution, compromise, persuasion, and decision making.
3. The process will begin with both management and labor submitting their contract proposals. These proposals must be presented in toto.
4. Each side may utilize two five-minute "cooling off" periods during the negotiation.
5. All information not otherwise specified is open to interpretation by the individual groups.
6. If desired, negotiating groups may break into subcommittees.

7. At the conclusion of the negotiating sessions, a proposal endorsed by both sides should be submitted to the instructor.

8. Profit-sharing, vacation, retirement benefits, wages, overtime, job security, and insurance are some of the areas that should be discussed and resolved.

The following negotiation information should also be provided: Glitz Gadget Company is the fifth leading domestic Gadget maker, accounting for 10 percent of the Gadgets sold in the United States. During fiscal year 1976, Glitz lost twenty-six million dollars. For the first six months of fiscal year 1977, Glitz lost thirty-three million. A contract with the leading Gadget maker called for salaries and benefits totalling seven dollars and fifty cents per hour for assembly line workers and ten dollars per hour for skilled workers. Glitz employees now earn five dollars and seventy-five cents per hour and eight dollars and seventy-five cents per hour, respectively. To cut costs, Glitz has called for a moratorium on overtime. Glitz employees have not struck since 1957, the first year they came under union representation. To become financially solvent, Glitz proposes to cut its work force by 10 percent, a loss of 5,000 persons. (This would be done not by firing any present workers, but by not filling vacancies when they occur.) A new thirteen-million-dollar contract has been awarded to Glitz to manufacture Gadgets for government workers. Until recently, Glitz employees have enjoyed the "one big happy family" atmosphere of their plants. Glitz has plans to extend to Europe, but has decided to automate a large portion of these new facilities. Glitz company president, Arnold Fern, warns that "a strike of any duration would be fatal." Employees have voted overwhelmingly to strike if demands are not met. Negotiations have been reconvened at the request of management in order to present a new proposal. Glitz employees currently work five eight-hour shifts a week. Labor leaders have called for "creative efforts" to end the stalemate. Most industry experts predict a big upsurge in the Gadget market during the next five years. Salaries at Glitz have consistently been below average for the industry, due, in part, to its small size. Employees are seeking more input to decision-making committees in the company. The Union Strike Fund is at a ten-year low, and benefits would run out quickly in the event of a strike.

Glitz employees feel very strongly that they are being badly treated by their employer. In contrast to other workers in the industry, they feel they are at the "bottom of the heap"—and deserve better in light of their loyalty and productivity over the past years. Management, on the other hand, believes that, if it is to survive, it cannot meet the wage standards set by the other top companies. If it does, it will go bankrupt—and there will be no jobs. Employees think this is the result of poor management and are willing to take risks in order to become equal to others in the industry.

### Management Contract Proposal

*Wages*:   $6.00/hour for assembly-line workers
            $9.00/hour for skilled workers
*Vacation*:   Six paid holidays/year
              Two weeks paid vacation—1-5 years experience
              Three weeks paid vacation—5-9 years experience
              Four weeks paid vacation—10-14 years experience
*Insurance*: Employer will pay 50% Blue Cross—No dental

### Labor Contract Proposal

*Wages*:   $7.50/hour for assembly-line workers
            $10.50/hour for skilled workers
*Vacation*:   Twelve paid holidays
              Three weeks paid vacation—1-5 years experience
              Four weeks paid vacation—5-9 years experience
              Five weeks paid vacation—10-14 years experience
*Insurance*: Employer will pay 100% Blue Cross
             Employer will pay 50% dental
*Retirement Benefits*:   Employer will pay 75% to pension fund
                         (The possibility of profit-sharing will be discussed.)

### Debriefing

For "management," the following questions may be asked: Did you have any strategies designed to gain, for the company, the maximum benefit from the negotiations? Describe them, particularly those related to communication. Did you change your strategy as you became involved in the negotiations? As you look back at the exercise, can you think of some communication principles you might have employed to improve your position? How did you feel at the beginning of the negotiations? In the middle? At the end? Did any of these feelings get in the way of your understanding of what the employees were asking for? At any time, did you try to "put yourself in the shoes" of your employees? If so, did it make a difference? Can you think of other situations where you might need negotiating skills?

Essentially the same questions as above can be directed toward "employees," with a few additional questions, focused more on labor's point of view: Did you feel that management had more power than you did? How did this affect your negotiations? Did management ever indicate to you that they understood your position? Your feelings? Did you try to tell management how you felt? If not, why not?

For the observer: Describe what you saw take place. Did you think that the communication skills of either management or labor gave them an advantage (or disadvantage) in the process? In what ways do you think communication on either side might have been improved? If you had been allowed to be actively involved in the negotiations, do you think you could have reached agreement in a shorter length of time?

Many commercial simulation games are available. However, these may not fit the particular needs of your class. Simulation games are relatively easy to construct. The guidelines presented in table 7.1 should help you in constructing your own games, simulations, or simulation games.[24]

*Table 7.1* *Guidelines for constructing games and simulations.*

| | Typical questions to be answered |
|---|---|
| 1. Objectives | 1. |
|   a. list your educational objectives |   a. What do you want the participants to learn? Skills, information, feelings, concepts, system constraints, system process? |
|   b. translate educational objectives into behavioral ones |   b. What kind of behavior should participants perform in order to demonstrate that they achieved the educational objective? |
| 2. Real-life situation | 2. What is the most specific description you can give of the situation to be modeled? |
| 3. General model of the game determine the roles needed | 3. What roles, if any, are to be represented? (Some games have none.) Are the roles to be individuals, groups, institutions, nations? |
| 4. Interactions | 4. |
|   a. determine the game structure |   a. Who deals with whom? Can everyone interact with everyone else? If not, what are the restrictions? |
|   b. determine the game's procedures |   b. In what way are the parties to interact? Do they buy and sell, fight, debate, cooperate, compete? What exactly are they to do with each other? |
|   c. consider the kind of learning desired when determining 4a and 4b |   c. Does the game intend to teach information, skills, feelings, processes? If information, then some type of classifying scheme should be included, or the teaching of a skill for using the information. If a concept is to be learned, then the game should allow for the application of the concept in different situations. If the game emphasizes feelings, then getting points for satisfaction or frustration should be emphasized. If skills are important, opportunities for practice will be needed. |

*(Continued)*

| | **Typical questions to be answered** |
|---|---|
| 5. Resources | 5. |
| a. determine the media of interaction | a. What means or sources of power are appropriate for the roles through which the participants can express themselves and conduct their affairs? Are the resources money, shares, votes, troops, knowledge, etc.? |
| b. determine the quantity of resources | b. How much of these resources is to be allocated to each role at the start of the game? Have you considered the inequalities found in reality when determining the allocation? |
| 6. Schedule of events determine a sequence for performing the game's activities | 6. In what order do players make their moves? Is the sequence of moves clear to all participants? How is the game to start? Who makes the first move and what will this be? |
| 7. Rules | 7. |
| determine the rules governing the interaction in the game | a. What laws or other limitations govern the real-life situation represented in the game? |
| | b. How can the laws affecting the real-life system be translated into rules of the game? |
| | c. Are there any specific acts which players may not perform? |
| | d. Are the rules simple and few in number so they can be easily learned and observed and not inhibit the game's progress? |
| 8. Scoring Criteria | 8. |
| a. determine how a team or individual can win | a. Does the game have an internal winner, such as: the most satisfied person, the first to reach a given goal, the one who gets his way, the nation which conquers the most territory, the candidate who gets the most votes? Are the criteria for winning clearly related to the players' resources? |
| b. determine the way players learn of their success or failure | b. Do players receive information about their position during each round, at the end of each round, or only once at the end of the game? How will the timing of this information affect their conduct in the game? |
| 9. Materials | 9. What equipment is needed to facilitate the functioning of the game's processes? Does the game require a playing board, role profiles, a scenario, a data bank, score cards, information cards, dice, spinners, special signs, toys? |

*(Continued)*

*Table 7.1 Guidelines for constructing games and simulations. (Continued)*

| | **Typical questions to be answered** |
|---|---|
| 10. Write and design the materials and game components listed above | 10. |
| | a. Write an outline of the scenario (if one is included in the materials). |
| | b. Write role profiles. Prepare one index card for each profile, and list on the card where each player is located and what he does in each stage of the game. Group cards according to their first appearance in the game sequence. On separate sheets of paper list all the ideas you want to transmit, to be discussed or to be investigated during the game. Divide these ideas among the role profiles, keeping in mind when the players will be exchanging ideas during the game. |
| | c. Expand each role profile to more life-like proportions. For example, you might include information about family background, economic background, character, feelings, attitudes, strivings and goals, friends, enemies, affiliations. |
| 11. Write instructions for the game leader and participants | 11. The instructions should include a description of the materials included in the game, its objectives, the roles for participating, and procedures for playing the game. Also, directions should be offered on how to use the game with different numbers of players, the physical facilities required, and how to lengthen or shorten the game according to the level of the students. Suggestions should be made to the game leader as to how she can ensure that the game proceeds smoothly. <br><br> Write instructions for players, if necessary. Include the game's objectives, preparations for the game, procedures, and any special rules. |
| 12. Test the game and rewrite items as necessary. | |

## ACTIVITY 7.7

Create a simulation game for your particular subject matter area. Have the class "play." Restructure the simulation game as needed.

The distinction between one kind of task and another is quite arbitrary. Tasks are presented separately here for purposes of clarity. However, they can and probably should be combined. For example, roles plays are often utilized in simulation games. A research group may become a discussion group as it determines what work must be done and how the group should proceed to complete the research task. The important idea to remember is that tasks should be appropriate to your students' needs and your objectives.

## OUTCOME

A group's outcomes depend on two factors—task work and interpersonal relations. The quality, appropriateness, and efficiency of the solution or decision are task considerations. The task outcome affects the group's future interactions. So, too, a group's interpersonal relations affect not only the task outcome but also the group's subsequent interactions. Collins and Guetzkow[25] suggest that member satisfaction results from task success as well as success in solving socioemotional problems.

---

### ACTIVITY 7.8

Choose any of the tasks you completed in a small group in activities 7.6–7.8. Analyze the outcome of your task. Were you successful in completing the task? Why or why not?

---

## GROUP ATMOSPHERE

The climate of the group may be hostile or friendly, as affected by the task, the environment, and the group composition. Three areas of group atmosphere—cohesiveness, conformity, and conflict—will be discussed in this section.

### Cohesiveness

Cohesiveness is the feeling group members hold about the group. Cohesiveness emphasizes each individual's relationship to the group. Cohesiveness can be measured by summing up each individual's feelings about the group. A highly cohesive group is one in which members feel a sense of belongingness and are committed to the group. Cohesiveness is important to both the morale of group members and the productivity of the group. Students who feel more involved in the group are more satisfied than students who do not feel involved. In addition, in classes in which small groups are utilized, communication among students is more open and spontaneous and efficient.[26]

---

**ACTIVITY 7.9** [27]

Read the following case study and analyze why it is likely that this class will learn to be open and spontaneous.

Mr. Leavitt was finishing up the committee assignments in his seventh grade class.

"Now let's see—Joe will be in George's group."

"Do we have to have him again?" and "Aw gee" came from the classroom.

"Well, I gather that some people have objections to working with you, Joe," said Mr. Leavitt.

"I don't care. I don't want to work with any of them anyway. I'd rather work by myself," responded Joe.

"Let's see if we can't talk a bit about this. I'd like to hear what some of the reasons are for not wanting to work with Joe," Mr. Leavitt requested.

"Well, he's always butting in when anyone else talks. And he thinks he's the only one who has any good ideas."

"Yeah, and if you don't agree with him he tells you you're dumb and you don't know anything. "

"If he can't have his own way, he spoils things for everyone. No wonder we don't want to work with him."

"I guess you're saying," said Mr. Leavitt, "that working with people in groups can cause difficulty. People don't always agree with one another, and some committee members want their own way. And people sometimes think that their ideas are better than other people's ideas. In order for a group to work together, though, people have to listen to each other and sometimes change their own ideas or even give up their own ideas."

"Right! And Joe never gives up his own ideas."

Mr. Leavitt continued. "Why is it that people usually think the ideas they have are good ones? And have you noticed that some people give in more easily than others?"

"Yeah—my brother never gives in. What a pest!"

"Well, I think that people think their own ideas are good just because they're theirs. Like you usually think your country is best, or your town."

"Well, I stick up for my ideas because I really think they're good," said Joe. "Otherwise I wouldn't suggest them. And you know, Mr. Leavitt, you've told me many times that I contribute some of the best suggestions in class. Some people really have more ideas or better ideas than other people, and if they're better then they should stick up for them."

"I guess we've all noticed that some people put up more of a fight for what they want to say than others," said Mr. Leavitt. "And certainly we've all noticed that some people talk much more than other people do. We know that in a democracy everyone should be allowed to contribute the best that he can, while at the same time considering the rights of others. In our groups we want to practice democracy—give everyone a chance to contribute, and utilize as many ideas and skills as we can. Does anyone have any suggestions for ways for working out the kind of problem we have been talking about here in class?"

"Well, what's the use of giving Joe a chance, he doesn't even want to change."

"Maybe we could try some role playing—you know, like we did last week about the kids picking on the other kids who can't play baseball too good. I liked that."

"All right," said Mr. Leavitt. "Any suggestions for situations?"

"Well, we could have the kids who are really on the committee with Joe go up and start to work together. Joe could play the chairman, and somebody else could play Joe."

"What do you say, Joe?" asked Mr. Leavitt.

"Well, I'll do it, but I'd still rather work alone," replied Joe.

"I think it might be good to give this a try, and then we'll decide," said Mr. Leavitt. "Who would like to be . . . ?"

## Conformity

Conformity is closely related to cohesion. Individuals in a highly cohesive group are more likely to conform to group norms than are individuals in a group that is not cohesive. Conformity also increases with increases in group size (up to four members), group interaction, task difficulty, and ambiguity of the situation.[28]

## Conflict

Conflict is often thought to be destructive, and many groups try to avoid conflict. The truth is that conflict, if managed well, can be an impetus to creativity, flexibility, personal and group change, and the examination of problems.

Conflict is inevitable. Conflicts exist whenever incompatible activities occur. Because group members are individuals with differing likes, dislikes, perceptions, attitudes, and values, it's inevitable that incompatibility will occur from time to time. It's not the conflict per se but rather how the conflict is managed that's the problem. Whether a conflict turns out to be constructive or destructive depends, to a great extent, on the context in which it occurs. Contexts for controversy are of two types: cooperative and competitive. A cooperative context fosters constructive criticism whereas a competitive context promotes destructive controversy in the following ways:[29]

1.   In order for controversy to be constructive, information must be accurately communicated. Communication of information is far more complete, accurate, encouraged, and utilized in a cooperative context than in a competitive context.

2.   Constructive controversy requires a supportive climate in which group members feel safe enough to challenge each other's ideas. Cooperation provides a far more supportive climate than competition.

3.   In order for controversy to be constructive, it must be valued. Cooperative experiences promote stronger beliefs that controversy is valid and valuable.

4.   Constructive controversy requires dealing both with feelings and with ideas and information. There is evidence that cooperativeness is positively related and competitiveness is negatively related to the ability to understand what others are feeling and why they are feeling that way.

5.   How controversies are defined has a great impact on how constructively they are managed. Within a cooperative context, controversies are defined as problems to be solved, while in a competitive situation controversies tend to be defined as "win-lose" situations.

6.   Constructive controversy requires a recognition of both the similarities and differences between positions. Group members participating in a controversy within a cooperative context identify more of the similarities between their positions than do members participating in a controversy with a competitive context.

*I was brought up in a traditional school setting, in which the roles of the teacher and students were clearly defined. The teacher bawled into our ears for fifty minutes, perhaps on the fox-hunting outfits in* Silas Marner, *and we took notes. Or the teacher demanded a 485-word essay—no fewer words—on "roadside beauty," and we students obliged. Later, when I began to teach, I did exactly the same thing. It was "teach as I was taught": the lessons were ground out, the desks were evenly spaced, a feet-on-the-floor atmosphere was maintained at all times . . . About this time, I came upon the gospel of James Moffett. I was appalled. The man advocated a student-centered language arts curriculum, one in which students generated the ideas to be used in the classroom; one in which students taught each other through cross-teaching techniques; one in which the emphasis was on student cooperation and collaboration. The man was obviously a kook. Wouldn't my kids hoot and take advantage of the ensuing chaos? Wouldn't they tear each other up much worse than in their daily battles on the playground and in the halls? Terms*

*like cooperation and collaboration weren't part of their vocabulary. And as*
*for their teaching each other, wouldn't it be a case of the blind leading the*
*blind? They didn't know a comma from a semiquaver.*[30]

In the above quotation, Richard Whitworth describes his trepidation about
using collaborative learning. His description will be familiar to many teachers
who "teach as they were taught." However, collaborative learning, the grouping
and pairing of students for the purpose of achieving an academic goal, has been
widely researched and advocated throughout the educational literature.

The collaborative learning method has been characterized as "a form of
indirect teaching in which the teacher sets the problem and organizes students
to work it out colaboratively."[31] One of the basic features of collaborative learning is student talk. In fact, students are supposed to talk with one another as
they work through various classroom activities and projects. Students assimilate
their ideas and information through their talk. Thus, collaborative learning is a
deliberate attempt to take advantage of differing viewpoints and perspectives
through interaction of individuals and their ideas in a reciprocal or alternating
action.[32] Merely putting students into groups, however, does not mean that collaborative learning is taking place. Specifically, "students put into groups are
only students grouped and are not collaborators, unless a task that demands
learning unifies the group activity."[33] They need guidance. As Golub indicates,
the role of the teacher changes from "information giver" to "guide on the side."[34]
The teacher is a facilitator, which involves questioning, suggesting, and directing
the discussion.

In sum, as Bruffee so aptly describes:

*The basic idea of collaborative learning is that we gain certain kinds of*
*knowledge best through a process of communication with our peers. What*
*we learn best in this way is knowledge involving judgment. We can sit by*
*ourselves and learn irregular French verbs, benzene rings, the parts of*
*an internal combustion engine, or the rhetorical devices which are useful*
*in eloquent or effective prose. But when we want to know how to use this*
*discrete knowledge—to speak French, to combine organic compounds, to*
*find out why an engine won't start and then to fix it, or actually to write*
*eloquent prose—we have to learn quite differently. . . . The best way to*
*learn to make judgments is to practice making them in collaboration with*
*other people who are at about the same stage of development as we are.*[35]

Johnson and Johnson[36] outline four elements necessary for effective collaborative learning:

1.  Positive interdependence: There must be a clear structure to ensure that
    the group works together. In other words, the group must understand
    exactly what it is they are to accomplish.

2. Face-to-face interaction: The Johnsons refer to this as "eye-to-eye and k-to-k (knee-to-knee)." Students must sit looking and facing one another.

3. Individual responsibility. Although the entire group learns collaboratively, each student must be responsible for some task. Too often, if this is not the case, one or more students may "go along for the ride," but do not really contribute.

4. Appropriate interpersonal skills: The teacher should not assume that students know how to communicate in groups. Students need to be taught interpersonal skills such as paraphrasing, clarifying, listening, responding, agreeing, disagreeing, etc.

The values of cooperative learning are well established.[37] Collaborative learning promotes higher mastery, retention, and transfer of concepts. It promotes a higher quality of reasoning strategies than do competitive and individualistic structures. It promotes healthier cognitive, social, and physical development and higher levels of self-esteem. It results in more positive student-student relationships that are characterized by mutual liking, positive attitudes toward one another, and mutual feelings of obligation, support, acceptance and respect.

In addition, the "socialness" of the collaborative learning method may be its most important value. The group process is the life process. As Resnick and Klopfer suggest:

> But most important of all, the social setting may let students know that all the elements of critical thought—interpretation, questioning, trying possibilities, demanding rational justifications—are socially valued. The social setting may help to shape a disposition to engage in thinking. There is not much research on how intellectual dispositions are socialized, but we do know how other traits such as aggressiveness, independence, or gender identification develop. By analogy with these traits, we can expect intellectual dispositions to arise from long-term participation in social communities that establish expectations for certain kinds of behavior. Through participation in communities, students would come to expect thinking all the time, to view themselves as able, even obligated, to engage in critical analysis and problem solving.[38]

The teacher may find that the collaborative learning method is not "neat and tidy" in either practice or in assessing its outcomes. It is somewhat chaotic. However, as Berthoff suggests, the learning is well worth the chaos:

> Now, chaos is scary: the meanings that can emerge from it, which can be discerned taking shape within it, can be discovered only if students who are learning to write can learn to tolerate ambiguity. It is to our teacherly advantage that the mind doesn't like chaos; on the other hand, we have to be alert to the fact that meanings can be arrived at too quickly, the possibility

*of other meanings being too abruptly foreclosed. What we must realize our-*
*selves and make dramatically evident to our students is what I. A. Richards*
*means when he calls ambiguities "the hinges of thought."* [39]

## ENVIRONMENT

All that a group says and does occurs within an environment. One aspect
of environment that affects small group interaction is furniture arrangements
and room size. Students in a circle arrangement talk to those students opposite them rather than those on either side. Students seated at the corners
of a rectangular table contribute less to the discussion, while central and
head positions appear to be dominant.[40] Sommer[41] found that, as room size
increased, the distance between people decreased.

Time is another environmental factor affecting small groups. As the allotted
time runs out, members will get more and more frustrated if their task is not
near completion. As a teacher, you need to be aware that time of day can affect
your classroom interaction greatly. Near the end of the school day, students may
need special motivational incentives in order to expend the energy that effective
small group interaction requires.

Such environmental factors as time and furniture arrangement can help or
hinder small group interaction. In addition, the place can affect small group interaction. Recall the discussion in chapter 4 of beautiful versus ugly rooms. If
your classroom is "ugly," you may want to "spruce it up" to create an environment in which students will enjoy working.

---

### ACTIVITY 7.10

Arrange to meet your group in different environments. Meet in different sized
rooms, attractive and unattractive rooms, meet at differing times. How did environmental changes change group interaction?

---

## OBSERVING AND EVALUATING
## SMALL INSTRUCTIONAL GROUPS

If students are to learn effectively from small group interaction, they must increase their small group interaction skills. One of the best ways to enable students
to increase these skills is to have them evaluate themselves and their group, and
to observe and evaluate other groups.

Through observation and evaluation, students can eliminate their errors, strengthen their strong points, and correct weak points. Following every small group experience, students should discuss their own experience in the group. Each of the components of the small group should be analyzed—the group composition, the structural and operating variables, task, outcome, group atmosphere, and environment. You might ask students to evaluate their experience in a small group by providing them with an evaluation form such as the one shown in table 7.2.

**Table 7.2** *Small group evaluation form.*

*Instruction:* Circle the number which best indicates your reactions to the following questions about the discussion in which you participated.

1. *Adequacy of Communication:* To what extent do you feel members were understanding each others' statements and positions?

   0    1    2    3    4    5    6    7    8    9    10

   Much talking past each                    Communicated directly with
   other, misunderstanding                   each other, understanding well

2. *Opportunity to Speak:* To what extent did you feel free to speak?

   0    1    2    3    4    5    6    7    8    9    10

   Never had a                               All the opportunity to
   chance to speak                           talk I wanted

3. *Climate of Acceptance:* How well did members support each other, show acceptance of individuals?

   0    1    2    3    4    5    6    7    8    9    10

   Highly critical                           Supportive and receptive
   and punishing

4. *Interpersonal Relations:* How pleasant and concerned were interpersonal relations?

   0    1    2    3    4    5    6    7    8    9    10

   Quarrelsome, status                       Pleasant, empathic,
   differences emphasized                    concerned with persons

5. *Leadership:* How adequate was the leader (or leadership) of the group?

   0    1    2    3    4    5    6    7    8    9    10

   Too weak ( ) or                           Shared, group-centered,
   dominating ( )                            and sufficient

6. *Satisfaction with Role:* How satisfied are you with your personal participation in the discussion?

   0    1    2    3    4    5    6    7    8    9    10

   Very dissatisfied                              Very satisfied
                                                  *(Continued)*

7. *Quality of Product:* How satisfied are you with the decisions, solutions, or learnings that came out of this discussion?

| 0 | 1 | 2 | 3 | 4 | 5 | 6 | 7 | 8 | 9 | 10 |
|---|---|---|---|---|---|---|---|---|---|----|

Very displeased                                                    Very satisfied

8. *Overall:* How do you rate the discussion as a whole apart from any specific aspect of it?

| 0 | 1 | 2 | 3 | 4 | 5 | 6 | 7 | 8 | 9 | 10 |
|---|---|---|---|---|---|---|---|---|---|----|

Awful, waste of time                                          Superb, time well spent

From J. Brilhart, *Effective Group Discussion*, 5th edition (Dubuque, IA: Wm. C. Brown, 1986) 173.

## IN SUM

This chapter has analyzed small group communication. A general model was presented. Group composition, structural variables, and operating variables were discussed. The types of small group tasks were explained. Group atmosphere, environment, and outcomes were discussed as they relate to classroom communication.

## ACTIVITY 7.11

In a microteaching situation, teach using the small group approach. Divide the class into groups. Choose a task for the groups to complete. How effective were you in utilizing this approach? Did you feel comfortable? Did your groups find the experience worthwhile? What changes would you make if you used this approach again?

## NOTES

1. G. Homans, *The Human Group* (New York: Harcourt Brace, 1950) 1.

2. L. Rosenfeld, *Human Interaction in the Small Group Setting* (Columbus, OH: Charles E. Merrill, 1973) 7.

3. J. E. McGrath and I. Altman, *Small Group Research: A Synthesis and Critique of the Field* (New York: Holt, Rinehart and Winston, 1966) 56.

4. S. B. Kahn and J. Weiss, "Teaching of Affecting Responses," *Second Handbook of Research in Teaching,* ed. R. Travers (Chicago: Rand McNally, 1973) 759–804.

5. T. Scheidel, *Speech Communication in Human Interaction* (Glenview, IL: Scott, Foresman, 1972) 270.

6. P. Slater, "Contrasting Correlates of Group Size," *Sociometry* 28 (1965): 335–348.

7. H. J. Leavitt, "Some Effects of Certain Communication Patterns on Group Performance," *Journal of Abnormal and Social Psychology* 46 (1951): 38–50.

8. H. H. Jennings, *Sociometry in Group Relations: A Guide for Teachers*, 2d ed. (Washington, D.C.: American Council on Education, 1959) 11.

9. Adapted from Rosenfeld, *Human Interaction*, 175–76.

10. E. F. Borgotta, "A Diagnostic Note on the Construction of Sociograms and Action Diagrams," *Group Psychotherapy* 3 (1951): 300–308.

11. M. Poole and J. Doelger, "Developmental Processes in Group Decision Making," *Communication and Group Decision Making*, ed. R. Hirokawa and M. Poole (Beverly Hills: Sage, 1986) 35–62; and S. Tubbs, *A Systems Approach to Small Group Interaction*, 3rd ed. (New York: Random House, 1988).

12. B. A. Fisher, "Decision Emergence: Phases in Group Decision-Making," *Speech Monographs* 37 (1970): 53–66.

13. Fisher, 61.

14. J. Luft, *Group Processes: An Introduction to Group Dynamics* (Palo Alto, CA: National Press Books, 1970) 33.

15. See, for example, K. Benne and P. Sheats, "Functional Roles of Group Members," *Journal of Social Issues* 4 (1948): 41–49; and E. Flynn and J. E LaFaso, *Group Discussion as a Learning Process: A Source Book* (New York: Paulist Press, 1972).

16. R. Bales, *Interaction Process Analysis: A Method for the Study of Small Groups* (Cambridge: Addison Wesley, 1950); *Personality and Interpersonal Behavior* (New York: Holt, Rinehart and Winston, 1970).

17. Adapted from S. Littlejohn, *Theories of Human Communication*, 3rd ed. (Belmont, CA: Wadsworth, 1989) 213.

18. Adapted from B. A. Fisher and D. Ellis, *Small Group Decision Making*, 3rd ed. (New York: McGraw-Hill, 1990) 235–239.

19. See, for example, M. Dunkin and B. Biddle, *The Study of Teaching* (New York: Holt, Rinehart and Winston, 1974).

20. D. W. Johnson, *The Social Psychology of Education* (New York: Holt, Rinehart and Winston, 1970).

21. J. Brophy, "On Motivating Students," *Talks to Teachers*, ed. D. Berliner and B. Rosenshine (New York: Random House, 1987) 201–245.

22. J. Callahan and L. Clark, *Teaching in the Middle and Secondary Schools*, 3rd ed. (New York: Macmillan, 1988) 221.

23. A. Covert and G. Thomas, eds. "Communication Games and Simulations," *Theory into Practice* (Urbana, IL: ERIC Clearinghouse on Reading and Communication Skills, 1978) 26–29.

24. S. Sharon and Y. Sharon. *Small Group Teaching* (Englewood Cliffs, NJ: Educational Technologies Publications, 1965) 201–205.

25. B. E. Collins and H. Guetzkow, *A Social Psychology of Group Processes for Decision-Making* (New York: Wiley, 1964).

26. E. Bormann and N. Bormann, *Effective Small Group Communication*, 4th ed. (Edina, MN: Burgess, 1988).

27. E. Amidon and E. Hunter, *Improving Teaching* (New York: Holt, Rinehart and Winston, 1966) 36–38.

28. S. Tubbs, *A Systems Approach*, 291.

29. D. Johnson and F. Johnson, *Joining Together: Group Theory and Group Skills*, 3rd ed. (Englewood Cliffs, NJ: Prentice-Hall, 1987), 243.

30. R. Whitworth, "Collaborative Learning and Other Disasters," *Focus on Collaborative Learning*, ed. J. Golub (Urbana, IL: National Council of Teachers of English, 1988) 13.

31. K. Bruffee, "Collaborative Learning and the Conversation of Mankind," *College English* 46 (1984): 637; J. Golub, ed. *Focus on Collaborative Learning* (Urbana: NCTE, 1988) 5–6.

32. C. Sills, "Interactive Learning in the Composition Classroom," *Focus on Collaborative Learning*, ed. J. Golub (Urbana, IL: NCTE, 1988) 21.

33. H. Weiner, "Collaborative Learning in the Classroom: A Guide to Evaluation," *College English* 48 (1986): 55.

34. Golub, *Focus*, 5.

35. K. Bruffee, *A Short Course in Writing*, 2nd ed. (Boston: Little, Brown, 1980) 103.

36. See, for example, D. Johnson and F. Johnson, *Joining Together Group Theory and Group Skills*: D. Johnson and R. Johnson, *Cooperative Learning* (New Brighton, MN: Interaction, 1984); and D. Johnson, R. Johnson, and E. Johnson-Holube, *Circles of Learning: Cooperation in the Classroom* (Edina, MN: Interaction, 1986).

37. See, for example, D. Johnson and R. Johnson, "Organizing the School's Social Structure for Mainstreaming," *Mainstreaming: Our Current Knowledge Base*, ed. P. Bates (Minneapolis: U of Minnesota, 1981); and research studies reviewed in K. Jongsma, "Collaborative Learning," *The Reading Teacher* (Jan. 1990): 346–347.

38. L. Resnick and L. Klopfer, eds., *Toward the Thinking Curriculum: Current Cognitive Research* (Annandale, VA: Association for Supervision and Curriculum Development, 1988) 9.

39. A. Berthoff, *The Making of Meaning: Metaphors, Models, and Maxims for Writing Teachers* (Montclair, NJ: Boynton/Cook, 1981) 70–71.

40. A. Hare and R. F. Bales, "Seating Position and Small Group Interaction," *Sociometry* 26 (1963): 440–446.

41. R. Sommer, "The Distance for Comfortable Conversation: A Further Study," *Sociometry* 25 (1962): 111–116.

## SUGGESTIONS FOR FURTHER READING

Barker, L., K. Whalers, and R. Kibler. *Group in Process: An Introduction to Small Group Communication*. 3rd. ed. Englewood Cliffs, NJ: Prentice Hall, 1987.

Bormann, E. G., and N. C. Bormann. *Effective Small Group Communication*. 4th ed. Edina, MN: Burgess, 1988.

Brilhart, J. *Effective Group Discussion*. 5th ed. Dubuque, IA: Wm. C. Brown, 1986.

Cathcart, R., and L. Samovar, eds. *Small Group Communication: A Reader*. 5th ed. Dubuque, IA: Wm. C. Brown, 1988.

Cohen, E. *Designing Groupwork: Strategies for the Heterogeneous Classroom*. Wolfeboro, NH: Teachers CP, 1986.

Engelhard, G., and J. Monsaas. "Academic Performance, Gender, and the Cooperative Attitudes of Third, Fifth, and Seventh Graders." *Journal of Research and Development in Education* 22 (1989): 13–19.

Ferguson, P. "Cooperative Team Learning: Theory into Practice for the Prospective Middle School Teacher." *Action in Teacher Education* XI (Winter 1989-90): 24–29.

Flynn, L. "Developing Critical Reading Skills through Cooperative Problem Solving." *The Reading Teacher* (May 1989): 664–666.

Gouran, D. "The Paradigm of Unfulfilled Promise: A Critical Examination of the History of Research on Small Groups in Speech Communication." *Speech Communication in the Twentieth Century*. Ed. T. Benson. Carbondale, IL: Southern Illinois UP, 1986. 90–108; 386–392.

Hendrick, C. ed. *Group Processes*. Beverly Hills: Sage, 1987.

Johnson, D., and R. Johnson. "Classroom Conflict: Controversy versus Debate in Learning Groups." *American Educational Research Journal* 22 (1985): 237–256.

Manera, E., and H. Glockhamer. "Cooperative Learning: Do Students 'Own' the Content?" *Action in Teacher Education* X (Winter 1988–89): 53–56.

Moore, H. "Effects of Gender, Ethnicity, and School Equity on Students' Leadership Behaviors in a Group Game." *The Elementary School Journal* 88 (1988): 515–521.

Neumann, Y., and E. Finaly. "The Problem-solving Environment and Students' Problem-solving Orientation." *Journal of Research and Development in Education* 22 (1989): 22–27.

Nicholls, J. *The Competitive Ethos and Democratic Education.* Cambridge, MA: Harvard UP, 1989.

Noddings, N. "Theoretical and Practical Concerns about Small Groups in Mathematics." *The Elementary School Journal* 89 (1989): 607–612.

Phillips, G., and S. Santoro. "Teaching Group Discussion via Computer-Mediated Communication." *Communication Education* 38 (1989): 151–161.

Prescott, S. "Teachers' Perceptions of Factors that Affect Successful Implementation of Cooperative Learning." *Action in Teacher Education* XI (Winter 1989–90): 30–34.

Thibaut, J., and H. Kelley. *The Social Psychology of Groups.* 2nd ed. New Brunswick, NJ: Transaction Books, 1986.

Vangelisti, A. "Problem Solving: Issues for the Classroom." *Communication Education* 36 (July 1987): 296–304.

Wood, J., B. Phillips, and D. Pedersen. *Group Discussion: A Practical Guide to Participation and Leadership.* 2nd ed. New York: Harper and Row, 1986.

# 8 TEACHER INFLUENCE IN THE CLASSROOM

## OBJECTIVES

After reading this chapter and completing the activities, you should be able to:

- Designate the relationship between influence and learning
- Differentiate between a teacher who views education as an influencing process and a teacher who does not view education in this way
- Define teacher credibility
- Differentiate between positive and negative consequences in classroom climate
- Define communicator style
- Relate communicator style to teaching effectiveness and classroom climate
- Discuss the effects of humor in the classroom
- Define sources of conflict in the classroom
- Discuss the ways to manage conflict
- Discuss the effect of teacher power in the classroom
- Define empathy
- List the two steps of empathy
- Describe the competent child
- Describe the competent adolescent
- Describe a communicatively competent teacher
- List five communication acts

- List four characteristics of a competent communicator
- Describe how communication competence relates to a teacher's influence in the classroom
- Discuss guidelines for effective parent/teacher conferences

## INTRODUCTION

*I have come to a frightening conclusion. I am the decisive element in the classroom. It is my personal approach that creates the climate. It is my daily mood that makes the weather. As a teacher I possess tremendous power to make a child's life miserable or joyous. I can be a tool of torture or an instrument of inspiration. I can humiliate or humor, or hurt or heal. In all situations, it is my response that decides whether a crisis will be escalated or de-escalated, a child humanized or dehumanized.*[1]

As teachers we are not simply "fountains of knowledge." Learning does not occur only on the intellectual level. Student attitudes and teacher attitudes influence the learning process. Whether we like it or not, we have great influence over our students—the knowledge they acquire, the skills they master, and their attitudes toward self, others, and learning. In very subtle ways—by who we are, the way we communicate, and the teaching methods we employ—we influence our students. We need to strive to influence our students positively, since student attitudes influence their self-concepts[2] and their learning.[3] In addition, we influence the parents of our students, our administrators, and our colleagues. This chapter examines how we can make our influence positive rather than negative.

---

### ACTIVITY 8.1

Consider the teacher who has influenced you the most. What sort of person was this teacher? Why was this teacher's influence so great?

---

### INFLUENCE AND LEARNING

In all learning, we must acquire new information, organize the information, and interpret the information. Obviously, communication is involved in all three aspects. The most important aspects of learning are curiosity and questioning. Once you have learned how to ask questions—relevant and appropriate and substantial questions—you have learned how to learn and no one can keep you from learning whatever you want or need to know.[4] At the crux of this inquiry method is the influencing of student attitudes and behavior through involvement of the student's cognitive and affective processes.

Teachers who do not view learning as a process are more concerned with covering the material than with student learning. Teachers who are concerned with influencing their students continually ask themselves questions like the following.[5]

1. What behavior do I seek from the student that tells me he has learned something? What reason do I have to believe that this behavior is relevant to learning? Is it reasonable to expect that the student can demonstrate this behavior? Will demonstrating the behavior injure him in any way?
2. What must the student know and be able to do before she expresses the behavior I seek? What alternatives are there that I will find acceptable?
3. Will the activities I am doing bring about the desired behavior? What do I need to know about the student (students) in order to bring this about? What do I know (from my research or experience) that leads me to believe that my method will work?
4. Of what use is this particular behavior to the student? How can I make him understand its use?

Teachers who are concerned with influencing their students regard their students as "real" people—as unique individuals. They realize that influencing student attitudes and behaviors is at the core of the learning process.

Teachers who do not view learning as a process of influencing the attitudes and behaviors of their students tend to believe the following.[6]

1. The concept of absolute, fixed, unchanging "truth," particularly from a polarizing good-bad perspective.
2. The concept of certainty. There is always one and only one "right" answer, and it is absolutely "right."
3. The concept of isolated identity, that "A is A," period, simply, once and for all.
4. The concept of fixed states and "things," with the implicit concept that if you know the name you understand the "thing."
5. The concept of simple, single, mechanical causality; the idea that every effect is the result of a single, easily identifiable cause.
6. The concept that differences exist only in parallel and opposing forms: good-bad, right-wrong, yes-no, short-long, up-down, etc.
7. The concept that knowledge is "given," that it emanates from a higher authority, and that it is to be accepted without question.

## MEANS OF INFLUENCE

Learning begins with motivation. People don't learn unless they are motivated to learn. Several theories of motivation exist.[7]

Curwin and Mendler [8] examine motivation from the perspective of attribution theory. Using the work of other researchers, they define motivation with three facets: self-concept, achievement motivation, and locus of control (a person's generalized expectation about control over her life: people who believe that outcomes in their life are due to chance, fate, or the power of others have an external locus of control; those who believe that outcomes in their life are controlled by their own behavior have an internal locus of control).

The researchers offer thirteen strategies for increasing student motivation:

1. Increase student response. Ask more low-risk, open-ended questions.
2. Monitor your behavior to see that low-ability students have an equal chance to respond. Make sure they are called on as often as high-achieving students.
3. Encourage students to persist with difficult problems and to finish projects.
4. Foster excitement about new ideas.
5. Assign more in-depth projects, activities, or independent studies.
6. Incorporate student self-evaluation in your grading system.
7. Involve students more in scheduling classroom learning.
8. Exhibit high expectations for your students.
9. Increase your students' readiness to learn. Begin lessons with intriguing questions. Use special objects or activities to help children focus on the concept.
10. Increase involvement and interest.
11. Cooperative assignments increase motivation, but you must also teach communication skills.
12. Audiences are great motivators. Invite the principal, parents, or other classes to activities.
13. Check to see that your low-ability students are "school wise." Do they need instruction on how to organize their desks, take down assignments, or memorize facts?

The authors then outline ten characteristics of motivating lessons:[9]

1. Students are actively involved in their learning.
2. Teacher uses feedback more than judgmental evaluation.
3. Students control their own learning whenever possible.

4. Students are asked to use higher level thinking skills.
5. Teacher uses cooperative learning structures.
6. Teacher keeps pace with the natural attention span of students.
7. Teacher integrates all domains of learning: cognitive, affective, and psychomotor.
8. Students feel a strong sense of purpose to the lesson.
9. The teacher uses competition carefully, stressing achievement more than winning, and does not have high negative consequences for the losers.
10. The teacher strives to create classes that are fun and validate a true sense of joy in learning.

## Teacher Credibility

Teachers influence student motivation. Your students' motivation will depend, in part, on their estimates of your worth and competence as a person, or your credibility. What factors constitute credibility? Traditionally credibility has been composed of three factors—competence, trustworthiness, and dynamism. Some researchers indicate that teacher credibility is composed of five factors—competence, composure, extroversion, character, and sociability.[10] Teachers who are rated high on all these factors by students will influence student attitudes and behaviors more than will teachers who are rated low on these factors.

A teacher credibility scale is presented in table 8.1. Items 1 and 2 measure competence, items 3 to 6 measure extroversion, items 7 and 8 measure character, items 9 to 11 measure composure, and items 12 to 14 measure sociability.[11]

*Table 8.1 Measuring teacher credibility.*

---

*Instructions:* The following are a series of attitude scales. You are asked to evaluate your instructor in terms of the adjectives on each scale. For example, if you think your instructor is very tall, you might mark the following scale as below:

Tall : X : : : : : : Short

Of course, if you consider your instructor to be shorter you would mark your "X" nearer the "short" adjective. The middle space on each scale should be considered "neutral." Mark this space if you feel neither adjective on the scale applies to your instructor or if you feel both apply equally.

| | | | | | | | | |
|---|---|---|---|---|---|---|---|---|
| 1. | Expert | : | : | : | : | : | : | : | Inexpert |
| 2. | Unreliable | : | : | : | : | : | : | : | Reliable |
| 3. | Meek | : | : | : | : | : | : | : | Aggressive |
| 4. | Verbal | : | : | : | : | : | : | : | Quiet |
| 5. | Bold | : | : | : | : | : | : | : | Timid |
| 6. | Silent | : | : | : | : | : | : | : | Talkative |

*(Continued)*

***Table 8.1*** *Measuring teacher credibility. (Continued)*

| | | | | | | | | | | |
|---|---|---|---|---|---|---|---|---|---|---|
| 7. | Unselfish | : | : | : | : | : | : | : | : | Selfish |
| 8. | Kind | : | : | : | : | : | : | : | : | Cruel |
| 9. | Poised | : | : | : | : | : | : | : | : | Nervous |
| 10. | Tense | : | : | : | : | : | : | : | : | Relaxed |
| 11. | Anxious | : | : | : | : | : | : | : | : | Calm |
| 12. | Unsociable | : | : | : | : | : | : | : | : | Sociable |
| 13. | Cheerful | : | : | : | : | : | : | : | : | Gloomy |
| 14. | Irritable | : | : | : | : | : | : | : | : | Good-natured |

## ACTIVITY 8.2

Complete the teacher credibility scale for the instructor in this class. Complete the scale for a teacher in a different class. Compare the results. Which teacher influences you the most? How is your learning affected? How is your attitude toward learning affected?

## Classroom Climate

The classroom climate can also be a factor in influencing students positively. Read the following poem:

### Third Grade Arithmetic by the Window*

The Sun ached for summer with me—
Glaring at the last stubborn scabs of snow
Clouds teased the light—
And changed my book
From bright to dusk to bright.
Beyond the window
New leaves move,
And paper scraps blow across the black top lot.

A woman clothespins sheets
Across the street,
Her dress flaps on her legs.
A child struggles in for nap.
A car gravels down the road.
One man, one hand resting on the wheel.
The woman takes her basket in.

And I am summoned
To put the answer on the board.

\* Patricia Walsh, used by permission of the author.

The child of the previous poem is obviously not interested in school—at least at the moment. What can we do as teachers to insure our students are affected positively by their experiences in our classrooms? As teachers we cannot "teach" our pupils anything. We can only facilitate their learning. The best means of facilitating learning is to create a positive classroom atmosphere. As a result, students' attitudes will be more positive.[12]

---

### ACTIVITY 8.3

What are some behaviors you engage in when you enjoy a class (arriving on time? asking questions?) What are some behaviors you engage in when you don't enjoy a class (arriving late? hesitating to participate?)

---

Several research findings suggest that when students are free from disruptive anxieties, fears, anger, or depression, they are more likely to make more desirable cognitive and affective gains.[13] More than any other person, the teacher sets the classroom climate. Ryans[14] found that productive pupil behavior was related to the following teacher characteristics: understanding-friendly teacher behavior, stimulating-imaginative teacher behavior, student-centered educational philosophy, favorable attitudes toward students, and democratic classroom procedures.

All this sounds good, but what, specifically and behaviorally, can you do as a teacher to create a positive classroom climate and, thus, positive attitudes in your students? The words of an old song are applicable here, "You've got to accentuate the positive, eliminate the negative, latch on to the affirmative and don't mess with the in-between." Mayer[15] defines these concepts for us. An aversive or negative consequence is "any event that causes physical or mental discomfort. It is any event that causes a person to think less highly of himself, that leads to a loss of self-respect or dignity, or that results in a strong anticipation of any of these. In general, any condition or consequence may be considered aversive if it causes a person to feel smaller or makes his world dimmer."[16]

Pain, anxiety, fear, frustration, embarrassment, boredom, and physical discomfort are all aversive stimuli and encourage a defensive classroom climate. More specifically, aversive stimuli include the following.[17]

1. Loss of self-esteem, as in failing to understand an idea or solve a problem correctly.

2.  Physical discomfort, such as sitting too long, trying to hear in a room with poor acoustics, or having to see a blackboard or a screen that is too far away for the size of what is being shown.
3.  Frustration from not being able to obtain reinforcement.
4.  Being told that one is unlikely to understand something.
5.  Having to stop work in the middle of an interesting activity.
6.  Taking tests over material and ideas that have not been taught.
7.  Trying to learn material that is too difficult for one's present level of ability or understanding.
8.  Having one's request for help go unmet by the teacher.
9.  Having to take a test made up of trivial or incomprehensible questions.
10. Not being told by the teacher how well one is doing except at the end of a course when it is too late to remedy defects.
11. Having to go too fast to keep up with students better than oneself at what is being learned.
12. Having to compare in a situation where only some of the students can succeed (for example, get an A or B) no matter how well one learns or achieves the objectives of a course; in short, being graded on a curve.
13. Being grouped in a section of inferior students.
14. Having to sit through a dull teacher presentation, one that is repetitive, boring, insufficiently challenging, banal, platitudinous, or too easy. (A teacher reading aloud from a textbook or manuscript is likely, in most instances, to have aversive consequences for students.)
15. Being exposed to a teacher who seems to be uninterested in the subject matter.
16. Having to behave in a way other than the way a prestigious model (the teacher or a student leader) behaves.

A positive consequence or condition is "any pleasant event that exists during the time the student is in the presence of the subject matter, or that follows his approach to the subject matter. In the way that an aversive condition or consequence causes the student's world to become dimmer or causes him to think less highly of himself, a positive condition or consequence causes the student to think a little more highly of himself, causes his world to become a little brighter."[18] Specifically, positive stimuli include the following.[19]

1.  Acknowledging students' responses, whether correct or incorrect, as attempts to learn, and following them by accepting rather than rejecting comments ("No, you'll have to try again," rather than "How could you make such a silly error!").

2. Reinforcing or rewarding subject approach responses.

3. Providing instruction in increments that will allow success most of the time.

4. Eliciting learning responses in private rather than in public.

5. Providing enough signposts so that the student always knows where she is and where she is expected to go.

6. Providing the student with statements of your instructional objectives that he can understand when he first sees them.

7. Detecting what the student already knows and dropping that from her curriculum, thus not boring her by teaching her what she already knows.

8. Providing feedback that is immediate and specific to the student's response.

9. Giving the student some choice in selecting and sequencing subject matter, especially where you maintain rigid control over the goals of the instruction, thus making positive involvement possible.

10. Providing the student with some control over the length of the instructional session.

11. Relating new information to old, within the experience of the student.

12. Treating the student as a person rather than as a number in a faceless mass.

13. Using active rather than passive words during presentations.

14. Making use of those variables known to be successful in attracting and holding human attention, such as motion, color, contrast, variety, and personal reference.

15. For administrators only: Allowing only those instructors who like and are enthusiastic about their subjects (and students) to teach.

16. Making sure the student can perform with ease, not just barely, so that confidence can be developed.

17. Expressing genuine delight at seeing the student succeed.

18. Expressing genuine delight at seeing the student (Delighted to see you again!).

19. Providing instructional tasks that are relevant to your objectives.

20. Using only those test items relevant to your objectives.

21. Allowing students to move about as freely as their physiology and their curiosity demand.

Anadam and his associates[20] conducted research suggesting that the freedom to verbalize feelings can improve classroom climate. Third-grade students who were allowed to freely express their feelings had increased pupil involvement in lessons, increased teacher-pupil interaction, and increased pupil-pupil interaction.

Teacher interrupting behavior has also been linked to classroom climate.[21] Children whose classroom activity is constantly interrupted show significantly

**Table 8.2** *Guidelines for effective and ineffective praise.*

| Effective Praise | Ineffective Praise |
| --- | --- |
| 1. Is delivered contingently | 1. Is delivered randomly or unsystematically |
| 2. Specifies the particulars of the accomplishment | 2. Is restricted to global positive reactions |
| 3. Shows spontaneity, variety, and other signs of credibility; suggests clear attention to the student's accomplishment | 3. Shows a bland uniformity, which suggests a conditioned response made with minimal attention |
| 4. Rewards attainment of specified performance criteria (which can include effort criteria, however) | 4. Rewards more participation, without consideration of performance processes or outcomes |
| 5. Provides information to students about their competence or the value of their accomplishments | 5. Provides no information at all or gives students information about their status |
| 6. Orients students toward better appreciation of their own task-related behavior and thinking about problem solving | 6. Orients students toward comparing themselves with others and thinking about competing |
| 7. Uses students' own prior accomplishments as the context for describing present accomplishments | 7. Uses the accomplishments of peers as the context for describing students' present accomplishments |
| 8. Is given in recognition of noteworthy effort or success at difficult (for this student) tasks | 8. Is given without regard to the effort expended or the meaning of the accomplishment (for this student) |
| 9. Attributes success to effort and ability, implying that similar successes can be expected in the future | 9. Attributes success to ability alone or to external factors such as luck or easy task |
| 10. Fosters endogenous attributions (students believe that they expend effort on the task because they enjoy the task and/or want to develop task-relevant skills) | 10. Fosters exogenous attributions (students believe that they expend effort on the task for external reasons—to please the teacher, win a competition or reward, etc.) |
| 11. Focuses students' attention on their own task-relevant behavior | 11. Focuses students' attention on the teacher as an external authority figure who is manipulating them |
| 12. Fosters appreciation of and desirable attributions about task-relevant behavior after the process is completed | 12. Intrudes into the ongoing process, distracting attention from task-relevant behavior |

less task persistence than children who are not constantly interrupted. Constant interruption may communicate a lack of respect for students.

In contrast, personal feedback and evaluative comments on returned test papers[22] and the use of praise and the lack of blame[23] increase student participation and performance. These practices probably communicate respect for students, or indicate to students that they are valued.

It's important to remember that simply providing feedback or praise is not sufficient in itself. The feedback must be effective. Guidelines for effective praise are presented in table 8.2.[24]

Table 8.3 lists the factors that Civikly[25] finds necessary for a supportive classroom climate. Analyze your classroom climate by answering the questions posed in the table.

## Teachers Communication Concerns and Behaviors

Several researchers have examined teachers' communication concerns and behaviors in an effort to determine how a teacher's communication strategies affect classroom interaction. This research has been conducted from two perspectives: (1) what do students view as effective teacher communication strategies and (2) what do teachers view as effective teacher communication strategies?

### *Students' Views*

In terms of the first perspective, research suggests that students are attracted to classes where teachers communicate well.[26] Students rate clarity, rapport, and effective delivery as important communication variables.[27] In addition, McLaughlin and Erikson found that interpersonal communication was also important when students described their "ideal instructor":[28] perceived integrative behaviors ("participates," "gives approval," "accepts differences," etc.) are regarded to be closer to their concept of an "ideal instructor" than are perceived dominative behaviors ("relocates," "postpones," "disapproves," etc.). Moreover, evaluative personality trait items such as "understanding," "gives approval," and "sincere" are more representative of student perceptions of the "ideal instructor" than items such as "narrow-minded," "makes warnings," or "sarcastic." Similarly, activity trait items such as "easy going" and "participates in joint activity" are more representative of an "ideal instructor" than items such as "shy," "introvert," and "emotional."

As discussed in chapter 4, nonverbal immediacy has been found to be perceived positively by students. In addition to nonverbal immediacy, researchers have examined verbal immediacy. For example, Gorham found that students' perceptions of teacher immediacy are influenced by verbal behaviors, and these behaviors contribute positively to learning:

> *The teacher's use of humor in class appears to be of particular importance, as are his/her praise of students' work, actions, or comments and frequency of initiating and/or willingness to become engaged in conversations with students before, after, or outside of class. In addition, a teacher's self-disclosure ("uses personal examples or talks about experiences she/he has had outside of class"); asking questions or opinions; following up on student-initiated topics ("gets into discussions based on something a student brings up even when this doesn't seem to*

*Table 8.3 Analyzing classroom climate.*

| Classroom Factor | Summary | Questions to Pose to Self |
|---|---|---|
| Challenge | "A good way to create challenge is to wait until the chances of success are good, and then say, 'This is hard work, but I think that you can do it.'" | — Do I provide challenging problems to the students and encourage their effort at solving the problem?<br>— Do I encourage creative alternative solutions to problems and questions? |
| Freedom | "What freedom means to the teacher is that students will learn, provided the material appears to be relevant to their lives and provided they have the freedom to explore and to discover its meaning for themselves." | — Do I encourage students to try something new and to join in new activities?<br>— Do I allow students to have a voice in planning and do I permit them to help make the rules they follow? |
| Respect | "The rule seems to be that whenever we treat a student with respect, we add to his self-respect, and whenever we embarrass or humiliate him, we are likely to build disrespect in him both for himself and for others." | — Do I have genuine respect for the student and for the student's contribution to the class?<br>— Do I communicate this respect to the students and demonstrate this respect in classroom discussions and one-to-one interactions with each student? |
| Warmth | "A warm and supportive educational atmosphere is one in which each student is made to feel that he belongs in school and that teachers care about what happens to him. It is one in which praise is used in preference to punishment, courtesy in preference to sarcasm, and consultation in preference to dictation." | — Do I spread my attention around and include each student, keeping special watch for the student who may need extra attention?<br>— Do I notice and comment favorably on the things that are important to students?<br>— Do I practice courtesy with my students? |
| Control | "Classroom control does not require ridicule and embarrassment. The secret seems to be in the leadership qualities of the teacher. When he (she) is prepared for class, keeps on top of the work and avoids the appearance of confusion, explains why some things must be done, and strives for consistency, politeness and firmness, then classroom control is likely to be maintained." | — Do I remember to see small disciplinary problems as understandable, and not as personal insults?<br>— Do I have, and do my students have, a clear idea of what is not acceptable in my class? |

*(Continued)*

| Classroom Factor | Summary | Questions to Pose to Self |
|---|---|---|
| Success | "Perhaps the single most important step that teachers can take in the classroom is to provide an educational atmosphere of success rather than failure." | — Do I permit my students some opportunity to make mistakes without penalty?<br>— Do I set tasks which are, and which appear to the student to be, within his or her abilities?<br>— Do I provide honest experiences of success for my students? |

*be a part of his/her lecture plan"); reference to class as "our" class and what "we" are doing; provision of feedback on students' work; asking how students feel about assignments, due dates, or discussion topics; and invitations for students to telephone or meet with him/her outside of class if they have questions or want to discuss something all contribute meaningfully to student-reported cognitive and affective learning.[29]*

### Teacher's Views

Researchers have also examined how teachers view their own communication. One of the variables examined is communicator style as it relates to effective teaching.

Communicator style is "the way an individual verbally and paraverbally interacts to signal how literal meaning should be taken, interpreted, filtered, or understood."[30] Communicator style can be classified in terms of eleven independent variables: whether the speaker is precise, contentious, relaxed, dominant, dramatic, open, attentive, animated, and friendly, and in terms of voice and the impression she leaves. Communicator style also consists of one dependent variable—communicator image. In his research, Norton found strong evidence that students' perceptions of effective teaching are related to a teacher's communicator style.[31] The effective teacher was rated as attentive, impression leaving, relaxed, not dominant, friendly, and precise.

To give you a better understanding of each communicator style variable, the items related to each variable are presented in table 8.4.

Norton examined the question of which of these variables strongly profile the ineffective teacher. He found that the ineffective teacher is not very animated or lively, does not show enough attentiveness or friendliness, does not have a very precise style, is not very relaxed and does not use a dramatic style.[32]

In addition, Norton examined the dramatic style more closely and found that the teacher with a highly dramatic style always scored high on three variables: (1) uses energy, (2) catches attention, and (3) manipulates moods. Norton sug-

*Table 8.4 Communicator style variables.*

| Communicator Style Variable | Questionnaire Item |
|---|---|
| Attentive | —This person can always repeat back to someone else exactly what was said. |
| | —This person deliberately reacts in such a way that people know that he or she is listening to them. |
| | —This person really likes to listen very carefully to people. |
| | —This person is an extremely attentive communicator. |
| Impression leaving | —What this person says usually leaves an impression on people. |
| | —This person leaves people with an impression that they definitely tend to remember. |
| | —The way this person says something usually leaves an impression on people. |
| | —This person leaves a definite impression on people. |
| Relaxed | —This person has no nervous mannerisms in his speech. |
| | —This person is a very relaxed communicator. |
| | —The rhythm or flow of this person's speech is not affected by nervousness. |
| | —Under pressure this person comes across as a relaxed speaker. |
| Not dominant | —In most social situations this person (does not) generally speak very frequently. |
| | —This person is (not) dominant in social situations. |
| | —This person (does not) try to take charge of things when she is with other people. |
| | —In most social situations this person (does not) tend to come on strong. |
| Friendly | —This person readily expresses admiration for others. |
| | —To be friendly, this person habitually acknowledges others' contributions verbally. |
| | —This person is always an extremely friendly communicator. |
| | —Whenever this person communicates, he tends to be very encouraging to people. |
| Precise | —This person is a very precise communicator. |
| | —In an argument this person insists upon very precise definitions. |
| | —This person likes to he strictly accurate when she communicates. |
| | —Very often this person insists that other people document or present some kind of proof for what they are arguing. |

gests the following recommendations to help ineffective teachers do a better job of teaching:

- **Use more energy when teaching.** The primary problem at this point is operationalizing what constitutes energy. It probably entails being more dynamic, active, open, mentally alert, enthusiastic, and forceful. The dynamic speaker employs vocal variety (emphasis, intonation, rate) and nonverbal variety (gestures) to increase expressiveness.

- **Anticipate how to catch attention.** The genre of communicative behaviors to do this includes use of humor, curiosity, suspense, emotion, analogy, metaphors, surprise, and narratives.

- **Learn how to make a class laugh.** This is not to say that the teacher needs to become a comic or clown. The more important dynamic entails audience analysis. Learning how to make someone laugh requires understanding shared premises. Even if laughter is never evoked, thinking about the problem is useful. A teacher might use humor to reduce tension, facilitate self-disclosure, relieve embarrassment, disarm others, save face, entertain, alleviate boredom, or communicate good will. The assumption is that humor enhances student/teacher relationships and, thus, enhances learning.

Bryant and his colleagues studied the use of humor and its relationship to student's evaluations of teachers.[33] They classified instructors' use of humor into six categories: joke, riddle, pun, funny story, humorous comment, and "other" (a category which included broad visual/vocal comedy such as Donald Duck sound effects). The researchers also examined (1) whether each humorous segment was spontaneous or prepared, (2) whether it involved the instructor, a student in class, another person, or no character, (3) whether the referent of hostile humor episodes was the instructor himself, a student, or someone else, (4) the degree to which the humor was sexual, hostile, or nonsense in nature, and (5) the degree to which it contributed to or distracted from the educational point. They found that most of the humor was in the form of stories or brief comments, with male instructors using more stories and female instructors using more brief comments. Few puns or riddles were coded. When jokes were used, they were more likely told by male teachers. Approximately half of the humorous comments were nonsense and half sarcastic/ tendentious, with females somewhat more likely to use tendentious humor. Most humor was spontaneous and related to the educational point. Males were more inclined to use self-disparagement, while females were more inclined to balance the referent of their comments among self, students, and others. In general, male teachers who more frequently used humor tended to receive higher evaluations, whereas females who frequently used humor tended to receive lower evaluations.

In a recent study, Gorham[34] found that the amount of humor teachers perceived to use is positively related to the students' perceptions of how much they learn and how positive they feel about the course content, instructor, and the behaviors recommended in the course. Examining students' perceptions of teachers' humor, Gorham and Christophel[35] found that male and female students perceive humor differently, and the effect of humor on learning differs by student gender. Females seem to prefer the use of stories or anecdotes, particularly personal stories related to the topic. Male students seem to prefer tendentious comments, reporting these as things their teachers did to "show he/she had a sense of humor."

Observational and experimental research indicates humor is capable of improving student perception of teachers, facilitating student/teacher rapport, reducing negative affective states, and enhancing perceptions of competence, appeal, delivery, perceived intelligence, character, and friendliness.[36] One note of caution is necessary. Downs and associates[37] found that award winning college teachers used less humor than did a comparison group of nonaward winning teachers. The researchers suggest that "too much humor or self-disclosure is inappropriate and moderate amounts are usually preferred. Perhaps the award winning teachers were able to differentiate moderate from excessive use of these verbal behaviors, thus contributing to their ability to relate to students and to overall perceived effectiveness."[38]

- **Learn what entertains a class.** Again, the advice is not to become an entertainer, but to learn what it would take to entertain the class. It can be easily adapted to any subject matter. A good chemistry teacher can vividly describe the chemical composition of an object, which can be entertaining in its own right.

- **Learn how to manipulate the mood of a class.** The effective teacher knows how to do this. It entails many complexities, including a strong sense of timing, a quickness at seeing connections to all sorts of things and processes, and a confidence to try such maneuvering.[39]

In addition to being related to students' perceptions of effective teaching, communicator style has also been shown to be a predictor of student learning[40] and student positive affect towards the teacher and the course.[41]

Victor and Otis[42] examined the relationship among teacher personality variables, teacher attitudes, and teacher behaviors. The researchers found that the personality characteristic of dogmatism (being closed to new ideas) was related to the teacher's (1) emphasis on subject matter and (2) preference for

*Table 8.5 Categories and frequencies of various behaviors perceived to be related to effective teaching.*

| Category | Rank | Frequency |
|---|---|---|
| A. Personality characteristics | 1 | 229 |
| B. Interpersonal skills and relationships | 2 | 216 |
| C. Planning skills | 3 | 206 |
| D. Professional attitudes and activities | 4 | 180 |
| E. Educational background and training | 5 | 149 |
| F. Teaching strategies | 6 | 147 |
| G. Evaluation abilities | 7 | 130 |
| H. Management skills | 8 | 116 |

teacher-student social distance. Teachers who scored highly on these two scales had a tendency to fail to establish rapport with students, express warmth, or show enthusiasm. In their interactions with students, these teachers did not utilize positive reinforcement or adapt their teaching strategies or language levels to the level of the student.

On the other hand, the personality characteristics of interpersonal openness and interpersonal flexibility were related to attitudes of concern and consideration for students and a preference for student direction during the teaching process. Teachers with these beliefs used an interactive or student-centered teaching style.

When secondary school speech and drama teachers were asked to rate categories of behaviors in terms of their importance to effective teaching, they rated them as shown in table 8.5.[43]

Teachers seem to have three major concerns about their communication—self, task, and impact—and their classroom behavior reflects these concerns.[44] In a case study of college and university teachers, Staton-Spicer and Marty-White found:[45]

1. A teacher who expresses the self-concern of credibility is likely to seek to build his credibility by
   a. engaging in self-disclosures related to humanness, intentions, and competence
   b. attempting to be viewed as personable by learning and using student names
2. A teacher who expresses the self-concern of flexibility is likely to engage in various behaviors reflective of a person willing to
   a. make schedule changes
   b. make assignment changes
   c. reteach
   d. digress

3.  A teacher who expresses the task concern of how to make abstract concepts concrete is likely to engage in the use of examples.
4.  A teacher who expresses the task concern of finding the right approach to teaching is likely to select and consistently engage in a method with which she feels comfortable.
5.  A teacher who expresses the impact concern of student understanding is likely to engage in a variety of behaviors to facilitate such understanding by
    a.  use of lecture pattern
    b.  use of interaction pattern
    c.  use of comprehension checks
    d.  eliciting student responses
    e.  use of questions
    f.  use of organizers: objectives, transitions, review
    g.  use of board
6.  A teacher who expresses the impact concern of establishing a nonthreatening environment is likely to engage in a variety of behaviors
    a.  reinforcement
    b.  self-disclosure
    c.  comprehension checks
    d.  conveying of expectations

In a later study, Staton-Spicer and Darling[46] analyzed the topics discussed by preservice teachers and found patterns of talk related to the three concerns of self, task, and impact. For example, in terms of the self-concern, preservice teachers talked about topics such as the pressures of teaching, role discrepancies, personal goals, relationships with teachers, other interns, and significant others, and evaluation of their teaching performance. Task talk focused on lesson planning, procedures, and getting ideas about how to perform discipline tasks and manage classrooms. Impact topics included such topics as feelings about students' poor performance and general perspectives on teaching and learning issues.

Zahorik[47] investigated two research questions in relation to the verbal behavior of elementary school teachers:

1.  What verbal behaviors do teachers recommend and what verbal behaviors do teachers not recommend?
2.  What reasons do teachers give for using the verbal behaviors that they recommend and what reasons do teachers give for not using the verbal behaviors that they do not recommend?

The results of Zahorik's study are summarized in tables 8.6 and 8.7.

*Table 8.6* Perceived importance of teacher verbal behaviors by elementary teachers.

| Behaviors | Very Important | Important | Neutral | Unimportant | Very Unimportant |
|---|---|---|---|---|---|
| Directions | 22 | 5 | 3 | | |
| Lecturing | 5 | 6 | 6 | 7 | 7 |
| Questioning | 14 | 9 | 5 | 2 | |
| Recall | 6 | 5 | 5 | 9 | 5 |
| Thought | 26 | 5 | | | |
| Answering | 18 | 6 | 6 | | |
| Praise | 20 | 9 | 2 | | |
| Reproof | 8 | 7 | 3 | 10 | 3 |
| Clarification | 9 | 11 | 10 | | |

$N = 31$

*Note:* Row totals are less than 31 for some behaviors because one teacher was not able to indicate their comparative importance.

*Table 8.7* Reasons given by elementary teachers for recommended and not recommended teacher verbal behaviors.

| | REASONS | | | |
|---|---|---|---|---|
| Behaviors | Motivation | Involvement | Thinking | Self-Concept |
| Directions | +,− | | | |
| Lecturing | +,− | +,− | | |
| Questioning | + | | +,− | |
| Answering | | | + | +,− |
| Praise-Reproof | | | +,− | +,− |
| Clarification | | | + | − |

+ = reason given for recommending use of specific type of behavior
− = reason given for not recommending use of specific type of behavior

Using the Index of Teacher's Affective Communication, researchers found that a teacher's mean scores were good predictors of his classroom communication patterns. Teachers with high (positive) scores had greater relative amounts of nondirect talk, higher rates of praise, and lower rates of criticism.[48]

All of this research on teacher effectiveness (both from the student's and the teacher's perspective) seems to suggest that communication variables such as humor, warmth, openness, enthusiasm, and attentiveness are extremely important in classroom interaction and in building a positive classroom climate.

One word of caution is necessary. Creating a positive classroom climate—positively influencing students—won't be easy. One reason this is so is exemplified in the following two poems.

That child seems to do everything wrong.
He's messy. He daydreams. He passes notes.
I don't know why I'm so patient with him, but I am.
Maybe it's the way he grins at me
just after he's done something devilish.
That smile makes up for a lot![49]

_____

I don't know why I don't like that Kid—
but I don't.
I like all the others,
even the noisy ones.
There's just something about the Kid
that makes me hope she'll make another mistake.[50]

It's important to recognize that there are students we will like and students we will dislike. We need to be aware that we influence both. Regardless of how we feel toward students, we should try to make our classrooms positive places.

---

## ACTIVITY 8.4

Think about the classrooms in which you've been a student. Consider the most negative experience you've had in the classroom. Why was it so negative? What could the teacher have done to make it less negative? Consider the most positive experience you've ever had as a student. Why was it so positive? What role did the teacher play in making it so positive?

---

## CLASSROOM CONFLICT

No matter how positive a classroom climate you create, you must realize that conflicts between you and your students will occur. You will influence not only student attitudes toward you and your class, but student attitudes toward themselves by the way you handle conflict situations.

### Causes of Classroom Conflict

In chapter 1, I discussed the evaluative characteristics of the classroom environment. The constant emphasis on evaluation and competition for grades, recognition, etc., does not necessarily "bring out the best" in students, as many teachers seem to believe. A common practice in elementary grades is to display the "best" piece of art work or the "most outstanding" paper. Children compete for the teacher's recognition. What happens to children whose work is never displayed as the "best"? Frustration or hostility leading to conflict may be the result. Perhaps, even worse, these students may withdraw completely.

In addition to the evaluative characteristics of the classroom environment, the perceived power differences between students and teachers can cause conflict. Since students often feel powerless and defensive, these feelings can give rise to conflict. The larger the perceived differences, the greater the chances for conflict.

A great deal of research in the communication field has focused on power in an attempt to determine the strategies teachers use to gain student on-task compliance. Seven major studies have examined the power variable. In the first of these, McCroskey and Richmond[51] described five bases of teacher power: coercive, reward, legitimate, expert, and referent power. In a later study, the researchers found that cognitive and affective learning were found positively related to the perceived use of referent and expert power and negatively related to the perceived use of coercive and legitimate power.[52] The next two studies,[53] in the sequence of seven, examined the types of behavior alteration techniques teachers and students perceive that teachers use in effective classroom management. The result was a twenty-two-item list of behavior alteration techniques (BAT) and representative behavior alteration messages (table 8.8).[54]

Using the BAT typology, McCroskey and his associates[55] found that how students perceived their teachers' use of BATs was related to student affective learning in grades 7–12. Affective learning was defined as "positive attitudes toward the course, its content, the instructor, as well as increased likelihood of engaging in behaviors taught in the class, and taking additional classes in the subject matter." Those BATs that contributed to positive affect were Immediate Reward from Behavior, Deferred Reward from Behavior, Self-Esteem, and Teacher Feedback. Those BATs that were associated with negative affect were Punishment from Teacher, Legitimate Teacher Authority, Peer Modeling, and Responsibility to Class and Debt. Later research by Plax[56] and his associates found a similar relationship between student perceptions of teacher use of BATs and affective learning for college students.

Richmond and her associates examined teachers' use of BATs to student cognitive learning. Results indicated that students perceived good teachers to use certain BATs more often than poor teachers.

*Good teachers were perceived to use the following BATs: Immediate Reward from Behavior; Deferred Reward from Behavior; Reward from Teacher; Reward from Others; Self-Esteem; Personal (Student) Responsibility; Responsibility to Class; Debt; Altruism; Expert Teacher; and Teacher Feedback. Poor teachers were associated with other BATs: Punishment from Behavior; Punishment from Teacher; Legitimate-Teacher Authority; and Teacher Modeling.*[57]

*Table 8.8 Behavior Alteration Techniques*

| Technique | Sample Messages |
|---|---|
| 1. Immediate Reward from Behavior | You will enjoy it. It will make you happy. Because it's fun. You'll find it rewarding/interesting. It's a good experience. |
| 2. Deferred Reward from Behavior | It will help you later on in life. It will prepare you for college (or high school, job, etc.). It will prepare you for your achievement tests. It will help you with upcoming assignments. |
| 3. Reward from Teacher | I will give you a reward if you do. I will make it beneficial to you. I will give you a good grade (or recess, extra credit) if you do. I will make you my special assistant. |
| 4. Reward from Others | Others will respect you if you do. Others will be proud of you. Your friends will like you if you do. Your parents will be pleased. |
| 5. Self-Esteem | You will feel good about yourself if you do. You are the best person to do it. You are good at it. You always do such a good job. Because you're capable! |
| 6. Punishment from Behavior | You will lose if you don't. You will be hurt if you don't. It's your loss. You'll feel bad if you don't. |
| 7. Punishment from Teacher | I will punish you if you don't. I will make it miserable for you. I'll give you an "F" if you don't. If you don't do it now, it will be homework tonight. |
| 8. Punishment from Others | No one will like you. Your friends will make fun of you. Your parents will punish you if you don't. Your classmates will reject you. |
| 9. Guilt | If you don't, others will be hurt. You'll make others unhappy if you don't. Your parents will feel bad if you don't. Others will be punished if you don't. |
| 10. Teacher/Student Relationship: Positive | I will like you better if you do. I will respect you. I will think more highly of you. I will appreciate you more if you do. I will be proud of you. |
| 11. Teacher/Student Relationship: Negative | I will dislike you if you don't. I will lose respect for you. I will think less of you if you don't. I won't be proud of you. I'll be disappointed in you. |
| 12. Legitimate—Higher Authority | Do it, I'm just telling you what I was told. It is a rule, I have to do it and I will have to give you an "F" if you don't. If you don't do it now, it will be homework tonight. |
| 13. Legitimate—Teacher Authority | Because I told you to. You don't have a choice. You're here to work! I'm the teacher, you're the student. I'm in charge, not you. Don't ask, just do it. |

*(Continued)*

| Technique | Sample Messages |
|---|---|
| 14. Personal (Student) Responsibility | It is your obligation. It is your turn. Everyone has to do her share. It's your job. Everyone has to pull her own weight. |
| 15. Responsibility to Class | Your group needs it done. The class depends on you. All your friends are counting on you. Don't let your group down. You'll ruin it for the rest of the class (team). |
| 16. Normative Rules | We voted, and the majority rules. All of your friends are doing it. Everyone else has to do it. The rest of the class is doing it. It's part of growing up. |
| 17. Debt | You owe me one. Pay your debt. You promised to do it. I did it the last time. You said you'd try this time. |
| 18. Altruism | If you do this, it will help others. Others will benefit if you do. It will make others happy if you do. I'm not asking you to do it for yourself; do it for the good of the class. |
| 19. Peer Modeling | Your friends do it. Classmates you respect do it. The friends you admire do it. All your friends are doing it. |
| 20. Teacher Modeling | This is the way I always do it. When I was your age, I did it. People who are like me do it. I had to do this when I was in school. Teachers you respect do it. |
| 21. Expert Teacher | From my experience, it is a good idea. From what I have learned, it is what you should do. This has always worked for me. Trust me—I know what I'm doing. I had to do this before I became a teacher. |
| 22. Teacher Feedback | Because I need to know how well you understand this. To see how well I've taught you. To see how well you can do it. It will help me know your problem areas. |

From J.C. McCroskey, V.P. Richmond, T.G. Plax, and P. Kearney, "Power in the Classroom V: Behavior Alteration Techniques, Communication Training, and Learning," *Communication Education* 34 (1985): 217.

In addition, results from this study indicated that BATs were correlated with cognitive learning.

> *Those BATs positively associated with cognitive learning were Immediate Reward from Behavior; Deferred Reward from Behavior; Reward from Teacher; Reward from Others; Self-Esteem; Personal (Student) Responsibility; Responsibility to Class; Debt; Altruism; Expert Teacher; and Teacher Feedback. Those BATs negatively associated with cognitive learning were Punishment from Teacher; Teacher/Student Relationship: Negative; Legitimate-Teacher Authority; and Teacher Modeling.*[58]

Examining which BATs teacher-evaluators perceived good, average, and poor teachers to be using, Allen and Edwards[59] found that Immediate Reward from Behavior, Deferred Reward from Behavior, Reward from Others, and Teacher

Feedback were the BATs principals reported good teachers use most often when encouraging students to comply with their demands. In addition, principals perceive that good and average teachers use Expert Teacher more frequently than poor teachers. Poor teachers are perceived as using Punishment from Teacher, Punishment from Others, Legitimate-Higher Authority, Legitimate-Teacher Authority, and Guilt more often than best teachers. Worst teachers and average teachers also are reported to use Debt more frequently than good teachers.

In addition to examining the behaviors teachers use to gain compliance, researchers have also examined the compliance-resistance behaviors of students. This research indicates that students are more likely to resist teachers who employ antisocial, as opposed to prosocial, techniques.[60] College students report greater likelihood of resisting nonimmediate (those perceived as cold, distant, and unfriendly) as opposed to immediate teachers (those perceived as warm, relaxed, and approachable).[61] Table 8.9 lists nineteen compliance resistance techniques and the messages students might use.[62]

Differences in perceptions can also lead to conflict. We discussed perception and the consequence of misperceptions in chapter 2. Suppose a student frequently misbehaves in your class. You may begin to perceive nearly all of that student's behavior as disruptive. If a student perceives your class is too difficult, she may use disruptive behavior as a result.

Combs and Snygg suggest that

> *people do not behave according to facts as others see them. They behave according to the facts as they see them. What governs behavior from the point of view of the individual himself are his unique perceptions of himself and the world in which he lives, the meanings things have for him.*[63]

This "perceptual field" includes the individual, other people, and the environment. Thus how students view a situation depends on their perceptual fields. How you view a situation depends on your perceptual field. Conflicts can arise from the way we view ourselves, others, or the environment.

Nye[64] suggests, "Anxious people who are not accepting of themselves are not apt to be accepting of others and may even take hostile action against them, thereby generating conflict." If a student feels she is academically inadequate, misbehavior may be the student's way of indicating this low self-concept.

When we fail to share the perceptions of others, communication is hampered and conflicts can arise. For example, I have a concept of my role as a teacher. You have a perception of your role as a student. We also each have a perception of the other's role. If our perceptions don't "mesh," conflict can develop. Suppose your idea of a teacher's role is "facilitator" and mine is one of "formal authority." My main teaching method is lecture. You think discussion is the best way to facilitate the gaining of knowledge. No doubt conflict will arise because you find it difficult to function in my classroom.

*Table 8.9 Compliance-resistance techniques and messages.*

1. **TEACHER ADVICE:**
   Prepare yourself better so you give better lectures.
   Be more expressive; everything will work out to your advantage.
   You should relate more with students before trying to give any advice.
   If you open up, we'll tend to be more willing to do what you want.

2. **TEACHER BLAME:**
   The teacher is boring.
   The teacher makes me feel uneasy.
   It is boring; I don't get anything out of it.
   Your teaching methods do not motivate me.
   You don't seem prepared yourself.
   If you weren't so boring, I would do what you want.

3. **AVOIDANCE:**
   I would drop the class.
   I won't participate as much.
   I won't go to class.
   I might keep the class but quit attending.
   I'll sit in the back of the room.

4. **RELUCTANT COMPLIANCE:**
   I'll do only enough work to get by.
   Although I would comply with the teacher's demands, I would do so unwillingly.
   I'll come prepared but not interested at all.
   I would be unwilling to do this but would probably comply.
   Grudgingly, I'll come prepared.

5. **ACTIVE RESISTANCE:**
   I won't come prepared at all.
   I'll leave my book at home.
   I'll keep coming to class unprepared.
   I would not go along with the teacher.
   I'll never come prepared.
   I'll continue to come unprepared to get on the teacher's nerves.

6. **DECEPTION:**
   Act like I'm prepared for class even though I may not be.
   I may be prepared, but play dumb for spite.
   I'll make up lies about why I'm not performing well in class.
   I would cheat off someone else.
   I might tell the teacher I would make an effort to comply but would not.
   I'll pretend to be prepared, but instead, borrow from others in class.

7. **DIRECT COMMUNICATION:**
   Go to the teacher's office and try to talk to her.
   After class, explain my behavior.
   Tell the teacher of the communication problem he has.
   I would talk to the instructor and tell her the way she is perceived by the class.
   Talk to the teacher and explain how I feel.

*(Continued)*

*Table 8.9 Compliance-resistance techniques and messages (Continued)*

**8. DISRUPTION:**

I would be noisy in class.

I'll disrupt the class by leaving to get needed materials.

I'll talk to friends in class while the teacher is lecturing.

I'll ask questions in a monotone voice without interest.

I'll be a wise-guy in class.

**9. EXCUSES:**

I don't feel well.

I don't understand the topic.

I would keep giving excuses.

I can remember things without writing stuff down.

I forgot and I'm sorry.

The class is so easy I don't need to stay caught up.

My car broke down.

**10. IGNORING THE TEACHER:**

I probably wouldn't say anything; just do what I was doing before.

Ignore the teacher's requests, but come to class.

I would simply let the teacher's request go in one ear and out the other.

I would just ignore the remark and keep up the same habit.

**11. PRIORITIES:**

I have other homework so I can't prepare well for this one.

I have kids and they take up my time.

I'm too busy.

This class is not as important as my others.

This class doesn't have anything to do with my major.

Due to a heavy class load, I just don't have the time.

I only took this class for general education requirements.

**12. CHALLENGE THE TEACHER'S BASIS OF POWER:**

I would ask the teacher if others in class were asked to do the same.

No one else is doing it, so why should I have to?

Do you really take this class seriously?

How does the teacher know what will be good or bad for me?

Why will this help or hurt me?

If this is such a good idea, why don't you prove it?

**13. RALLY STUDENT SUPPORT:**

I would talk to other students to see if they feel the same (there is safety in numbers).

Try to get the class to rally around the teacher's unprofessional style or unrealistic demand.

I would tell my classmates not to go to class.

I might get other students to go along with me in not doing what the teacher wants.

Get the rest of the class to support my behavior that the teacher is trying to change.

**14. APPEAL TO POWERFUL OTHERS:**

I might complain to the department head that this instructor is incompetent and can't motivate the class.

*(Continued)*

I would make a complaint to the Dean of the school about the teacher's practices.
I would talk to my advisor.
I would speak to the Department head.
Threaten to go to the Dean.

15. **MODELING TEACHER BEHAVIOR:**
I would participate more if you were more enthusiastic about what you're doing.
You aren't enjoying it, so how can I?
If the teacher was not going to make the effort to teach in an interesting way, I
    would not make an effort to listen.
Simply say that with the effort the instructor puts forth, why should I prepare for
    class?
You don't do it, so why should I?

16. **MODELING TEACHER AFFECT:**
You don't seem to care about this class, why should I?
You don't care.
The teacher doesn't care about students, so why should I care about what the teacher
    wants?
The teacher doesn't seem to care except when there are problems.
You have no concern for this class.

17. **HOSTILE DEFENSIVE:**
I'm old enough to know how I can do in this class.
Tell the teacher what she can do with this class!
Tell the teacher that my behavior is my business.
Right or wrong, that's the way I am.
I'm surprised you even noticed I'm in your class.
Lead your own life!

18. **STUDENT REBUTTAL:**
I don't need this grade anyway.
I'm doing fine right now without changing my behavior.
We'll see when the test comes up.
I have my own way of doing things.
I know what works; I don't need your advice.

19. **REVENGE:**
I'll express my dissatisfaction with the teacher/course on evaluations at the end of
    the term.
I won't recommend this teacher/class to others.
I'll steal or hide the teacher's lecture notes/tests.
I'll tear assigned articles out of books or journals in the library.
I'll write a letter to put in the teacher's file.

From N.F. Burroughs, P. Kearney, and T. Plax, "Compliance-Resistance in the College Classroom,"
*Communication Education* 38 (July 1989): 221-223.

Finally, differing perceptions of context can cause conflict. A classroom context requires certain behaviors. Suppose I am the drama coach and you come to play tryouts. You get a part in the school play. In addition, I am your English teacher. What's appropriate behavior between you and me at drama practice may not be appropriate in the classroom. Perhaps I allow you to call me by my first name at drama practice. If I did not find that appropriate behavior in the classroom context, and you did, a conflict would result.

## Managing Classroom Conflict

Whatever the cause for classroom conflict, the teacher must make a decision concerning how to manage the conflict. Several options are possible. Hocker describes five styles of managing conflict ranging from competition to collaboration.[65] Hocker suggests that collaboration is most effective since it shows high concern for self, other, and the relationship. It is a style which is cooperative and highly involving. As a result, it produces solutions that are likely to be accepted by all parties.[66]

Collaboration tactics include:

1.  *Description.* "I noticed that your grades have declined for the past three quarters," not "You must not have been working."
2.  *Disclosure.* "You don't have any way to know this, but past experience leads me to conclude that students have trouble finishing incompletes. So I am fairly prejudiced against the practice," not "You'll never finish it."
3.  *Negative inquiry* (soliciting complaints about self). "You said you were disappointed with the class. What makes you say that? I'd like to know," not "You should have read the syllabus more carefully."
4.  *Emphasizing common interests.* "I know both of us are interested in your doing well in the course. How are you studying for the exams?" not "I can't help you if you don't study."[67]

How we manage conflict can have far-reaching effects on our classroom interaction. The results of research on classroom management indicate that the quality of a teacher's classroom management is consistently associated with student achievement.[68] As a result, researchers are examining the behaviors of effective classroom managers.[69] For example, Lasley[70] found that effective classroom managers had clearly defined, workable rules and had developed definitions of inappropriate behavior that enabled them to respond quickly and consistently to those behaviors.

Managing classrooms is no easy task. However, there are several techniques which can make managing your classroom easier for you and more pleasant for your students. We've already discussed collaboration tactics. (I discussed the importance of creating a positive classroom climate earlier.) In addition, in ed-

*Table 8.10 Positive versus negative language.*

| Positive Language | Negative Language |
| --- | --- |
| Close the door quietly. | Don't slam the door. |
| Try to work these out on your own without help. | Don't cheat by copying your neighbor. |
| Quiet down—you're getting too loud. | Don't make so much noise. |
| Sharpen your pencil like this (demonstrate). | That's not how you use a pencil sharpener. |
| Carry your chair like this (demonstrate). | Don't make so much noise with your chair. |
| Sit up straight. | Don't slouch in your chair. |
| Raise your hand if you think you know the answer. | Don't yell out the answer. |
| When you finish, put the scissors in the box and bits of paper in the wastebasket. | Don't leave a mess. |
| These crayons are for you to share—use one color at a time then put it back so others can use it too. | Stop fighting over those crayons. |
| Use your own ideas. When you do borrow ideas from another author, be sure to acknowledge them. Even here, try to put them in your own words. | Don't plagiarize. |
| Speak naturally, as you would when talking to a friend. | Don't just read your report to us. |
| Note the caution statements in the instructions. Be sure you check the things mentioned there before proceeding to the next step. | Take time when doing this experiment, or you'll mess it up. |
| Be ready to explain your answer—why you think it is correct. | Don't just guess. |

ucation, as in medicine, "an ounce of prevention is worth a pound of cure." You can utilize many techniques to prevent conflict in your classroom. Another principle to keep in mind is to reinforce positive behavior and ignore negative behavior. Reinforcement of positive behavior can be done by your use of language. None of us likes to constantly be told what we should not do. Good and Brophy[71] provide excellent examples of the use of positive versus negative language (table 8.10).

It's important to remember that you need not intervene every time a problem arises in your classroom. Some problems are minor. For example, if one student briefly whispers to another, there's no reason to call attention to it. When behavior continues or threatens to spread to other students, you can no longer ignore it. Good and Brophy suggest that minor misbehavior is fairly easy to eliminate by any one or a combination of the following.[72]

1.   *Eye Contact.* If eye contact can be established, it usually is enough by itself to return attention to the task at hand. To make sure the message is received, the teacher may want to add a head nod or other gesture such as looking at the book the student is supposed to be reading.

Eye contact becomes doubly effective for stopping minor problems when the teacher regularly scans the room. Because students will know that the teacher regularly scans the room, they will tend to look at the teacher when they are misbehaving (to see if they are being watched). This makes it easier for the teacher to intervene through eye contact. Teachers who do not scan the room properly will have difficulty using eye contact in these situations, because they usually will have to wait longer before students look at them.

2.   *Touch and gesture.* When the students are close by, the teacher does not need to wait until eye contact can be established. Instead, the teacher can use a simple touch or gesture to get their attention. This is especially effective in small group situations. A light tap, perhaps following with a gesture toward the book, will get the message across without any need for verbalization.

Gestures and physical signals are also helpful in dealing with events going on in different parts of the room. If eye contact can be established, the teacher may be able to communicate messages by shaking the head, placing a finger to the lips, or pointing. These gestures should be used when possible, because they are less disruptive than leaving the group or speaking to students across the room. In general, touch and gesture are most useful in the early grades, where much teaching is done in small groups and where distraction is a frequent problem. Touching would be unwise with some adolescents who resent any attempt by a teacher to touch them.

3.   *Physical closeness.* When the teacher is checking seat work or moving about the room, he can often eliminate minor student behavior problems simply by moving close to the students involved. If the students know what they are supposed to be doing, the physical presence of the teacher will motivate them to get busy. This technique is especially useful with older elementary students.

4.   *Asking for responses.* During lessons or group activities, the simplest method of returning students' attention may be to ask them a question or call for a response. This request automatically compels attention, and it does so without mentioning the misbehavior.

## Handling Disruptive Students

Sometimes punishment is unavoidable. You, however, not the principal, should do the punishing. Sending a student to the principal may work on a short-term basis, but sooner or later you must "come to grips" with behavior problems in your classroom. You must take responsibility for them. Deferring to someone else should be done as a last resort.

When punishment becomes necessary, communicate to the student that you are punishing him only because he has left you no other alternative. Your actions and paralanguage should communicate concern for the student as well as regret that punishment must be utilized. In other words, it should be clear to the student that he has no one to blame but himself. His own behavior is the cause for the punishment.

When punishing, several guidelines are important. Make the reasons for the punishment clear, as well as type of punishment. Don't make threats or punishments you can't "make good." In addition, "make the punishment fit the crime." In other words, the punishment should be related to, and proportional to, the offense. If a student plagiarizes, she should receive no credit for that particular paper, but should not fail the course.

Curwin and Mendler[73] suggest that teachers need to think in terms of consequences rather than punishment. Consequences are simple, direct, related to the rule that's been broken, and instructive. They also preserve a student's dignity. Punishment, on the other hand, is not related to a natural extension of the rule and tends to generate anxiety, resentment, and hostility in the student. Below are some examples of the difference between consequences and punishments:[74]

### Rule

All trash must be thrown in the basket.

| *Consequence* | *Punishment* |
|---|---|
| Pick your trash up off the floor. | Apologize to the teacher in front of the whole class. |

### Rule

Tests and homework must be completed by yourselves unless group work is assigned. There is no copying other student's work.

| *Consequence* | *Punishment* |
|---|---|
| Do the test or homework again under supervision. | Write 100 times "I will not copy other students' work." |

### Rule

No talking when someone else is talking. If you want to speak, wait until the current speaker has finished.

| *Consequence* | *Punishment* |
|---|---|
| Wait five minutes before speaking. | Sitting in the hall for the entire period. |

### Rule

You must be in your seat by five minutes after the bell.

| Consequence | Punishment |
|---|---|
| You are responsible to get any missed information or make up any work missed while you are late. | Miss entire class sitting in the principal's office, then make up work. |

Whenever conflict arises, control your anger. Pause before you react to the disruptive behavior. You can think for a moment so you don't overreact and designate a punishment you can't enforce. In addition, the momentary pause may give the student time to "settle down"—to get over his anger or resentment.

Perhaps the best means of handling disruptive students is to remove them. Give the class an assignment and remove the student to the hall for a conference. If this is not possible, indicate to the student that her behavior is inappropriate, she is disrupting other students, and you'll discuss this with her after school (the next period, during recess, etc.).

During the conference with the student, you should follow these guidelines.[75]

1. *Clearly "own" your messages by using first person singular pronouns: I, my.* Personal ownership includes clearly taking responsibility for the ideas and feelings that are expressed. People disown their messages when they use terms like "most people," "some of our friends," and "our group."

2. *Make your messages complete and specific.* Include clear statements of all necessary information the student needs in order to comprehend the message. Being complete and specific seems so obvious, but often people do not communicate the frame of references they are using, the assumptions they are making, the intentions they have in communicating, or the leaps in thinking they are making.

3. *Make your verbal and nonverbal messages congruent.* Every face-to-face communication involves both verbal and nonverbal messages. Usually these messages are congruent, so if a person is saying that he has appreciated your help, he is smiling and expressing warmth nonverbally. Communication problems arise when a person's verbal and nonverbal messages are contradictory.

4. *Be redundant.* Repeating your messages more than once and using more than one channel of communication (such as pictures and written messages as well as verbal and nonverbal cues) will help the student understand your messages.

5. *Ask for feedback concerning the way your messages are being received.* In order to communicate effectively you must be aware of how the student is interpreting and processing your messages. The only way to be sure is to continually seek feedback as to what meaning the receiver is attaching to your messages.

6. *Make sure your feedback is helpful and nonthreatening:*

a. *Focus your feedback on the person's behavior, not on her personality.* Refer to what the person does, not to what you imagine his traits to be. Thus you might say, "you talked too much in class" rather than saying "you are a loudmouth." The former is an observation of what you see and hear, and the latter is an inference about, or interpretation of, the person's character.

b. *Focus your feedback in descriptions rather than on judgments.* Refer to what occurred, not to your judgments of right or wrong, good or bad, or nice or naughty. You might say, "you speak too softly to be heard," rather than "you are a poor public speaker." Judgments arise out of a frame of reference or value system and should be avoided, whereas description represents, as much as possible, neutral reporting.

c. *Focus your feedback on a specific situation rather than on abstract behavior.* What a person does is always related to a specific time and place. Feedback that ties behavior to a specific situation and is given immediately after the behavior has occurred increases self-awareness. Instead of saying, "Sometimes you have very interesting ideas," say "When you have done your homework and thought about the assignment, you have very interesting ideas."

d. *Focus your feedback on the "here and now" not on the "there and then."* The more immediate the feedback, the more helpful it is. Instead of saying, "Three weeks ago you didn't hand in your homework," say "You didn't hand in your homework today. Is something wrong?"

e. *Focus your feedback on sharing your perceptions and feelings rather than on giving advice.* By sharing perceptions and feelings you leave other people free to decide for themselves—in the light of their own goals in a particular situation at a particular time—how to use the perceptions, reactions, and feelings. When you give advice, you tell other people what to do with the information and thereby take away their freedom to determine for themselves what is for them the most appropriate course of action. Let other people decide for themselves what behavior they want to change. You can give feedback such as, "You don't do well in this class when you don't do your homework," without giving advice such as "You are failing. Do your homework."

f. *Do not force feedback on other people.* Feedback is given to help people become more self-aware and to improve their effectiveness in relating to other people. If other people do not want to hear your feedback, do not force it on them. Even if you are upset and want more than anything else to give a student some feedback, do not give it if the student is too defensive or uninterested to understand it.

g. *Do not give people more feedback than they can understand at the time.* If you overload other people with feedback, it reduces the chances that they will use it.

7.   *Make the message appropriate to the receiver's frame of reference.* The same information will be explained differently to an expert in the field than to a novice, to a child than to an adult, or to your boss than to a co-worker.

8.   *Describe your feelings by name, action, or figure of speech.* When communicating your feelings, it is especially important to be descriptive. You may describe your feelings by name ("I feel sad"), by actions ("I feel like crying"), or by figures of speech ("I feel down in the dumps"). The description will help communicate your feelings clearly and unambiguously.

9.   *Describe other people's behavior without evaluating or interpreting.* When reacting to the behavior of other people, be sure to describe their behavior ("You keep interrupting me") rather than evaluating it ("You're self-centered and won't listen to anyone else's ideas").

Conflict management skills are very important for a teacher to develop. The teacher who manages conflict well influences the growth of positive attitudes toward learning, self, and others.

---

**ACTIVITY 8.5** [76]

Read the following case study and answer the questions.

"Some of the members of this class have been doing quite a bit of noisy fooling around lately, and it's becoming annoying," said Ms. Hughes to her fifth grade class as the school day drew to a close. "I keep speaking to the same children over and over again. It seems too bad that the rest of us have to be constantly interrupted and bothered by these few. Maybe some of you have some suggestions for what to do about this problem."

"You could make the kids who talk all the time sit on the floor in the back of the room."

"Or you could send them to the principal. That's what Mr. Grey used to do."

"They shouldn't be allowed to come to school if they can't behave."

"You could make them stay in the coat room or out in the hall."

"They could stand by their desks until they could be quiet, and also their mothers should have to come to school."

"They could have extra pages of work, and extra homework."

"They could stay after school."

"Well, we have a number of suggestions," said Ms. Hughes. "But you know, I've noticed that those kinds of punishments often don't work—especially with those who make the most noise or pay the least attention. I remember when I was in school, the same children stayed after school day after day, but they didn't change. And that was true if they were sent to the principal or even sent home. Their behavior didn't seem to improve. Maybe we could come up with some new ideas—something besides punishment."

"But, if you don't punish them they'll do it more."

"It's not fair to get away with things."

"Yeah, but you're right about the same kids getting all the punishments and they're still the same way they were in kindergarten."

"So what'll we do—give the bad kids some prizes?"

"Well, perhaps we could start by finding out why they are so noisy and why they don't pay attention more," suggested Ms. Hughes. "But the bell's about to ring, so let's think about this overnight, and tomorrow morning, first thing, we'll talk more about this. Maybe we'll really be able to do some important problem solving. Those who have been reprimanded so often lately can think about why this has happened to you, and we'll all talk the thing over together."

### Questions

What might be some effects of this open discussion on the behavior of the children who are causing problems in the classroom? What seem to be some of this teacher's assumptions about methods of disciplining?

Why is it that many children who are reproved and punished most seem not to improve, and even may display increased misbehavior?

### Skill Session

Role play the next session of this class, with the first statement of the teacher being, "Yesterday we said that we would go on with our discussion about why some of you have been noisier than you should be. I suggested that the people who have been reprimanded so often lately might think about why this has happened. And we'll see what suggestions we have for trying to change behavior. Who would like to begin?"

Finally, as I discussed earlier, a sense of humor can be very important in classroom management. Civikly reviewed research on humor and teaching. Although humor is not always appropriate, it can serve

> *as a social corrective and can be an effective persuasive tool to hint at or evoke desired changes. When joking rather than direct threat is used to enforce norms, the negative side effects of a direct hostile confrontation are often avoided.*[77]

## THE TEACHER AS COUNSELOR

As a teacher you influence students outside the classroom as well as inside it. Often your students will approach you for advice. In other words, you will undoubtedly find yourself in the role of a counselor. One of the most important skills in this context is empathy.

### Empathy

When students come to you to discuss a personal problem, you need to keep in mind that childhood and adolescence are difficult times. Both periods are characterized by change. Adolescence, in particular, is a time characterized by rapid physical growth, desire for independence, increased sexual awareness, search for self-identity, and a search for a "philosophy of life." One of the first things a teacher must do is to empathize, or stand in the other person's shoes. From a transactional perspective, empathy involves two steps.[78]

1. Predicting accurately the motives and attitudes of others.
2. Communicating in ways that are rewarding to the other person who is the object of prediction.

   Let's examine each of these.

### *Predicting Accurately*

The first step—predicting accurately—involves an awareness of what childhood and adolescence is and what can realistically be expected from these age groups. The Speech Communication Association has completed a project that outlines communication competencies of children and adolescents. The competent child:[79]

1. Gains and maintains the attention of adults in socially acceptable ways
2. Uses adults as resources when a task is clearly too difficult
3. Expresses both affection and hostility to adults
4. Assumes control in peer-related activities or follows the lead of others
5. Expresses both affection and hostility to peers
6. Competes with peers—that is, exhibits interpersonal competition
7. Praises oneself and/or shows pride in one's accomplishments
8. Involves oneself in adult role-playing behaviors or otherwise expresses the desire to grow up
9. Gives evidence of opinion to support a claim
10. Presents a variety of arguments to support a plan of action

11. Takes into account another person's point of view in talking with that person, especially if asked to do so

12. Presents and understands information in messages related to objects and processes not immediately visible

13. Reads effectively the feedback of others to one's messages; supplies relevant feedback to others when they communicate

For adolescents, the above competencies are prescribed along with five additional communication competencies:[80]

1. Evaluates the messages of others critically and makes appropriate comments regarding such evaluations

2. Takes the role of another person effectively without being pushed to do so

3. Constructs contrary-to-fact propositions

4. Presents a conceptualization on one's own thought, as well as the thoughts of others

5. Gives, as well as understands, complex referential messages; adapts referential messages to the needs of others

---

**ACTIVITY 8.6**

Think about your own childhood. Describe yourself. What did you like to do? Who were your friends? What kind of things did you worry about? How did you view school? Your teachers?

Think about your own adolescence. Describe yourself. What did you like to do? Who were your best friends? What kind of things did you worry about? How did you view school? Your teachers?

---

In addition to understanding students, you must also accept them. Combs and his associates indicate that, for many people, the very experience of being accepted is most important.

*A child who expresses a shocking or naughty attitude may be told, "Why, Johnny, you mustn't feel that way!" Thus his feelings, the very things he must explore to get over his difficulty, are barred from examination.*[81]

Acceptance does not mean agreement. You can accept students' feelings, ideas, and behavior as legitimate and still not agree with them. However, students appreciate empathic understanding—the realization that they are understood, not evaluated or judged, but understood from their own point of view rather than the teacher's.

Research evidence suggests the importance of empathy in student-teacher relationships. Emmerling's[82] research indicated that, when high school teachers were asked to identify the problems they regarded as their most urgent, they could be divided into two groups. The "positively oriented" group considered the most serious problems to be:

1. Getting students to participate
2. Helping students to think for themselves and be independent
3. Helping students to express individual needs and interests
4. Learning new ways of helping students develop their maximum potential

The students perceived these teachers as significantly more real, more empathic, and more accepting than the "negatively oriented" teachers.

"Negatively oriented" teachers saw their most urgent problems in terms of student deficiencies, such as:

1. Students who aren't able to do the work required for their grade
2. Getting students to listen
3. Teaching students who lack the desire to learn
4. Trying to teach students who don't have the ability to follow directions

It appears, then, that teachers whose orientation is toward releasing students' potentials exhibit more empathy than teachers whose orientation is toward the shortcomings of students. What does such a finding indicate about classroom communication? When teachers are empathic, liking and affection are fairly evenly distributed throughout the classroom. In addition students have more positive attitudes toward self and toward school.[83] Finally, student achievement is affected. Working with third graders, Aspy[84] found that students of "positively oriented" teachers had significantly greater gains in reading scores than did students of "negatively oriented" teachers.

### Communicating Empathy

In terms of the second component of empathy indicated by Miller and Steinberg— communicating empathy to students—several guidelines should be followed.[85]

1. **Be willing to become involved with the student.** When students who are graduating from high school or college are asked to identify the best teachers they had, they often identify teachers who were available or accessible to them. The willingness to become involved with another person can be more important

at times than the quality of the interaction itself. Knowing that someone who is important to you cares enough about you to devote time to the relationship and to focus on matters of mutual interest can make quite a difference.

2.   Communicate positive regard for the student. Positive regard for another person is expressed not so much by the specific content of our remarks when we interact as it is by the general way we treat that person. If we are manipulative, if we attempt to control or to coerce the other person, or if we prevent the other person from saying or doing things that displease us, then we are not displaying positive regard. Positive regard for another person can be said to exist when we treat that person with a basic respect and as a person of integrity, regardless of the specific things that person says or does.

3.   Communicate a permissive psychological climate. A permissive psychological climate is not necessarily one in which individuals agree with and praise everything that everyone says or does. However, it is one in which the emphasis is on understanding, rather than on judging the behavior of others. Furthermore, a permissive climate is one in which the love that we have for others and the acceptance that we show them are not withdrawn whenever their behavior displeases us.

4.   Have a capacity to listen. Listening is not a passive process. It requires commitment and the capacity to focus on many of the things that the other is saying with his words, inflections, voice, facial expressions, and the like. Effective listening requires that we respond to the content of the message and the metacommunication, or the information about the message, as well. Furthermore, constructive listening includes communicating to the other person that she was understood.

5.   Accurately reflect and clarify feelings. There is a tendency to respond more to the content of what others say—the ideas, thoughts, opinions, and attitudes conveyed—than to the feelings that others are expressing. Feelings are harder to respond to because most of us in our culture have had less experience responding to feelings than to ideas.

6.   Be genuine and congruent. We are not as likely to develop a good relationship with others if we communicate in a false and misleading way. Facades are difficult to maintain and ultimately not very attractive. A constructive relationship is one in which the participants respond to each other in an honest and genuine manner. Our communication is congruent when the things that we do and say accurately reflect our real thoughts and feelings.

### ACTIVITY 8.7

Read the following case study. What would you do? Say? Why?

Jane is in the eleventh grade. She has done fairly well in your class all semester. She will probably finish the course with a "C." It's November and Jane comes to talk to you about quitting school. She indicates she hates going home after school. Her parents are always fighting. She feels they don't care about her. They don't seem to have any confidence in her ability to finish school. Her brothers and sisters (she has two of each) are younger and are always noisy. This makes studying very difficult. She says she enjoys your class, but it's the only one. Her friends are all considering dropping out too, so they may all leave the city—go off "on their own." She wants your advice.

## OTHER AREAS OF INFLUENCE

Not only do you influence your students, you also influence parents, administrators, and fellow teachers. Sometimes your communication interactions with these various groups will be under less than ideal circumstances. For example, a parent may need to be consulted concerning a student's behavior or academic difficulty. An administrator may discuss a student's dissatisfaction with your class. A fellow teacher may complain to you about the lack of fairness of the educational system, about a student he dislikes, or his work load. On other occasions your interactions will be very enjoyable. Regardless of the circumstances surrounding your interactions, the more competent a communicator you are, the more effective you can be.

### Communication Competence

What is a competent communicator? According to Wood,

> *when people work to develop communication competence, they are concerned with "putting language to work" for them in the following ways: (1) enlarging their repertoire of communication acts; (2) selecting criteria for making choices from the repertoire; (3) implementing the communication acts chosen; and (4) evaluating the effectiveness of communication employed.*[86]

To be effective communicators, we must be flexible, or possess a repertoire of communication acts. Different communication behaviors may be required depending on the situation, the people involved, the topic being discussed, and the task at hand. According to Wood, the competent communicator can perform five different types of communication acts.[87]

1.  *Controlling*—You might need to persuade parents that their child needs counseling; convince the principal that your band members, not the football team, should get new uniforms this year; or persuade your team teacher to let you present a lecture he thinks should be omitted from the unit of study.

2.  *Feeling*—often we need to express our feelings and attitudes or respond to those of others. You might, for example, praise another teacher, express your attitude concerning new discipline procedures in the school, or indicate to a parent your approval or disapproval of her child's classroom work.

3.  *Informing*—These are communication acts in which you seek or give information. You may need to ask a counselor for a student's score on an aptitude test or explain your grading procedures to a parent.

4.  *Ritualizing*—These communication acts serve to maintain social relationships and to facilitate social interaction. Included here are the actions of greeting, leave-taking, taking turns in conversations, and demonstrating culturally appropriate amenities. To understand the importance of these communication acts, think how frustrating it is to communicate with someone who never lets you have a chance to talk or who continually moves toward the door, but never actually leaves!

5.  *Imagining*—These are communicative acts in which you cast yourself and the other participants into imaginary situations. It might be helpful to speculate or theorize with parents concerning why their son or daughter misbehaves. You might then use the imagining act to speculate on what behaviors you and the parents could utilize to help the student, and what the student's reactions to those behaviors might be.

In terms of classroom communication, the Speech Communication Association has outlined the communication competencies teachers need in order to be effective. These are listed in table 8.11.[88] We know that effective teachers:

1.  Make clear their instructional goals.
2.  Know their content and the strategies for teaching it.
3.  Communicate to their students what is expected of them and why.
4.  Use existing instructional material expertly to devote more time to practices that enrich and clarify content.
5.  Know their students, adapt instruction to their needs, and anticipate misconceptions in their existing knowledge.
6.  Teach students metacognitive strategies and give them opportunities to master them.
7.  Address higher as well as lower level cognitive objectives.

8.   Monitor students' understanding by offering regular, appropriate feedback.

9.   Integrate their instruction with that in other subject areas.

10.  Accept responsibility for student outcomes.

11.  Reflect on their practice.[89]

Being competent communicators in the five areas listed in table 8.11 will enable teachers to be effective. As Norton indicates, "teacher effectiveness is . . . intrinsically related to the way one communicates."[90]

The basis of communication effectiveness is the appropriateness of the communication act. The competent communicator carefully examines the components of the communication situation—the participants, the setting, the topic, and the task. Based on an analysis of these components, the competent communicator chooses the appropriate communication act.

Imagine for a moment that you and another teacher, Ms. Smith, are alone in the faculty lounge after school. Ms. Smith is complaining loudly to you about a student who is disruptive in class—refuses to work, arrives late to class every day, whispers constantly to other students, and "talks back" when Ms. Smith tells him to "behave." You have the student in class and have had no difficulties with him. You know that Ms. Smith has the reputation among students of being "incompetent" and is perceived by the faculty as unable to "keep order" in her classroom. Ms. Smith, after complaining at length, turns to you and asks, "What shall I do?" Several communication choices are open to you. Among them are: persuade Ms. Smith to quit teaching, inform her of how students and faculty perceive her, accept her feelings of anger and tell her you understand, or theorize with her about what she might do to solve the problem. Based on your analysis of the communication situation, you will choose one of the possible choices—the one you think most appropriate.

After choosing from the repertoire of possible communicative acts, you'll implement the one you've chosen. Finally, you'll evaluate the effectiveness of the choice you implemented. Was it appropriate to the communication situation? Was it satisfactory to you? To the other person? The judgments you make concerning the effectiveness of your communication choice will depend on feedback from others as well as information from your personal experiences.

Poor parent/teacher, administrator/teacher, and teacher/teacher communications can seriously interfere with your relationship with your students. Remember the systems perspective. If you respond inappropriately to a parent, for example, you may create defensiveness or hostility that the parent, intentionally or not, may communicate to the student. This, in turn, affects how the student behaves in your classroom. Thus, possessing a large repertoire of communicative acts—controlling, feeling, informing, ritualizing, and imagining acts—and utilizing them appropriately will enhance your communication interaction with others in the educational environment.

*Table 8.11  Communication competencies for teachers.*

---

I. **Informative Messages.** Teachers should demonstrate competence in sending and receiving messages that **give or obtain information.**

   A. To **send** these messages effectively:
1. Structure information by using devices such as preview questions and comments, transitions, internal summaries, and concluding summaries.
2. Amplify information graphically through the use of verbal and audio-visual supporting materials.
3. Ask incisive questions to assess how well students understand the information given in lectures.
4. Present information in an animated and interesting way.

   B. To **receive** these messages effectively:
1. Identify the main point of students' informative messages.
2. Discern structural patterns and problems in the information they present.
3. Evaluate the adequacy of one's verbal and audio-visual supporting material in terms of the students' responses.
4. Formulate questions that probe for informative content.
5. Differentiate between informative messages that students deliver in an interesting manner and those that are dull—but still say something.

II. **Affective Messages.** Teachers should demonstrate competence in sending and receiving messages that **express or respond to feelings.**

   A. To **send** these messages effectively:
1. Reveal positive and negative feelings about self to students.
2. Express positive and negative feelings about students to students.
3. Offer opinions about classroom content, events, and real world occurrences.
4. Demonstrate openness, warmth, and positive regard for students.

   B. To **receive** these messages effectively:
1. Recognize verbal and nonverbal cues that reveal students' feelings.
2. Invite students to express their feelings.
3. Be nonjudgmental in responding to their feelings.
4. Ask open-ended questions in response to their expressions of feelings.
5. If necessary, offer advice tactfully.

III. **Imaginative Messages.** Teachers should demonstrate competence in sending and receiving messages that **speculate, theorize, or fantasize.**

   A. To **send** these messages effectively:
1. Use vivid descriptive language.
2. Use expressive vocal and physical behavior when creating or recreating examples, stories, or narratives.

   B. To **receive** these messages effectively:
1. Respond to students' use of imagination with appreciation.
2. Be nondirective when encouraging their creativity.

IV. **Ritualistic Messages.** Teachers should demonstrate competence in sending and receiving messages that **maintain social relationships and facilitate interaction.**

   A. To **send** these messages effectively:
1. Demonstrate appropriate behavior in performing everyday speech acts such as greeting, taking turns in conversation, and leave taking.

*(Continued)*

---

*Table 8.11 Communication competencies for teachers. (Continued)*

      **2.** Model appropriate social amenities in ordinary classroom interaction.

      **3.** Demonstrate speaking and listening competence when participating in or role-playing interviews, conversations, problem-solving and legislative groups, and public ceremonies.

  B. To **receive** these messages effectively:

      1. Comment favorably when students perform everyday speech acts appropriately.

      2. Acknowledge appropriate performance of social amenities; diplomatically correct inappropriate behavior.

      3. Recognize competence and incompetence when students participate in interviews, conversations, problem solving and legislative groups, and public ceremonies.

**V. Persuasive Messages.** Teachers should demonstrate competence in sending and receiving messages that **seek to convince.**

  A. To **send** these messages effectively:

      1. Differentiate between fact and opinion.

      2. Be aware of audience factors that may encourage or constrain acceptance of ideas, such as peer pressure, fatigue, bias, etc.

      3. Offer sound reasons and evidence in support of ideas.

      4. Recognize underlying assumptions in one's own arguments.

  B. To **receive** these messages effectively:

      1. Admit one's own bias in responding to ideas.

      2. Question the adequacy of reason and evidence given.

      3. Evaluate audience evidence and reasons presented.

      4. Recognize underlying assumptions in the arguments of others.

## ACTIVITY 8.8

In triads, role play the following communication interactions. Two people should role play and one should observe. Discuss what occurs.

*Teacher/Administrator:* The principal has called you in to discuss a student in your class. The student has complained that your grading practices are unfair. The student in question has caused considerable problems for you in the past. You don't particularly like the student.

*Parent/Teacher:* A student in your class consistently performs poorly. You think the student should be retained a second year. You have called the parent in to discuss this possibility.

*Teacher/Teacher:* You are in the faculty lounge. The school year is just beginning, and you are reading your class lists. Another teacher begins to discuss one of the students on your list—one who was "academically slow" and a "behavior problem" for the teacher the year before.

## Parent-Teacher Conferences

Because interaction between the school and the home seems to be increasing, the home environment affects the influence a teacher may have,[91] and because parents and teachers each hold the other primarily responsible for school-related problems,[92] parent-teacher conferences deserve special attention. Your goal during a parent-teacher conference is to discuss a student's progress. In order to meet that goal, you and the parents must communicate effectively. Several guidelines should prove helpful, for example:[93]

1. Know the child's home background. Does she live in a single-parent home or with a parent or stepparent? Such information will often influence how you structure the conference.
2. Create a positive atmosphere. Make sure your meeting room is clean and attractive. Choose furniture that is all the same height. If you sit in a higher chair or remain seated behind your desk, parents may feel intimidated.
3. Make the right comments. Don't outline all of a student's shortcomings. Choose those which are essential to the student's improvement. State your "problem" in positive terms ("Jane did not finish her assignment because she was reading the school newspaper" rather than "Jane is lazy").
4. Offer practical, realistic suggestions. Ask parents for their suggestions and solutions for solving a problem. Your attitude ought to be: How can we best work together to help Jane?
5. Listen to parents. Don't get defensive. If a conflict arises, remember the behaviors we discussed earlier about managing conflict and apply them to this situation.
6. Conclude the conference by asking parents questions that will tell you whether or not your message was clearly understood. Make sure you understood them correctly also.
7. Don't leave a parent "hanging." Request a follow-up conference if necessary or report back to parents on their child's progress.

Parent/teacher conferences can be very enjoyable and helpful. Much of what occurs during the conference will be your responsibility. By following these guidelines, most of your conferences should prove to be very productive.

---

### ACTIVITY 8.9

Read the following letter. As a teacher, how would you respond? Write a letter to the parent responding to her concerns.

Dear Mrs. McCrea,

About that conference next week. . . . It's a week until our conference about David, and I already have a knot in my stomach. Even having sat behind the desk as a teacher doesn't make it any easier when it's my child. I still have a knot.

I guess I'm like most people in that I don't deal very well with the unknown. I start weaving dreadful fantasies, anticipating the worst. Oh, I know David is a terrific kid. The question is, do you? I also know I shouldn't get anxious; when I'm anxious, I don't listen very well, and that's not a great way to go into a conference that's supposed to be for my benefit, is it? So I've been trying to think of ways to make our getting together a little easier for me, and maybe for you too. Here are a few suggestions:

Information in advance about what we'll be talking about would definitely help loosen that knot in my stomach. You might send a general note to all the parents outlining the topics you usually cover—and maybe even ask us what we'd like to hear about on a tear-off at the bottom (that way you won't have to wait and wonder what I'm going to spring on you!). If you have a sense of what's on the agenda, I can pull my thoughts together and formulate reasonable-sounding questions (my words just get jumbled up if I don't have a chance to plan a bit). I could also talk with David's father about his ideas, and bring them along, since he can't always get away for daytime meetings.

It would help if you went over, at the outset of the meeting, what you plan to cover during the meeting—as well as what you don't plan to discuss. That way I'll know what to expect and can dispel those dreadful fantasies right from the start. At the same time, it would be useful if you told me how you want to structure the meeting. Should I interrupt with questions or wait until you ask for them? Will there be things for me to look at or read? How much time will we have? Much as I hate to admit it, we parents are a bit like students when it comes to parent-teacher conferences. The more that's laid out for us at the beginning of the lesson, the more we're apt to learn.

What I really want to know about David is how he's doing—both in relation to his own ability (and certainly I want to know if he's slacking off), and in comparison with other children. I know comparisons aren't supposed to be important, but I do wonder where he stands. Eventually he'll be getting some kind of comparative grades; I don't want to be taken by surprise. Hearing for years that "he's working up to his ability" in spelling won't prepare me for his official low grade in the subject. I want to know as much as you can tell me about my child's schoolwork.

If you do have bad news for me, tell me at the start, so I don't have to spend my time waiting for the other shoe to drop. Let me know exactly what you see to be the problem. Show me the papers, tell me the episodes, put everything out for me to look at. I'll probably be upset, but I'll react more calmly if I get clear, specific information. I'd like to know how serious you think the problem is, too. Is it a big issue that you think will have long-term effects, or do you see it as a minor annoyance that will go away by itself? Is it a part of a larger concern, or is it an isolated event? Help me to keep my perspective by telling me just how worried I should be.

Please tell me, too, what you plan to do about any problem David is having—and how I can help. The worst feeling for me is helplessness. If you can give me some guidance about what David needs (a special tutor, less help with homework, whatever), I'll have something to do besides worry.

Which brings me to another point. Even though I think I know what "fine motor skills" and "set theory" mean, some real-world examples will help me to be sure we agree on their meaning and purpose. I like seeing David's work. I'm also interested in what you see in his writing and art. Don't worry about boring me with lots of examples; where my child's progress is concerned, I'd rather see his work than listen to lots of fancy talk about it.

Finally, please plan to reserve some time to listen to me. I want to be able to tell you how I think David's doing, to ask you some questions, to respond to what you've told me. I know that I do go on at times, so I won't mind if you remind me that we have only a few minutes left and ask if I have any last things to say. If I feel there's a lot more to talk about, I hope we can schedule another conference.

If all this makes you think I'm an over concerned parent, well, maybe I am. I admit I'm something of a zealot where David's skills, competence, and progress are concerned. I want what's best for him, of course. I've put him under your care and tutelage for six hours a day. Now I expect to know what's been going on during that time, how he's doing, and what I can do to help. I think we can be a terrific team—if I can just untie that knot in my stomach.

Kalle Gerritz, *Learning* (February 1983): 46.

## IN SUM

As teachers, we have great influence in the educational environment. The importance of our influence necessitates that it be positive rather than negative. The guidelines suggested in this chapter should enable you to make your influence positive and to avoid the feelings of the teacher in the following poem.

> Spelling's done.
> Arithmetic—sort of.
> We covered Asia.

And sandwiched in creative writing.
Thank God it's Friday!
The horror show is over![94]

## NOTES

1. H. Ginott, *Teacher and Child* (New York: Macmillan, 1972) 16–17.

2. M. Kash and G. Borich, *Teacher Behavior and Pupil Self-Concept* (Reading, MA: Addison-Wesley, 1978).

3. R. M. Gagne and L. J. Briggs, *Principles of Instructional Design* (New York: Holt, Rinehart and Winston, 1974).

4. N. Postman and C. Weingartner, *Teaching as a Subversive Activity* (New York: Dell, 1969) 23.

5. G. Phillips, D. Butt, and N. Metzger, *Communication in Education: A Rhetoric of Schooling and Learning* (New York: Holt, Rinehart and Winston, 1974) 101–102.

6. Postman and Weingartner, *Teaching as a Subversive Activity*, 217.

7. See, for example, R. Wlodkowski, *Enhancing Adult Motivation to Learn* (San Francisco: Jossey-Bass, 1986); J. Brophy, "Synthesis of Research on Strategies for Motivating Students to Learn," *Educational Leadership* 45(2) (1987): 40–48; and J. Brophy and T. L. Good, "Teacher Behavior and Student Achievement," *Handbook of Research on Teaching*, 3rd ed., ed. M. C. Wittrock (New York: Macmillan, 1986) 328–375.

8. R. Curwin and A. Mendler, *Discipline with Dignity* (Alexandria, VA: ASCD, 1988) 161–162.

9. Curwin and Mendler, 162.

10. J. C. McCroskey, W. Holdridge, and J. K. Toomb, "An Instrument for Measuring the Source Credibility of Basic Speech Communication Instructors," *Speech Teacher* 23 (1974): 26–34.

11. McCroskey, et al., "An Instrument for Measuring the Source Credibility of Basic Speech Communication Instructors," 30.

12. See P. Cooper and K. Galvin, *Improving Classroom Communication* (Washington, D.C.: Dingle Associates, 1983).

13. See, for example, M. Dunkin and B. Biddle, *The Study of Teaching* (New York: Holt, Rinehart and Winston, 1974); J. Brophy and T. Good, *Teacher-Student Relationships: Courses and Consequences* (New York: Holt, Rinehart and Winston, 1974); P. Leth, "Self-Concept and Interpersonal Response in the Classroom: An Exploratory Study" (Ph.D. diss., Purdue U, 1977).

14. D. G. Ryans, "Research on Teacher Behavior in the Context of the Teacher Characteristics Study," *Contemporary Research on Teacher Effectiveness*, ed. B. J. Biddle and W. J. Ellena (New York: Holt, Rinehart and Winston, 1964).

15. R. Mayer, *Developing Attitude Toward Learning* (Palo Alto, CA: Fearon, 1968) 47.

16. Mayer, 49.

17. N. L. Gage and D. C. Berliner, *Educational Psychology* (Chicago: Rand McNally, 1974) 350–351.

18. Mayer, *Developing Attitude Toward Learning*, 58.

19. Mayer, 58–59.

20. K. Anadam, M. Davis, and W. Poppen, "Feelings—To Fear or Free?" *Elementary School Guidance and Counseling* 5 (1971): 181–189.

21. S. Famham Diggory and B. Ramsey, "Play Persistence: Some Effects of Interruption, Social Reinforcement, and De-

fective Toys," *Developmental Psychology* 4 (1971): 297-98.

22. E. Page, "Teacher Comments and Student Relationships Performance: A Seventy-Four Classroom Experiment in School Motivation," *Journal of Educational Psychology* 49 (1958): 173-181.

23. W. Brown, L. Payne, C. Lankewich, and L. Cornell, "Praise, Criticism, and Race," *Elementary School Journal* 70 (1970): 373-377.

24. J. Brophy, "Teacher Praise: A Functional Analysis," *Review of Educational Research* 51 (Spring 1981): 26.

25. J. Civikly, "Self-Concept, Significant Others, and Classroom Communication," *Communication in the Classroom*, ed. L. Barker (Englewood Cliffs, NJ: Prentice Hall, 1982) 161-162.

26. J. Jordon, "The Professor as Communicator," *Improving College and University Teaching* 30 (Summer 1982): 120-125.

27. J. Minterez, "Overt Teaching Behaviors and Student Ratings of Instructors," *Journal of Experimental Education* 48 (Winter 1979/80): 145-153; J. Allen, "Classroom Management: Students' Perspectives, Goals and Strategies," *American Educational Research Journal* 23 (1986): 437-459.

28. M. McLaughlin and K. Erikson, "A Multidimensional Analysis of the 'Ideal Interpersonal Communication Instructor'," *Communication Education* 30 (Oct. 1981): 397-98.

29. J. Gorham, "The Relationship Between Verbal Teacher Immediacy Behavior and Student Learning," *Communication Education* 37 (1988): 47-48.

30. R. W. Norton, "Foundation of a Communicator Style Construct," *Human Communication Research* 4 (1978): 99.

31. R. W. Norton, "Teacher Effectiveness as a Function of Communicator Style," *Communication Yearbook 1*, ed. B. D. Rubin (New Brunswick, NJ: Transaction, 1977).

32. R. Norton, *Communicator Style: Theory, Applications, and Measures* (Beverly Hills, CA: Sage, 1983).

33. J. Bryant, P. Comisky, J. Crane, and D. Zillmann, "Relationship Between College Teachers' Use of Humor in the Classroom and Students' Evaluations of Their Teachers," *Journal of Educational Psychology* 74 (1980): 511-519; J. Bryant, P. Comisky, and D. Zillmann, "Teachers' Humor in the College Classroom," *Communication Education* 28 (1979): 110-118.

34. Gorham, "The Relationship Between Verbal Teacher Immediacy and Student Learning."

35. J. Gorham and D. Christophel, "The Relationship of Teachers' Use of Humor in the Classroom to Immediacy and Student Learning," *Communication Education* 39 (Jan. 1990): 46-62.

36. Gorham and Christophel.

37. V. C. Downs, M. Javidi, and J. F. Nussbaum, "An Analysis of Teachers' Verbal Communication Within the College Classroom: Use of Humor, Self-Disclosure, and Narratives," *Communication Education* 37 (1988): 127-141.

38. Downs, et al., 139.

39. Norton, *Communicator Style*, 260.

40. J. F. Nussbaum and M. D. Scott, "Instructor Communication 'Behaviors and Their Relationship to Classroom Learning'," *Communication Yearbook 3*, ed. D. Nimmo (New Brunswick, NJ: Transaction Books, 1979).

41. J. Andersen, R. Norton, and J. Nussbaum, "Three Investigators Exploring Relationships between Perceived Teacher Communication Behaviors and Student Learning," *Communication Education* 30 (Oct. 1981): 377-392.

42. J. Victor and J. Otis, "Teacher Strength and Sensitivity Behavior: Attitude Personality Correlates," *Journal of Experimental Education* 49 (Fall 1980): 14.

43. M. Swinton and R. Bassett, "Teachers' Perceptions of Competencies Needed for Effective Speech Communication and Drama Instruction," *Communication Education* 30 (April 1981): 149.

44. A. Staton-Spicer and C. Marty-White, "A Framework for Instructional Commu-

nication Theory: The Relationship between Teacher Communication Concerns and Classroom Behavior," *Communication Education* 30 (Oct. 1981): 354–366.

45. Staton-Spicer and Marty-White, 365.

46. A. Staton-Spicer and A. L. Darling, "Communication in the Socialization of Preservice Teachers," *Communication Education* 35 (July 1986): 215–230.

47. J. Zahorik, "Teacher Experimental Knowledge about Teacher Verbal Behavior," *Journal of Teacher Education* 31 (Jan./Feb. 1980): 44–49.

48. M. McLaughlin, K. Erickson, and M. Ellison, "A Scale for the Measurement of Teachers' Affective Communication," *Communication Education* 29 (Jan. 1980): 21–32.

49. A. Cullum, *Blackboard, Blackboard on the Wall, Who is the Fairest One of All?* (New York: Harlin Quist, 1978) 50.

50. Cullum, 38.

51. J. C. McCroskey and V. P. Richmond, "Power in the Classroom I: Teacher and Student Perceptions," *Communication Education* 32 (1983): 176–184.

52. V. P. Richmond and J. C. McCroskey, "Power in the Classroom II: Power and Learning," *Communication Education* 33 (1984): 125–136.

53. P. Kearney, T. Plax, V. Richmond, and J. McCroskey, "Power in the Classroom III: Teacher Communication Techniques and Messages," *Communication Education* 34 (1985): 19–28; and P. Kearney, T. Plax, V. Richmond, and J. McCroskey, "Power in the Classroom IV: Teacher Communication Techniques as Alternatives to Discipline," *Communication Yearbook 8*, ed. R. Bostrom (Beverly Hills, CA: Sage, 1984)

54. J. C. McCroskey, V. P. Richmond, T. G. Plax, and P. Kearney, "Power in the Classroom V: Behavior Alteration Techniques, Communication Training, and Learning," *Communication Education* 34 (1985): 217.

55. McCroskey, et al., 214–226.

56. T. G. Plax, P. Kearney, J. C. McCroskey, and V. P. Richmond, "Power in the Classroom VI: Verbal Control Strategies, Nonverbal Immediacy and Affective Learning," *Communication Education* 35 (1986): 43–55.

57. V. P. Richmond, J. C. McCroskey, P. Kearney, and T. Plax, "Power in the Classroom VII: Linking Behavior Alteration Techniques to Cognitive Learning," *Communication Education* 36 (1987): 1–12.

58. Richmond, et al.

59. T. Allen and R. Edwards, "Evaluators' Perceptions of Teachers' Use of Behavior Alteration Techniques," *Communication Education* 37 (July 1988): 187–197.

60. T. G. Plax, P. Kearney, T. M. Downs, and R. A. Stewart, "College Student Resistance Toward Teacher's Use of Selective Control Strategies," *Communication Research Reports* 3 (1986): 20–27.

61. P. Kearney, T. Plax, V. Smith, and G. Sorensen, "Effects of Teacher Immediacy and Strategy Type on College Student Resistance," *Communication Education* 37 (1988): 54–67.

62. W. Burroughs, P. Kearney, and T. Plax, "Compliance-Resistance in the College Classroom," *Communication Education* 38 (July 1989): 221–223.

63. A. Combs and D. Snygg, *Individual Behavior* (New York: Harper and Row, 1959) 17.

64. R. W Nye, *Conflict Among Humans* (New York: Springer, 1973) 3.

65. J. L. Hocker, "Teacher-Student Confrontations," *Communicating in College Classrooms*, ed. J. M. Civikly (San Francisco: Jossey-Bass, 1986) 71–82.

66. J. L. Hocker and W. W. Wilmot, *Interpersonal Conflict*, 2nd ed. (Dubuque, IA: Wm. C. Brown, 1985).

67. Hocker, "Teacher-Student Confrontations," 78.

68. See, for example, J. E. Brophy, "Teacher Behavior and Its Effects," *Journal of Educational Psychology* 71 (1979): 733–750; W. Doyle, "Research on Classroom Contexts," *Journal of Teacher Education* 32 (Nov./Dec. 1981): 3–6; T. Good, "Teacher Effectiveness in the Elementary

School," *Journal of Teacher Education* 30 (1979): 52–64; and J. S. Kounin, *Discipline and Group Management in Classrooms* (New York: Holt, Rinehart and Winston, 1970).

69. See, for example, E. T. Emmer, C. M. Evertson, and L. M. Anderson, "Effective Classroom Management at the Beginning of the School Year," *Elementary School Journal* 80 (1980): 219-231; C. M. Evertson, "Differences in Instructional Activities in Average and Low-Achieving Junior High Classes," *Elementary School Journal* 82 (1982): 309-327.

70. T. Lasley, "Research Perspectives on Classroom Management," *Journal of Teacher Education* 32 (March/April 1981): 14-17.

71. T. Good and J. Brophy, *Looking in Classrooms* 4th ed. (New York: Harper and Row, 1987) 234-235.

72. Good and Brophy, 261-262.

73. Curwin and Mendler, *Discipline with Dignity*, 70.

74. Curwin and Mendler, 70-71.

75. Adapted from D. Johnson, *Reaching Out,* 4th ed. (Englewood Cliffs, NJ: Prentice Hall, 1990) 38-39; 112-113.

76. E. Amidon and E. Hunter, *Improving Teaching* (New York: Holt, Rinehart and Winston, 1966) 135-37.

77. J. Civikly, "Humor and The Enjoyment of College Teaching," *Communicating in College Classrooms*, ed. J. Civikly (San Francisco: Jossey-Bass, 1986) 69.

78. G. Miller and M. Steinberg, *Between People* (Chicago: Science Research Associates, 1975).

79. B. Wood, ed., *Communication Competencies: Pre-K–Grade 6* (Urbana, IL: ERIC/SCA, 1977) 2.

80. B. Wood, ed., *Communication Competencies: Grade 7–12* (Urbana, IL: ERIC/SCA, 1977) 2.

81. A. Combs, D. Avila, and W. Purkey, *Helping Relationships: Basic Concepts for the Helping Professions* (Boston: Allyn and Bacon, 1978) 149.

82. E. C. Emmerling, "A Study of the Relationships between Personality Characteristics of Classroom Teachers and Pupil Perceptions" (Ph.D. diss., Auburn U, Auburn, AL, 1961).

83. R. Schmuck, "Some Relationships of Peer Liking Patterns in the Classroom to Pupil Attitudes and Achievement," *The School Review* 71 (1963): 337-359.

84. D. N. Aspy, "A Study of Three Facilitative Conditions and Their Relationship to the Achievement of Third Grade Students" (Ed.D. diss., U of Kentucky, 1965).

85. Adapted from A. Barbour and A. A. Goldberg, *Interpersonal Communication:* Teaching Strategies and Resources (Urbana, IL: ERIC/SCA, 1974) 38-39.

86. Wood, *Communication Competencies,* 5-6.

87. Wood, 4-5.

88. P. Cooper, ed. "Communication Competencies for Teachers," Speech Communication Association, Annandale, VA, 1988.

89. A. C. Porter and J. Brophy, "Synthesis of Research on Good Teaching: Insights from the Work of the Institute of Research on Teaching," *Educational Leadership* 45(8) (1988): 74-85.

90. R. W. Norton, "Teacher Effectiveness as a Function of Communicator Style," *Communication Yearbook 1*, ed. B. D. Ruben (New Brunswick, NJ: Transaction, 1977) 526.

91. See, for example, P. Friedman, *Communicating in Conferences: Parent-Teacher-Student Interaction* (Urbana, IL: ERIC/SCA, 1980); R. Bradley, "Preschool Home Environment and Classroom Behavior," *Journal of Experimental Education* 49 (Summer 1981): 196-199; B. Iverson and H. Walberg, "Home Environment and School Learning: A Quantitative Analysis," *Journal of Experimental Education* 50 (Spring 1982): 144-51; research reviewed in L. Stafford "Parent Teacher Communication," *Communication Education* 36 (1987): 182-187.

92. E. Vernberg and F. Medway, "Teacher and Parent Perceptions of School Problems," *American Educational Research Journal* 18 (Spring 1981): 29–38.

93. Adapted from "Parent Conferences: The Connecting Link between Home and School," *Practical Ideas for Reading Teachers* 1 (March/April 1983): 2–3, 17–18.

94. Cullum, *Blackboard, Blackboard,* 26.

## SUGGESTIONS FOR FURTHER READING

Allen, J. "Classroom Management: Students' Perspectives, Goals, and Strategies." *American Educational Research Journal* 23 (Fall 1986): 437–459.

Allen, R., K. Brown, and J. Yatkin. *Learning Language through Communication: A Functional Approach.* Belmont, CA: Wadsworth, 1986.

Applegate, J. "Adaptive Communication in Educational Contests: A Study of Teachers' Communicative Strategies." *Communication Education* 29 (May 1980): 158–70.

Berliner, D. "Simple Views of Effective Teaching and a Simple Theory of Classroom Instruction." *Talks to Teachers.* Ed. D. Berliner and B. Rosenshine. New York: Random House, 1987. 93–110.

Book, C., and K. W. Simmons. "Dimensions and Perceived Helpfulness of Student Speech Criticism." *Communication Education* 29 (May 1980): 158–170.

Borich, G. D. *The Appraisal of Teaching: Concepts and Process.* Reading, MA: Addison-Wesley, 1977.

Brophy, J. "Research on Teacher Effects: Uses and Abuses." *The Elementary School Journal* 89 (1989): 3–21.

Brophy, J., and T. Good. "Teacher Behavior and Student Achievements." *Handbook of Research and Teaching.* Ed. M. C. Wittrock. New York: Macmillan, 1986. 328–375.

Bryant, J., P. W. Comisky, J. S. Crane, and D. Zillman. "Relationship Between College Teachers' Use of Humor in the Classroom and Students' Evaluations of their Teachers." *Journal of Educational Psychology* 72 (1980): 511–519.

Centra, J. A., and D. A. Potter. "School and Teacher Effects: An Interrelational Model." *Review of Educational Research* 50 (Summer 1980): 273–291.

Charles, C. M. *Building Classroom Discipline: From Models to Practice.* New York: Longman, 1981.

Charles, C.M. *Elementary Classroom Management: A Handbook for Excellence in Teaching.* New York: Longman, 1983.

Civikly, J. M., ed. *Communicating in College Classrooms.* San Francisco: Jossey-Bass, 1986.

Cody, M. J., M. L. McLaughlin, and W. J. Jordan. "A Multidimensional Scaling of Three Sets of Compliance-Gaining Strategies." *Communication Quarterly* 28 (Summer 1980): 34–46.

Cohen, P. "Student Ratings of Instruction and Student Achievement: A Meta-analysis of Multisection Validity Studies." *Review of Educational Research* 51 (Fall 1981): 281–309.

Coladarci, T. "The Relevance of Educational Research for Identifying Master Teachers." *N.A.S.S.P. Bulletin* 72(504) (1988): 90–98.

Combs, A. W. *A Personal Approach to Teaching.* Boston: Allyn and Bacon, 1982.

Cornett, C. "Learning Through Laughter: Humor in the Classroom." *Phi Delta Kappa Educational Foundation.* Bloomington, IN, 1986.

Hamilton, E. "A Model for Resolving Classroom Conflict and Enhancing Student Commitment." *Organizational Behavior Teaching Review* 12(2) (1987–88): 40–50.

Johnson, C. "An Introduction to Powerful and Powerless Talk in the Classroom." *Communication Education* 36 (April 1987): 167–173.

Kearney, P. "Power in the Classroom." *Journal of Thought* 22 (1987): 45–50.

Kearney, P., and T. Plax. "Situational and Individual Determinants of Teachers' Reported Use of Behavior Alteration Techniques." *Human Communication Research* 14 (1987): 145–166.

McCaleb, J. "Selecting a Measure of Oral Communication as a Predictor of Teaching Performance." *Journal of Teacher Education* (Sept./Oct. 1984): 33–38.

McCroskey, J., and V. Richmond. "Power in the Classroom I: Teacher and Student Perceptions." *Communication Education* 32 (April 1983): 175–184.

McQuillan, J., and D. Higgenbotham. "Children's Reasoning about Compliance-Resisting Behaviors." *Communication Yearbook 9.* Ed. M. McLaughlin Beverly Hills, CA: Sage, 1986. 673–690.

Mannin, M. L. "Contemporary Studies of Teaching Behavior and Their Implication for Middle Level Teacher Education." *Action in Teacher Education* XI (Winter 1989–90): 1–5.

Norton, R. "Communicator Style in Teaching: Giving Good Form to Content." *Communicating in College Classrooms.* Ed. J. Civikly. San Francisco: Jossey-Bass, 1986. 33–49.

Norton, R. *Communicator Style: Theory, Application, and Measures.* Beverly Hills, CA: Sage, 1983.

Norton, R. W., and J. Nussbaum. "Dramatic Behaviors of the Effective Teacher." *Communication Yearbook 4.* Ed. D. Nimmo. New Brunswick, NJ: Transaction, 1980.

Nussbaum, J. F., and M. D. Scott. "The Relationship among Communicator Style, Perceived Self-Disclosure, and Classroom Learning." *Communication Yearbook 4.* Ed. D. Nimmo. New Brunswick, NJ: Transaction, 1979.

Plax, T., P. Kearney, and L. Tucker. "Prospective Teachers' Use of Behavior Alteration Techniques on Common Student Behaviors." *Communication Education* 35 (1986): 32–42.

Plax, T., P. Kearney, J. McCroskey, and V. Richmond. "Power in the Classroom VI: Verbal Control Strategies, Nonverbal Immediacy, and Affective Learning." *Communication Education* 35 (1986): 43–55.

Porter, A. C., and J. Brophy. "Synthesis of Research on Good Teaching: Insights from the Work of the Institute of Research on Teaching." *Educational Leadership* 45 (1988): 74–85.

Richmond, V., J. McCroskey, P. Kearney, and T. Plax. "Power in the Classroom VII: Linking Behavior Alteration Techniques to Cognitive Learning." *Communication Education* 36 (1987): 1–12.

Rosenfeld, L. "Communication Climate and Coping Mechanisms in the College Classroom." *Communication Education* 32 (April 1983): 167–174.

Ross, D. D., and D. W. Kyle. "Helping Preservice Teachers Learn to Use Teacher Effectiveness Research." *Journal of Teacher Education* 38(2) (1987): 40–44.

Rubin, D., J. Daly, J. C. McCroskey, and N. Mead. "A Review and Critique of Procedures for Assessing Speaking and Listening Skills among Preschool through Grade Twelve Students." *Communication Education* 31 (1982): 285–303.

Rubin, R. "Assessing Speaking and Listening Competence at the College Level: The Communication Competence Assessment Instrument." *Communication Education* 31 (1982): 19–32.

Rubin, R., ed. *Improving Speaking and Listening Skills.* San Francisco, Jossey-Bass, (1983).

Rubin, R., and J. Feezel. "Elements of Teacher Communication Competence." *Communication Education* 35 (1986): 254–268.

Schwarz, G. "We Are Not Machines." *Educational Leadership* 46(2) (1988): 83.

Shulman, L. "The Wisdom of the Practitioner." *Talk to Teachers.* Ed. D. Berliner and B. Rosenshine. New York: Random House, 1987. 375–386.

Sprowl, J. "Humor Theory and Communication Research." *World Communication* 16 (1987): 47–65.

Stewart, R., P. Kearney, and T. Plax. "Locus of Control as a Mediator: A Study of College Students' Reactions to Teachers' Attempts to Gain Compliance." *Communication Yearbook 9.* Ed. M. McLaughlin. Beverly Hills, CA: Sage, 1986. 691–706.

Stohl, C. "Perceptions of Social Attractiveness and Communicator Style: A Developmental Study of Preschool Children." *Communication Education* 30 (Oct. 1981): 367–376.

Trenholm, S., and T. Rose. "The Compliant Communicator: Teacher Perceptions of Appropriate Classroom Behavior." *Western Journal of Speech Communication* 45 (Winter 1981): 13–26.

Woolfolk, A. E., and L. McCune-Nicolich. *Educational Psychology for Teachers.* 2nd ed. Englewood Cliffs, NJ: Prentice Hall, 1984.

# 9 COMMUNICATION BARRIERS

## OBJECTIVES

After reading this chapter and completing the activities, you should be able to:

- Define communication apprehension
- Describe a highly communication-apprehensive student
- List the effects of high communication apprehension
- Define receiver apprehension
- List the effects of receiver apprehension
- Define sexism
- Describe the extent of sexism in the classroom
- Describe the effects of sexism on classroom interaction
- Define teacher expectancy
- Describe the process of teacher expectancy
- Outline how teacher expectancies can be communicated
- Describe necessary teacher expectancies
- Define student expectancy
- Describe ways to handle cultural diversity
- Define students with special needs

## INTRODUCTION

The teaching-learning process is primarily a communication process that relies largely on the interactive behaviors of students and teachers. Any variable that prohibits effective communication can adversely affect the learning process. In this chapter, we'll discuss several barriers to effective communication—communication apprehension, receiver apprehension, sexism, teacher expectancy, student expectancy, cultural diversity, and students with special needs.

## COMMUNICATION APPREHENSION

### Definition

Practically speaking, communication apprehension is a serious concern for educators. The presence of highly apprehensive students can baffle even the best teacher. There's nothing more disheartening than a student who has something worthwhile to contribute, but, because of communication apprehension, is both unwilling and fearful of sharing that knowledge with others.

What exactly is communication apprehension and how extensive is it? The student with high communication apprehension is one who attaches high levels of punishment to the communication encounter.[1] The individual is fearful of communication and will go to great lengths to avoid communication situations, and when by chance or necessity he is placed in them, the student feels uncomfortable, tense, embarrassed, and shy.

Chances are that you'll have many students with this problem. One out of every five students experiences high communication apprehension and an additional 20 percent are affected to some degree.[2] Shaw[3] found that between 15 and 25 percent of the elementary school students he examined reported high apprehension. Similar results have been found at other age levels.[4] The problem has reached such proportions that some authors[5] suggest that when compared to other learning handicaps, communication apprehension ranks first in terms of the number of people affected.

### Causes of Communication Apprehension

The specific causes of communication apprehension are not known. Four explanations have been posited: genetic predisposition, skills acquisition, modeling, and reinforcement.[6]

The *genetic predisposition explanation* for communication apprehension holds that certain genetic components such as sociability, physical appearance, body shape, and coordination and motor abilities may contribute to the development of communication apprehension.[7] However, as is true with many research findings concerning inherited characteristics, the environment can either enhance or decrease the hereditary predisposition towards communication apprehension.

A child may also develop communication apprehension because she fails to acquire the necessary *skills for effective social interaction* at the same rate as her peers. The child with high communication apprehension is slow to develop such necessary social skills as reciprocity, language use, referential communication skills, sensitivity to verbal and nonverbal social cues, interaction management skills, and the use of verbal reinforcers. A vicious cycle emerges: as the apprehensive child continues to fall behind her less apprehensive (more skillful) peers, she develops more communication apprehension because of her lack of skills.

A third explanation for the development of communication apprehension involves *modeling.* The child may imitate others in his environment. If a parent or teacher is communication apprehensive, the child may observe the parent's or teacher's behavior and then imitate that behavior.

The explanation most often set forth for the development of communication apprehension relates to the theory of *reinforcement.* If a child receives positive reinforcement, he finds communication a desirable, rewarding experience. He will develop little if any communication apprehension. If, on the other hand, the child has been taught to be "seen but not heard"—if he has not been reinforced for communicating—he will find communication an unrewarding, undesirable experience, and communication apprehension may be high.

As the child progresses through life, communication apprehension is self-fulfilling. As you recall from chapter 2, a self-fulfilling prophecy is a prophecy that comes true because we expect it to come true. Individuals with high apprehension fear they won't succeed in social interactions. They thus avoid interaction, and the avoidance results in the loss of valuable practice time in communicating. As a consequence, when the individual is placed in an interaction, she performs more poorly than others. This failure then reinforces the individual's apprehension. In short, the individual expects to fail, shapes her environment so that she does fail, and is more convinced than ever that communication is punishing.

In the classroom, communication apprehension can be caused or increased by the teacher's communication. The following research demonstrates how this might happen.

*Twenty percent of the children in a certain elementary school were reported to their teachers as showing unusual potential for intellectual growth. The names of these 20 percent were drawn by means of a table of random numbers. . . . Eight months later these unusual or "magic" children showed significantly greater gains in IQ than did the remaining children who had not been singled out for the teachers' attention. The change in the teachers' expectations regarding the intellectual performance of these allegedly "special" children had led to an actual change in the intellectual performance of these randomly selected children.[8]*

Obviously, no single explanation—genetic predisposition, reinforcement, skills acquisition, or modeling—is probably sufficient to explain why a child develops communication apprehension. Instead, all four explanations work together to explain the development of communication apprehension.

---

### ACTIVITY 9.1

Think about your educational experiences. In which classes did you communicate most? Least? How did you feel about the classes in which you communicated most? Least? Analyze the variables of the educational environment in each class. Why did you communicate? Why didn't you communicate?

---

Two influential environments in a child's life—home and school—may contribute to the development of communication apprehension. McCroskey and his associates[9] and Daly and Friedrich[10] reviewed literature that suggests that home environmental factors such as the amount of family talk and parent-child interaction styles predict children's communication behavior. Based on the previous work of Davey[11] and Daly and Friedrich,[12] McCroskey and his associates probed the school environment as a potential cause of increased communication apprehension in some students. They found that children in grades K–3 reported lower levels of communication apprehension than children in grades 4–12. The biggest change in the levels of communication apprehension occurred during grades three and four. The researchers conclude that although biological and/or social factors unrelated to the school environment may cause these changes, the school cannot be discounted as a potential causal agent.[13]

### The Effects of Communication Apprehension

Communication apprehension can have a significant impact on a person's life. Research reviewed by Daly[14] revealed that, in comparison to low communication-apprehensive people, those with high communication apprehension:

1. Select occupations they perceive as requiring little communication
2. Are offered jobs less frequently and are offered lower salaries
3. Are seen by others as less socially attractive
4. Are rated lower on composure, competence, extroversion, and sociability
5. Disclose significantly less
6. Rate self-esteem and self-credibility lower

7. Feel isolated and seclusive
8. Lack trust in others

In addition, high communication apprehension has been found to be positively correlated with anxiety, dogmatism, and external control; and negatively correlated with emotional maturity, dominance, adventurousness, confidence, self-control, tolerance for ambiguity, and need to achieve.[15] After reviewing the research concerning the effects of communication apprehension on group interaction, McKinney concluded: Since communication-apprehensive group members participate less in their group's interaction, they are perceived as (1) less effective in their interactions; (2) less competent; and (3) less likely to emerge as group leaders than nonapprehensive group members.[16]

In 1978, Norton[17] published his foundations of a communication style construct. (For a review of this construct, see chapter 8.) Since that time the construct has been examined in relation to communication apprehension. Andersen[18] found that highly communication-apprehensive persons perceived others as less immediate, less dramatic, less animated, less impression leaving, less attractive, less open, and less friendly in their communication styles than did those with lower levels of communication apprehension. In addition Porter[19] found that individuals who reported their level of communication apprehension as high were perceived by their communication partners as "talking less" and not "taking charge."

## Student Communication Apprehension

Many of the behaviors discussed above are evidenced in the classroom as well. Daly's[20] research review indicates that highly communication-apprehensive students interact less frequently. In addition, highly apprehensive students:

1. Do not assume positions of leadership in groups[21]
2. Do not volunteer to participate in classroom question/answer sessions[22]
3. Drop classes requiring a large amount of communication[23]
4. Are perceived by teachers as having less likelihood of success in almost every subject area regardless of intelligence, effort, or academic ability[24]
5. Are perceived to have less success potential in deportment[25]
6. Have low self-esteem[26]
7. Express a preference for seating arrangements that inhibit communication interaction[27]
8. Have lower grade point averages and score lower on student achievement tests than low communication apprehensive students[28] (Recent research indicates that as communication apprehension

increases, attitudes toward school become more negative, and, therefore, final grades are detrimentally affected.[29])

9. Show more tension and less interest and talk less[30]

From the previous research findings, a picture of the highly communication-apprehensive student can be drawn. Generally, this student is withdrawn; has a hard time expressing self; is quiet, reserved, dissatisfied, easily annoyed, and strongly affected by emotions; lacks leadership; is a follower; is submissive; has a low task orientation; is restrained; avoids people and participation in groups; dislikes interaction; is shy; is an ineffective speaker; has little success in groups; is indecisive, tense, frustrated, and closed-minded; has a low tolerance for ambiguous or uncertain situations, low need to achieve, and low self-esteem; chooses occupations requiring little communication; and sees others as controlling his life.

In general, a review of the communication apprehension research indicates that students with high levels of communication apprehension from the elementary to college levels are less academically successful than students with low levels of communication apprehension, as measured by final grades, GPA, and standardized achievement tests.[31] In addition, teachers expect students with high levels of communication apprehension to be less academically and socially successful.[32]

The low communication-apprehensive student presents quite a different picture. He is generally perceived as a high interactor, mature, independent, self-assured, assertive, competitive, talkative, determined, enjoys people, is chosen for leadership, decisive, open-minded, tolerant of ambiguous or uncertain situations, has a high need to achieve, sees himself as being in control of his own life, seeks occupations requiring a large amount of communication, and has high self-esteem.

## Teacher Communication Apprehension

Thus far we've talked primarily of students. However, teachers can be high in communication apprehension also. Approximately one in three teachers at the lower elementary level is suffering from communication apprehension.[33] Teachers who are communication apprehensive may gravitate to lower grades because teaching younger children may be less threatening to them.

Although little research has been conducted on the effect of communication apprehension on teaching effectiveness, one fact seems clear. Teachers with communication apprehension prefer instructional systems that reduce the amount of student-teacher and student-student communication.[34] Research does suggest that teachers may have an impact on the development of communication apprehension. Based on their findings that students increase in communication apprehension as they progress through elementary school, McCroskey and his associates tested two hypotheses:[35]

1.  That there is a higher proportion of teachers with high communication apprehension in the lower elementary grades (K–4) than at other grade levels
2.  That there is a higher proportion of teachers with high communication apprehension in the lower elementary grades (K–4) than there are teachers with low communication apprehension in those grades.

Both hypotheses were confirmed. Thus, the researchers concluded that highly communication-apprehension teachers may have an effect on the development of communication apprehension in their students.

---

### ACTIVITY 9.2

Analyze yourself. Determine your own level of communication apprehension by completing the questionnaires below. First complete the Verbal Activity Scale (VAS). This will give you an idea of your normal verbal activity level.

### *Verbal Activity Scale (VAS)*

The following ten statements refer to talking with other people. If the statement describes you very well, circle "1." If it somewhat describes you, circle "2." If you are not sure whether it describes you or not, or if you do not understand the statement, circle "3." If the statement is a poor description of you, circle "4." If the statement is a very poor description of you, circle "5." There are no right or wrong answers. Work quickly; record your first impression.

1 2 3 4 5    1.  I enjoy talking.
1 2 3 4 5    2.  Most of the time I would rather be quiet than talk.
1 2 3 4 5    3.  Other people think I am very quiet.
1 2 3 4 5    4.  I talk more than most people.
1 2 3 4 5    5.  Talking to other people is one of the things I like best.
1 2 3 4 5    6.  Most of the time I would rather talk than be quiet.
1 2 3 4 5    7.  I don't talk much.
1 2 3 4 5    8.  Other people think I talk a lot.
1 2 3 4 5    9.  Most people talk more than I do.
1 2 3 4 5    10. I talk a lot.

To obtain your VAS score, complete the following steps:

1.  Add your scores for the following items: 2, 3, 6, 7, and 9.

2. Add your scores for the following items: 1, 4, 5, 8, and 10.
3. Add 30 to your score for step 1.
4. Subtract your score for step 2 from your score for step 3. Your score should be between 10 and 50.

If your score is above 38, this indicates you are more verbally active than most people. Be careful not to dominate the communication in your classroom! If you score below 22, this indicates you are more quiet than most people. You'll need to work at becoming more verbally active, thus stimulating verbal activity on the part of your students. If your score falls between 22-38, you're "normal" in your verbal activity.

To determine your level of communication apprehension, complete the Personal Report of Communication Apprehension (PRCA) below.

### Personal Report of Communication Apprehension (PRCA)

This instrument is composed of twenty-five statements concerning your communication with other people. Indicate the degree to which each statement applies to you by marking whether you (1) strongly agree, (2) agree, (3) are undecided, (4) disagree, or (5) strongly disagree with each statement. There are no right or wrong answers. Work quickly; record your first impression.

_____ 1. While participating in a conversation with a new acquaintance, I feel very nervous.

_____ 2. I have no fear of facing an audience.

_____ 3. I talk less because I'm shy.

_____ 4. I look forward to expressing my opinions at meetings.

_____ 5. I am afraid to express myself in a group.

_____ 6. I look forward to an opportunity to speak in public.

_____ 7. I find the prospect of speaking mildly pleasant.

_____ 8. When communicating, my posture feels strained and unnatural.

_____ 9. I am tense and nervous while participating in a group discussion.

_____ 10. Although I talk fluently with friends, I am at a loss for words on the platform.

_____ 11. I have no fear about expressing myself in a group.

_____ 12. My hands tremble when I try to handle objects on the platform.

_____ 13. I always avoid speaking in public if possible.

_____ 14. I feel that I am more fluent when talking to people than most other people are.

_____ 15. I am fearful and tense all the while I am speaking before an audience.

_____ 16. My thoughts become confused and jumbled when I speak before an audience.

_____ 17. I like to get involved in group discussions.

_____ 18. Although I am nervous just before getting up, I soon forget my fears and enjoy the experience.

_____ 19. Conversing with people who hold positions of authority causes me to be fearful and tense.

_____ 20. I dislike using my body and voice expressively.

_____ 21. I feel relaxed and comfortable while speaking.

_____ 22. I feel self-conscious when I am called upon to answer a question or give an opinion.

_____ 23. I face the prospect of making a speech with complete confidence.

_____ 24. I'm afraid to speak up in conversations.

_____ 25. I would enjoy presenting a speech on a local television show.

To determine your score, complete the following steps:

1. Add up your scores for items 2, 4, 6, 7, 11, 14, 17, 18, 21, 23, and 25.
2. Add up your scores for items 1, 3, 5, 8, 9, 10, 12, 13, 15, 16, 19, 20, 22, and 24.
3. Add 84 to the total for step 1.
4. Subtract the total for step 2 from the total for step 3. Your score should be between 25 and 125.

If your score is between 62 and 88, you fall within the normal range of communication apprehension. If you score above 88, you have a high level of communication apprehension and may have difficulty helping your students who also suffer from this problem. If you score below 62 you have a low level of communication apprehension. You may have difficulty understanding your students with communication apprehension, since this problem is unfamiliar to your own experience.

From J. McCroskey, *Quiet Children and the Classroom Teacher* (Urbana, IL: ERIC, 1977) 16–18.

## Identifying the Highly Communication-Apprehensive Student

The first step in identifying the highly communication apprehensive student is observation. Reexamine the characteristics of this type of student. If you have a student who exhibits several of these characteristics, she may be a highly communication-apprehensive person. You might also use an independent observer, such as your principal, speech therapist, or another teacher, to share his observations of your students with you.

You can also administer the VAS to your students. The scale can be administered orally if students are in the lower elementary grades. The VAS can indicate which students will be highly verbal. Although little research has been conducted examining overly talkative children, they can be very frustrating to the classroom teacher. In addition, teachers must be careful when "toning down" the overly talkative student in order to avoid causing communication apprehension in this student.

Not every student who is quiet will be communication apprehensive. Some quiet students may lack certain communication skills, feel alienated from society, or be from a different ethnic or cultural background. To identify whether a quiet child is communication apprehensive, you can administer the Personal Report of Communication Fear (PRCF). This questionnaire can be administered orally to young children.

---

**ACTIVITY 9.3**

*Personal Report of Communication Fear (PRCF)*

The following fourteen statements concern feelings about communicating with other people. Please indicate the degree to which each statement applies to you by circling your response. Mark "YES" if you strongly agree, "yes" if you agree, "?" if you are unsure, "no" if you disagree, or "NO" if you strongly disagree. There are no right or wrong answers. Work quickly; record your first impression.

YES yes ? no NO    1.   Talking with someone new scares me.

YES yes ? no NO    2.   I look forward to talking in class.

YES yes ? no NO    3.   I like standing up and talking to a group of people.

YES yes ? no NO    4.   I like to talk when the whole class listens.

YES yes ? no NO    5.   Standing up to talk in front of other people scares me.

YES yes ? no NO    6.   I like talking to teachers.

YES yes ? no NO    7.   I am scared to talk to people.

YES yes ? no NO    8.   I like it when it is my turn to talk in class.

YES yes ? no NO    9.   I like to talk to new people.

YES yes ? no NO    10.   When someone asks me a question, it scares me.

YES yes ? no NO    11.   There are a lot of people I am scared to talk to.

YES yes ? no NO    12.   I like to talk to people I haven't met before.

YES yes ? no NO    13.   I like it when I don't have to talk.

YES yes ? no NO    14.   Talking to teachers scares me.

*Scoring*: YES = 1, yes = 2, ? = 3, no = 4, NO = 5

To obtain the score for the PRCF, complete the following steps:

1.  Add the scores for the following items: 2, 3, 4, 6, 8, 9, and 12.
2.  Add the scores on the following items: 1, 5, 7, 10, 11, 13, and 14.
3.  Add 42 to the total of step 1.
4.  Subtract the total of step 2 from the total of step 3. Your score should be between 14 and 70.

The normal range on the PRCF is between 28 and 47. Students scoring above 47 are probably highly communication apprehensive. They will need special encouragement to communicate. Those students scoring below 28 are very low in communication apprehension.

J. McCroskey, *Quiet Children and the Classroom Teacher* (Urbana, IL: ERIC, 1977) 20-21.

## Treating the Highly Communication-Apprehensive Student

Research indicates that personalized systems of instruction[36] and small classes[37] do not prove effective for students with high communication apprehension. These students seem to do better academically in mass lecture courses.[38] However, it is not likely that students will always be in lecture classes. What, then, can the classroom teacher do to help the highly communication apprehensive student?

Although clinical approaches to reducing communication apprehension (systematic desensitization, cognitive modification, skills training, and visualization)[39] have been found to reduce apprehension, such methods are rarely at the classroom teacher's disposal. Reinforcement—a method in which individuals are conditioned to talk more by a series of reinforcing events—has also been found to reduce apprehension and is more readily available to the classroom teacher.

One of the best ways to help the communication-apprehensive student is to provide a friendly, nonthreatening classroom climate.[40] On the first day, make clear to students exactly what is expected of them. Set ground rules that foster honest, open communication (for example, "you don't 'cut down' another student's comment"). Engage in some get-acquainted exercises. For example, you might use the exercise in which you and your students share your full name and the significance of it.

Don't grade on oral participation. Although taking a speech course has been shown to reduce the average student's communication apprehension, the same is not true for the student with high communication apprehension.

Vary the task assignments for students with high and low communication apprehension. Booth-Butterfield's[41] research suggests that students with high communication apprehension need more structured tasks than students with low communication apprehension. The more concrete the assignment for highly communication-apprehension students the better their performance will be.

In addition some research suggests that students may benefit from working in small group or interpersonal settings with acquaintances.[42] Also, communication apprehension is reduced when (1) student perceptions of dissimilarity are reduced; (2) a noncritical, attentive classroom atmosphere is produced and maintained; (3) students present short, rather than long, speeches; and (4) performance criteria are few.[43]

---

### ACTIVITY 9.4

*Creating a Supportive Communication Climate*

Observe two instructors. Using Gibb's supportive and defensive climate categories (chapter 6), jot down behaviors each instructor engages in under each category. If one instructor seems to create a supportive climate and the other a defensive climate, interview several students from each instructor's class. Ask them to comment on how willing they feel to express their ideas, how comfortable they are in class, how well they think they're learning, and so on.

---

## RECEIVER APPREHENSION

Another communication barrier in the classroom is receiver apprehension.[44] Receiver apprehension is the degree to which students are fearful about misinterpreting, inadequately processing, and/or being unable to psychologically adjust to messages.

Students suffering from receiver apprehension perform less well on objective examinations and class projects. They also have difficulty taking notes. As a result, students with a high level of receiver apprehension may do less well academically.

Research by Wheeless and Scott[45] indicates that receiver apprehension has a significant negative effect on information gain in the classroom. Beatty[46] provided further evidence that suggested that receiver apprehension is a function of assimilated information affected by processing difficulties.

Based on previous research, Beatty and Payne[47] speculated that a significant negative relationship exists between an individual's level of cognitive complexity and level of receiver apprehension. Cognitive complexity is represented on a continuum of information-processing ability. On one end of the continuum are persons who use several dimensions and a complex set of rules for combining these dimensions into overall judgments and impressions. On the opposite end of the continuum are persons who utilize only a few dimensions and a simple set of rules. Beatty and Payne's research confirmed the negative relationship between cognitive complexity and receiver apprehension. Evidently "complex" individuals experience less receiver apprehension than their less complex counterparts because complex individuals process information more easily.

In a recent study, Preiss and Kerssen suggest:

> *A profile of apprehensive receivers is beginning to emerge in the literature. Apprehensive receivers do not enjoy processing information and they prefer low-content messages. They perceive the environment to be saturated with information, yet they employ few cues when rendering judgments and evaluating performance. Highly apprehensive individuals distrust messages and are less cognitively complex when decoding and responding to incoming information. The result is a rigid processing style characterized by an uncritical evaluation of information and intolerance for new or novel ideas. In light of this profile, it seems clear that educators need to respond to the information processing style of apprehensive receivers. Much like teachers attempt to ameliorate the stage fright experience in public speaking classes, educators need to develop techniques for reducing receiver apprehension.*[48]

We know very little about the causes and consequences of receiver apprehension. We know even less about effective means of treatment. Perhaps the most effective treatment for the student who is apprehensive about receiving communication is to create a supportive communication climate in your classroom. You might give the student training in the skills he lacks, for example, in note taking. You might utilize alternative methods of testing and instruction. Positive reinforcement and personal conferences in which you discuss the problem in a friendly, supportive climate might also help.

## ACTIVITY 9.5

To determine your level of receiver apprehension, complete the following questionnaire. This questionnaire can also be administered to your students.

### The Receiver Apprehension Test (R.A.T.)*

The following statements refer to how various people feel about receiving communication.

Indicate how much these statements relate to how you feel by marking whether you (1) strongly disagree, (2) disagree, (3) are undecided, (4) agree, or (5) strongly agree with each statement. Record your first impression. There are no right or wrong answers.

_____ 1. When listening to people in authority I always find it easy to put together exactly what was said.

_____ *2. I occasionally have difficulty listening in a group discussion because I am worried about adjusting and adapting to the ideas.

_____ *3. I sometimes have difficulty concentrating on what others are saying.

_____ 4. I find it easy to concentrate on what is being said.

_____ *5. At times I have difficulty concentrating on instructions others give me.

_____ *6. It is sometimes difficult for me to make sense out of what others are saying.

_____ *7. I sometimes feel uncomfortable when listening to other's ideas.

_____ 8. I almost never have difficulty understanding test items that I have to read.

_____ *9. It is at times hard to listen or focus on what other people are saying unless I know them well.

_____ *10. At times I feel tense when listening as a member of a social gathering.

_____ *11. Receiving new information sometimes makes me feel somewhat afraid.

_____ 12. I have no fear of misunderstanding what I read.

_____ *13. My thoughts occasionally become confused and jumbled when reading important information.

_____ *14. I am sometimes afraid that I will misread instructions.

_____ 15. I have no fear of listening and adjusting to others' views.

_____ *16. I am sometimes afraid that I will not completely understand what is said.

## Scoring Procedure

1. Add scores for items with asterisks (Total 1)
2. Add scores for items without asterisks (Total 2)
3. Complete the following formula: RAT Score = 66 − (Total 1) + (Total 2)

## Interpretation

Students with scores above 62 are probably suffering from receiver apprehension. Students with scores between 53 and 62 have a moderate level of receiver apprehension.

*From L. R. Wheeless, "An Investigation of Receiver Apprehension and Social Context Dimensions of Communication Apprehension," *The Speech Teacher* 24 (1975): 265.

## SEXISM IN THE CLASSROOM

Much research indicates the negative effects of sexism (discrimination on the basis of biological sex) in the classroom.[49] It is beyond the scope of this text to review even a significant portion of extant research. However, even a cursory review of research indicates gender differences for teachers and students. Male students generally receive more praise, more academic response opportunities, more instruction, lower grades, and more contact with teachers than do female students.[50] In addition, several studies indicate that teachers (regardless of their sex):[51]

1. Use a harsh tone when reprimanding boys and a conversational tone when reprimanding girls
2. Reprimand boys more often than girls
3. Respond to a girl's reading failure by providing a second response opportunity or a clue, but call on someone else or provide the word to boys
4. Overestimate the achievement levels of girls and underestimate achievement levels for boys
5. Have more negative attitudes toward boys in terms of their potential for disruptive behavior and school motivation

In addition, females are discouraged from pursuing such "masculine" subjects as math, and males have difficulty with "feminine" subjects such as reading.[52]

Differences have also been found in male and female teachers' classrooms. As Brophy and Good indicate in their research review:

> *First, the female teachers' classes seemed to be more active, with greater student willingness to initiate interaction with the teachers. Students initiated more comments and questions in the female teachers' classes, had more response opportunities, and initiated more private contacts with teachers. Also, they were more likely to take a guess when unsure of their response, while they were more likely to remain silent in a male teacher's classroom. Thus, the students apparently felt safer in guessing in the female teachers' classes.*[53]

Brophy and Good go on to say:

> *Male teachers more often failed to give feedback to students, but this happened mostly after correct or part-correct answers. Female teachers, in contrast, more often failed to give feedback after the student had responded incorrectly or had failed to answer. Following wrong answers or failures to respond, male teachers were more likely to provide process feedback to give explanations, or clear up the student's misunderstanding. In general, in failure situations male teachers were more likely to provide abstract feedback or to provide a second response opportunity by asking another question, while female teachers were more likely to give the answer or call on someone else.*[54]

In their extensive research review, Hall and Sandler [55] found several ways in which teachers treat male and female students differently, and thus reinforce traditional sex-role stereotypes. Teachers do this by:

- Making eye contact more often with males than with females
- Nodding and gesturing more often in response to males' questions and comments than to females'
- Assuming a posture of attentiveness (for example, leaning forward) when men speak, but the opposite (such as looking at the clock) when women make comments
- Habitually choosing a location near male students (Proximity in the classroom may invite comments primarily from those sitting close by.)
- Giving males detailed instructions in how to complete a particular problem or lab assignment in the expectation they will eventually succeed on their own, but doing the assignment for females—or allowing them to fail with less instruction
- Ignoring female students while recognizing male students, even when women clearly volunteer to participate in class
- Calling directly on male students but not on female students
- Calling male students by name more often than female students
- "Coaching" male but not female students in working toward a fuller answer by probing for additional elaboration or explanation
- Waiting longer for males than for females to answer a question before going on to another student
- Interrupting female students (or allowing them to be disproportionately interrupted by peers)
- Asking female students questions that require factual answers (lower order questions) while asking male questions that demand personal evaluation and critical thinking (higher order questions)
- Responding more extensively to males' comments than to females' comments
- Crediting males' comments to the speaker ("as Bill pointed out") but not giving credit to females for their comments
- Phrasing classroom examples in a way that reinforces a stereotyped and negative view of females' psychological traits
- Using classroom examples that reflect stereotyped ideas about males' and females' social and professional roles
- Using the generic "he" or "man" to represent both males and females

**ACTIVITY 9.6**

*Teachers' Self-Evaluation Questionnaire*

To increase your awareness of stereotypes, spend some time observing your behavior in the classroom and then complete the questionnaire. If you are not presently teaching, observe a teacher's classroom interaction and complete the questionnaire.

1. Do you group children according to gender and/or pit one gender against the other in competition?
2. Do you make value judgments about children based on their appearances?
3. Do you expect behavioral differences in boys and girls (do you expect boys to be loud and rough and girls to be more quiet and gentle)?
4. Do you expect differences in the academic preferences of boys and girls (do you feel boys favor math and science and girls prefer reading and art)?
5. Do you emphasize the attractiveness of girls and the strength and abilities of boys?
6. Do you make an effort to change sex-stereotyped material that you must use in the classroom (do you involve the class in rewriting stereotyped material? Do you draw attention to stereotyped statements)?
7. Do you make an effort to free your language from sexist terminology (do you try to refrain from using male terms for all humanity or when referring to a teacher in the abstract; do you use the pronouns *she* and *her*)?
8. Do you discipline boys more harshly than girls?
9. Do you give boys more instructional time?
10. Do you involve fathers as much as mothers in your communication with children's homes?
11. Do you do all you can to see that all extracurricular activities include both boys and girls?
12. Do you use resource people in the classroom to show changes in sex roles?
13. Do you supplement your classes with current material on new openings in careers for males and females?
14. Do you call on only boys to do chores involving strength (for example, carrying stacks of books or moving tables)?
15. Do you encourage dominant roles for girls as well as boys (do you place girls in leadership positions or encourage boys to follow and receive help from girls)?
16. Do you encourage friendships between the sexes (do you assign joint projects and group the class according to interests)?

17.  Do you write to publishers to complain when material you receive does not represent the sexes fairly or equally?

18.  Do you encourage all children to use a variety of materials for recreation and learning (are bats and balls, dolls, trucks, hammers, jump ropes, measuring cups and spoons, and so on equally available to boys and girls)?

19.  Do you encourage children to try a variety of roles in play (parent, fire fighter, truck driver, cook, and so on)?

20.  Do you accept and encourage an equal display of anger and pain in boys and girls (do you accept it when girls hit and fight and when boys cry)?

21.  Are there specific classroom areas for boys and girls to play in (whether labeled as such or not)? For example, do you have a housekeeping area with kitchen toys for girls and a construction area for boys, or a separate book section for boys' books or girls' books? What happens when a boy heads for the kitchen corner or reads girls' books? Or when the girls head for the construction corner? (Note the students' response; note your own.)

22.  Do you plan different activities, or different roles within an activity, for boys and for girls? How are they different?

23.  Who do you ask to do secretarial chores and special tasks? Is this group predominantly male or female? Do you ask for a "strong boy" or a "good girl?"

24.  Notice the verbal cues for sex-role behavior that you use during the day. For instance, "Boys should _____." "Big boys don't _____." "Nice girls won't _____."

Adapted from KNOW, Inc., P.O. Box 86031, Pittsburgh, PA 15221.

## Gender Differences in Communication

It is generally accepted that males and females communicate differently and that these communication differences may be carried into the classroom. Research demonstrates that in groups containing both males and females, males:[56]

- Talk more, and what they say carries more weight
- Talk for longer periods of time
- Take more turns at speaking
- Exert more control over the topic of conversation
- Interrupt females more frequently than females interrupt males

Females are more likely to use "correct" linguistic forms, questions (especially "tag" questions such as "That was an easy test, don't you think?"), intensifying adjectives and adverbs, references to self, and incomplete assertions, and they interpret nonverbal cues more effectively than males.[57]

In terms of communication style, males tend to be more dominant in conversation, to be more relaxed, to argue more, and to be more dramatic and more precise. Females tend to be more friendly and attentive (employing smiles, head nods, positive reactions), and more open and animated in their display of feelings and emotions.[58]

In 1974, Bem[59] published her concept of androgyny—a psychological identification of sex. Androgenous individuals, regardless of their biological sex, identify with both "masculine" characteristics (aggressiveness, independence, dominance, and so on) and "feminine" characteristics (sensitivity, expressiveness, dependence, and so forth). As a result, androgenous individuals are more adaptable and more free from pressure to restrict their social behavior to stereotyped sex roles.

In terms of communication competence, androgynous individuals demonstrate a high level of adaptability (ability to be flexible and feel comfortable with a variety of people) and rewarding impressions (being other-oriented and providing positive feelings toward others). Generally, adaptability is associated with "maleness" and rewarding impressions with "femaleness." An individual who identifies with both masculine and feminine characteristics is generally a more competent communicator than an individual who identifies with only male or only female characteristics.[60]

According to a team of Harvard researchers, females make choices based on keeping the peace rather than making their opinions known and asserting themselves. Females place the highest priority on maintaining a relationship and not harming anyone. This "ethic of care," as the researchers refer to it, may influence how girls compete in class and cause them to fall behind males academically. Males tend to base their decisions on the "ethics of justice," centered on absolutes of right and wrong. Thus, males are more likely to take a stand and make clear arguments to support their ideas.[61]

In a recent study, the types of questions male and female students at various grade levels asked in mathematics and language arts classes were charted. The results suggest that, in advanced secondary mathematics classes, female students ask fewer questions than males. In addition, teachers subtly discouraged female students from participating.[62]

Richmond and Gorham, in their study of current generic-referent usage among 1,529 public school children in grades 3 through 12, found that the masculine generic usage is still prevalent.[63] In addition, a heavy dependence on masculine referents were associated with self-image. Males used significantly more masculine referents than did females. Males who selected traditionally male careers used more masculine referents than did males who selected a gender non-specific career. Females selecting stereotypically feminine careers used the most feminine referents.

Findings such as those just outlined have far-reaching implications for classroom teachers. For example, Rosenfeld and Jarrard[64] examined how the perceived sexism of professors affected classroom climate. They found that classes of perceived high sexist male teachers were described as less supportive and less innovative than those of perceived nonsexist male teachers.

In a follow-up study, the researchers examined coping mechanisms used by students in classes taught by sexist and nonsexist teachers. Coping mechanisms used by students in sexist male teachers' classes were passive (not doing what the teacher asks and hiding feelings) when students liked the class. If students did not like the class, and perceived the male teacher as sexist, students used an active coping mechanism—forming alliances against the teacher. Generally, teachers in disliked classes were perceived as more sexist than teachers in liked classes. Also, male teachers were perceived as more sexist than female teachers.[65]

Sexism is a two-edged sword—harming both males and females—and teachers may inadvertently communicate their own sex-role biases to students. Students may in turn model the sexist behavior of their teachers. Thus teachers are a significant element in the development and continuation of sexism.[66] On the other hand, students may model the nonsexist behaviors of their teachers. As a result, teachers can also be a significant element in the reduction of sexism.

## Sexist Curriculum Materials

Not only teacher behaviors but also the curriculum materials teachers use can perpetuate sex-role stereotypes. From the preschool level on, students are exposed to sexist materials. For example, Weitzman and her associates[67] examined how sex roles were treated by the winners of both the Caldecott Medal and Newbery Award. The Caldecott Medal is given by the Children's Service Committee of the American Library Association for the most distinguished picture book of the year. The Newbery Award is sponsored by the American Library Association for the best book for school-age children. The eighteen Caldecott winners and runners-up from 1967 to 1972 were analyzed in Weitzman's study. The researchers found that the ratio of pictured males to pictured females was 11:1. When females were illustrated, their traditional sex-role characterizations were reinforced: girls are passive, boys active; girls follow and serve others, boys lead and rescue others. Adult men and women in these books were also sex stereotyped: women were presented as wives and mothers; men in a variety of occupations. Newbery Award winners didn't fare much better. The ratio of male-to-female main characters was 3:1.

In an update of the Weitzman et al. study, Kolbe and LaVoie[68] analyzed Caldecott winners from 1972 to 1979. Although the ratio of male-to-female pictures had improved drastically (1.8:1), the role portrayal of males and females had not. Female roles continued to be stereotypically portrayed. Cooper's[69] research of Caldecott and Newbery Winners from 1980–1987 showed similar results to the Weitzman and Kolbe and LaVoie studies, as did her research of the images of parents and stepparents in children's literature.[70]

Two other recent studies of Caldecott Medal winners suggest similar patterns. Heinz[71] examined the occupations of characters in Caldecott Medal winners from 1971 to 1984. Males were shown in three times as many occupations as females. Almost half of the females shown in an occupation were depicted in a homemaker role. Dougherty and Engel[72] analyzed Caldecott winners and honor books from 1981 to 1985 and found that although numerical disparities had decreased considerably, stereotyped sex-role images had not.

In a random sampling of 1,380 school library books in grades K–6, female athletes frequently fell victim to sex-role stereotyping.[73] Boys were shown participating in a variety of individual sports, and girls predominated only in traditionally feminine activities, such as dance. In team sports, 34 out of 38 baseball players were male, as were 7 out of 8 basketball players.

Since the lack of female characters can communicate that females are unimportant in society, these ratios are disturbing. However, even more problematic is the way in which females were portrayed. For the most part, women and girls were portrayed as emotional, fearful, and incompetent (relying on others to solve their problems and comfort them.) They were constantly concerned with their appearances and spent the majority of their time cooking, sewing, or watching as boys played sports, made things, solved problems, or experienced adventures. They often demeaned themselves and accepted ridicule from boys. Boys, on the other hand, were portrayed as clever, adventurous, and brave.

Teen romances are an extremely popular form of fiction for female adolescents. They are one of the three types of books most widely read by young girls; a single title may sell as many as 90,000 copies through book clubs. Teen romances constitute 35 percent of B. Dalton's and Waldenbooks's combined nonadult sales.[74] Reading romances is the primary leisure-time activity for many adolescent girls.[75] Teenagers read romance novels for three reasons: escape, enjoyment, and education.[76]

Weitzman and Rizzo[77] studied the most used elementary school textbooks in grades one through six and found that males and females were portrayed stereotypically, particularly in the illustrations. In science texts, females appeared in only 26 percent of the illustrations. In social studies texts, 33 percent of the illustrations included females. In a reading series, 102 stories were about boys and only 35 were about girls. Math texts pictured the mathematically competent boy and the mathematically incompetent female. Such illustrations present negative images for females and communicate what is considered "appropriate" behavior for each sex.

In general, despite the adoption of nonsexist guidelines during the past decade, textbook publishers have made relatively few changes to increase the visibility of females and decrease the stereotyping of males and females. For example, in elementary school textbooks, stories about females are only included in one or two books in a series or added to a single grade level.[78]

The "nonbiased" material is sometimes added to the center or end of a text without any attempt to integrate it into the overall format of the rest of the book. Basal readers appear to be doing little to present the idea that men and women may share occupational roles and both may bring positive qualities to these roles.[79] After reading stories in which nontraditional roles for both males and females were depicted, students (grades four, seven, eleven) were more likely to believe that both males and females should and could do the activity of the main character than after reading traditional stories. Neither comprehension nor interest were adversely affected by the nonbiased materials.[80]

Boys rate stories less interesting when the main character is female. Although their preference was less pronounced, females found stories in which the main character was male less interesting.[81]

Secondary textbooks do not appear to be much better. Nilsen[82] examined sciences curriculum materials and found that in the majority of the books the word "man" is used to describe people in general and few books depicted women in scientific careers.

Judith Bazler examined the seven best selling high school science texts. According to Bazler, only one of the texts provided a balance of pictures of men and women. Calling for a change, Bazler says.

*If women do not see women in science, if their teachers are 95 percent men, and if textbooks are predominantly male, they won't go into science unless they're specifically out to break down those barriers.*[83]

The typical history text devotes one of its 500 to 800 pages to women and their achievements.[84] When women are discussed in history textbooks, passages frequently include misleading words or phrases that detract from the significance of women and their accomplishments. For example, one text informs readers that no women were members of the Senate in 1972 when, in fact, Margaret Chase Smith served as a senator at that time.[85] In a survey of English literature textbooks, the 171 anthologized selections included 147 male authors and 24 female authors. Another survey of 400 selections counted 94 female authors and 306 male authors.[86] Apparently many subject matter areas are sex biased since studies of math, science, and social studies texts reveal similar results.[87]

Allen[88] suggests that educators will see little change in textbooks as long as sex-typing in the division of labor in publishing continues. Although the number of women who have moved into important editorial positions has increased, women are still not as evident as men in positions that actually exercise control over the goals and policies of publishing.

---

**ACTIVITY 9.7**

Analyze textbooks or readers to determine the level of sexism in each. Take note of how women are portrayed. Are there more boys than girls? Are males and females doing stereotypical things?

---

## The Effects of Sexism

One might ask, "So what? What effect does sexist curriculum material have on students?" Much research suggests that these materials influence student sex-role stereotypes and behavior.[89] Of particular interest to communication education scholars is the effect of sexism on student self-concept.

In a study comparing the self-concept scores of tenth grade girls with the scores of their male peers, Bohan[90] found girls had a significantly lower self-concept rating than did males. Tenth grade girls also showed significantly lower self-concept scores than girls in all other age groups. Bohan posits two interpretations for these findings: (1) that the adolescent years involve a reevaluation of self, and it may be that adolescent girls find themselves wanting in relation to the values they hold or believe to be important; (2) since adolescence is the period of the most intense role evaluation as well as the apex of sex-role development, the adolescent girl may come to recognize that the role she is expected to assume as a female is relatively inferior in status and prestige to the male role. Accordingly, she may decrease her evaluation of herself. Petersen[91] also found that the achievement of girls declined from seventh to twelfth grade. A recent study by Gilligan et al. verifies this decrease.[92]

Equally as disconcerting as the decline in the self-concept of adolescent girls are test results that seem to indicate that these girls decrease in their IQ scores while boys increase.[93] Studies indicate that girls with better grade averages than boys in high school generally do not believe that they have the ability to do college work. Of the brightest high school graduates who do not go on to college, 75 to 90 percent are women.[94]

In a recent major study, Earle, Roach, and Fraser[95] studied female dropouts. The report concludes that the majority of female students who drop out are not pregnant, as had previously been assumed. The report, "Female Dropouts: A New Perspective," speculates that current school practices encourage girls to leave school by depressing their overall achievement. For example, studies have shown that teachers talk less to female than to male students, counsel them less, and provide them with fewer directions and rewards. Also, schools provide limited opportunities for students to work cooperatively, though girls may perform better than boys in such situations.

Licht and her associates[96] review research demonstrating that girls are more likely than boys to attribute their failure to insufficient ability and are less likely to attribute their success to high ability. When females receive negative feedback about their performance they are less likely than boys to respond by increasing their efforts. Although, in general, girls report lower confidence in their abilities, this emerges most often when there is an uncertainty of success (when tasks are unfamiliar or difficult and when past performance feedback has been ambiguous or infrequent).

In addition to affecting self-concept, sexism also affects curriculum choices. The sex-role stereotyping in education also affects the course of study students pursue. Traditionally, female students have perceived math and science courses, spatial ability, and problem solving as male domains.[97] Males traditionally have viewed home economics, secretarial skills, and reading as feminine activities.[98] Research examining differences in male/female math and science performance suggests that males are more likely to take higher-level math and science courses and that this is particularly true in physics, trigonometry, and calculus.[99]

Finally, sexism affects choice of occupation. A recent report on girls' lower SAT scores,[100] "Sex Bias in College Admission Tests: Why Women Lose Out," suggests the long-term impact a lack of math and science background is having—a real dollar loss for females in later life. Females get less prestigious jobs, earn less money, and have fewer leadership opportunities. Male-dominated occupations are higher-paying, on average, than those dominated by females.[101]

---

**ACTIVITY 9.8**

Interview young children (younger than age ten) and assess the level of sex-role stereotyping in their self-concepts. Have them answer questions such as: (1) How do they play? With whom? (2) What do they want to be when they grow up? (3) What is their role in the family? (4) Who are their heroes?

## What Teachers Can Do

The first step to eliminating sexism in our classrooms is awareness of our behavior. Asking our students to complete a questionnaire like the one below could tell us a great deal about our teaching behavior as it relates to issues of gender.

---

**ACTIVITY 9.9**                                    **Student Perception Questionnaire**

*Directions:*

Answer each of the following questions. Choose only one answer for each question.

1.  Your age _____

2.  Sex of student
    (1)   Male
    (2)   Female

3.  Sex of Instructor
    (1)   Male
    (2)   Female

4.  How often do you voluntarily answer questions or contribute to class discussions in class?
    (1)   Never
    (2)   One to three times during the course
    (3)   An average of once a week
    (4)   An average of two to three times a week
    (5)   An average of one or more times a day

5.  How often does the teacher call on you or ask you to respond to a question or comment?
    (1)   Teacher does not call on anyone
    (2)   One to three times during the course
    (3)   An average of once a week
    (4)   An average of two to three times a week
    (5)   Never

6.  How does the teacher most frequently call on you?
    (1)   By name
    (2)   By pointing
    (3)   By eye contact/looking directly at me
    (4)   Teacher never calls on me

7. How many times have you raised your hand to ask a question or make a comment and found that the teacher does not respond?
   (1) Once or twice during the course
   (2) Three or more times during the course
   (3) I am called on when I raise my hand
   (4) I never raise my hand

8. Why do you think the teacher does not respond when you raise your hand? (Select the one answer which best reflects your opinion.)
   (1) Too many students want to speak
   (2) Others beat me to it
   (3) Teacher does not see or hear me
   (4) Teacher ignores me
   (5) This situation never occurs

9. How many times have you wanted to participate in class by asking a question or making a comment but chosen not to do so?
   (1) Once or twice during the course
   (2) Three or more times during the course
   (3) Nearly every day
   (4) Not at all, because I participate when I want to
   (5) I usually do not want to participate

10. If you have wanted to participate in class by asking a question or making a comment but did not do so, what was your reason for not doing so? (Select the one response that most closely corresponds with your feelings.)
    (1) Felt insecure, inadequate, or uncertain
    (2) Another student asked question or commented first
    (3) Too many students in class
    (4) Disagreed with teacher but chose not to speak out

11. In your opinion, which students most frequently participate in class? (Select the one answer that best represents your opinion.)
    (1) Those who are most knowledgeable or most interested in the subject
    (2) Those who are seeking clarification or want more information
    (3) Those who are trying to show off or get attention
    (4) I have not noticed

12. In your opinion, which students ask the most questions and make the most comments in class?
    (1) Male student(s)
    (2) Female student(s)
    (3) Male and female students equally
    (4) I have not noticed

13. How does the teacher react to the questions you ask in class?
    (1) Encourages me to question or comment again
    (2) Discourages me from commenting or asking a question again
    (3) Neither encourages nor discourages me
    (4) I never participate

14. In your opinion, how does the teacher react to opinions and comments given by other students in the class?
    (1) Respects the opinions of students in this class
    (2) Does not respect the opinions of students in this class
    (3) Embarrasses or "puts down" students for their opinions
    (4) I did not notice

15. Does the instructor make humorous references that you feel are offensive, embarrassing, or belittling to any individuals or groups?
    (1) Never
    (2) Once or twice
    (3) Occasionally
    (4) Frequently

16. How often do students participate in this class by asking questions or making comments?
    (1) Never
    (2) Rarely
    (3) Occasionally
    (4) Frequently

Adapted from J. Gappa and J. Pearce, *Sex and Gender in the Social Sciences: Reassessing the Introductory Course* (San Francisco: San Francisco State University, 1982).

In addition to using student evaluations, we can ask colleagues to observe our classrooms or we can videotape our classroom interactions to help analyze how we relate to our students on the basis of gender.

**ACTIVITY 9.10**

In a microteaching session, complete either part A or B of the Student-Faculty Communication Checklist.

### *Student-Faculty Communication Checklist*

It may be difficult for an instructor to be conscious of the interactional dynamics in the classroom while transmitting a lecture or guiding a discussion. For this reason, the following techniques are suggested to help faculty analyze the interaction in their classes.

### A. Classroom Observation

Having a friend, colleague, or teaching assistant observe some of your classes on a random basis can be helpful. Classroom observation can be used to answer questions such as:

1. How many males do you call on to answer questions? How many females?
2. Which students (male or female) participate in class more frequently through answering questions or making comments? Is the number disproportionate enough that you should encourage some students to participate more frequently?
3. Do interruptions occur when an individual is talking? If so, who does the interrupting?
4. Is your verbal response to students positive? aversive? encouraging? Is it the same for all students? If not, why? (Valid reasons occur from time to time for reacting or responding to a particular student in a highly specified manner.)
5. Do you tend to face or address one section of the classroom more than others? Do you establish eye contact with certain students more than others? What gestures, postures, or facial expressions do you use and are they different for men, women, or minority students?

### B. Audiotaping of Class Section

Have a student tape record some of your class sessions. Self-analysis of the tapes could provide answers to questions such as:

1. Which students do you call by name?
2. What language patterns are you using? Do you regularly use male referencing or the generic "he" or "man"? Are stereotypical assumptions about men and women revealed in your classroom dialogue?
3. Are examples and anecdotes drawn from men's lives only?
4. Can differential patterns of reinforcement be detected from the tapes?

Reprinted from J. Gappa and J. Pearce, *Sex and Gender in the Social Sciences: Reassessing the Introductory Course* (San Francisco: San Francisco State University, 1982).

In addition to becoming aware of how we may inadvertently be perpetuating sex-role stereotypes, we also need to model the nonsexist behavior we wish our students to develop. For example, if we avoid using sexist language such as the generic "he," our students may begin to model this behavior.[102] Since research suggests that the classroom is a "chilly" climate for females, concentrate on creating a climate that will encourage females to communicate. Hall and Sandler[103] make the following recommendations:

1. Pay particular attention to classroom interaction patterns during the first few weeks of class, and make a special effort to draw females into discussion during that time. Participation patterns are likely to be established during this period that often continue throughout the term.

2. Make a specific effort to call directly on females as well as on male students.

3. In addressing the class, use terminology that includes both males and females in the group.

4. Respond to female and to male students in similar ways when they make comparable contributions to class discussion by:
   a. crediting comments to their author ("as Jeanne said . . .")
   b. "coaching" for additional information

5. Intervene in communication patterns among students that may shut out females. For example, if male students pick up on each other's points, but ignore an appropriate comment offered by a female, slow the discussion, and pick up on the comment that has been overlooked.

6. Note patterns of interruption to determine if female students are interrupted more than males—either by yourself or by other students. Make a special effort to ensure that all students have the opportunity to finish their comments.

7. Ask females and males qualitatively similar questions—that is, ask students of both sexes critical as well as factual questions.

8. Give male and female students an equal amount of time to respond after asking a question.

9. Give females and males the same opportunity to ask for and receive detailed instructions about the requirements for an assignment.

10. When talking about occupations or professions in class discussion, use language that does not reinforce limited views of male and female role and career choices.

11. Avoid using the generic "he" whenever possible.

12. Avoid placing professional women in a "special category," for example, "woman (or worse, 'lady') doctor."

13. Make eye contact with females as well as with male students after asking a question to invite a response.

14. Watch for and respond to nonverbal cues that indicate female students' readiness to participate in class, such as leaning forward or making eye contact.

15. Use the same tone in talking with female as with male students (for example, avoid a patronizing or impatient tone when speaking with females, but a tone of interest and attention when talking with males.)

16. Finally, eliminate sexist materials from your curriculum. As Sprague points out:

> As long as teachers rely solely on existing teaching materials and linguistic codes, women will be discouraged from exploring the independent, assertive, forceful aspects of their personalities while men will be discouraged from exploring the tenderness, dependence, and compliance that is part of them as human beings. Women will have trouble considering the role of engineer, senator, or laborer, and men will find it difficult to consider seriously how they might fit into roles such as nurse, partner in home tasks, or elementary teacher. Unless students of both sexes display a variety of individual personality styles and careers, their self-concepts and their human potential will be limited.[104]

## TEACHER EXPECTANCY

With the publication of Rosenthal and Jacobson's *Pygmalion in the Classroom* in 1968, a controversy began about the effect of teachers' expectations on students.[105] Basically the expectancy process works as follows.

1. Teachers expect certain behaviors from certain students.

2. These expectations influence the teacher's behavior towards these students.

3. The teacher's behavior indicates to the students what the teacher expects of them. These expectations affect the student's self-concept, motivation to achieve, and achievement.

4. If the teacher's behavior is consistent over time and the student does not resist it, high expectation students will achieve well and low expectation students will not.

Although much disagreement has been generated over the teacher expectancy issue, the evidence does suggest that teacher expectations can be self-fulfilling. Rosenthal[106] reviews the studies dealing with the Pygmalion effect and indicates that of 242 studies, 84 supported the effect. The proportion of significant results was the same for experimental studies (34 percent) as for field studies (37 percent). Recent studies indicate similar results.[107]

## ACTIVITY 9.11

Formulate two descriptions of two students. One description should describe a student as physically attractive, highly verbal in class, well dressed, and from a high socioeconomic status. The other description should describe a student who is just the opposite. Show both descriptions to ten teachers. Ask the question, "Which of the following would you expect to do well academically and why?" What do the results of this mini-experiment tell you about teacher expectancy?

One of the clearest models of teacher expectancy is one proposed by Braun.[108] Basically, the model suggests that, based on teacher's perceptions of student ability and background (input), expectations are formed (see figure 9.1). These expectations are then communicated to students in various ways (output). Students read and internalize the teacher's output and form a self-expectation. The student's output, based on the self-expectation, produces new input (represented by the dotted line box in the model) and the cycle continues.

Brophy and Good outline several specific methods by which expectations can be communicated.[109]

1. *Waiting less time for lows to answer.* Teachers have been observed to provide more time for high achieving students to respond than for low achieving students. The determinants of this behavior could include excessive sympathy for the student, teacher anxiety, and lack of probing skills, among others. As with the other variables that appear below, the determinants of such behavior are largely unknown.

2. *Staying with the lows in failure situations.* In addition to waiting less time for lows to begin their response, teachers in replicated studies have been found to respond to lows' (more so than highs') incorrect answers by giving them the answer or calling on another student to answer the question. High achieving students in failure situations are much more likely to have the teacher repeat the question, provide a clue, or ask them a new question. Thus, teachers have been found to accept mediocre performance from lows but to work with and demand better performance from highs.

3. *Rewarding inappropriate behavior of lows.* In some studies, teachers have been found to praise marginal or inaccurate student responses. Praising inappropriate substantive responses (as opposed to perseverance, and so on) when the children's peers know the answer may only dramatize the academic weakness of such students.

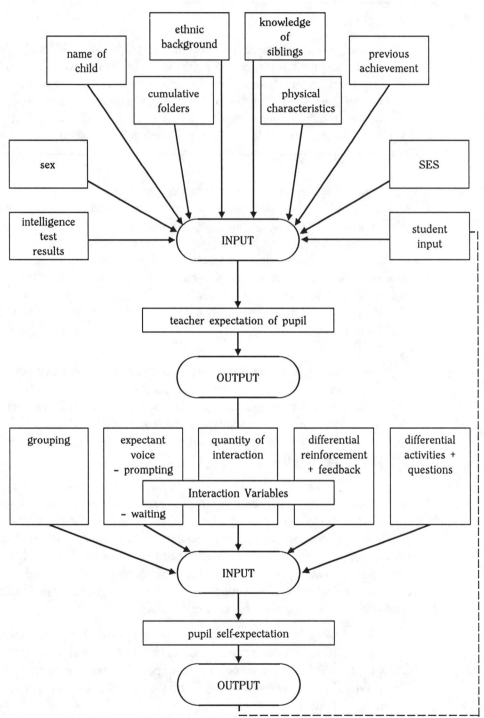

***Figure 9.1** A model of the expectation process.*

4. *Criticizing lows more frequently than highs.* Somewhat at odds with the above findings is that in some studies teachers have been found to criticize lows proportionately more frequently than highs when they provide wrong answers. This is indeed a strong finding, for it suggests that lows' expression of risk-taking behavior and general initiative is being discouraged. One would expect that lows might receive more negative feedback (but not necessarily criticism) simply because they emit more wrong answers. But the analysis alluded to here were controlled for the frequency of wrong answers and found that on a percentage basis, lows were more likely to be criticized than highs. It is possible that the quality of lows' responses may have been lower, but criticism for a serious attempt to respond is an inappropriate strategy in any case. The seeming discrepancy between variables three and four may reside in differing teachers' personalities. Teachers who praise inappropriate answers from lows may be mired in sympathy for these students, whereas hypercritical teachers may be irritated at them for delaying the class and/or providing evidence that the teaching has not been completely successful.

5. *Praising lows less frequently than highs.* Also in contrast to (3) above, some research has shown that when lows provide correct answers, they are less likely to be praised than highs even though they provide fewer correct responses. The situation is clear for lows in certain classes. If they respond, they are more likely to be criticized and less likely to be praised; thus, the safest strategy is to remain silent, because here the teacher is likely to call on someone else.

6. *Not giving feedback to public responses of lows.* Teachers in some studies have been found to respond to lows' answers (especially correct answers) by calling on another student to respond. Failing to confirm their answers seems undesirable in that these students more than other students may be less sure about the adequacy of their response.

7. *Paying less attention to lows.* Studies have shown that teachers attend more closely to highs (and, as we noted above, provide more feedback). Some data exists to suggest that teachers smile more often and maintain greater eye contact with highs than lows. Studies also show that teachers miss many opportunities to reinforce lows simply because they do not attend to their behavior. Such studies provide support for part of Rosenthal and Jacobson's original explanation of the Pygmalion results: positive expectations increase a student's salience and his opportunity for appropriate reinforcement.

8. *Calling on lows less often.* Relatedly, teachers have been found to call on high achieving students more frequently than low achieving students. Although much of the difference can be explained by student differences, the data

show that few teachers compensate for these student differences. The difference in public participation becomes more sharply differentiated with increases in grade level.

9.    *Differing interaction patterns of highs and lows.* Interestingly, contact patterns between teachers and lows are different in elementary and secondary classrooms. In elementary classrooms highs dominate public response opportunities, but highs and lows receive roughly the same number of private teacher contacts. In secondary classrooms highs become even more dominant in public setting, but lows begin to receive more private contacts with the teacher. Perhaps at this level private conferences with teachers are a sign of inadequacy, especially if the teacher does not initiate many private contacts with highs.

10.    *Seating lows farther from the teacher.* Studies have suggested that when students are grouped randomly within classrooms, undesirable discrepancies in teacher behavior between high and low achievers are less likely. Perhaps this is because lows are sitting next to highly salient or "liked" students so that teachers are more likely to notice them and to maximize treatment of them as individual learners. Seating pattern studies have sometimes found that lows tend to be placed away from the teacher (creating a physical barrier). Random placement seems to reduce the physical isolation of lows and the development of sharp status differences among peers.

11.    *Demanding less from lows.* Several studies have suggested that this is a relevant variable. It can be seen as an extension of the more focused "giving up" variable discussed above. This is a broader concept suggesting such activities as giving these students easier tests (and letting the students know it) or simply not asking the student to do academic work. Also, sometimes if a low achieving student masters the elementary aspects of a unit, she may be neglected until the elementary aspects of the next unit are dealt with. Teachers set different mastery levels for students. At times, however, being less demanding may be appropriate if initial low demands are coupled with systematic efforts to improve performance.

In his recent review of the last two decades of research on teacher expectation effects in the classroom, Good substantiates these behaviors and suggests:

> *To the extent that such differentiation exists in a classroom, expectation effects on student achievement are likely to occur both directly through opportunity to learn (differences in the amount and nature of exposure to content and opportunities to engage in various academic activities) and indirectly through differential treatment likely to affect students' self-concepts, attributional inferences, or motivation.*[110]

Should the teacher strive to have only positive expectations? The preceding section may seem to suggest this. However, appropriate expectations, not necessarily high expectations, are what you as a teacher should strive for:

*Expectations should be appropriate rather than necessarily high, and they must be followed up with appropriate behavior. This means planned learning experiences that take students at the level they are now and move them along at a pace they can handle. The pace that will allow continued success and improvement is the correct pace and will vary with different students. Teachers should not feel guilty or feel that they are stigmatizing slower learners by moving them along at a slower pace. As long as students are working up to their potential and progressing at a steady rate, the teacher has reason to be satisfied. There will be cause for criticism only if the slower children are moved along at a slower pace than they can handle because the teacher's expectations for them are too low, are never tested out or re-evaluated, and consequently, are unalterable.*[111]

Certain teacher expectations are recommended for an effective learning experience. Without them, teachers would not be very effective. Listed below are some of these expectations.[112]

1. *The teacher should enjoy teaching.* Teaching brings many rewards and satisfactions, but it is a demanding, exhausting, and sometimes frustrating job. It is hard to do well unless you enjoy doing it. If you enjoy teaching, you'll show this in your classroom behavior.

2. *Teachers should understand that their main responsibility is to teach.* Your job involves many roles besides that of instructing students. Many of these have been discussed in previous chapters. Although these other roles are necessary aspects of your job, they are subordinate to and in support of the major role of teaching—instruction.

3. *Teachers should understand that the crucial aspects of teaching are task presentation, diagnosis, remediation, and enrichment.* Failure to be clear about crucial aspects of teaching characterizes teachers who favor high achievers over low achievers or who pay more attention to answers than to the thinking processes a student goes through in reaching an answer. Such teachers sometimes act as if the students are expected to learn on their own with no help from them. If a student does not catch on immediately after one demonstration or does not do his work correctly after hearing the instructions one time, they react with impatience and frustration.

4. *Teachers need to assess students understanding.* There may be disparity between what teachers think they have communicated and what students actually

heard. Teachers should regularly monitor the work of their students and talk to them about their understanding of classroom instruction. Unfortunately, many teachers become relatively passive during seatwork and deny themselves the opportunity to discover gaps or confusion in student understanding. It is important for teachers to assess the effects of instruction immediately (rather than waiting for an exam), to prevent students from practicing errors and developing misunderstandings.

5.   *Teachers should expect all students to meet at least the minimum specified objectives.* Although all students cannot be reasonably expected to do equally well, reasonable minimal objectives can be established for each of your classes. Naturally, most students will be capable of going considerably beyond minimal objectives, and you should try to stimulate this development as far as their interests and abilities allow. However, remember that remedial work with students who have not yet met minimal objectives should not be delayed in favor of enrichment activities with those who have.

6.   *Teachers should expect students to enjoy learning.* Teachers can and should expect students to enjoy learning activities and communicate this expectation to students. This is one of the most common areas where teacher expectations become self-fulfilling. When you do have the appropriate attitude toward your subject, you present it in ways that make your students see it as enjoyable.

7.   *The teacher should expect to deal with individuals, not groups or stereotypes.* As a rule, you should think, talk, and act in terms of individual students. You may practice grouping or use terms such as slow learner. These practices and labels should be practiced only as a means to meet the needs of individual students and/or to think about ways to teach individuals better. In the final analysis, you are teaching Johnny and Susie, not Group A or "slow learners." The way you talk about your students is an indication of how you think about them and how you'll relate to them.

8.   *The teacher should assume good intentions and a positive self-concept.* Teachers must communicate to their students the expectation that the students want to be, and are trying to be, fair, cooperative, reasonable, and responsible. This includes even those who consistently present the same behavior problems. Your basic faith in the student's ability to change is a necessary (but often not sufficient) condition for such change. If students see that you do not have this faith in them, they will probably lose whatever motivation they have to keep trying.

9.   *The teacher should expect to be obeyed.* Obedience is usually obtained rather easily if you establish fair and appropriate rules, are consistent in what you say, say only what you really mean, and follow up with appropriate action whenever this is necessary. This produces credibility and respect; the students

are clear about what you expect of them and know that they are accountable for meeting these expectations.

---

### ACTIVITY 9.12

Microteach a five-minute lesson. Choose any teaching method you desire. Try to communicate the positive expectations previously outlined. When you're finished microteaching, consider the following:

1. How did you communicate your expectations?
2. Did you feel comfortable communicating these expectations? Why or why not?

---

## STUDENT EXPECTANCIES

Remember that expectancies exist on the part of students, as well as teachers. Students avoid some teachers and flock to others based on their expectations for what a particular teacher's class will be like. The expectancies a student has for a teacher will affect communication in the classroom. Students will communicate more with teachers they expect will be positive in responding. Student expectancies can affect student perceptions of a teacher's messages. If students expect to receive negative feedback, chances are they'll perceive messages from the teacher as negative. If they expect to receive positive messages, they'll perceive the teacher's communication as positive. For example, if a student raises her hand and is not called on, she may perceive the message negatively—"Ms. Miller never calls on me"—if she expects a negative message. If a positive expectation is present, the student could interpret the message, "Ms. Miller wanted to give someone else a chance to talk."

Finally, student expectations can affect learning. Consider how learning might be affected by such expectations as, "You never have to do anything. Just go to class and you'll get an A," or "Mr. Brommel really knows his stuff. You'll learn a lot."

---

### ACTIVITY 9.13

What expectations did you have for this class? From where did these expectations come?

Do you think you communicated these expectations to your teacher? How? What effect did these expectations have on

1. Your perceptions
2. Your learning
3. Your communication
4. Other variables, such as your motivation, satisfaction with the class, where you sat in the class, how much out of classroom contact you had with the teacher, etc.

## CULTURAL DIVERSITY

Although there is a wide diversity of cultural backgrounds in classrooms, most teachers are not trained to deal with multicultural settings. In fact, as Condon[113] argues, the classroom culture is, to a great extent, an extension of mainstream American culture. For example, the values of the classroom are those of mainstream America—independence, competition, individualism, and concern for relevance and application. As a result, students whose backgrounds are different from this dominant culture, such as inner city Blacks, Hispanics, Southeast Asian refugee children, Native Americans, and other ethnic minorities, may have a difficult time adjusting to the classroom culture.

This is true because as Bowman[114] tells us, culture influences both behavior and psychological processes. It affects the way we perceive the world. Culture "forms a prism through which members of a group see the world and create 'shared meanings'."[115]

This creating of shared meanings can be frustrating and fraught with misunderstanding. One way to improve the possibility that communication will be effective is to be sensitive to the "stumbling blocks" to intercultural communication. These have been defined as[116]

1. *Assuming similarity instead of difference.* There seem to be no universals of "human nature" that can be used as a basis for automatic understanding. Each of us is so unconsciously influenced by our own culture that we assume the basic needs, desires, and beliefs of others are the same as our own.

2. *Language.* Even "yes" and "no" cause trouble. When a Japanese hears, "Won't you have some tea?" she listens to the literal meaning of the sentence and answers. "No," meaning she wants some. "Yes, I won't" would be a better reply because this tips off the hostess that there may be a misunderstanding. Also in some cultures, it is polite to refuse the first or second offer of refreshment. Many foreign guests have gone hungry because their U.S. host or hostess never presented the third offer—another case of "no" meaning "yes".[117]

3. *Nonverbal misinterpretations.* When we enter into another culture, we need to be able to hear its "special hum and buzz of implication."[118] When we do not comprehend or misinterpret the nonverbal cues, communication will be ineffective.

4. *Preconceptions and stereotypes.* These reduce the chance for effective communication because they interfere with our ability to objectively view the situation.

5. *Tendency to evaluate.* When we approve or disapprove the actions or statements of another, rather than try to comprehend, effective communication is difficult. We need to remain openminded. Otherwise, communication may be "cut-off" before we really understand the other person.

6. *High anxiety.* Going into new, unfamiliar and/or uncertain situations is difficult for many of us. We become anxious, and as a result, may become defensive. Jack Gibb tells us that defensiveness prevents us from concentrating on the message. In addition:

> *Not only do defensive communicators send off multiple value, motive, and affect cues, but also defensive recipients distort what they receive. As a person becomes more and more defensive, he becomes less and less able to perceive accurately the motives, the values, and the emotions of the sender.*[119]

The cultural differences of our students are important to understand for two major reasons (1) cultural differences may result in differences in learning style and (2) understanding cultural differences can help us communicate more effectively with our students.

Gay[120] indicates that two cognitive patterns are evident from research on ethnic learning styles. The analytic style is detail specific, impersonal, requires sustained attention, and utilizes an elaborate syntactic code. This style seems to be characteristic of Anglo and Jewish Americans. The relational style employs self-centered orientations, determines word meanings by situational contexts, focuses on global characteristics of stimuli, uses a descriptive mode of abstracting information from stimuli, and utilizes a restricted syntactic code. This style seems to be characteristic of Mexican Americans, Asian Americans, Black Americans, and some American Indians.

It would be impossible to outline the cultural characteristics of every ethnic group here. Teachers must identify the groups present in their classrooms and learn about the characteristics of each. In terms of our focus, the communication variables which "are identifiable as culturally determined, as constituting ethnic communication styles, and as being influential in shaping interactions among members of different ethnic groups"[121] are:

attitudes

social organization (status of people within the structure)

patterns of thought

role prescription (how people are supposed to behave)

language

use and organization of space

vocabulary

time conceptualizations

nonverbal expressions

Thus, the above list constitutes the categories of knowledge you will need about a particular ethnic group in order to communicate effectively with that group.

Anderson and Powell,[122] in their article on cultural influences on education processes, review research that highlights intercultural differences. For example, there is virtually no classroom interaction in Vietnamese, Mexican, or Chinese classrooms. In contrast, in an Israeli kibbutz students talk among themselves, address teachers by their first names, and criticize teachers when they feel teachers are wrong.

In Italian classrooms, children greet their teacher with a kiss on both cheeks, and students and teachers touch one another frequently. Black children use back channeling—a vocal response that is meant to encourage or reinforce the speaker ("yeah," "go on," "right on," etc.). Often Anglo-American teachers view this interaction as an interruption rather than a reinforcer. Looking at the teacher is a sign of disrespect in Jamaican and Black African cultures, but a sign of respect in the United States.

While the Anglo-American culture values punctuality and a monochronic view of time, other cultures may not. This can cause problems in the educational process. For example, Hispanic students are not conditioned to use every moment in a productive, task-oriented way. American Indians have a polychronic view of time—things are done when the time is right, not by a time on a clock or a date on a calendar.

In the past decade, considerable research has focused on students' learning styles:[123] Students appear to have preferences for the ways in which they process information (for example, concretely or abstractly) as well as the ways in which they receive information (for example, listening or seeing).

In general, the research supports the conclusions that Hispanic American, Native American, Black, and female students respond better to teaching methods that emphasize holistic thinking, cooperative learning, a valuing of personal knowledge, a concrete orientation, the oral tradition, and a reliance on imagery and expressiveness. This learning style is quite different from most college instructors, Asian Americans, and traditional students whose learning style is characterized by an abstract, independent, written, technical orientation.

Remember that although general statements such as these can be made as a result of this research, careful attention must be given to individual differences so that stereotyping can be avoided.

In order to understand our communication in the culturally diverse classroom, it is necessary to consider:

1. Our expectations for appropriate student behavior. We may, for example, expect students to use Standard English in both speaking and writing.

2. The student's actual behavior. The student may or may not use Standard English.

3. Our feeling about the student's behavior as well as the basis for this feeling. "I'm angry because the student refuses to learn Standard English."

4. Our explanations for the behavior. "The student isn't motivated to learn." These explanations reflect our cultural values.

5. Our response to the student's behavior. We may reprimand the student—either publicly or privately. Again, our response reflects our cultural values and norms.[124]

When we are aware of the cultural differences in our classrooms, understand our attitudes concerning them and the five steps outlined above, we can begin to structure our classroom so that we communicate effectively with multicultural students. We can, for example, respect the ethnic background of our students. We could read stories with varied ethnic and racial content in literature class. We might have students study world events from different cultural perspectives in social studies class. However, multicultural education is not content alone. Your attitude toward culturally different students and how you communicate that attitude is extremely important.[125]

Gail Sorensen suggests that although there is much research in multicultural issues, little of it is helpful in guiding teachers. She shares an example of what she learned from public school teachers in Fresno, California:

*First, never touch Hmong children on the top of the head. This is where the spirits reside and they become angry when touched. Second, allow children to wear strings around their wrists and ankles. Blue string keeps the good spirits in, while red string keeps the evil spirits out. Third, watch for signs of a sore throat and subsequent distress. Many of the Asians treat sore throats by having their children eat sand. Fourth, contact the family if students are absent for prolonged periods. When a member of the family is believed to be dying children may be kept home to protect the ailing person from evil spirits. Fifth, if homework is rarely completed, check on the living conditions at home. Many refugees come here in extended families. No matter what housing arrangements are made, they may be living with more than 10 people in a two bedroom apartment. Additionally, it has been discovered that some refugees have brought in dirt and "gro lights" to raise their own food in one room of the apartment. The school children may have no place to do their work.[126]*

What this example tells us is that teaching in a culturally diverse classroom is not an easy task. Teachers need special training.

In preparing to teach a diverse group, Chism and her associates[127] suggest the following:

1.  Understand nontraditional learning styles
2.  Learn about the history and culture of nontraditional groups
3.  Research the contributions of women and ethnic minorities
4.  Uncover your own biases
5.  Learn about bias in instructional materials
6.  Learn about your school's resources for nontraditional students

Finally, use a variety of teaching methods. Provide opportunities for students to work cooperatively as well as individually. Supplement lectures with audio-visual materials, use discussion, simulation, role-plays, and active, hands-on experiences. Give students choices in how to complete an assignment—a paper, an art project, an oral report.

---

### ACTIVITY 9.14

Read the following example. In a small group, discuss how the teacher could have avoided the problem described.

A teacher in a large city public school scolded a young Puerto Rican boy. "Look at me when I talk to you," shouted the angry teacher. The boy lowered his head even more; his eyes stared at the ground. "Did you hear me?" said the teacher. "Look at me!" The boy shook his head to acknowledge that he did indeed hear the teacher's words, but his head remained down. "You're absolutely impossible," the teacher said in exasperation. Unfortunately, the teacher did not realize that in Puerto Rican culture it is a sign of disrespect for a person to look at the person while being scolded.

---

## STUDENTS WITH SPECIAL NEEDS

No doubt you are aware that you will find all types of students in your classroom. Some may be learning disabled. With mainstreaming mandated by Federal law (Public Law 94-142) some of your students may be handicapped. Space does not allow an in-depth discussion of students with special needs; however, books have been written on each of these categories of students and I have included several references for further reading at the end of this chapter. Following is a brief discussion of each category and some suggestions for teaching students with special needs.

### The Learning Disabled Student

Learning disabled students often have low self-concepts[128] and are less accepted and more overtly rejected than their peers without learning disabilities; they frequently have problems interacting with teachers and parents and have problem behaviors in general. Many youth with learning disabilities exhibit negative verbal interactions and misinterpret nonverbal communications. Furthermore, in adolescence, some youth with learning disabilities are at risk for juvenile delinquency.[129]

In recent years research demonstrates that learning disabled students benefit from interactive settings when cooperative efforts among peers and teachers are encouraged.[130]

Students with a learning disability usually demonstrate a discrepancy between their actual level of performance and intellectual potential. These students have difficulty in processing auditory and visual stimuli, the result of which is a faulty interpretive response. Learning disabilities can occur in the following areas:

*Memory*—inability to remember newly presented information

*Visual-auditory discrimination*—inability to see or hear likenesses and differences

*Visual-auditory association*—inability to associate visual and auditory stimuli

*Perceptual-motor skills*—inability of visual, auditory, tactile, and kinesthetic
channels to interact appropriately with motor activity

*Spatial orientation*—inability to master temporal, spatial, and orientation factors

*Verbal expression*—inability to express ideas, communicate, or request information

*Closure-generalization*—inability to extrapolate beyond an established set of data
or information

*Attending*—inability to attend selectively or focus upon tasks

Generally, learning disabled students need a structured classroom environment. Following are general guidelines for working with the learning disabled student:[131]

1.  Increase attention span by removing distractions, including any materials other than those necessary for the assigned task.
2.  Teach the student how to organize her desk belongings and materials.
3.  Try to improve one behavior at a time, rewarding appropriate behavior, and involving the student in recording behavioral progress. Discuss appropriate ways to expend extra energy.
4.  Carefully structure the learning environment and tasks with specific standards, limits, and rules.
5.  Consistency is an important ingredient—in rules, directions, and the like. Make consequences for rule infractions clear.
6.  Assign one task at a time, at first using a step-by-step procedure. This means short, sequential assignments, with breaks between tasks.
7.  Use a variety of media to present content (films, tapes, printed material, etc.)
8.  Utilize active methods (simulation games, experiments, role playing, etc.) in the instructional strategies.
9.  Employ materials for differing learning patterns (pictures, tapes, concrete objects).

## The Intellectually Gifted Student

Intellectually gifted students often progress academically one and a fourth or more years within one calendar year.[132] Usually gifted students possess some of the following characteristics:

1.  An interest in books and reading
2.  Large vocabularies and ability to express themselves verbally in a mature style
3.  A wide range of interests
4.  A high level of abstract thinking
5.  A curiosity to learn[133]

Instructional materials and programs for the gifted are numerous.[134] In general, the following instructional procedures should prove helpful:

1.  Make use of trade (library) books in the program.
2.  Develop units of work that provide opportunity for in-depth and long-term activities, as well as library research.
3.  Utilize special tables and bulletin boards for interesting and challenging problems, puzzles, worksheets, etc.

4. Use special enrichment materials appropriate to the content areas.

5. Encourage oral and written reports on topics under discussion and related topics.

6. Challenge creative thinking by using games and simulation.

7. Provide opportunity for participation in special clubs or groups designed to challenge gifted students.[135]

In terms of teaching gifted students, several traits of effective teachers of the gifted have been identified.[136] These include building and maintaining interpersonal relationships with students, skill in problem-solving strategies, skill in conducting group discussions, using debate and controversy to involve students in discussion, communicating with children at their level of understanding, and asking questions to elicit higher level cognitive responses.

The voluminous research on gifted and talented youth demonstrates that gifted students need accelerated, challenging instruction in core subject areas that parallel their special aptitudes, opportunities to work with other gifted students, and highly competent teachers.[137]

Although I have focused on the intellectually gifted student, it is important to note that the gifted student may be defined in several ways. Although programs for identified gifted students have generally been limited to well-adjusted, high achieving, well-rounded students, there is an awareness that there are some gifted students who were also emotionally disturbed or learning disabled.[138]

## The Mainstreamed Student

Mainstreaming is the practice of integrating students, who had previously been enrolled in special education classes, into the regular classroom. Prior to these students entering your classroom, an Individualized Educational Program (IEP) must be devised for each disabled pupil.

According to law, each IEP should be made up by a team of specialized personnel, parents, and classroom teachers yearly. It should contain (1) a statement of the pupil's present educational levels, (2) the educational goals for the year, (3) specifications for the services to be provided and to what extent the pupil should be expected to take part in the regular program, and (4) the type, direction, and evaluative criteria for the services to be provided. You should have an active role in the preparation of these specifications for the disabled students assigned to your classes. You will have the major responsibility for carrying out the specifications.

Regardless of the nature of the disability, the following guidelines should prove helpful in dealing with the mainstreamed student:[139]

1.   *Build rapport with the disabled student.* Let the student know you are genuinely interested in seeing that he overcomes her difficulties. A comfortable, relaxed atmosphere also enhances rapport.

2.   *Formulate a plan for alleviating the difficulty as much as possible.* Instruction must be tailored to meet the needs of the individual student. Skills to be taught must relate to the student's learning characteristics and potential. Different approaches will succeed with different students, so you must be flexible in your approaches and familiar with many different approaches.

3.   *Adjust the length of the instructional session to fit the student's attention span.* In fairly long sessions, you will need frequent changes of activities. Repeated drill may be necessary because of slower retention.

4.   *Identify the basic life skills and relate them to subject content.* For example, in mathematics, note skills related to such everyday areas as these: newspaper advertisements; price tags; money values; calendar; road signs; road maps; recipes; timetables; measurement units; thermometers; clocks; sales slips; making change; budgeting money; planning meals; and personal checks.

5.   *The mainstreamed students' interests need to be utilized.* Where a student is interested in a particular topic (hobby, game, sport, or the like), she will tend to put forth a great deal of effort to master a particular concept or skill that relates to the interest.

In a very real sense, all of the groups discussed previously are at-risk. However, for our purposes, the at-risk student is defined as "one who is in danger of failing to complete his or her education with an adequate level of skills."[140] Risk factors include low achievement, behavior problems, poor attendance, retention in grade, low socioeconomic status, and attendance at schools with large numbers of poor students.[141]

According to Slavin and Madden:

> *Each of these factors is closely associated with the dropout rate; and by the time students are in 3rd grade, we can use these factors to predict with remarkable accuracy which students will drop out of school and which will stay to complete their education.*[142]

At-risk students are characterized by:[143]

- Academic difficulties
- Lack of structure (disorganized)
- Inattentiveness

- Distractibility
- Short attention span
- Low self-esteem
- Health problems
- Excessive absenteeism
- Dependence
- Discipline problem
- Narrow range of interest
- Lack of social skills
- Inability to face pressure
- Fear of failure (feels threatened by learning)
- Lack of motivation

Not all of these characteristics need be present for a student to be identified as at-risk.

In their book on at-risk learners, Lehr and Harris[144] identify the necessary skills/competencies necessary to teach at-risk students:

### Personal Skills/Competencies

Teachers of low-achieving students need to be

1. Accepting
2. Caring, concerned, empathetic, loving, respecting, humanistic
3. Enthusiastic and energetic
4. Humorous
5. Patient
6. An effective communicator with students and parents
7. Creative
8. Flexible

### Professional Skills/Competencies

Teachers of low-achieving students need to

1. Be professional (reliable, punctual, dedicated)
2. Utilize resources from other teachers and community

### Materials

Teachers of low-achieving students need to

1. Adapt materials to appropriate levels
2. Develop and utilize manipulatives
3. Utilize a wide range and variety of materials

### Methods

Teachers of low-achieving students need to

1. Possess organizational skills
   - Planning
   - Time Management
   - Record Keeping
2. Set realistic goals and objectives for students (high expectations)
3. Diagnose, prescribe, and evaluate students (formally and informally)
4. Make learning relevant
5. Individualize instruction
6. Utilize small group instruction
7. Utilize a variety of techniques and methods
8. Reteach and give students time to practice the skill or concept—meaningful repetition is essential
9. Know how to teach reading and language arts skills
10. Have a thorough knowledge of all content areas
11. Have training in special education

### Learning Environment

Teachers of low-achieving students need to

1. Be a "cheerleader":
   - Be positive
   - Use motivational strategies
   - Reward
   - Enhance self-concepts
   - Ensure successful experiences
2. Create a warm, inviting learning environment
3. Be firm, consistent, and fair in classroom management
4. Consider the total child (mental, physical, and emotional)

In addition, cooperative learning has been found to improve academic and social skills of students at-risk. Slavin summarizes the effectiveness of cooperative learning:

*The research on cooperative learning methods supports the usefulness of these strategies for improving such diverse outcomes as student achievement at a variety of grade levels and in many subjects, inter-group relations, relations between mainstreamed and normal-progress students, and student self-esteem. Their widespread and growing use demonstrates that in addition to their effectiveness, cooperative learning methods are practical and attractive to teachers. The history of the development, evaluation, and dissemination of cooperative learning is an outstanding example of educational research resulting in directly useful programs that have improved the education experience of thousands of students and will continue to affect thousands more.*[145]

Finally, teachers need to consider how to motivate at-risk students. Brophy[146] outlines thirty-three principles for motivating students (figure 9.2). These are particularly necessary for at-risk students.

***Figure 9.2*** *Highlights of research on strategies for motivating students to learn.*

Research on student motivation to learn indicates promising principles suitable for application in classrooms, summarized here for quick reference.

*Essential Preconditions*

1. Supportive environment
2. Appropriate level of challenge/difficulty
3. Meaningful learning objectives
4. Moderation/optimal use

*Motivating by Maintaining Success Expectations*

5. Program for success
6. Teach goal setting, performance appraisal, and self-reinforcement
7. Help students to recognize linkages between effort and outcome
8. Provide remedial socialization

*Motivating by Supplying Extrinsic Incentives*

9. Offer rewards for good (or improved) performance
10. Structure appropriate competition
11. Call attention to the instrumental value of academic activities

*Motivating by Capitalizing on Students' Intrinsic Motivation*

12. Adapt tasks to students' interests

*(Continued)*

***Figure 9.2*** *Highlights of research on strategies for motivating students to learn. (Continued)*

13.  Include novelty/variety elements
14.  Allow opportunities to make choices or autonomous decisions
15.  Provide opportunities for students to respond actively
16.  Provide immediate feedback to student responses
17.  Allow students to create finished products
18.  Include fantasy or simulation elements
19.  Incorporate game-like features
20.  Include higher-level objectives and divergent questions
21.  Provide opportunities to interact with peers

*Stimulating Student Motivation to Learn*

22.  Model interest in learning and motivation to learn
23.  Communicate desirable expectations and attributions about students' motivation to learn
24.  Minimize students' performance anxiety during learning activities
25.  Project intensity
26.  Project enthusiasm
27.  Induce task interest or appreciation
28.  Induce curiosity or suspense
29.  Induce dissonance or cognitive conflict
30.  Make abstract content more personal, concrete, or familiar
31.  Induce students to generate their own motivation to learn
32.  State learning objectives and provide advance organizers
33.  Model task-related thinking and problem solving

J. E. Brophy, "Synthesis of Research on Strategies for Motivating Students to Learn," *Educational Leadership* 45, no. 2 (October 1987).

## IN SUM

The fewer the barriers to effective communication in your classroom, the greater the chances for effective learning. There are many variables that can be barriers to communication in your classroom. We discussed these in previous chapters—language, meaning, perception, low self-concept. This chapter has focused on seven others—communication apprehension, receiver apprehension, sexism, teacher expectancies, student expectancies, cultural diversity, and the student with special needs.

## NOTES

1. J. C. McCroskey, *Quiet Children and the Classroom Teacher* (Urbana, IL: ERIC Clearinghouse on Reading and Communication Skills, 1977) 7; J. C. McCroskey and J. Daly, (eds.), *Avoiding Communication* (Beverly Hills: Sage, 1984); J. A. Daly, "Communication Apprehension in the College Classroom," *Communicating in College Classrooms*, ed. J. M. Civikly (San Francisco: Jossey-Bass, 1986) 21–32.

2. J. C. McCroskey, "The Problems of Communication Apprehension in the Classroom," *Communication Education* 26 (1977): 27–33.

3. I. R. Shaw, "Speech Fright in the Elementary School: Its Relationship to Speech Ability and Its Possible Implications for Speech Readiness," *Speech Monographs* 34 (1967): 319.

4. See research reviewed by J. Daly, "Communication Apprehension in the Classroom: A Review," Speech Communication Association Convention, Houston, TX, 1976.

5. J. C. McCroskey and T. Leppard, "The Effects of Communication Apprehension on Nonverbal Behavior," Eastern Communication Association Convention, New York, 1975.

6. J. A. Daly and G. Friedrich, "The Development of Communication Apprehension: A Retrospective Analysis of Contributory Correlates," *Communication Quarterly* 29 (1981): 243–255.

7. See research reviewed in Daly and Friedrich, 1981.

8. R. Rosenthal and L. Jacobsen, *Pygmalion in the Classroom* (New York: Holt, Rinehart and Winston, 1968) vii-viii.

9. J. McCroskey, J. Andersen, V. Richmond, and L. Wheeless, "Communication Apprehension of Elementary and Secondary Students and Teachers," *Communication Education* 30 (April 1981): 122–132.

10. Daly and Friedrich, 1981.

11. W. Davey, "Communication Performance and Reticence: A Diagnostic Case Study in the Elementary Classroom," Western States Speech Communication Association Convention, Seattle, 1975.

12. Daly and Friedrich, 1981.

13. McCroskey, Andersen, Richmond, and Wheeless, 122-132.

14. Daly, "Communication Apprehension in the Classroom: A Review," 7; Daly, "Communication Apprehension in the College Classroom."

15. J. C. McCroskey, J. Daly, and G. Sorensen, "Personality Correlates of Communication Apprehensions." Western Speech Association Convention, Seattle, 1975.

16. B. McKinney, "The Effects of Reticence on Group Interaction," *Communication Quarterly* 30 (Spring 1982): 124-128.

17. R. Norton, "Foundations of a Communicator Style Construct," *Human Communication Research* 4 (1978): 99–112.

18. J. R Andersen, "Perceptions of Immediacy and Communicator Styles as Altered by Communication Apprehension Level." Western Speech Communication Association Convention, Los Angeles, 1979.

19. T. Porter, "Communicator Style Perceptions as a Function of Communication Apprehension," *Communication Quarterly* 30 (Summer 1982): 237-244.

20. Daly, "Communication Apprehension in the Classroom: A Review," 10.

21. L. Crowell, A. Ketcher, and S. Miyamoto, "Self-Concept of Communication Skill and Performance in Small Group Discussions," *Speech Monographs* 22 (1955): 20-27.

22. A. Paivo, L. Baldwain, and S. Berger, "Measurement of Children's Sensitivity to Audiences," *Child Development* 32 (1961): 721-730.

23. J. C. McCroskey, D. C. Ralph, and J. E. Barrick, "The Effect of Systematic De-

sensitization on Speech Anxiety," *Speech Teacher* 19 (1970): 32–36.

24. See, for example, J. C. McCroskey and J. Daly, "Teachers' Expectations of the Communication Apprehensive Child in the Elementary School," *Human Communication Research* 3 (1976): 67–72; and J. C. McCroskey and J. F. Andersen, "The Relationship between Communication Apprehension and Academic Achievement among College Students," *Human Communication Research* 3 (1976): 73–81.

25. W. C. Bowers and A. T. Dunathan, "Student Teacher Success Expectancies for Communication-Apprehensive Students." International Communication Association Convention, Chicago, 1978.

26. J. C. McCroskey, J. Daly, and V. Richmond, "Studies of the Relationship between Communication Apprehension and Self-Esteem," *Human Communication Research* 3 (1977): 269–277.

27. J. C. McCroskey and R. McVetta, "Classroom Seating Arrangements: Instructional Communication Theory vs. Student Preferences," *Communication Education* 27 (1978): 99–112; and J. C. McCroskey and M. Sheehan, "Seating Position and Participation: An Alternative Theoretical Explanation." International Communication Association Convention, Portland, OR, 1976.

28. J. C. McCroskey, "Classroom Consequences of Communication Apprehension," Speech Communication Association Convention, Houston, 1976; and J. C. McCroskey and J. R Andersen, "The Relationship between Communication Apprehension and Academic Achievement among College Students," 73–81.

29. H. T. Hurt and R. Preiss, "Silence Isn't Necessarily Golden: Communication Apprehension, Desired Social Choice, and Academic Success Among Middle School Students," *Human Communication Research* 4 (1978): 315–329; and M. Scott and L. Wheeless, "Toward a Reconceptualization of the Relationship between Communication and Learning: A Critical Review." International Communication Association Convention, Chicago, 1978.

30. P. R. Hamilton, "The Effect of Risk Proneness on Small Group Communication Apprehension and Self-Disclosure," thesis, Illinois State U, 1972.

31. See, for example, M. E. Comadena and D. T. Prusank, "Communication Apprehension and Academic Achievement Among Elementary and Middle School Students," *Communication Education* 37 (1988): 270–277; Hurt and Preiss, "Silence Isn't Necessarily Golden," 1978, 315–329; and D. T. Prusank, "Communication Apprehension: A Summary of Research in Elementary Schools," *Journal of Thought* 22 (1987): 38–43.

32. J. C. McCroskey and J. A. Daly, "Teachers Expectations of the Communication Apprehensive Child in the Elementary School," *Human Communication Research* 3 (1976): 67–72; J. C. McCroskey, J. F. Andersen, V. P. Richmond, and L. R. Wheeless, "Communication Apprehension of Elementary and Secondary Students and Teachers," *Communication Education* 30 (1981): 122–132; M. J. Smythe and W. G. Powers, "When Galatea Is Apprehensive: The Effect of Communication Apprehension on Teacher Expectations," *Communication Yearbook 2* (New Brunswick, NJ: Transaction Books, 1978); and A. Watson and E. Monroe, "Academic Achievement: A Study of Relationships of IQ Communication Apprehension, and Teacher Perception," *Communication Reports* 3 (Winter 1990): 28–36.

33. McCroskey, *Quiet Children and the Classroom Teacher*, 12.

34. See, for example, McCroskey, *Quiet Children and the Classroom Teacher*; and T. J. Coates and C. E. Thorenson, *Teacher Anxiety: A Review with Recommendations* (Stanford, CA: Stanford UP, 1974).

35. McCroskey, Andersen, Richmond, and Wheeless, "Communication Apprehen-

sion of Elementary and Secondary Students and Teachers," 130.

36. M. Scott, M. Yates, and L. Wheeless, "An Exploratory Investigation of the Effects of Communication Apprehension in Alternative Systems of Instruction," International Communication Association Convention, Chicago, 1975).

37. M. L. Scott and L. B. Wheeless, "An Exploratory Investigation of Three Types of Communication Apprehension on Student Achievement," *Southern Speech Communication Journal* 42 (1977): 246-255.

38. J. C. McCroskey and J. Andersen, "The Relationship between Communication Apprehension and Academic Achievement among College Students." *Human Communication Research* 3 (1976): 73-81; L. Kelly, "Implementing a Skills Training Program for Reticent Communicators," *Communication Education* 38(2) (April 1989): 85-118; J. Ayres and T. S. Hopf, "Visualization: A Means of Reducing Speech Anxiety," *Communication Education* 34 (1985): 318-323; J. Ayres and T. S. Hopf, "Visualization, Systematic Desensitization, and Rational Emotive Therapy: A Comparative Evaluation," *Communication Education* 36 (1987): 236-240; J. Ayres and T. S. Hopf, "Visualization: Is it More than Extra-Attention?" *Communication Education* 38 (1989): 1-5; and J. Ayres and T. S. Hopf, "The Long-Term Effect of Visualization in the Classroom: A Brief Research Report," *Communication Education* 39 (Jan. 1990): 70-78.

39. See, for example, J. C. McCroskey, D. Ralph, and J. E. Barrack, "The Effects of Systematic Desensitization for Communication Apprehension," *Speech Teacher* 19 (1970): 32-36; J. C. McCroskey, "The Implementation of a Large-Scale Program of Systematic Desensitization for Communication Apprehension," *Speech Teacher* 21 (1972): 255-264; and W.J. Fremouw and M. B. Harmatz, "A Helper Model for Behavioral Treatment of Speech Anxiety," *Journal of Consulting and Clinical Psychology* 43 (1975): 652-

660; K. Harris, "The Sustained Effects of Cognitive Modification and Informed Teachers on Children's Communication Apprehension," *Communication Quarterly* 28 (1980): 47-56; S. Glaser, "Oral Communication Apprehension and Avoidance: The Current Status of Research," *Communication Education* 30 (1981): 321-341; D. Peterson, "Systematic Desensitization as a Model for Dealing with the Reticent Student," *Communication Education* 29 (1980): 229-233; the entire issues of *Communication Education,* 29(3) (1980) and 31(3) (1982); K. Foss, "Overcoming Communication Anxiety," *Improving Speaking and Listening Skills*, ed. R. Rubin (San Francisco: Jossey-Bass, 1983): 25-36.

40. For information on improving classroom climate, see P. Cooper and K. Galvin, *Improving Classroom Communication,* (Washington, D.C.: Dingle Association, 1982).

41. M. Booth-Butterfield, "Stifle or Stimulate? The Effects of Communication Task Structure on Apprehensive and Non-Apprehensive Students," *Communication Education* 35 (October 1986): 337-348.

42. S. Booth-Butterfield, "Instructional Interventions for Reducing Situational Anxiety and Avoidance." *Communication Education* 37 (July 1988): 214-224.

43. M. Beatty, "Situational and Predispositional Correlates of Public Speaking Anxiety," *Communicating Education* 37 (Jan. 1988): 28-39.

44. L. R. Wheeless, "An Investigation of Receiver Apprehension and Social Context Dimensions of Communication Apprehension," *The Speech Teacher* 24 (1975): 261-268; D. Bock and E. H. Block, "The Effects of Positional Stress and Receiver Apprehension on Leniency Errors in Speech Education: A Testing of the Rating Paradigm," *Communication Education* 33 (1984): 338-341; M. Beatty, R. Behnke, and L. Henderson, "An Empirical Validation of the Receiver Apprehension Test as a Measure of Trait Lis-

tening," *Western Journal of Speech Communication* 44 (1980): 132–136; M. Beatty, "Effects of Anticipating Listening (State) Anxiety on the Stability of Receiver Apprehension Scores," *Central States Speech Journal* 36 (1985): 72–76.

45. L. Wheeless and M. D. Scott, "The Nature, Measurement and Potential Efforts of Receiver Apprehension," International Communication Association Convention, Portland, April 1976.

46. M. Beatty and S. Payne, "Receiver Apprehension as a Function of Cognitive Backlog," *Western Journal of Speech Communication* 45 (1981): 275–279.

47. M. Beatty and S. K. Payne, "Receiver Apprehension and Cognitive Complexity," *Western Journal of Speech Communication* 45 (Fall 1981): 363–369.

48. R. Preiss and J. Kerssen, "Receiver Apprehension and Educational Skills: Five Tests of the Limited Cognitive Capacity Hypothesis," SCA Convention, Sacramento, 1990.

49. E. Maccoby and C. Jacklin, *The Psychology of Sex Differences* (Stanford, CA: Stanford U, 1974); M. Guttentog and H. Gray, *Undoing Sex Stereotypes: Research and Resources for Educators* (New York: McGraw-Hill, 1976); M. Sadker and D. Sadker, *Sex Equity Handbook for Schools* (New York: Longman, 1982); J. Stockard, et al., *Sex Equity in Education* (New York: Academic Press, 1980).

50. See research reviewed in C. H. Foxley, *Nonsexist Counseling* (Dubuque, IA: Kendall/Hunt, 1979) 39–100; J. Brophy and T. Good, *Teacher-Student Relationships: Causes and Consequences* (New York: Holt, Rinehart and Winston, 1974) 199–239; M. Mooney Marini and E. Greenberger, "Sex Differences in Educational Aspirations and Expectations," *American Educational Research Journal* 45 (Winter 1978): 67–79.

51. J. Brophy and T. Good, *Teacher-Student Relationships: Causes and Consequences* (New York: Holt, Rinehart and Winston, 1974).

52. D. Gunderson, "Sex Differences in Language and Reading," *Language Arts* 53 (1976): 300–306.

53. Brophy and Good, *Teacher-Student Relationships*, 235.

54. Brophy and Good, 236.

55. R. Hall and B. Sandler, "The Classroom Climate: A Chilly One for Women?" (Washington, D.C.: Project on the Status of Education of Women, Association of American Colleges, 1982) 7–9.

56. See research reviewed in B. Eakins and R. Gene Eakins, *Sex Differences in Human Communication* (Boston: Houghton Mifflin, 1978); and C. Berryman and J. Wilcox, "Attitudes toward Male and Female Speech Experiments on the Effects of Sex-Typical Language," *Western Journal of Speech Communication* 44 (Winter 1980): 50–59; B. Thome and N. Henley, eds., *Language and Sex: Difference and Dominance* (Rowley, MA: Newberry House, 1975); W. Todd-Mancillas, "Masculine Generics—Sexist Language: A Review of Literature and Implications for Speech Communication Professionals," *Communication Quarterly* (Spring 1981): 107–115; V. Wheeless and L. Wheeless, "Language and Female/Male Communication: An Overview," Speech Communication Association Convention, Los Angeles, 1981; J. Bernard, *The Sex Game: Communication between the Sexes* (New York: Antheneum, 1975); M. Isenhart, "An Investigation of the Relationship of Sex and Sex Role to the Ability to Decode Nonverbal Cues," *Human Communication Research* 6 (Summer 1980): 309–318.

57. See research reviewed in L. Stewart, P. Cooper, and S. Friedley, *Communication Between the Sexes*, 2nd ed. (Scottsdale, AZ: Gorsuch-Scarisbrick, 1990); J. C. Pearson, "Communication Between Women and Men," *Bridges Not Walls*, ed. J. Stewart (New York: Random House, 1986) 283–300.

58. R. Norton and B. Montgomery, "Sex Differences and Similarities in Communication Style," *Communication Monographs* 48 (June 1981): 121–132; M. Tal-

ley and V. P. Richmond, "The Relationship between Psychological Gender Orientation and Communicator Style," *Human Communication Research* 6 (Summer 1980): 326-339.

59. S. Bem, "The Measurement of Psychological Androgyny," *Journal of Consulting and Clinical Psychology* 42 (1974): 155-162.

60. V. Wheeless and R. Duran, "Gender Orientation as a Correlate of Communicative Competence," *The Southern Speech Communication Journal* 48 (Fall 1982): 51-64.

61. C. Gilligan, "Seeking to Connect: New Insights and Questions for Teachers," (Cambridge, MA: Harvard Graduate School of Education, 1989).

62. T. Good and R. Slavings, "Male and Female Student Question-Asking Behavior in Elementary and Secondary Mathematics and Language Arts Classes," *Journal of Research in Childhood Education* 3 (1988): 5-23.

63. V. Richmond and J. Gorham, "Language Patterns and Gender Role Orientation Among Students in Grades 3-12," *Communication Education* (1988): 142-150.

64. L. B. Rosenfeld and M. W. Jarrard, "The Effects of Perceived Sexism in Female and Male College Professors on Students' Descriptions of Classroom Climate," *Communication Education* 34 (1985): 205-213.

65. L. B. Rosenfeld and M. W. Jarrard, "Student Coping Mechanisms in Sexist and Nonsexist Professor's Classes," *Communication Education* 35 (1986): 157-162.

66. V. Richmond and P. Dyba, "The Roots of Sexual Stereotyping: The Teacher as Model," *Communication Education* 31 (Oct. 1982): 265-274.

67. L. Weitzman, D. Eifler, E. Hokada, and C. Ross, "Sex-Role Socialization in Picture Books for Preschool Children," *American Journal of Sociology* 77 (1972): 1125-1151.

68. R. Kolbe and J. LaVoie, "Sex-Role Stereotyping in Children's Picture Books," *Social Psychology Quarterly* 44 (1981): 369-374.

69. P. Cooper, "Children's Literature: The Extent of Sexism," *Beyond Boundaries: Sex and Gender Diversity in Education*, ed. C. Lont and S. Friedley (Fairfax, VA: George Mason U, 1989) 233-250.

70. P. Cooper, "Sex Role Stereotypes of Stepparents in Children's Literature," *Communication, Gender and Sex Roles in Diverse Interaction Contexts*, ed. L. Stewart and S. Ting-Toomey (Norwood, NJ: Ablex, 1987).

71. K. Heinz, "An Examination of Sex and Occupational Role Presentations of Female Characters in Children's Picture Books," *Women's Studies in Communication* 11 (1987): 67-78.

72. W. Dougherty and R. Engel, "An 80s Look for Sex Equality in Caldecott Winners and Honor Books," *The Reading Teacher* 40 (1987): 394-398.

73. See research by K. Weiller and C. Higgs reviewed in *Learning 90* (March 1990): 18.

74. L. K. Christian-Smith, "Girls' Romance Novel Reading and What to Do About It," *The New Advocate* 1 (1988): 177-185.

75. M. A. Moffitt, "Understanding the Appeal of the Romance Novel for the Adolescent Girl: A Reader-Response Approach," ICA Convention, Montreal, 1987.

76. Christian-Smith, "Girls' Romance Novel Reading," 180.

77. L. Weitzman and D. Rizzo, "Images of Males and Females in Elementary School Textbooks in Five Subject Areas," *Biased Textbooks* (Washington, D.C.: Resource Center on Sex Roles in Education, National Foundation for the Improvement of Education, 1974).

78. M. deNys and L. Wolfe, "Learning Her Place: Sex Bias in the Elementary Classroom," *Peer Report* 5 (1985): 1-10; Elisha Y. Babad, "Some Correlates of Teachers' Expectancy Bias," *American Educational Research Journal* 22(2) (Summer 1985): 175-183; A. Badini and

R. Rosenthal, "Visual Cues, Student Sex, Material Taught, and the Magnitude of Teacher Expectancy Effects," *Communication Education* 38 (April 1989): 162–167; and J. Dusek, *Teacher Expectancies* (Hillsdale, NJ: Erlbaum, 1985).

79. S. Silvern, "Connecting Classroom Practice and Research," *Journal of Research in Childhood Education* 4 (1989): 69–71; and C. Vaughn-Roberson, G. Thompkins, M. Hitchcock, and M. Oldham, "Sexism in Basal Readers: An Analysis of Male Main Characters," *Journal of Research in Childhood Education* 4 (1989): 62–68.

80. K. Scott, "Effects of Sex-Fair Reading Materials on Pupils' Attitudes, Comprehension and Interest," *American Educational Research Journal* 23 (1986): 105–116.

81. M. Bleakley, V. Westerberg, and K. Hopkins, "The Effect of Character Sex on Story Interest and Comprehension in Children," *American Education Research Journal* 25 (Spring 1988): 145–155.

82. A. Nilsen, "Three Decades of Sexism on School Science Materials," *School Library Journal* (1987): 117–122.

83. "Chem Text Photos Discourage Women," *NEA Today* (Nov. 1989): 33.

84. P. Arlow and M. Froschl, "Women in the High School Curriculum: A Review of U.S. History and English Literature Texts," *High School Feminist Studies*, ed. C. Ahlum, J. Fralley, and F. Howe (Old Westbury, NY: 1976).

85. D. Kirby and N. Julian, "Treatment of Women in High School U.S. History Textbooks," *Social Studies* 72 (1981): 203–207.

86. Both studies are cited in Arlow and Froschl, "Women in the High School Curriculum."

87. See research cited in Foxley, "Nonsexist Counseling; Sex Equity in Education," Stockard, et al.; J. Brooks-Gunn and W. J. Matthews, *He and She: How Children Develop Their Sex-Role Identity* (Englewood Cliffs, NJ: Prentice Hall, 1979); and D. Spender, *Invisible Women* (London: Writers and Readers, 1982); Stewart et al., *Communication Between the Sexes.*

88. M. Allen, "Making Knowledge Legitimate: Power, Profit, and the Textbook," *Current Thought on Curriculum* (Alexandria, VA: Association for Supervision and Curriculum Development, 1985) 73–90.

89. A. Bandura, *Psychological Modeling: Conflicting Theories* (Chicago: Aldine-Atherton, 1971); V. Flerx, D. Fidler, and P. Roger, "Sex-Role Stereotypes: Developmental Aspects and Early Intervention," *Child Development* 47 (1976): 998–1007; L. Weitzman, *Sex-Role Socialization* (Palo Alto, CA: Mayfield, 1979); Scott, Foresman, *Improving the Image of Women in Textbooks* (Glenview, IL: Scott, Foresman, 1974); L. T. Arthur and S. Eisen, "Achievement of Male and Female Storybook Characters as Determinants of Achievement Behavior of Boys and Girls," *Journal of Personality and Social Psychology* 33 (1976): 467–473.

90. J. Bohan, "Age and Sex Differences in Self-Concept," *Adolescence* (Fall 1973): 115–119. See also Stockard, et al., *Sex Equity in Education.*

91. A. Petersen, "Those Gangly Years," *Psychology Today* (Sept. 1987): 28–34.

92. C. Gilligan, N. Lyons, and T. Hammer, *Making Connections* (New York: Troy, 1989).

93. P. Campbell, "Adolescent Intellectual Decline," *Adolescence* 11 (Winter 1976): 20–25; See also Stockard, et al., *Sex Equity in Education*; and J. Pearson, *Gender and Communication* (Dubuque, IA: Wm. C. Brown, 1985).

94. C. M. Jacko, "Classroom Teachers and Sex-Role Stereotyping," *Journal of Instructional Psychology* 7 (Spring 1980): 201–207; H. G. Levine and K. Mann, "The Nature and Functions of Teacher Talk in a Classroom for Mentally Retarded Learners," *The Elementary School Journal* 86(2) (1985: The U of Chicago): 185–190; J. D. Hawkins, H. J. Doueck, and D. M. Lishner, "Changing Teaching

Practices in Mainstream Classrooms to Improve Bonding and Behavior of Low Achievers," *American Educational Research Journal* 25(1) (Spring 1988): 31–50; M. P. Brady, R. D. Taylor, and R. Hamilton, "Differential Measures of Teachers' Questioning in Mainstreamed Classes: Individual and Classwide Patterns," *Journal of Research and Development in Education* 22(4) (Summer 1989): 400–408; J. Crawford, "Teaching Effectiveness in Chapter 1 Classrooms," *The Elementary School Journal* 90(1) (1989): 210–214; and M. P. Brady, P. R. Swank, R. D. Taylor, and H. J. Freiberg, "Teacher-Student Interactions in Middle School Mainstreamed Classes: Differences with Special and Regular Education Students," *Journal of Educational Research* 81 (July/Aug. 1980): 332–340.

95. J. Earle, V. Roach, and K. Fraser, *Female Dropouts: A New Perspective*. (Alexandria, VA: National Association of State Boards of Education, 1987).

96. B. Licht, S. Stader, and C. Swenson, "Children's Achievement-Related Beliefs: Effects of Academic Area, Sex, and Achievement Level," *Journal of Educational Research* 82 (1989): 253.

97. D. Goleman, "Girls and Math: Is Biology Really Destiny?" *New York Times Educational Life* 2 (Aug. 1987): 42–46.

98. C. H. Foxley, *Nonsexist Counseling* (Dubuque: Kendall/Hunt, 1979); and C. H. Foxley, "Sex Equity in Education: Some Gains, Problems, and Future Needs," *Journal of Teacher Education* 33 (1982): 6–9.

99. S. L. Bem, "The Measurement of Psychological Androgyny," *Journal of Counseling and Clinical Psychology* 42 (1974): 155–162; Goleman, "Girls and Math."

100. D. Carmody, "SATs Are Biased Against Girls, Report by Advocacy Group Says," *The New York Times* 17 Apr. 1987; B2.

101. U.S. Dept of Labor, "Jobs for the Future," (Washington, D.C.: U.S. Government Printing Office, 1988).

102. Richmond and Dyba, "The Roots of Sexual Stereotyping"; A. Flanagan and W. Todd-Mancillas, "Teaching Inclusive Pronoun Usage: The Effectiveness of an Authority Innovation-Decision Approach versus an Optional Innovation-Decision Approach," *Communication Education* 31 (Oct. 1982): 275–284.

103. Hall and Sandler, "The Classroom Climate," 16.

104. J. Sprague, "The Reduction of Sexism in Speech Communication Education," *Speech Teacher* 24 (Jan. 1975): 41.

105. L. Rosenthal and L. Jacobson, *Pygmalion in the Classroom* (New York: Holt, Rinehart and Winston), 1968.

106. R. Rosenthal, "The Pygmalion Effect Lives," *Psychology Today* (Sept. 1973): 56–63.

107. H. Cooper, "Pygmalion Grows Up: A Model for Teacher Expectation Communication and Performance Influence," *Review of Educational Research* 49 (Summer 1979): 396; H. Cooper and D. Y. H. Tom, "Teacher Expectation Research: A Review with Implications for Classroom Instruction," *The Elementary School Journal* 85 (1984): 77–89.

108. C. Braun, "Teacher Expectation: Sociopsychological Dynamics," *Review of Educational Research* 46 (1976): 206.

109. Brophy and Good, *Teacher-Student Relationships: Causes and Consequences*, 330–333.; T. Good and J. Brophy, *Looking in Classrooms*, 4th ed. (New York: Harper and Row, 1987).

110. T. L. Good, "Two Decades of Research on Teacher Expectations: Findings and Future Directions," *Journal of Teacher Education* 37 (1987): 37.

111. Good and Brophy, *Looking in Classrooms*, 128–134.

112. Adapted from Good and Brophy, 147–152.

113. J. Condon, "The Ethnocentric Classroom" *Communicating in College Classrooms*, ed. J. M. Civikly (San Francisco: Jossey-Bass, 1986): 11–20.

114. B. Bowman, "Educating Language-Minority Children: Challenges and Oppor-

tunities," *Phi Delta Kappan* (Oct. 1989): 118–120.

115. Bowman, 118.

116. L. Barna, "Stumbling Blocks in Intercultural Communication," *Intercultural Communication: A Reader*, ed. L. Samovar and R. Porter (Belmont, CA: Wadsworth, 1988) 322–330.

117. Barna, 326.

118. C. Frankel, "The Neglected Aspect of Foreign Affairs," (Washington, D.C.: Brookings Institute, 1965) 103.

119. J. Gibb, "Defensive Communication," *Journal of Communication* 2 (Sept. 1961): 141–148.

120. G. Gay, "Viewing the Pluralistic Classroom as a Cultural Microcosm" *Educational Research Quarterly* 2 (Winter 1978): 52.

121. Gay, 52.

122. J. Anderson and R. Powell, "Cultural Influences on Educational Processes," *Intercultural Communication: A Reader*, ed. L. Samovar and R. Porter (Belmont, CA: Wadsworth, 1988) 207–214.

123. See research reviewed in P. Kuriowa, "The 'Invisible' Students," *Momentum* 63 (1975): 34–36; M. Belenky and others, *Women's Ways of Knowing: The Development of Self, Voice and Mind.* (New York: Basic Books, 1987); A. G. Hilliard, "Teachers and Cultural Styles in a Pluralistic Society," *NEA Today* Washington, D.C.: National Education Association, 1989. J. A. Banks, *Multiethnic Education: Theory and Practice.* (Newton, MA: Allyn & Bacon, 1988); G. Pemberton, *On Teaching the Minority Student: Problems and Strategies.* (Brunswick, ME: Bowdoin College, 1988); and J. A. Anderson, "Cognitive Studies and Multicultural Populations," *Journal of Teacher Education* 39(1) (1988): 2–9.

124. Adapted from Condon, "The Ethnocentric Classroom," 12.

125. For specific suggestions see Christine Bennett, "Teaching Students as They Would Be Taught: The Importance of

the Cultural Perspective," *Educational Leadership* (1979): 260–268.

126. G. Sorensen, "Teaching Teachers from East to West: A Look at Common Myths," *Communication Education* 38 (Oct. 1989): 331–332.

127. N. Van Note Chism, J. Cano, and A. Pruitt, "Teaching in a Diverse Environment: Knowledge and Skills Needed by TAs," *Teaching Assistant Training in the 1990s, New Directions for Teaching and Learning*, no. 39, ed. J. Nyquist, R. Abbott, and D. Wulff (San Francisco: Jossey-Bass, 1989) 23–35.

128. J. Chapman, "Learning Disabled Children's Self-Concepts," *Review of Educational Research* 58 (Fall 1988): 347–371.

129. See research reviewed in C. Trapani and M. Gettinger, "Effects of Social Skills Training and Cross-Age Tutoring on Academic Achievement and Social Behaviors of Boys with Learning Disabilities," *Journal of Research and Development in Education* 22 (1989): 321.

130. See for example, E. Reyes, M. Gallego, G. Duran, and D. Scanlon, "Integration of Internal Concepts and External Factors: Extending the Knowledge of Learning Disabled Adolescents," *Journal of Early Adolescence* 9 (1989): 112–124; C. Giles and M. Van Dover, "The Power of Collaboration," *Focus on Collaborative Learning*, ed. J. Golub (Urbana, IL: National Council of Teachers of English, 1988) 29–34.

131. B. Roe, E. Ross, and P. Bums, *Student Teaching and Field Experiences Handbook* (Columbus, OH: Charles E. Merrill, 1984) 187–188.

132. Roe, et al., 182.

133. Roe, et al., 182–183.

134. See descriptions and resources in E. P. Torrance, "Teaching Creative and Gifted Learners," *Handbook of Research on Teaching*, ed. M. C. Wittock (New York: Macmillan, 1986) 630–647.

135. Roe, et al. *Student Teaching and Field Experiences*, 183.

136. See research reviewed in C. Martin-White and A. Staton-Spicer, "Instructional Communication in the Elementary Gifted Classroom," *Communication Education* 36 (1987): 259-271.

137. J. Feldhusen, "Synthesis of Research on Gifted Youth," *Educational Leadership* (March 1989): 6-11.

138. Torrance, "Teaching Creative and Gifted Learners," 630-647.

139. Roe, et. al. *Student Teaching and Field Experiences*, 197-198.

140. R. Slavin and W. Madden, "What Works for Students at Risk: A Research Synthesis," *Educational Leadership* (Feb. 1989): 4.

141. R. Slavin, "Students at Risk for School Failure: The Problem and Its Dimensions," *Effective Programs for Students at Risk*, ed. R. Slavin, N. Karweit, and N. Madden. (Needham Heights, MA: Allyn and Bacon, 1989).

142. Slavin and Madden, "What Works for Students at Risk," 4.

143. J. Lehr and H. Harris, *At-Risk, Low Achieving Students in the Classroom* (Washington, D.C.: National Education Association 1988) 11.

144. Lehr and Harris, 56-61.

145. R. Slavin, *Using Student Team Learning*, 3rd ed. (Baltimore: Johns Hopkins U, 1986) 126.

146. J. Brophy, "Synthesis of Research on Strategies for Motivating Students to Learn," *Educational Leadership* 45 (Oct. 1987): 4-13.

## SUGGESTIONS FOR FURTHER READING

Acker, S., ed. *Teachers, Gender and Careers*. Bristol, UK: Falmer, 1989.

Allen, M., J. E. Hunter, and W. A. Donohue. "Meta-Analysis of Self-Report Data on the Effectiveness of Public Speaking Anxiety Treatment Techniques." *Communication Education* 38 (Jan. 1989): 54-77.

Behnke, R. R., C. R. Sawyer, and P. E. King. "The Communication of Public Speaking Anxiety." *Communication Education* 36 (April 1987): 138-142.

Booth-Butterfield, M., and F. Jordan. "Communication Adaptation among Racially Homogeneous and Heterogeneous Groups." *Southern Communication Journal* 54 (1989): 213-234.

Borisoff, D., and L. Merrill. *The Power to Communicate*. Prospect Heights, IL: Waveland, 1985.

Bowers, J. W., and Members of 36C:099, "Classroom Communication Apprehension: A Survey." *Communication Education* 35 (Oct. 1986): 372-378.

Burgoon, J., M. Pfau, T. Birt, and V. Manusou. "Nonverbal Communication Performance and Perceptions Associated with Reticence: Replications and Classroom Implications." *Communication Education* 36 (April 1987): 119-131.

Buriel, R., and D. Cardoza. "Sociocultural Correlates of Achievement Among Three Generations of Mexican American High School Seniors." *American Educational Research Journal* 25(2) (Summer 1988): 177-192.

Burke, P. "Gender, Identity, Sex and School Performance." *Social Psychology Quarterly* 52 (1989): 159-169.

Burstein, N. D., and B. Cabello. "Preparing Teachers to Work with Culturally Diverse Students: A Teacher Education Model." *Journal of Teacher Education* (Sept.-Oct. 1989): 9.

Calabrese, R., and L. Wallich. "Attribution: The Male Rationale for Denying Women Access into School Administration." *The High School Journal* 72 (1989): 105–110.

Carelli, A., ed. *Sex Equity in Education: Readings and Strategies*. Springfield, IL: Charles C Thomas, 1986.

Chapman, A. *The Difference It Makes: A Resource on Gender for Educators*. Boston: National Association of Independent Schools, 1986.

Clark, A. J. "Communication Confidence and Listening Competence: An Investigation of the Relationships of Willingness to Communicate, Communication Apprehension, and Receiver Apprehension to Comprehension of Content and Emotional Meaning in Spoken Messages." *Communication Education* 38 (July 1989): 237–249.

Cole, D. A., T. Vandercook, and J. Rynders. "Comparison of Two Peer Interaction Programs: Children With and Without Severe Disabilities." *American Educational Research Journal* 25(3) (Fall 1988): 415–439.

Collier, M. J. "A Comparison of Conversations Among and Between Domestic Culture Groups: How Intra and Intercultural Competencies Vary." *Communication Quarterly* 36 (1988): 122–144.

Condon, J. "'. . . So Near the United States': Notes on Communication between Mexicans and North Americans." *Intercultural Communication: A Reader*. 5th ed. Ed. L. A. Samovar and R. E. Porter. Belmont, CA: Wadsworth, 1988.

Cristensen, C. A., M. M. Gerber, and R. B. Everhart. "Toward a Sociological Perspective on Learning Disabilities." *Educational Theory* 36(4) (Fall 1986): 317–332.

"Dealing with Diversity: At-Risk Students." Special issue of *Educational Leadership* 46 (Feb. 1989).

Firestone, W. "Beyond Order and Expectations in High Schools Serving At-Risk Students." *Educational Leadership* 46 (1989): 41–45.

Forman, A., and G. Pressley. "Ethnic Culture and Corporate Culture: Using Black Styles in Organizations." *Communication Quarterly* 35 (Fall 1987): 293–307.

Forness, S., and K. Kavale. "Effects of Class Size on Attention, Communication and Disruption of Mildly Retarded Children." *American Educational Research Journal* 22 (Fall 1985): 403–412.

Frymier, J., and B. Gansneder. "The Phi Delta Kappa Study of Students At-Risk." *Phi Delta Kappan* (Oct. 1989): 142–145.

Fuchs, D., and L. S. Fuchs. "Bias in the Assessment of Handicapped Children." *American Educational Research Journal* 22(2) (Summer 1985): 185–198.

Gallegos, E. M. "Beyond *Board of Education v. Rowley*: Educational Benefit for the Handicapped?" *American Journal of Education* 1989: 258–288.

Gannon, S. R., and R. A. Thompson. "Cross-Culturalism in Children's Literature: Proceedings and Selected Papers from the 1987 International Conference of the Children's Literature Association." New York: Pace University, 1987.

Garrison, J. P., and K. R. Garrison. "Measurement of Oral Communication Apprehension Among Children: A Factor in the Development of Basic Speech Skills." *Communication Education* 28 (1979) 119–128.

"The Gender Card: How It's Played in Education." *New York Times: Education Life*, 6 Aug. 1989, 4A.

Grant, C. A. "The Persistent Significance of Race in Schooling." *The Elementary School Journal* 88(5) (1988): 561–572.

Grant, C., and C. Sleeter. "Race, Class, and Gender in Education Research: An Argument for Integrative Analysis." *Review of Educational Research* 56 (Summer 1986): 195–211.

Grauerholz, E., and B. Pescosolido. "Gender Representation in Children's Literature: 1900–1984." *Gender and Society* 3 (March 1989): 113–126.

Greer, R., and W. Husk. *Recruiting Minorities into Teaching*. Fastback 290. Bloomington, IN: Phi Delta Kappa, 1989.

Haberman, M. *Preparing Teachers for Urban Schools*. Fastback 267. Bloomington, IN: Phi Delta Kappa, 1988.

Hamby, J. "How to Get an 'A' on Your Dropout Prevention Report Card." *Educational Leadership* 46 (1989): 21–25.

Hecht, M., S. Ribeau, and J. K. Alberts. "An Afro-American Perspective on Interethnic Communication." *Communication Monographs* 56 (1989): 385–410.

Heslep, R. D. "Education in PL94-142." *Journal of Research and Development in Education* 22(4) (Summer 1989): 1–13.

Johnson, R., and G. Shulman. "Gender-Role Composition and Role Enactment in Decision Making Groups." *Gender and Society* 3 (Sept. 1989): 355–372.

Johnson, S., and V. Johnson. *Motivating Minority Students*. Springfield, IL: Charles C Thomas, 1988.

Keller, C. *Learning Disabilities*. Washington, D.C.: NEA, 1987.

Klein, S. "Sex Education and Gender Equity." *Educational Leadership* (March 1988): 69–74.

Kochman, T. "Black Style in Communication." *Intercultural Communication: A Reader*. 5th ed. Ed. L. A. Samovar and R. E. Porter. Belmont, CA: Wadsworth Publishing, 1988. 130–138.

Kounin, J. *Discipline and Group Management in Classrooms*. New York: Holt, Rinehart and Winston, 1970.

Kreidler, W. *Creative Conflict Resolution*. Glenview, IL: Scott, Foresman, 1984.

LaFrance, M. "The School of Hard Knocks: Nonverbal Sexism in the Classroom." *Theory into Practice* 24(1) (1985): 40–44.

Levine, H., and K. Mann. "The Nature and Functions of Teacher Talk in a Classroom for Mentally Retarded Learners." *The Elementary School Journal* 86 (Nov. 1985): 185–198.

Levine, T. R., and J. C. McCroskey. "Measuring Trait Communication Apprehension: A Test of Rival Measurement Models of the PRCA-24." *Communication Monographs* 57(1) (March 1990): 62–73.

Levy, G. D., and D. B. Carter. "Gender Schema, Gender Constancy, and Gender Role Knowledge: The Roll of Cognitive Factors in Preschoolers' Gender-Role Stereotype Attributions." *Developmental Psychology* 25 (1989): 444–449.

McCroskey, J. C. "The Communication Apprehensive Perspective." *Avoiding Communication*. Ed. J. A. Daly and J. C. McCroskey. Beverly Hills, CA: Sage, 1984. 13–38.

McCroskey, J. C., and M. J. Beatty. "Oral Communication Apprehension." *Shyness: Perspectives on Research and Treatment*. Ed. W. H. Jones, J. M. Cheek, and S. R. Briggs. New York: Plenum Press, 1986. 279–293.

McCroskey, J. C., S. Booth-Butterfield, and S. K. Payne. "The Impact of Communication Apprehension on College Student Retention and Success." *Communication Quarterly* 37 (1989): 100–107.

McCroskey, J. C., and L. L. McCroskey. "Self-Report as an Approach to Measuring Communication Competence." *Communication Education* 5(2) 1988: 108–113.

Maher, F., and C. Rathbone. "Teacher Education and Feminist Theory: Some Implications for Practice." *American Journal of Education* (1986): 214–235.

Mannix, D. *Oral Language Activities for Special Children*. West Nyack, NY: Center for Applied Research in Communication, 1990.

Margolis, H., and E. Schwartz. "Facilitating Mainstreaming through Cooperative Learning." *The High School Journal* 72 (1989): 83–88.

Marsh, H., J. Parker, and J. Barnes. "Multidimensional Adolescent Self Concepts: Their Relationship to Age, Sex, and Academic Measures." *American Educational Research Journal* 22 (Fall 1985): 422–444.

Martin, C. L. "Children's Use of Gender-Related Information in Making Social Judgements." *Developmental Psychology* 25 (1989): 80–88.

Miller, M. D. "The Relationship of Communication Reticence and Negative Expectations." *Communication Education* 36 (July 1987): 228–236.

Miller, S. E., G. Leinhardt, and N. Zigmond. "Influencing Engagement Through Accommodation: An Ethnographic Study of At-Risk Students." *American Educational Research Journal* 25(4) (Winter 1988): 465–487.

Neer, M. "The Development of an Instrument to Measure Classroom Apprehension." *Communication Education* 36 (April 1987): 154–167.

Olneck, M. R. "The Recurring Dream: Symbolism and Ideology in Intercultural and Multicultural Education." *American Journal of Education* 98(2) (Feb. 1990): 117–175.

O'Reilly, P., and K. Borman. "Sexism and Sex Discrimination in Education." *Theory into Practice* 24(1) (1985): 110–116.

Orfield, G. "Hispanic Education: Challenges, Research, and Policies." *American Journal of Education* 95(1) (Nov. 1986): 1–26.

Osborne, S. "Effects of Teacher Experience and Selected Temperament Variables on Coping Strategies Used with Distractible Children." *American Educational Research Journal* 22 (Spring 1985): 79–86.

Pagano, J. A. "Teaching Women." *Educational Theory* 38 (Summer 1988): 321–342.

Pearson, C., D. Shavlik, and J. Touchton. *Educating the Majority: Women Challenge Tradition in Higher Education.* Washington, D.C.: American Council on Education and Macmillan, 1989.

Pearson, J. *Gender and Communication.* Dubuque, IA: Wm. C. Brown, 1985.

Pelias, M. H. "Communication Apprehension in Basic Public Speaking Texts: An Examination of Contemporary Textbooks." *Communication Education* 38(1) (Jan. 1989): 41–54.

Pelias, M., and R. Pelias. "Communication Apprehension in the Basic Course in Performance of Literature." *Communication Education* 37 (April 1988): 118–126.

Phinney, J. S. "Stages of Ethnic Identity Development in Minority Group Adolescents." *Journal of Early Adolescence* 9(1–2) (May 1989) 34–49.

Pingree, S., R. Hawkins, M. Butler, and W. Paisley. "A Scale for Sexism." *Journal of Communication* 26 (Autumn 1976): 193–200.

Pogrow, S. "Challenging At-Risk Students: Findings from the HOTS Program." *Phi Delta Kappan* (Jan. 1990): 389–399.

Presseisen, B. Z., ed. *At-Risk Students and Thinking Perspectives from Research.* West Haven, CT: National Education Association Professional Library, 1989.

Pritchard, R. J. "Special Students in Regular Secondary Classes: Selected Annotated Bibliography." *Journal of Teacher Education* 35 (March/April 1984): 51–54.

Proctor, C. P. "Teacher Expectations: A Model for School Improvement." *The Elementary School Journal* 84 (March 1984): 469–481.

Randall, P. "Sexist Language and Speech Communication Texts: Another Case of Benign Neglect." *Communication Education* 34 (1985): 128–134.

Rendon, L., and M. Taylor. "Hispanic Students: Action for Access." *AACJC Journal* (Dec./Jan. 1989/90): 18–23.

Reynolds, M. "Students with Special Needs." *Knowledge Base for the Beginning Teacher.* Ed. M. Reynolds. New York: Pergamon Press, 1989, 129–142.

Richmond, V. P., and J. C. McCroskey. *Communication: Apprehension, Avoidance, and Effectiveness.* Scottsdale, AZ: Gorsuch Scarisbrick, Publishers, 1985.

Riddell, S. "Pupils, Resistance and Gender Codes: A Study of Classroom Encounters." *Gender and Education* 1 (1989): 183–198.

Rolison, M., and F. Medway. "Teachers' Expectations and Attributions for Student Achievement: Effects of Label, Performance Pattern, and Special Education Intervention." *American Educational Research Journal* 22 (Winter 1985): 561–574.

Rosenfeld, L., and M. Jarrard. "Student Coping Mechanisms in Sexist and Nonsexist Professors' Classes." *Communication Education* 35 (April 1986): 157–162.

Roy, P., and M. Schen. "Feminist Pedagogy: Transforming the High School Classroom." *Women's Studies Quarterly* XV (Fall/Winter 1987): 110–115.

Ruben, B. D. "Human Communication and Cross-Cultural Effectiveness." *Intercultural Communication: A Reader.* Ed. L. Samovar and R. Porter. Belmont, CA: Wadsworth, 1988. 331–338.

Schorr, E. *Within Our Reach: Breaking the Cycle of Disadvantage.* New York: Anchor Press/Doubleday, 1988.

Scott, K. "Effects of Sex-Fair Reading Material on Pupils' Attitudes, Comprehension, and Interest." *American Educational Research Journal* 23 (Spring 1986): 105–116.

Shade, B. "Afro-American Cognitive Style: A Variable in School Success." *Review of Educational Research* 52 (Summer 1982): 219–245.

Shepard, L., M. L. Smith, and C. Vojir. "Characteristics of Pupils Identified as Learning Disabled." *American Educational Research Journal* 20 (Fall 1983): 309–331.

Simpson, A., and M. Erickson. "Teachers' Verbal and Nonverbal Communication Patterns as a Function of Teacher Race, Student Gender, and Student Race." *American Educational Research Journal* 20 (Summer 1983): 183–198.

Slavin, R. E. *Cooperative Learning.* New York: Longman, 1983.

———"Cooperative Learning and the Cooperative School." *Educational Leadership* (Nov. 1987): 7–13.

———"Cooperative Learning: Where Behavioral and Humanistic Approaches to Classroom Motivation Meet." *Elementary School Journal* 88 (1988): 29–38.

Sleeter, C., and C. Grant. *Making Choices for Multicultural Education.* Columbus, OH: Merrill Publishing, 1988.

Soldier, L. "Cooperative Learning and the Native American Student." *Phi Delta Kappan* (1989): 161–164.

"Special Report on the Education of Native Americans." *Education Week,* August 2, 1989.

Stadulis, J. "A Synthesis of Twenty-Five Years of Research on Black English and Its Effect in the Classroom." Speech Communication Association Convention, San Francisco, Nov. 1989.

Staley, C., and J. Cohen. "Communication Style and Social Style: Similarities and Differences Between the Sexes." *Communication Quarterly* 36 (Summer 1988): 192–202.

Strahan, D. "Life on the Margins: How Academically At-Risk Early Adolescents View Themselves and School." *Journal of Early Adolescence* 8(4) (1988): 373–390.

Tanner, C. K. "Probable Impacts of Education Policy on At-Risk Students." *Journal of Research and Development in Education* 22(2) (Winter 1989): 319.

Ting-Toomey, S. "Rhetorical Sensitivity Style in Three Cultures: France, Japan, and the United States." *The Central States Speech Journal* 39(1) (Spring 1988): 28–37.

Trujillo, C. M. "A Comparative Examination of Classroom Interactions Between Professors and Minority and Non-Minority College Students." *American Educational Research Journal* 23(4) (Winter 1986): 629–643.

Valentine, C., and N. Hoar, eds. "Women and Communicative Power: Theory, Research and Practice." Annandale, VA: SCA, 1988.

Viadero, D. "Minorities' Aspirations Found High in Early Grades." *Education Week* 5 (March 1, 1989), 17.

Wallace, C., and Y. Goodman. "Research Currents: Language and Literacy Development of Multilingual Learners." *Language Arts* 66(5) (Sept. 1989): 542–546.

Waxman, H. C. "Urban Black and Hispanic Elementary School Students' Perceptions of Classroom Instruction." *Journal of Research and Development in Education* 22(2) (Winter 1989): 57–62.

Wilkenson, L., and C. Merrett, eds. *Gender Influence in Classroom Interactions.* Orlando, FL: Academic Press, 1985.

Wood, J., and J. Seyforth. "A Study of Teacher Inservice Training and Changing Teacher Attitudes toward Handicapped Children." *Action in Teacher Education* 7 (Fall 1985): 65–72.

Ysseldyke, J. E., M. L. Thurlow, S. L. Christenson, and R. McVicar. "Instructional Grouping Arrangements Used with Mentally Retarded, Learning Disabled, Emotionally Disturbed, and Nonhandicapped Elementary Students." *Journal of Educational Research* 81(5) (May/June 1988): 305–311.

# 10  SYSTEMATIC OBSERVATION

## OBJECTIVES

After reading this chapter and completing the activities, you should be able to:

- Understand the complexity of teacher assessment
- Define systematic observation
- List the effects of the use of systematic observation on teacher behavior
- Distinguish between expert-prepared and teacher-prepared instruments
- Analyze your teaching using a systematic observation system

## INTRODUCTION

*Teaching is more than acquiring a repertoire of teaching techniques . . . . This does not negate the importance of helping potential teachers acquire a repertoire of teaching skills. This is obviously necessary—but not sufficient. Teachers must learn to discern the state of a classroom or pupil at a given point during an educational interchange. They must select the teaching behavior or patterns which are the most likely to be effective. This is the essence of teaching.*[1]

Educational reports and educational literature are contemplating the quality of American education. To say that we live in a time of increasing emphasis on teacher assessment is to state the obvious. In no other era has the emphasis on assessment been greater.[2]

The purposes of teacher assessment are four; these are shown in table 10.1.[3] Two of these purposes focus on the teacher—improving teacher performance and

*Table 10.1  Four purposes of teacher evaluation.*

| | Individual | Organization |
|---|---|---|
| | *Improve Teacher Performance* | *Improve Organizational Performance* |
| G<br>A<br>T<br>H<br>E<br>R<br>I<br>N<br>G<br><br>D<br>A<br>T<br>A | • Develop formative information about teaching performance.<br>• Assess hiring criteria and job specifications.<br>• Develop formative information about teacher characteristics and capacities.<br>• Identify supervision goals.<br><br>• Identify supervision approaches.<br>• Model decision-making processes. | • Gather data about the effectiveness of the staff development system.<br><br>• Gather data about the congruence between hypothetical and actual curriculum.<br>• Measure student access to range and variety of teaching methodologies.<br><br>• Identify organizational goals and action plans.<br>• Assess school climate/trust level. |
| | *Inform Personnel Decisions* | *Inform Organizational Decisions* |
| M<br>A   D<br>K   E<br>I   C<br>N   I<br>G   S<br>    I<br>    O<br>    N<br>    S | • Produce summative information related to evaluation criteria.<br>• Grant tenure.<br><br><br>• Award promotions, advancements to leadership roles.<br>• Administer disciplinary actions.<br>• Dismiss teachers. | • Design staff development program for subjects of teachers and administrators.<br>• Initiate systemwide changes in expectations for instructional methodology.<br>• Allocate budget resources for staff development, supervision, evaluation.<br>• Align curriculum. |

Of the 20 subfunctions of a comprehensive evaluation system, only one is for the sole purpose of dismissing teachers. However, many districts may be tempted to allow that motive to overwhelm other design considerations.

---

informing personnel decisions about teachers. The other two focus on the educational institution—improving the institution's performance and informing institutional decisions.

In this chapter, I am primarily concerned with the teacher focus. In this regard, assessment can be either formative or summative. The purpose of formative teacher assessment is to help form or modify the teacher's instructional behaviors. The purpose of summative assessment concerns more final decisions (tenure, termination, merit pay decisions, etc.).

The issues of teacher assessment are complex. For example, what type of assessment (systematic observation, pencil-paper tests, portfolios, etc.) should be used?[4] Who should be responsible for the assessment? What should be the minimum standard for performance? Will that be the same for all teaching levels and teaching areas? Should the standards be state or national? What should be assessed? Should the findings of educational research be incorporated into assessment policies? Who should control the allocation of funds necessary for assessment? What are the legal issues inherent in assessment?[5]

The focus of this chapter will not be answering these questions of assessment. To do so is beyond the scope of this text. Rather, our focus will be on ways to assess teacher communication competencies.

## WHY COMMUNICATION?

Certainly assessment can focus on numerous classroom and educational variables. However, remember that I began this text with the idea that communication is the crux of education. Elements of communication particularly important to effective teaching have been isolated, and I have discussed them throughout this text. Specific skills have been identified by the Speech Communication Association.[6] Researchers have written about communication competencies important for teachers.[7] In general, these authors have noted the validity of using observational and behavioral measures to identify the strengths and weaknesses of teachers as communicators and have stressed the value to be gained from systematic and multifaceted evaluations.[8]

Researchers from disciplines other than communication have also focused on communication's centrality to effective teaching.[9]

## WHY SYSTEMATIC OBSERVATION? AN OVERVIEW

Systematic observation systems are classificatory systems used to record

> *relevant aspects of classroom behaviors as (or within a negligible time after) they occur, with a minimum of quantification intervening between the observation of a behavior and the recording of it. Typically behaviors are recorded in the form of tallies, checks, or other marks which code them into predefined categories and yield information about which behaviors occurred, or how they occurred, during the period of observation.*[10]

Systematic observation is an effective way to assess teacher competency.[11] Through the use of systematic observation, you can analyze your communication in the classroom, your response style, types and levels of questions you ask, ways you reinforce student communication, and the general pattern of communication in your classroom. Utilizing the information you receive from the use of various appropriate observation instruments, you can alter your communication if you need to.

Systematic observation can answer three basic questions:

1. Is this how I want to teach?
2. Is it the best method of instruction for the goals and objectives of the course?
3. If this is not how I want to teach, how far am I from my goal?

In this chapter we'll examine types of systems available and spend considerable time on two systems. First, however, we'll discuss what systematic observation can do for you and your students.

## What's In It for Me?

Teachers are often reluctant to use systematic observation because

1. Teachers are unaware of the benefits of using systematic observation techniques.
2. Learning to use a systematic observation technique can be time consuming.
3. The observation instruments do not relate specifically to the evaluation instruments an administrator uses as she evaluates a teacher's instructional strategies.

However, numerous studies indicate that teacher use of systematic observation instruments can change teacher behavior. For example, teachers become more flexible, more accepting, less critical, more sensitive to pupil attitudes, and actively encourage student-initiated comments after using systematic observation.[12] In addition, the use of systematic observation by teachers has been linked to increased student learning.[13] Friedrich and Brooks explain these findings as

> the use of systematic observation systems provides the beginning instructor with (1) a model—in behavioral terms—of the kind of teaching behavior he may choose to develop, (2) the framework for conceptualizing and developing a variety of teaching roles, (3) feedback concerning progress toward the development of those teaching behaviors he has chosen, and (4) an opportunity to gain insight into principles of effective teaching through personal inquiry.[14]

Systematic observation is one method by which we can increase our effectiveness. True, systematic observation is time consuming (but then, no one ever said teaching doesn't take time), and may not relate specifically to the evaluation instruments our administrators use to evaluate our teaching. However, the use of systematic observation can provide insight into teaching and help us determine what changes we need to make to be more effective. The more effective we are, the more that effectiveness will be reflected in our classrooms, regardless of the instrument the administrator chooses to use to evaluate our teaching.

## What's Available?

A plethora of instruments are available from which you can choose. Mirrors for Behavior III[15] contains a description of ninety-nine systems. Other sources describe forty-eight additional systems.[16] These systems can be classified as:[17]

1. *Affective*—a category is said to be affective if it concentrates on the emotional component of behavior. The emotional component can concern either people or ideas.

2. *Cognitive*—a category is labeled cognitive if it focuses primarily on the intellectual component of behavior. The emphasis is on ideas and beliefs themselves rather than attitudes or feelings about those ideas or beliefs.

3. *Psychomotor*—categories that focus on description of behaviors by which people communicate when they are not using words are labeled psychomotor.

4. *Activity*—activity categories focus on recording activities in which people are engaged.

5. *Content*—a category is labeled content if it deals with what is being talked about. Such categories may focus on task-related or nontask-related behavior.

6. *Sociological structure*—if the category supplies a means to determine who is talking to whom, if it designates the role of the person or persons, if it notes the number of people interacting, or if it provides information about vital statistics of those interacting, such as gender, race, age, and so forth, the category is classified as dealing with a sociological structure.

7. *Physical environment*—the final set of categories, physical environment, describes the physical space in which the observation is taking place and notes specific materials and equipment being used.

Obviously, you can't observe everything at once. Each systematic observation instrument focuses on certain variables. You must decide which variables about your own teaching you want to examine, and then choose the appropriate instrument. You may even combine instruments or develop your own.

Basically there are two types of observation instruments—expert prepared and teacher made. Expert-prepared instruments are prepared by professionals in the field of observation. Teacher-made instruments are prepared by teachers for use in their own classrooms.

## EXPERT-PREPARED SYSTEMS

### A Verbal Observation System—Flanders

One of the best known and most often utilized expert-prepared systems is the one developed by Flanders and his associates.[18] The system divides classroom communication into three major categories: teacher talk, student talk, and noncodable. Each of these major categories is divided into smaller categories. The entire system is presented below.

#### Teacher Talk: Indirect Influence

1. *Accepts Feeling.* Accepts and clarifies the feeling tone of the student in a nonthreatening manner. Feelings may be positive or negative. Predicting or recalling feelings is included.

2. *Praises or Encourages.* Praises or encourages student action or behavior. Jokes that release tension, but not at the expense of another individual, nodding head, or saying, "Um hm?" or "Go on" are included.

3. *Accepts or Uses Ideas of Students.* Clarifying, building, or developing ideas suggested by a student. As teacher brings more of her own ideas into play, shift to Category 5.

4. *Asks Questions.* Asking a question about content or procedure with the intent that a student answer.

#### Teacher Talk: Direct Influence

5. *Lecturing.* Giving facts or opinions about content or procedures; expressing his own ideas, asking rhetorical questions.

6. *Giving Directions.* Directions, commands, or orders with which a student is expected to comply.

7. *Criticizing or Justifying Authority.* Statements intended to change student behavior from nonacceptable to acceptable pattern; bawling someone out; stating why the teacher is doing what she is doing; extreme self-reference.

#### Student Talk

8. *Student Talk—Response.* Talk by student in response to teacher. Teacher initiates the contact or solicits student statement.

9. *Student Talk—Initiation.* Talk by students which they initiate. If "calling on" student is only to indicate who may talk next, observer must decide whether student wanted to talk. If he did, use this category.

*Noncodable*

10. *Silence or Confusion.* Pauses, short periods of silence, and periods of confusion in which communication cannot be understood by the observer.

To use the instrument, the observer (another teacher, for example) sits in the back of the classroom and adjusts to the classroom (about ten–fifteen minutes). She then records behavior according to one of the categories every three seconds or as often as behavior changes. The numbers of the categories are recorded in sequence on a sheet like the one on pages 338–339. The observer should record for ten to fifteen minutes. A complete explanation of the Flanders System is found in Appendix E.

### A Nonverbal Observation System—Grant and Hennings

Flander's system focuses on verbal communication in the classroom. However, the use of a teacher's nonverbal communication seems particularly important to the classroom situation. It is imperative that your nonverbal behavior enhance instruction. If students are confused because of contradictions between verbal and nonverbal aspects of the classroom, the classroom climate, and thus learning, can be affected.

Grant and Hennings[19] have developed an instrument that focuses on nonverbal teacher behavior. The instrument divides nonverbal communication into four areas.

1. *Conducting*—motions that enable teacher to control student participation and obtain attending behavior
2. *Acting*—motions that amplify and clarify meanings
3. *Wielding*—motions in which teacher interacts with objects, materials, or parts of the room
4. *Personal motions*—motions not related to instruction

In addition to examining nonverbal communication, the instrument gives you an idea of how your nonverbal communication relates to your verbal communication. A complete explanation and inventory is included in Appendix E.

### TEACHER-PREPARED SYSTEMS

Often teachers have a specific behavior they want to examine—level and sequence of questions asked, types of reinforcement, or specific nonverbal behaviors such as movement or gesture. Regardless of what behavior the teacher wishes to observe, several steps must be followed when developing an observation tool. Gerald Bailey[20] suggests the following steps:

1. Identify the behaviors that will be observed.
2. Examine a number of expert-prepared instruments to get an idea of the design of observation instruments. The expert-prepared observation forms will assist in determining (1) the type of form to be designed, (2) techniques for identifying behavior, and (3) methods for interpreting and analyzing collected information.
3. Construct the observation form to illustrate one or more of these facets: (1) identification of a specific behavior, (2) the frequency of a behavior, and (3) the sequence of behaviors. Design the directions and format for actual data collection.
4. Audiotape or videotape a classroom session; analyze data in terms of how well the classroom interaction was collected.
5. Revise the observation form on the basis of the findings, record another classroom session, and use this recording to collect data on the revised form.

Suppose you want to know the level of questions you ask in your classroom and the level of questions your students ask. You might devise a form like the one below. An observer would simply check the appropriate column each time you or your students asked a question. You could also video- or audiotape a class period and then tally the results yourself.

|  | Knowledge | Comprehension | Application | Analysis | Synthesis | Evaluation |
|---|---|---|---|---|---|---|
| Teacher Questions |  |  |  |  |  |  |
| Student Questions |  |  |  |  |  |  |

Perhaps you are interested in what types and frequency of positive reinforcement you use in the classroom. A form such as the one below could be used. The observer would place a check after each behavior when it occurs in the designated three-minute interval.

| | 3 | 6 | 9 | 12 | 15 |
|---|---|---|---|---|---|
| Single Word Sentence | | | | | |
| Humor | | | | | |
| Movement Toward Student | | | | | |
| Gesture Toward Student | | | | | |
| Enthusiastic Vocal Tone | | | | | |

Teacher-made observation systems are not without their shortcomings. The process of constructing them is time consuming. The bias of the creator is difficult to avoid. As a result, reliability and validity are difficult to determine. However, these limitations may be less important than the advantage of creating an instrument tailor-made to observing the behaviors on which the teacher wishes to focus. Two teacher-prepared observation systems are included in Appendix E.

## IN SUM

This chapter has presented you with a brief discussion of teacher assessment and an overview of systematic observation and how it can help you analyze your teaching. A variety of instruments exist. Choose the one most appropriate to your needs or develop your own. However, remember that no observation system tells you whether you are a "good" teacher. It merely describes your behavior. What you do with what you learn is up to you.

## ACTIVITY 10.1

Using one of the two instruments described here, observe another teacher. Discuss what you find with him.

**ACTIVITY 10.2**

In a microteaching situation, have another student or teacher observe you, utilizing a systematic observation instrument. Discuss the observer's findings. What have you learned about your teaching? Which behaviors would you like to change? Why? Which behaviors would you like to maintain? Why?

## NOTES

1. M. I. Semmel, "Systematic Observation," *Journal of Teacher Education* 29 (March-April 1978): 27.

2. Association of Teacher Educators, *Teacher Assessment* (Reston, VA: Association of Teacher Educators, 1988).

3. A. Costa, R. Garmston, and L. Lambert, "Evaluation of Teaching: The Cognitive Development View," *Teacher Evaluation: Six Prescriptions for Success*, ed. S. Stanley and W. J. Popham (Alexandria, VA: ASCD, 1988) 148.

4. L. Shulman, "A Union of Insufficiencies: Strategies for Teacher Assessment in a Period of Education Reform," *Educational Leadership* (Nov. 1988): 36-46.

5. Association of Teacher Educators, 1988.

6. P. Cooper, ed. "Teacher Communication Competencies," Annandale, VA: SCA, 1988, pamphlet.

7. See, for example, R. B. Ruben, "The Communication Competency Assessment Instrument," SCA Convention, Washington, DC, 1983; R. B. Ruben and J. D. Feezel, "Elements of Teacher Communication Competence," *Communication Education* (1986): 254-268; J. L. McCaleb, "Selecting a Measure of Oral Communication as a Predictor of Teaching Performance," *Journal of Teacher Education* 35 (1984) 33-38; and V. C. Downs, J. Manoochehr, and J. F. Nussbaum, "Analysis of Teachers' Verbal Communication Within the College Classroom: Use of Humor, Self-Disclosure, and Narratives,"

*Communication Education* 37 (1988): 127-141.

8. J. L. McCaleb, ed., "How Do Teachers Communicate? A Review and Critique of Assessment Practices," *Teacher Education Monograph No. 7* (Washington, DC: ERIC Clearinghouse on Teacher Education, 1987).

9. See, for example, R. J. Bonstetter, "Teacher Behaviors That Facilitate New Goals," *Education and Urban Society* 22 (1988): 30-39; D. C. Davidson, "Perception of Instructor in Relation to Self and Evaluation of Instructor's Performance," *Perceptual and Motor Skills* 36 (1973): 533-534; G. Denemark and N. Nutter, *The Case for Extended Programs of Initial Teacher Preparation* (Washington, DC: ERIC Clearinghouse for Teacher Education, 1980); R. S. Meier and J. F. Feldhausen, "Another Look at Dr. Fox: Effect of Stated Purpose for Evaluation, Lecturer Expressiveness, and Density of Lecture Content on Student Ratings," *Journal of Educational Psychology* 71 (1979): 339-345; E. G. Pultorak, "How Valid Are Undergraduate Curricula in Preparing Teacher Candidates for the NTE?" *The Teacher Educator* 25 (1989): 18-26; and D. C. Smith, "Redesigning the Curriculum in Teacher Education," *Strengthening Teacher Education*, ed. C. P. Magrath and R. L. Egbert (San Francisco: Jossey-Bass, 1987) 87-96.

10. D. Medley and H. Mitsel, "Measuring Classroom Behavior by Systematic Observation," *Handbook of Research on Teaching*, ed. N. W. Gage (Chicago: Rand McNally, 1963) 253.

11. W. Wiersma and T. Gibney, "Observation as an Approach to Measuring Teacher Competency," *Action in Teacher Education* 7 (Spring/Summer 1985): 59–67.

12. E. J. Amidon and J. B. Hough, eds., *Interaction Analysis: Theory, Research and Application* (Reading, MA: Addison-Wesley, 1967) 11.

13. Amidon and Hough.

14. G. Friedrich and W. Brooks, "The Use of Systematic Observation Instruments for the Supervision of Teaching," *The Speech Teacher* 19 (Nov. 1970): 285.

15. A. Simon and E. G. Boyer, eds., *Mirrors for Behavior III: An Anthology of Observation Instruments* (Wyncote, PA: Communication Materials Center, 1974).

16. B. Rosenshine and N. Furst, "The Use of Direct Observation to Study Teaching," *Second Handbook of Research on Teaching*, ed. R. M. W. Travers (Chicago: Rand McNally, 1973) 128–184.

17. Simon and Boyer, 11–32.

18. E. J. Amidon and N. A. Flanders, *The Role of the Teacher in the Classroom: A Manual for Understanding and Improving Teacher Classroom Behavior* (Minneapolis: Association for Productive Teaching, 1967).

19. B. Grant and D. Hennings, *The Teacher Moves* (New York: Columbia U, 1971) 126–133.

20. G. Bailey, *Teacher Self-Assessment: A Means for Improving Instruction* (Washington, D.C.: National Education Association, 1981) 59.

## SUGGESTIONS FOR FURTHER READING

Brandt, R. "On the Assessment of Teaching: A Conversation with Lee Shulman." *Educational Leadership* 46 (1988): 42–46.

Buttram, J. L., and B. L. Wilson. "Promising Trends in Teacher Evaluation." *Educational Leadership* 45 (1987): 4–5.

Cashin, W. "Student Ratings of Teaching: A Summary of Research." Idea Paper No. 20. Kansas State U, Center for Faculty Evaluation and Development, Sept. 1988.

Fenton, R., and D. Nancarrow. "Improving Teacher-Supervisor Communication Through Modification of the Communication Context." Western Speech Communication Association Convention. Spokane, 1989. (ERIC Ed 302 875).

Friedrich, G. W., and W. J. Seiler. "The Influence of Differing Administrative Instructions on Student Ratings of Instructors." *Central States Speech Journal* 32 (1987): 111–117.

Lacefield, W. E. "Faculty Enrichment and the Assessment of Teaching." *The Review of Higher Education* 9 (1986): 361–379.

McCaleb, J., ed. *How Do Teachers Communicate?* Washington, DC: American Association of Colleges for Teacher Education, 1987.

McLaughlin, M., and R. Pfeifer. *Teacher Education*. New York: Teachers CP, 1988.

O'Shea, L. J. "The Supervision Throughout Model: Interpersonal Communication Skills and Problem-Solving Procedures for Effective Intern Supervision." *Teacher Education and Special Education* (Spring 1987): 71–80.

Perry, C. "Research Findings on Teaching—Misuse and Appropriate Use." *Action in Teacher Education* 11 (1989): 12–15.

Porter, A. "Understanding Teaching: A Model for Assessment." *Journal of Teacher Education* 39 (July/Aug. 1988): 2–6.

Shepherd, G., and D. Trank. "Individual Differences in Consistency of Evaluation: Student Perceptions of Teacher Effectiveness." *Journal of Research and Development in Education* 22 (1989): 45–51.

Shulman, L. S. "Assessment for Teaching: An Initiative for the Profession." *Phi Delta Kappan* 69 (1987): 38–44.

Stewart, D. "Materials on Evaluation of Teacher Education Programs in the ERIC Database." *Journal of Teacher Education* (1988): 23–25.

Thorson, J. R., R. K. Miller, and J. J. Bellon. "Instructional Improvement Through Personnel Evaluation." *Educational Leadership* (April 1987): 52–54.

Weimer, M. *How Am I Teaching?* Madison, WI: Magna Publications, 1988.

# JOURNAL ASSIGNMENT SUGGESTIONS

Journal writing is increasingly being utilized in education.[1] Keeping a journal enables you to reflect about and react to course material, analyze and synthesize materials and observations, generate new ideas, and promote self-awareness.[2]

Journals are most effective when we want to keep them. What follows are merely suggestions. You are free to put anything in your journal that you feel will help you become a better teacher. You may want to keep a diary of your teaching experiences. You may want to write poems expressing your feelings about teaching and students. You may want to jot down ideas for teaching in your subject area. You may want to collect recent articles in the newspaper that illustrate the importance of effective communication in everyday life. You may want to include comments students make. The possibilities are endless; consider the following suggestions.

## TEACHER EDUCATION PROGRAMS

Design the "ideal" teacher education program. You may find it helpful to work in small groups and then come together as an entire class to compare ideas. Outline the basic competencies, knowledge, and practical experiences to which a prospective teacher should be exposed.

Interview teachers who have been teaching a number of years. Compare their ideas with your group's. How do they differ? Why?

## PERSONAL CREDO

Read Robert Fulghum's "Credo" in *All I Ever Needed to Know I Learned in Kindergarten* (New York: Villard Books, 1988) and write your own personal credo.

## STORYTELLING JOURNAL

Start a storytelling journal to document your storytelling activities and to put copies of any stories you tell.

Keep notes for yourself about how the stories went, new story ideas that come to you, and any storytelling insights you had.

## TWENTY TIPS FOR TEACHERS

Barbara Rebbeck[3] asked her students to list the traits good teachers should possess. Among those listed were "Be versatile" and "Don't complain."

Conduct a survey in which you ask ten students to list the traits they believe are important. Compile the lists. What do the lists tell you about effective teachers?

## DIFFERENT THIS TIME

Often students procrastinate and find themselves wishing they had done things differently in order to make the semester, quarter, or year better. Write a short essay entitled "Different This Time" in which you outline the changes you'll make in order to enhance your education. Begin with the sentence, "School will be different this year because . . . ."

## SELF-ASSESSMENT[4]

### Directions

Complete the sentence stems on the accompanying Worksheets 1 and 2, leaving out any that are inappropriate for you. Try not to talk around the subject and give drawn-out answers: be concise and to the point. For example, rather than saying:

> *"I feel badly when I haven't taken all the steps necessary for having my lesson ready by the time when I have to teach it."*

say:

> *"I feel badly when I'm not prepared."*

Once you have completed the sentence stems, code them in the manner suggested below. No response should have more than one code. Try to select the most appropriate code for each sentence. Each code may be used any number of times. Some sentences may not have a code.

## Codings

Place P next to those sentences that make you proud.

Place C next to those sentences that make you feel comfortable.
Place UN next to those sentences that make you feel uncomfortable.
Place ME next to those sentences that you feel you have control over.
Place NO next to those sentences that you feel you have no control over.
Place D next to those sentences that you wish were different.

You may wish to modify or change the above coding system. You must use the codes that are most appropriate for you. Other possible codes include L for an item you learned in your teacher-education program, SCH-G for an item that reminds you of a pleasant experience you had when you were in the same grade as the one you are now teaching, or SCH-B for an unpleasant experience.

Repeat this activity at least four or five times over a period of a month or two. Do not read your past responses before you repeat this activity, since that might influence your completions. When you have done this activity a number of times and feel you have enough data, gather your worksheets and cut each sentence stem into a strip. Sort the strips according to the code in Worksheet 3. If you have modified the codes, change the worksheet accordingly. Next, examine each category on your worksheet by noting the sentences that have been grouped together. Then answer the following questions.

## Questions

1. What similarities do you notice in each category?
2. What differences do you notice between categories?
3. Are there any recurring items that dominate each category?
4. Which category has the most responses? Which the least? What significance does the distribution of items over the worksheet have for you?
5. What areas of your professional life give you your greatest satisfactions as indicated by the worksheet? How can you expand these areas?
6. What areas of your professional life appear to be in need of modification? What steps can you begin to take?

## Follow-up

Once you have identified the areas in your teaching life that you wish to change, the rest is up to you. You must be willing to make the investment in time and energy and to take responsibility for whatever changes you consider important. This is a very difficult task for all of us, however; New Year's resolutions are famous for being unfulfilled. One method of helping yourself change your behavior is to think of specific, direct steps that will accomplish your goal. You can then readily check to see how well you are succeeding. If you wish to be more self-disclosing, for example, you might resolve to talk about yourself at least twice each hour of the day. To further check your progress, repeat this activity after a month or so and notice what significant differences, if any, have occurred.

### Worksheet 1: Self-Assessment Sentence Stems

I feel good about myself when my students—
I feel bad about myself when my students—
I feel good about myself when other teachers—
I feel bad about myself when other teachers—
I feel discouraged about teaching when—
I feel encouraged about teaching when—
I feel I have been successful when—
I feel I have wasted students' time when—
I feel the students trust me when—
I feel the students are learning when—
I feel I am learning when—
I feel the students are not learning when—
I feel in a rut when—
I am glad to be a teacher when—
I lose my temper when—
I know it's time to put my foot down when—
I feel used when—
I like having classroom visitors when—
I am threatened when—

### Worksheet 2: Self-Assessment Sentence Stems

I am most patient in school when—
I am least patient in school when—
I am most at ease in school when—
I am least at ease in school when—
Students make me nervous when—

I react to other teachers—

I react to authority—

When I am in authority—

When people agree with me—

When people disagree with me—

Two things I can improve on as a teacher—

Three things I do exceptionally well as a teacher—

My students would describe me as—

My student's description of me makes me feel—

The student I like best—

The student I like least—

I listen—

I learn from my students—

*Worksheet 3*

| Place all Ps here | Place all Cs here | Place all UNs here | Place all MEs here | Place all NOs here | Place all Ds here |
|---|---|---|---|---|---|
|  |  |  |  |  |  |

## DIFFERING PERCEPTIONS

List three persons with whom you expect to have significant communication encounters in the next few days. For each person, describe as accurately as you can her view of the world. How does each person's view of the world differ from yours? What effect could these differences have on your communication encounter? What does this tell you about classroom communication? For example, if your "reality" is different from the "reality" of your students, how will learning be affected? How will the classroom climate be affected?

## A YEAR OFF

*Require every teacher to take a one-year leave of absence every fourth year to work in some "field" other than education.*

*Such an experience can be taken as evidence, albeit shaky, that the teacher has been in contact with reality at some point in his life. Recommended occupations: bartender, cab driver, garment worker, waiter. One of the common sources of difficulty with teachers can be found in the fact that most of them simply move from one side of the desk (as students) to the other side (as "teachers") and they have not had much contact with the way things are outside the school rooms.[5]*

1.  Do you agree with the idea expressed above? Why or why not?
2.  What areas would you choose to engage in if you were a teacher and had the opportunity to take a year off?

## A SYSTEMS PERSPECTIVE

Oftentimes we live in our "own little world" and forget there are others in the school environment. From a systems perspective, each person in the school system affects us as teachers. Observe various people in the school system—principal, secretary, cafeteria worker, a member of the janitorial staff, school nurse, school counselor, or a teacher of a subject matter different from your own. Take some time and follow each of these people as they go through their daily activities. Talk to them about their jobs. Answer the following questions when your observations are completed.

1.  What is each person's name?
2.  What are their responsibilities?
3.  What were the major problems and frustrations of each person? The major rewards?
4.  How does each person you observed affect you as a teacher?
5.  What did you learn about the school as a system?

## WEEKLY LOGS

- As a student teacher, keep a weekly reaction log to your experiences. Use the following questions as guidelines, but add others of your choice.

  Date _____

1. What were your objectives for the week? Did you accomplish them?
2. Which experiences, students, other teachers, etc., were the most rewarding? Which were the least rewarding? Why?
3. If you had this week to relive, what, if anything, would you do differently? Why?
4. Complete the following statement with three adjectives. This week, my classroom experience was _____, _____, and _____.

   Comments (feelings, frustrations, anxieties, joys, etc.):

   _____

   _____

- You might keep a similar log reacting to your classroom experiences as a student. We can learn much about being a teacher from analyzing our experiences as a student. For the remainder of the term, keep a weekly log. What do your experiences as a student tell you about being an effective teacher?

## TEACHER-STUDENT PARADOX[6]

### Procedure

The instructor will divide the class into groups of five or six. As a group, select two people to act as "teachers" and one person to act as "observer." The rest of the group will act as "students." The "teachers" will be assigned a lesson to teach the students. During this process, the observer will fill out Form A, noting specific verbal and nonverbal cues on the part of the "teachers" and "students."

Your observations on the exercise:

### Observer Form A

During the teaching activity, note specific verbal and nonverbal cues given by "teachers" and "students" that begin to erect barriers to the communication process.

|  | "Teachers" | "Students" |
|---|---|---|
|  | Examples of: | Examples of: |
|  | Teaching strategy that causes mistrust: | Response to teaching strategy used that caused mistrust: |
|  | Teaching strategy that improved trust: | Response to teaching strategy used that improved trust: |
|  | Nonverbal cues that helped or hindered communication: | Nonverbal cues that helped or hindered communication: |

## Journal Entry

1. How did your perceptions of the roles of "student" and "teacher" affect your ability to communicate in this situation?

2. Describe some barriers that currently exist between you and teachers in general. Analyze ways to overcome these barriers as you continue to communicate with your teachers.

3. Additional questions supplied by your instructor and your own comments and reactions.

## COMMUNICATION LOG — EDUCATIONAL ENVIRONMENT

For a period of one week, make notes on your communication activities with others on the following forms. At the end of the week, write a brief description of the type of communication you engage in most often.

Date: _____          Place: _____

From: _____ to _____

*Type of Contact:*
_____ Dyadic
_____ Discussion in group
_____ Memo
_____ Telephone
_____ Other (specify):

*Others Involved:*
_____ Administrators
_____ Students
_____ Other teachers
_____ Parents
_____ Other (specify):

*Type of Contact:*
_____ Classroom teaching
_____ Parent/teacher conference
_____ Student/teacher conference
_____ Inservice training
_____ Public relations
_____ Faculty conference
_____ Other (specify):

*Purpose of Communication:*
_____ Giving information
_____ Giving advice
_____ Receiving information
_____ Receiving advice
_____ Making a decision
_____ Solving a problem
_____ Other (specify):

*Attitude Toward Communication:*
_____ Worthwhile
_____ Boring
_____ Satisfactory
_____ Helpful
_____ Worthless
_____ Interesting
_____ Unsatisfactory
_____ Not Helpful

*Additional Comments:*

## TEACHER CHARACTERISTICS

Answer the following questions:

1. What would you most like to communicate to your students?
2. What would you most like your teachers to communicate to you?

Based on your answers, list five characteristics of effective teachers. Share your ideas with a classmate.

## LEARNING WISH LIST

Keep an "I Wish to Learn" log. Jot down ideas about teachers, schools, parents, students, and the teaching/learning process you'd like to know more about.

## LISTENING WELL

In your journal, consider the following: Think of a person who listens well. Analyze the behaviors of that person, verbal and nonverbal. How do you feel when talking or interacting with that person. What does this tell you about good listening?

## PHOTOGRAPHIC ESSAY

Create a photographic essay entitled "A Day In the Life of a Teacher." (You may choose to use videotape rather than photographs.) Share with this class. Discuss similarities and differences among your classmates' essays.

## COAT OF ARMS

Complete the Coat of Arms on page 353. In small groups, share your Coat of Arms. Periodically during the term, complete it again. Are there changes? What might account for these changes? How will the changes affect your teaching?

## EVALUATION OF STUDENTS: WHERE DO YOU STAND?[7]

### Part One

How many of the routine practices that you have initiated in your classroom have you thoroughly considered before doing? Most of us carefully analyze some of our practices, think sketchily about others, and consider some not at all. We have been learning teaching behavior all our lives: from our parents (our first and most pervasive teachers), our elementary and secondary teachers, our college instructors, our cooperating teachers and supervisors, and our colleagues. Frequently, however, we fail to think very deeply about whether or not this learned behavior truly constitutes our ideal conception of what teaching behavior ought to be. The following activity gives you an opportunity to think about your beliefs and attitudes as they relate to the matter of evaluating students.

### *Directions*

Use the statements headed, "Attitudes on Evaluation," and the sorting board to describe your conception of "good" and "not-so-good" practices related to evaluation. First record the forty-six attitude statements on small cards. With the sorting board before you, sort the cards into seven categories, putting the

# COAT OF ARMS

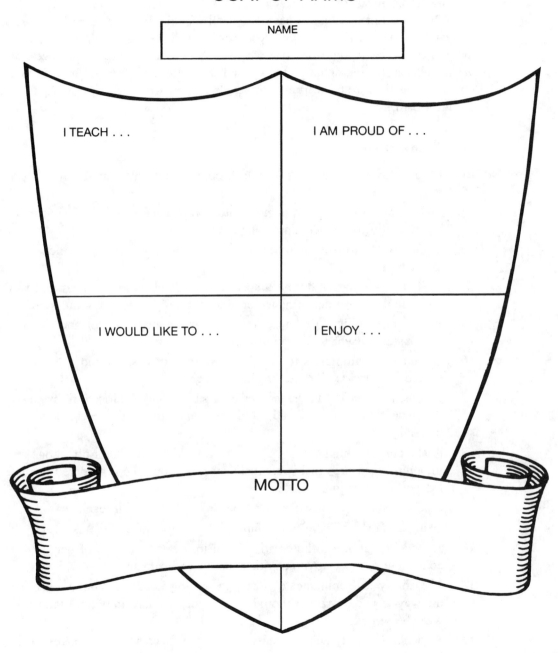

NAME

I TEACH . . .

I AM PROUD OF . . .

I WOULD LIKE TO . . .

I ENJOY . . .

MOTTO

following number of statements—1, 4, 9, 18, 9, 4, 1—in respective categories, ranging from "most ideal" in category A to "least ideal" in category G.

When you finish, you will have a general ranking of the statements. Those in categories A and B describe what you believe to be sound evaluative practices; those in categories F and G describe what you believe to be unsound practices, with the remainder ranging somewhere between the extremes. Place each card on the board as you read it and rearrange the cards as you work. (See page 362 for the Sorting Board.)

### Attitudes on Evaluation

1. It's best to consider and take into account a student's intelligence when evaluating his work.

2. Final exams or unit tests demonstrate competence and should contribute significantly to a student's evaluation.

3. The amount of effort a student expends should be reflected in her evaluation.

4. A student's progress during a specified marking period is measured well by a single major performance criterion, usually a test of some kind.

5. A student's ability to relate to others is an important factor and should be considered when evaluating him.

6. A student's willingness to contribute to class discussion and activity should be considered when evaluating her.

7. The feelings evoked in the teacher by a student are significant measures of the student's competency and should be considered in the teacher's evaluation.

8. A student's willingness and ability to follow the teacher's directions are important measures of his competency and should be considered in the teacher's evaluation.

9. Students should be discouraged from taking issue with teachers.

10. Using a standard curve is the fairest way to evaluate students.

11. A student's ability to be creative is an important measure of her competency, so creative activities should be evaluated.

12. The ability to communicate clearly in writing is of great importance, so the way a student writes should be considered more important than what he writes.

13. Students generally achieve more if they are faced with challenges, so it is best not to give too many As or superior evaluations.

14. Students need positive reinforcement in order to go beyond where they are, so it is best not to fail students.

15. Because students often are not motivated to work outside the classroom, it is a good idea to suggest that they will be quizzed on homework assignments.

16. Student opinion and interpretation are significant means and indications of learning and should be emphasized in tests and other methods of evaluation.

17. Students will not be able to apply knowledge until they have mastered the basics, so tests and other means of evaluation should emphasize the acquisition of factual material.

18. Because what a student knows is more important than how well she is able to communicate it in writing, content rather than style or grammar should be emphasized in students' writing.

19. Because it is important for students to learn to spell well, students should be penalized for spelling errors.

20. Good spelling is an asset and therefore should be encouraged by giving students extra points on tests and papers for perfect spelling.

21. Quizzes and tests that are unannounced are better measures of actual learning than those that are announced in advance.

22. Neatness should be encouraged by giving it consideration when evaluating student work.

23. Low grades and poor evaluations usually create incentives for students to work harder.

24. It is often helpful to solicit the opinions of other teachers about the students and to consider these opinions when evaluating the students.

25. High grades and good evaluations usually create incentive for students to work harder.

26. Students will work harder if they feel their work is appreciated, so it is helpful to openly appreciate what they do.

27. Because students should know where they stand in relation to other students, all grades should be public.

28. To de-emphasize grades, it is good practice not to tell a student what his grades are until the end of the term, when the school administration insists that they be shared.

29. Promptness should be encouraged by penalizing students for tardiness.

30. It is a significant learning experience for students to be allowed and encouraged to negotiate their evaluations with teachers.

31. Students contracting with teachers for grades prior to a unit of work is a meaningful, fair, and positive way to handle evaluation.

32. It is best to give many more positive than negative evaluations.

33. It is better to consistently criticize student work than to consistently praise it.
34. The last day of the week is a good time to evaluate student's progress for that week.
35. In order that students not lose ground over vacation periods, it is a good idea to assign homework then.
36. A good teacher should be accountable for the performance of her students.
37. Tests should be used diagnostically rather than evaluatively.
38. Standard grading procedures are generally detrimental and should be eliminated.
39. Alternatives to standard grading procedures should be explored and tried.
40. The parents of students who are not doing well should be notified.
41. All parents should be notified of their children's progress in school.
42. Teachers should be concerned about cheating.
43. Students who miss tests should be required to complete more difficult makeup work.
44. Students should be allowed and encouraged to evaluate themselves.
45. Students should be allowed and encouraged to evaluate one another.
46. A student's sex should be considered in evaluating his work.

## Questions

After you have sorted the ideal evaluative practices, answer the following questions:

1. What makes the statement in A so meaningful for you?
2. Do the statements in B have anything in common with one another? If so, what?
3. How are the statements in A and B similar for you?
4. Do the statements in C have anything in common with one another? If so, what?
5. How are the statements in C similar to or different from those in A and B?
6. As a result of your examination of the statements in A, B, and C, complete five statements beginning with the words "I believe _____."
7. What makes the statement in G so unacceptable to you?
8. Do the statements in F have anything in common with one another? If so, what?
9. How are the statements in F and G similar for you?
10. Do the statements in E have anything in common with one another? If so, what?
11. How are the statements in E similar to or different from those in F and G?

12. As a result of your examination of the statements in E, F, and G, complete five more statements beginning with the words "I believe _____."
13. Based on the information drawn from the sorting activity above, write a paragraph describing the characteristics and behavior concerning evaluation that are important to you.

## Part Two

How consistent with your statements of belief is your actual behavior? All of us at times fail to act on our beliefs, sometimes because we have not truly incorporated the beliefs we profess, other times because we have not consciously related our behavior to our professed beliefs. Sometimes we fail because we hold conflicting beliefs, and other times because it is simply easier to act inconsistently with beliefs, even though we are uncomfortable doing so. No matter how difficult it is to act in a way that is congruent with our beliefs, it is certainly worthwhile to work toward this kind of consistency in life. One of the hallmarks of the healthiest people in all societies is the congruence of their values, attitudes, beliefs, and behavior.

In Part One of this activity you examined your attitudes and beliefs as they relate to evaluating students. Now we ask you to describe your actual behavior in a similar fashion.

## Directions

As before, record the statements headed "Evaluation Practices" on cards; then shuffle and sort them in the same manner as you did in Part One, but this time ranging from "most characteristic" to "least characteristic" of you in the classroom. These statements all contain the personal pronoun "I" and are meant to describe your actual behavior.

### Evaluation Practices

1. I grade slower students differently from bright ones.
2. I weigh final exams and unit tests heavily, using them for 50 percent or more of a student's grade.
3. I give better evaluations to those who try harder.
4. I usually give one major test or other measure of evaluation each marking period.
5. I have been influenced in my evaluation of a student by how well she gets along with her peers.
6. Students who participate actively in class receive better evaluations from me than those who do not.

7. I trust my personal feelings for students and frequently use them to evaluate students.

8. I have graded students who agree with me differently from those who do not.

9. I have encouraged students to disagree with me in class.

10. I use a standard grading curve in assigning grades.

11. I have used letter or number grades in evaluating creative activities.

12. I have given considerable weight to the grammatical correctness of student papers.

13. I did not give very many As or superior evaluations last term.

14. I did not fail anyone last term.

15. I have used the threat of unannounced quizzes to motivate students to do homework.

16. Most of my tests rely on subjective questions that allow student opinion and interpretation.

17. Most of my test questions are objective, requiring students to respond with factual material.

18. In evaluating student work, I consider content more heavily than style or the correctness of usage.

19. I usually take points off a paper that contains numerous misspelled words.

20. I have given extra points to papers with no spelling errors.

21. I have given surprise quizzes.

22. I have lowered the evaluation of a paper because it was messy.

23. I have sometimes given students lower evaluations than I might have in order to motivate them to work harder.

24. I have sought out and listened to my colleagues' opinions about students when determining how to evaluate them.

25. I have given students higher grades than I might have in order to motivate them to work harder.

26. I have personally thanked or otherwise expressed my appreciation to students who have done excellent work.

27. I have posted or publicly announced student evaluations.

28. I have kept all grades and evaluations secret from students until the end of the marking period.

29. I have lowered the evaluation of a student paper or project for being turned in late.

30. I have negotiated with students for their evaluations, and both student and teacher have been satisfied with the final decision.

31. I have written grading contracts with students prior to a unit of work and have honored the contracts.

32. My students probably consider me an easy grader.

33. My students probably consider me a hard grader.

34. I frequently give exams or other means of evaluation on Fridays.

35. I have never assigned homework over a vacation period.

36. I have felt personally responsible for the poor performance of a student of mine.

37. I have used tests diagnostically; I have given tests before the end of a term, and without grading them, have used them to plan future activities.

38. I have used other than standard grading procedures and have worked in my school to make them acceptable.

39. I have looked for and considered alternate grading systems to the generally accepted ones.

40. I have sent progress reports to parents of students doing poorly.

41. I have sent progress reports to parents of all students.

42. I have taken specific measures to prevent cheating in my classes.

43. I have given makeup tests that have been purposely more difficult than the original.

44. I have allowed students to grade themselves on a project or for a term.

45. I have allowed students to grade one another on a project or for a term.

46. I have been, at times, influenced by the sex of my students in determining their evaluations.

### Questions for Analysis

1. What makes the statement in A so meaningful for you?

2. Do the statements in B have anything in common with one another? If so, what?

3. How are the statements in A and B similar for you?

4. Do the statements in C have anything in common with one another? If so, what?

5. How are the statements in C similar to or different from those in A and B?

6. As a result of your examination of the statements in A, B, and C, complete five statements beginning with the words "I am _____."

7. What makes the statement in G so unacceptable to you?

8. Do the statements in F have anything in common with one another? If so, what?

9. How are the statements in F and G similar for you?

10.  Do the statements in E have anything in common with one another? If so, what?

11.  How are the statements in E similar to or different from those in F and G?

12.  As a result of your examination of the statements in E, F, and G, complete five more statements beginning with "I am _____."

13.  Based on the information drawn from the sorting activity above, write a paragraph describing the characteristics and behavior concerning your procedures of evaluation.

### Follow-up

You now have two profiles, one that states your beliefs concerning the evaluation of students, another that enumerates your actual classroom practices. Compare the two, using the following questions as a guide.

1.  What strong similarities exist between the two profiles? In what ways are your beliefs and behaviors congruent?

2.  In what ways are the two profiles different? How are your beliefs and behaviors incongruent?

3.  Would you be willing to reconsider any of your stated beliefs? If so, which?

4.  In light of your stated beliefs, would you be willing to reconsider any of your behavior?

5.  Write a contract with yourself about something you will do to make your beliefs and behavior more congruent when it comes to evaluating students.

### DISCIPLINE

The mood of the anonymous person is, "If I cannot affect or touch anybody, I can at least shock you into some feeling, force you into some passion through wounds and pain; I shall at least make sure we both feel something, and I shall force you to see me and know that I am also here!" Many a child or adolescent has forced the group to take cognizance of him by destructive behavior, and though he is condemned, at least the community notices him. To be actively hated is almost as good as being actively liked; it breaks down the utterly unbearable situation of anonymity and aloneness.[8]

- What is your reaction to the ideas stated above?

- Knowing what you know about communication, what might you do to help a student with this attitude to find other ways of being recognized?

## CLASSROOM MANAGEMENT: WHAT IS YOUR STYLE?[9]

Whether you teach in a traditional setting or in one of the many variations being tried with youngsters of all ages, you "manage" that environment in one way or another. It is likely that your management style is uniquely yours. Unfortunately, however, many of us have adopted certain styles not through careful examination and selection of alternatives, but merely by imitation or by accident. This activity is designed to help you become better aware of how you manage your classroom.

## Directions

Use the statements headed, "Classroom Management Style," and the sorting board below to get a better idea of your management style. First record each of the forty-six statements about management practices on small cards. Then with the sorting board before you, sort the cards into the seven categories it illustrates. The number of cards put into the seven categories follows this order—1, 4, 9, 18, 9, 4, and 1—ranging from most characteristic of your behavior (one card) in category A to least characteristic of your behavior (also one card) in category G. When you finish you will have a general ranking of the statements, those in categories A and B describing your most characteristic behaviors, those in categories F and G describing behaviors that are least characteristic of you. The remainder will be arranged somewhere between these extremes.

If you have difficulty ranking some behaviors, you might add the element of importance to your ranking. Then you will rank the behavior that is more significant for you higher than the one that is less significant. It may be that you would prefer to place three or five behaviors in category A or in category G, instead of one. At that point you will have to force yourself to decide which one of those three or five is of greatest importance and concern to you. The statements must be grouped according to the group sizes indicated: 1, 4, 9, 18, 9, 4, 1. To facilitate arrangement, place each card on the board as you read it, then rearrange the cards as you work. It is considerably easier to rearrange on the board than to try to organize all forty-six cards before placing them.

### *Classroom Management Style*

1. Desks in my classroom are usually arranged in rows.
2. I encourage students to speak spontaneously, without necessarily raising their hands.
3. My students call me by my first name.
4. Papers being turned in follow a standard format in my classroom.
5. The bulletin boards in my classroom are usually decorated by me, rather than by the students.

**Sorting Board**

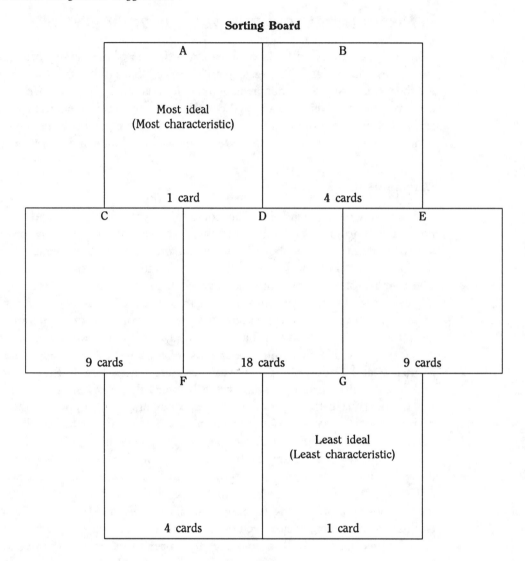

6. I usually follow and complete my lesson plans.
7. Students in my class are expected to ask permission to leave the room.
8. I allow students to go to the bathroom at just about any time.
9. My students may chew gum and eat most of the time.
10. My students usually sit in assigned places.
11. I often threaten punishment of one kind or another for misbehavior.
12. I frequently contact parents.
13. I do not tolerate swearing or other unacceptable language in my classroom.

14. When I monitor a study period, the students are quiet.
15. I often stand or sit behind a lectern or desk when teaching.
16. My students and I sit on the floor.
17. Students often remove their shoes in my class.
18. I believe in reasonable dress codes for students and teachers.
19. Students probably consider me traditional.
20. My principal probably considers me traditional.
21. I encourage students to work independently in self-directed activities.
22. The students in my class make decisions about classroom management.
23. I often depart from or discard my lesson plans.
24. I sometimes keep students after school when they misbehave.
25. I tell my students a great deal about myself.
26. Student's questions sometimes frighten me.
27. I find it difficult to say "I don't know."
28. I often ask students for feedback concerning my teaching.
29. I am likely to be asked to keep my students quieter.
30. My classroom would probably be classified as teacher-oriented.
31. I am likely to be asked by students to attend or chaperon their parties.
32. I am likely to be advising student groups, formally or informally.
33. I laugh a lot in class.
34. I enjoy team-teaching.
35. I am careful about checking attendance.
36. I usually reprimand students who are tardy.
37. I get tense when my principal comes into my room.
38. I probably let students take advantage of me.
39. I enjoy being friends with my students.
40. I frequently touch students.
41. I expect respect from students.
42. I have carefully read my students' cumulative records.
43. I feel and act differently with students outside of class.
44. I sometimes send students to see the principal, vice-principal, or counselor when they misbehave.
45. I sometimes use sarcasm to win a point with a student.
46. I often sit on the desk.

## Questions

1. What makes the statement in A so characteristic of you?

2. Do the statements in B have anything in common with one another? If so, what?

3. How are the statements in A and B similar for you?

4. Do the statements in C have anything in common with one another? If so, what?

5. How are the statements in C similar to or different from those in A and B?

6. As a result of your examination of the statements in A, B, and C, write five statements with this beginning: "I manage _____."

7. What makes the statement in C so uncharacteristic of you?

8. Do the statements in F have anything in common with one another? If so, what?

9. How are the statements in F and G similar for you?

10. Do the statements in E have anything in common with one another? If so, what?

11. How are the statements in E similar to or different from those in F and G?

12. As a result of your examination of the statements in E, F, and G, write five statements with this beginning: "I generally do not _____."

13. Based on the information drawn from the sorting activity above, write a paragraph describing the characteristics and behaviors of your personal style of classroom management.

## Follow-up

If you have the opportunity to work with a support group, you might use the group to discuss and compare your individual styles of classroom management. After sharing the paragraphs you wrote following the sorting activity, discussion might focus on the following questions:

1. In what ways are your various styles of classroom management similar? Are your similarities based on a common belief, on habit, or on some other factor?

2. In what ways do your styles differ? Are your differences important? Do you need to work them out? If not, why not? If so, why?

3. What are students likely to learn about each of you as a result of the way you manage your classroom? Are you pleased about what they may be learning?

4. Have you identified any behavior that you would like to change? If so, share your concerns with the other group members and elicit their help in designing a plan that will help you change.

## TEXTBOOK CONSULTANT

Assume you have been asked to serve as a consulting editor for a large publishing house of textbooks in your subject matter area. What suggestions would you give the authors in order to make their textbooks more useful to teachers?

## CHOOSE YOUR OWN TEACHING STRATEGY[10]

### #1

You are teaching a middle school class to an average group of students. Your topic is decision making. As you write on the board, you become aware of a distraction. Out of the corner of your eye, you notice that Pete Morgan who, totally oblivious to your lesson, is engrossed in what appears to be a cheap science fiction novel. You stroll over to his desk and ask for the book. The book is titled *By Balloon to the Sahara*, by D. Tennan. You notice that it is part of a series called "Choose Your Own Adventure," published by Bantam Books. It is not the first time you have had to interrupt your lesson because of one of the books from this series. How would you respond?

- If you would take the book away, admonish the student, and continue your lesson, read section #2.
- If you would ask the class to explain the series' popularity, read section #3.
- If you would begin to read the story aloud, read section #4.
- If you would ask to borrow the book, read section #5.

### #2

Only some of the students perk up as you resume your lesson. There are still a few students like Pete who do not seem interested in the topic. Yet, you regard decision making as a valuable skill, especially in these turbulent times. These students need to think about decision making, engage in it. What should you do?

- If you would continue the lesson in the same vein, read section #6.
- If you would try to personalize the lesson at that point, read section #8.

### #3

"What is this series all about?" you ask. Hands shoot into the air. The children all begin to speak at once.

"One at a time," you laugh. "Pete?"

"Oh, it's really neat! It's a regular story, but there's more than one ending. Whoever reads it decides what he would do and then turns to the page for that choice. The ending could be happy or sad, depending on your decision."

"And it's not predictable either," chimes in Nancy. "It's fun to figure out what to do!"

Pete adds, "Best of all, when I read it, it seems like I'm the main character!"

You have not seen so much excitement in your classroom since the white mice got loose. What should you do next?

- If you would return to your planned lesson, read section #6.
- If you would begin reading the story aloud, read section #4.
- If you would ask to borrow the book, read section #5.

## #4

You begin to read. It seems like a standard mystery story, until it is time for the character to make a tough decision. The author provides a list of choices.

"I'd ask for help," announces Pete.

"There's no time," counters Nancy. "You've got to get the clues right away."

Other students call out their choices.

"Hey, this is interesting, kids," you interrupt. "It's exactly what I was going to teach about today! How do you make these decisions?"

"I think it depends on the problem," suggests Robin. "You really have to know exactly what the problem is. I like to go back and make sure I have all the facts."

Pete agrees. "That's important all right! In the last book I read, I forgot an important fact and ended up in quicksand!"

Everyone laughs at how Pete confused himself with the novel's main character.

"That's good!" you say. "Clarifying the issue is the basic step in problem solving. But is that the only thing you need to do?"

"Well, you have to consider the consequences, don't you?"

"Exactly!" you respond. "Once you decide on which alternatives to consider, you have to pick the very best one. That depends on what you anticipate will happen. How do you decide that?"

"You could look for clues."

"You could base it on similar situations that you've experienced."

"You could check with an expert."

"Not bad," you say. These kids know more about the topic than you thought. "All right, you've looked at the consequences. Now what?"

"You put all your information together," responds Nancy. "You take all the possible consequences and all the reasons and . . . well, just think about it!"

"That's the hardest part," mutters Robin.

Pete is getting excited again. "Ya' know what I do? I write everything down. That way I can see what my choices are!"

"What a good idea!" the students shout. You are beaming with pleasure. The class is beginning to see the connections between decision making and the "Choose Your Own Adventure" series. You wrap up the lesson just before the bell. What do you do next?

- If you would ask to borrow Pete's book, read section #5.
- If you would start getting ready for your next class, read section #7.

## #5

You take the book home and enjoy the challenge of making such exciting decisions. It is fun to see the results of a controversial choice, especially in a fictional setting. Being a creative teacher, you consider possible ways of using the series in your classroom:

1.   The decision-making process can be analyzed in terms of each story. Each step in the procedure can be discussed: determining the problem, generating alternative choices, generating consequences, planning to gather data, gathering the data in relation to the consequences, examining and evaluating the consequences, choosing the alternative, and acting upon the decision. After seeing the results of their thinking, the students can review their own procedures for strengths and weaknesses.

2.   Students can evaluate their own decision-making processes and those of others. A class discussion of recent and current problems can be the real-life instrument for applying what was learned about problem solving. Student dilemmas ranging from academic course choices to family conflicts can be examined. The "Dear Abby" and "Dear Ann Landers" newspaper columns can also be utilized as discussion-starters.

3.   Students can apply the decision-making model by developing their own stories with alternative endings.

4.   Historical decisions can be rewritten by teachers and/or students in a realistic mode, thus making the children aware of the social, political, and religious considerations that influenced some controversial choices. Truman's Hiroshima decision and the Cuban missile crisis should lend themselves beautifully to such an exercise.

5.   The decisions of fictional characters can be studied. The stories of Huck Finn, Fern in *Charlotte's Web*, and Margaret in *Are You There God? It's*

*Me, Margaret* can be examined and rewritten with students developing alternative outcomes.

6.   You blew it! Some of the students will gain an appreciation of the decision-making process, but most will continue to be bored. You have passed up an ideal opportunity to relate the subject matter to your students' interests. Fortunately, however, this is not real life; you get a second chance. Try section #8.

### #6

You made a good move in discussing the book. Your students had fun and they learned, too. But you are making a mistake if you ignore the other possibilities this series offers.

- If you would still forget about the book, read section #6.
- If you would stop off at the bookstore to purchase the book, read section #5.

### #7

"Have any of you had the opportunity to make any difficult decisions lately?" you ask the class.

Pete raises his hand. "I don't mean any disrespect, you know, but that book you took away was just filled with hard decisions."

You realize Pete is sincere, but you are also worried about finishing your lesson. What should you do?

- If you would tell Pete that the subject of the book is closed, read section #6.
- If you would ask him to explain about his response, read section #3.

## QUOTATIONS

Keep a book of quotations related to teaching and communication. Here are some of my favorites.

> *One of the greatest problems in teaching is the illusion that learning is taking place.*
>
> —Bernard Shaw

> *My assumption is that the story of any one of us is in some measure the story of us all.*
>
> —Frederick Buechner

*God made man because he loves stories.*
        —Elie Wiesel

*In contrast to insects, as someone*
*once said, human beings start out as butterflies*
*and end up as cocoons.*
        —Marilyn Fergeson, *The Aquarian Conspiracy: Personal and Social Transfor-*
        *mation of Our Time.*

**Sir Thomas More's Advice to Richard Rich**

*Why not be a teacher?*
*You'd be a fine teacher.*
*Perhaps even a great one.*

*And if I was,*
*who would know it?*

*You,*
*your pupils,*
*your friends,*
*God.*

*Not a bad public that.*
        —Robert Bolt, *A Man for All Seasons*

*Teaching is not answering; it is asking questions and providing the means to find*
*answers.* (p. 39)

*. . . teaching is as noble, challenging, stimulating, and rewarding a job as one can*
*set one's heart and mind to—except on Fridays and during the month of February.*
(p. vii)
        —Eric Johnson, *Teaching School: Points Picked Up*

*HOLD YOUR POINT! Champion bird dogs are judged in part by how long they*
*"hold the point" when they detect a covey of birds. Similarly, champion teachers*
*are judged by the way they consistently and dependably send invitations to students.*
*Creating a positive classroom environment is a marathon, not a sprint.*
        —Parkey and Strahan

*The schools became a scene*
*Of solemn farce, where Ignorance on stilts,*
*His cap well lin'd with logic not his own,*
*With parrot tongue perform'd the scholar's part,*
*Proceeding soon a graduated dunce.*
        —Cowper

*"I want no man on board
who does not fear the whale."*
—Words of the captain in *Moby Dick*

*Only he who stands in awe can be trusted
with a great and difficult task.
Teaching is such a task—
yes, more, it is an art,
and no one does well
who thinks that he has mastered it.*
—G. E. Frost

*What cartloads of words
we heaped and tossed on
our towering conversation
and in this haystack of
talk, we lost the needle—communication.*
—G. Gailbraith

*To teach is to confront, interpret, and reflect.
It is to leave the person
respectfully alone
with troublesome meanings,
and then to wait
while he wrestles and decides.
it is even to honor
the search for escape
and the right to say "No!"*
—G. E. Frost

***Take All the Risks***
*When I reflect on teaching,
I can't forget the words
of an Olympic ski champion,
a man for whom two minutes is a career;
"Go faster than you think you can
on every part of the course;
take all the risks."
Take all the risks.
Great words for one who is to teach.
Take the risk of loving;
it means that you'll be hurt.
Take the risk of listening,
it means that you will learn
and will have to change.*

*Take the risk of responding;*
*little by little, it will cost you*
*your life!*

*Teaching is response.*
*learning occurs within relationships,*
*and relationship involves risk,*
*the risk of knowing and of being known.*
　　　　　　　　　　　—G. E. Frost

### Respect the Moment

*Like a person,*
*a question has to be warm*
*or it is dead.*

*One has to feel one's question.*

*Not, "We're coming to that,"*
*or, "We've had that."*
*In learning together*
*we've never had it.*
*we're always in it.*

*Teacher,*
*respect the moment.*
*It will never come again.*
　　　　　　　　　　　—G. E. Frost

*Therefore, if you would understand him, listen not to what he says, but rather to*
*what he does not say.*

　　　　　　　　　　　—Kahil Gibran

*Talking and communicating are not necessarily the same thing. Again and again*
*I have seen people "talking" to each other without giving one another any infor-*
*mation, any aspect of self, any aspect of feeling. They each mouthed words, artic-*
*ulated and sometimes enunciated beautifully, without conveying a single idea and*
*without changing one another, in any area, one iota.*

*. . . I have seen people who hardly talk at all who are obviously in excellent*
*communication. They are open to each other, receive each other, operate on the*
*same wavelength, so that it takes a minimum of verbal symbols—words—to con-*
*vey meanings, ideas, feelings, and subtle nuances. These people relate—tell each*
*other how they feel—and invariably have enough impact on one another so that*
*both have changed because of their talk.*

*. . . Communicating is certainly not a black or white activity. There are many*
*graduations and many varieties. But it is certainly the antithesis of compulsive*

*small talk, chatter and the mouthing of many words, which people often mistake for some kind of attempted communication. So, people talk and communicate; people don't talk or talk relatively little and communicate; and people do and don't talk and don't communicate.*

—Theodore Isaac Rubin, *The Winner's Notebook*

*I think how easy it is for the teacher*
*to police great meanings*
*right out the door.*
*How often, when newness and vision break in*
*and wait to be shared by some enchanted child*
*have we, the teachers, been preoccupied*
*with the orderly arrangement of class cards,*
*or with roll call, or rubbers,*
*or some other laudable trivia!*

—G. E. Frost

*Perhaps there is no effort*
*which is as total,*
*or which makes one so vulnerable*
*as teaching.*
*He who attempts it reaches beyond himself*
*and senses that his best is not good enough.*

—G. E. Frost

*The teacher is successful at the moment which his student becomes original.*

—Lane Cooper

*. . . and the exciting smell of chalk and varnished desks; the smell of heavy bread-sandwiches of cold fried meat and butter . . .*

—Thomas Wolfe

*No blackboard was black; all were indelibly clouded with ingrained layers of old chalk; the more you rubbed it out, the more you rubbed it in. Every desk was stained with generations of inkspots, cut deeply with initials and scratched drawings. What idle thoughts had been wandering for years through all those empty heads in all those tedious school hours!*

—George Sanayana, *Persons and Places*

*He who can, does. He who cannot, teaches.*
—Bernard Shaw, *Maxims for Revolutionists*

*Teaching is even more difficult than learning. We know that; but we rarely think about it. And why is teaching more difficult than learning? Not because the teacher must have a larger store of information, and have it always ready. Teaching is more difficult than learning because what teaching calls for is this: to let learn. The real teacher, intact, lets nothing else be learned than—learning. His conduct, therefore, often produces the impression that we properly learn nothing from him, if by "learning" we now suddenly understand merely the procurement of useful information. The teacher is ahead of his apprentices in this alone, that he has still far more to learn than they—he has to learn to let them learn.*

—Martin Heidegger, *What Is Called Thinking?*

### Religion Class

*They told me to write about life;*
*To discover new insights;*
*To probe my inner soul;*
*To meditate on my faith;*
*To reflect on my ideas;*
*And have it in by Friday.*

—Anonymous

*The ideal condition*
*Would be, I admit, that men*
*should be right by instinct;*
*But since we are all likely to*
*go astray,*
*The reasonable thing to do is to learn*
*from those who can teach.*

—Sophocles

### Listen

*When I ask you to listen to me*
*and you start giving advice*
*you have not done what I asked.*

*When I ask you to listen to me*
*and you begin to tell me why I shouldn't feel that way,*
*you are trampling on my feelings.*

*When I ask you to listen to me*
*and you feel you have to do something to solve my problem,*
*you have failed me, strange as that may seem.*
*Listen! All I asked, was that you listen.*
*not talk or do—just hear me.*
*Advice is cheap: 10 cents will get you both Dear Abby*
*and Billy Graham in the same newspaper.*
*And I can do for myself; I'm not helpless.*

*Maybe discouraged and faltering, but not helpless.*

*When you do something for me that I can and need to do*
*for myself, you contribute to my fear and weakness.*

*But, when you accept as a simple fact that I do feel what I feel,*
*no matter how irrational, then I can quit trying to convince*
*you and can get about the business of understanding what's*
*behind this irrational feeling.*
*And when that's clear, the answers are obvious and I don't need advice.*
*Irrational feelings make sense when we understand what's behind them.*

*Perhaps that's why prayer works, sometimes, for some people*
*because God is mute, and He doesn't give advice or*
*try to fix things. "They" just listen and let you*
*work it out for yourself.*

*So, please listen and just hear me. And, if you want to talk,*
*wait a minute for your turn; and, I'll listen to you.*

—Anonymous

## NOTES

1.See, for example, K. Danielson, *Dialogue Journals: Writing as Conversation*, Fastback 266 (Washington, D.C.: Phi Delta Kappa Educational Foundation, 1988); C. Adams, "The Teacher Journal: A Better Way to Show Your Success," *Learning 89* (Oct. 1989): 57-59; R. Ross, "Journal Writing as a Strategy for Learning from Experience in the Communication Classroom." Convention, San Francisco, 1989.

2.G. Simons, *Keeping Your Personal Journal* (New York: Ballantine Books, 1978).

3."20 Tips for Teachers—From Students," *Learning 86* (Feb. 1986): 65.

4.From R. Curwin and B. Fuhrman, *Discovering Your Teaching Self* (Englewood Cliffs, NJ: Prentice Hall, 1975) 53-61.

5.N. Postman and C. Weingartner, *Teaching as a Subversive Activity* (New York: Delta, 1969) 139-140.

6.From L. Phelps and S. DeWine, *Interpersonal Communication Journal* (St. Paul, MN: West Publishing, 1976) 261-266.

7.Curwin and Fuhrman, 114-119.

8.M. Rollo, *Love and Will* (New York: W. W. Norton, 1969) 31. Copyright 1969 by W. W. Norton & Company, Inc.

9.Curwin and Fuhrman, 46-51.

10.J. Passe, "Choosing Your Own Teaching Strategy," *The Clearinghouse 56* (April 1983).

# A   MICROTEACHING

Microteaching is a training concept that can be applied at various preservice and in-service stages in the professional development of teachers. Microteaching provides teachers with a practice setting for instruction in which the normal complexities of the classroom are reduced and in which the teacher receives a great deal of feedback on his performance. To minimize the complexities of the normal teaching encounter, several dimensions are limited. The length of the lesson is reduced. The scope of the lesson is narrowed. In microteaching, the teacher instructs only a few students instead of the normal twenty-five to thirty.

A casual observer might describe microteaching as follows: A teacher instructs four or five students for a short time and then talks it over with another adult. An experienced observer would emphasize the fact that the teacher concentrated on a specific training skill or technique and utilized several sources of feedback, such as the supervisor, the students, the teacher's own reflections and the playback of videotapes. The experienced observer would also note that the teacher has an opportunity to repeat the entire process by reteaching the lesson and again having her performance critiqued, and that in the second and subsequent cycles she teaches different students. Fundamentally, microteaching is an idea, at the core of which lie five essential propositions:

*First,* microteaching is real teaching. Although the teaching situation is a constructed one in the sense teacher and students work together in a practice situation, nevertheless, bona fide teaching does take place.

*Second,* microteaching lessens the complexities of normal classroom teaching. Class size, scope of content, and time are all reduced.

*Third,* microteaching focuses on training for the accomplishment of specific tasks. These tasks may be the practice of instructional skills, the practice of

From D. Allen and K. Ryan, *Microteaching* (Reading, MA: Addison-Wesley, 1969) 1–3, 39–41.

techniques of teaching, the mastery of certain curricular materials, or the demonstration of teaching methods.

*Fourth,* microteaching allows for the increased control of practice. In the practice setting of microteaching, the rituals of time, students, methods of feedback and supervision, and many other factors can be manipulated. As a result, a high degree of control can be built into the training program.

*Fifth,* microteaching greatly expands the normal knowledge-of-results or feedback dimension in teaching. Immediately after teaching a brief microlesson, the trainee engages in a critique of her performance. To give her a maximum insight into her performance, several sources of feedback are at her disposal. With the guidance of a supervisor or colleague, she analyzes aspects of her own performance in light of her goals. The trainee and the supervisor go over student response forms that are designed to elicit students' reactions to specific aspects of her teaching. When the supervisor has videotape available, he can use videotape playbacks to help show the teacher how she performs and how she can improve. All this feedback can be immediately translated into practice when the trainee reteaches shortly after the critique conference.

## Patterns of Training: The Microlesson

The five-minute lesson fits into a framework of a week's emphasis on a particular skill. A typical pattern is as follows. The trainees receive a live or tape demonstration of the skill to be used in their five-minute lessons throughout the week. Opportunities are given for them to get clarifications of the purpose and uses of the skill in a classroom. Then each trainee is scheduled for two forty-five-minute sequences during the week. A sequence begins with the trainee teaching a brief lesson she has developed to stress some concept or principle. She usually teaches this lesson to three or four students. The supervisor is present in the rear of the room; when possible, the lesson is videotaped. After the trainee has taught for four minutes, the video technician, or the supervisor, gives her a signal indicating that she has one more minute. The signal can be either the snapping of the fingers or a visual cue of some kind.

After the lesson, the supervisor hands out the rating forms to the students and the supervisor fills one out himself. Since the rating forms are simple and familiar to the students, this rarely takes longer than a minute or so. When the students have finished rating and handed their forms to the supervisor, they leave the room. In the meantime, the teacher-trainee collects her materials and readies the room for the next trainee. Normally the supervisor tries to get the trainee to estimate her success with respect to the particular skill being worked on. Then they move on to the students' and supervisor's rating reports, which deal with aspects of the skill still to be learned.

During the critique period the trainee and supervisor center their discussion on the performance of the skill and occasionally on one other item which the trainee is interested in improving. When a videotape recording is available, pertinent parts of it are reviewed. The intention of the critique period is to help the trainee think of ways of improving her performance for the next teaching session, which will follow shortly. The supervisor's main objectives are to help the trainee think and to offer alternative approaches. At the end of the ten-minute critique period the trainee leaves the room for a fifteen-minute planning period. During this time she is expected to recast her lesson in the light of the suggestions of the supervisor and the students and particularly her own fresh thoughts. While the trainee is rethinking her lesson, the supervisor is going through a five-minute teach-critique cycle with another trainee.

After the planning break, the first trainee begins the second phase: the reteach session. She teaches the same basic lesson, not to the original three or four students, but to a new group of students at the same grade level as the first. At the end of the lesson, the same procedures are followed. Rating forms are filled out and parts of the videotape are viewed. The supervisor helps the trainee to evaluate her progress from teach to reteach session, and suggests ways that the skill could be further improved. Then the second trainee begins his reteach session. The entire pattern from *first teach to second critique* takes forty-five minutes.

Two days later the trainee returns to the clinic and repeats the forty-five-minute pattern of teach, critique, planning, reteach and recritique. Although the trainee develops and teaches a different lesson, she works on the performance of the same skill. This particular pattern of five-minute lessons allows the trainee to practice each skill four times under conditions of maximum feedback, and it has been found to be adequate for most of the trainees for most of the skills. When a trainee has trouble with a particular skill, however, special arrangements are made. The supervisor schedules extra microteaching time for her. Normally, one day a week is set aside for make-up work and extra training sessions.

Many are shocked at the brief period of time allowed for practice in the microlesson. A common question is "what could possibly be taught in five minutes?" Since this question most frequently comes from college and high school teachers, one could surmise that these groups have been conditioned to think that knowledge comes in forty-five- or fifty-minute chunks. Still, most people, when they encounter microteaching for the first time, are constantly wanting to increase the class size and length of lesson.

A number of formal and informal experiments in this regard produced the consistent result that time is not really a very important variable. Specifically, we looked at the difference between four- and seven-minute lessons, and found no detectable differences. Perhaps there is a universal phenomenon that holds in the microteaching world as well as in the actual classroom: A teacher with four minutes wants five, and one with five would like seven, and one with seven would like ten, and one with ten would be more comfortable with fifteen. Is this not reminiscent of the teacher with forty minutes? He wants forty-five. And with forty-five, he wants fifty minutes, and with fifty minutes he is sure that fifty-five would be even better. We pay entirely too much attention to the variable of time in American education at all levels, microteaching included. The only real evidence we have to back up this opinion is that our trainees have rarely found the five-minute lesson a great limitation.

Our insistence on adhering to the five-minute microlesson pattern would seem arbitrary indeed, however, if all we could say for it was that our students could adjust to it. The length of the microlesson follows from its purpose. Recall that one of the major purposes of the clinic is to provide training in selected teaching skills. And although the short microlesson is not suitable for the practice of all skills, for many this time period seems ideal. Microteaching is designed to be a highly focused, highly concentrated experience. Five minutes of practice of a selected skill gives both the trainee and the supervisor much grist for the mill. The short teaching experience, as opposed to a longer session, allows for a greater possibility of recall of specific instances of the skill performance.

Looked at from another perspective, the short period of time allows little opportunity for extraneous problems to muddy the water. In longer microteaching lessons, of ten minutes or more, the trainee does many more things and gets involved in many more teaching behaviors. This, in turn, tends to make the critique session more diffused and apparently less effective.

Another feature of this short microlesson is that it allows for more frequent practice by the teacher. Instead of having one long training period followed by a long critique, the microteaching clinic proceeds on the premise that many short teaching periods followed immediately by critique periods can bring about more desirable results.

Finally, for pre-service teachers the microlesson is one link in a progressive chain to actual classroom teaching. The next link is the microclass.

# STUDENT
# EVALUATION FORMS

These forms can be used by students to evaluate your teaching.

Mark the appropriate space on the following continua:

For me, this class is:

| | | | | | |
|---|---|---|---|---|---|
| free | | | | | restricted |
| discouraging | | | | | encouraging |
| relevant | | | | | irrelevant |
| warm | | | | | cold |
| organized | | | | | disorganized |
| easy | | | | | difficult |
| slow | | | | | fast |
| boring | | | | | interesting |
| motivating | | | | | not motivating |
| comfortable | | | | | uncomfortable |

The following aspects of this lesson were good:

The following aspects of this lesson need improvement:

If I were teaching this lesson, I would:

Draw a picture of a good teacher. Include anything significant that you feel makes a good teacher. List any characteristics that a good teacher has. Which of these characteristics are exemplified by the teacher of this class?*

Draw a picture of a poor teacher. Include anything significant that you feel makes a poor teacher. List any characteristics that a poor teacher possesses. Which of those characteristics are exemplified by the teacher of this class?

* Adapted from R. Curwin and B. Fuhrman, *Discovering Your Teaching Self* (Englewood Cliffs, NJ: Prentice Hall, 1976) 212.

# COMMUNICATIVE READING

## OBJECTIVES

After reading this appendix and completing the activities you should be able to:

- Define communicative reading
- Define the components of communicative reading
- List considerations when selecting literature
- Outline the steps in preparing material for communicative reading
- Prepare a selection for communicative reading
- Present the selection

## INTRODUCTION

*After supper she (the Widow Douglas) got her book and learned me about Moses and the Bullrushers, and I was in a sweat to find out all about him.*[1]

No teacher should pass up the opportunity to read to her class. Reading aloud can be used to introduce a unit of instruction, to help explain a concept, to motivate students, and to simply provide enjoyment and appreciation of literature.

However, reading aloud—communicative reading—involves more than simply vocalizing words. "It requires an appreciation of one's material as a work of literary art and the ability to communicate that work of art through voice and body. It demands full intellectual and emotional response from the interpreter, and a control and channeling of the understanding and emotion to elicit the appropriate response from the audience."[2]

This chapter will examine two major areas of inquiry concerning communicative reading: (1) what communicative reading is, and (2) what procedures are used to insure good communicative reading.

## WHAT IS COMMUNICATIVE READING?

Communicative reading is reading aloud to communicate meaning to an audience. You want your audience to "see," in their minds, the images and ideas you create orally.

As the systems perspective suggests, you do not read in a vacuum. Your students are an integral part of the communicative reading process. When we share literature with others, we want them to understand and enjoy the selection. Thus, you need to be aware of three important components in the communicative reading situation. First, you need to understand the content of the material. You cannot communicate the message of the material if you do not understand it. Secondly, you need to understand the emotional quality of the selection—the "feelings" in the selection. Finally, you need to be aware of aesthetic entirety, or the manner in which the parts work together to create the whole.

Thus, a triadic relationship exists between you (the communicative reader), the literary selection, and the audience—your students. This relationship can be diagrammed as a triangle. This relationship, like all communicative relationships, is dynamic. Each component influences and is influenced by every other component.

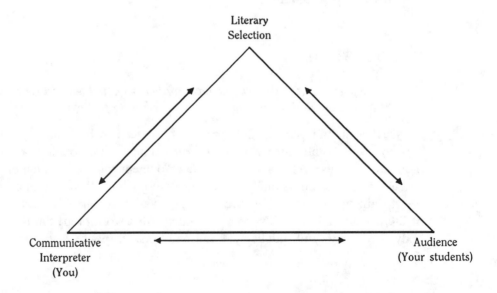

Literary
Selection

Communicative
Interpreter
(You)

Audience
(Your students)

**ACTIVITY C.1**

Think back over your school experiences. Consider a time when an instructor utilized communicative reading. For what purpose was it used? Did you enjoy it? Why or why not? What effect did the use of communicative reading have on your motivation to learn? Your feelings for the class? For the instructor?

## Components of Communicative Reading

As the diagram of the triangle indicates, three components are important in communicative reading—the communicative reader, the literary selection, and the audience. Each of these components will be discussed separately. Remember, however, that this separation is for analysis only. In actuality, the components cannot be separated; they work together to create the "aesthetic entirety" discussed earlier. In addition to these three components, some techniques of the oral presentation will be presented.

### The Communicative Reader

Think back to our discussion of self-concept in chapter 2. Remember that I indicated that we each reveal ourselves every time we communicate. The literature you choose to share with your students reveals a lot about you—your feelings, beliefs, and attitudes. It's important to choose material that you enjoy. Beginning public speakers are often told to choose a topic of interest to them. The same can be said of communicative reading. If you're not genuinely interested in the material, your students won't be either. Have a genuine desire to communicate with your students. Never read to your students simply to "fill up time." Communicative reading should be used because it can help students with motivation, learning, or attitudes. Consider your skills as an oral communicator. Consider your voice, gestures and bodily movements, eye contact, facial expressions, etc. Do you have any habits that might be distracting? Many things can distract your students from what you're reading, such as the time of day, noises outside as well as inside the classroom, and their internal states. You may not be able to control these factors, but you can eliminate the elements in you that could be distracting. Remember, the focus of your students should be on the thought, emotions, and attitudes of the selection, not on you as a reader.

## ACTIVITY C.2

1.  What types of literature do you like best—poetry, prose, drama? Jot down some of your favorite literary selections and authors.
2.  Analyze your strengths and weaknesses as an oral reader.

### *The Literary Selection*

You have a variety of literature from which to choose—poetry, prose fiction, nonfiction prose, and drama. Regardless of the type of literature, several guidelines should be followed when choosing literature for communicative reading.

Perhaps the first consideration when choosing literature is whether or not it's worth your time and effort. Does it have literary merit? Does it have unity and harmony of theme and style? Does it have sufficient variety and contrast to hold interest? Is the plot clear? Are the characters well developed? Does it have aesthetic qualities?

Having determined that the selection has sufficient literary merit to warrant your time and effort, your next consideration should be its appropriateness. Is it appropriate for your students? Would the selection hold their interest? Is it appropriate for their age level? Could they understand and appreciate it on the first reading?

Is the selection appropriate for the classroom situation? For example, what are the physical limitations such as time allotted for a particular subject or unit? Similarly, is the selection appropriate for your educational purpose? For example, suppose you want to instill an appreciation for poetry in your students by reading some poetry to them. It will be very important to choose poetry that they will enjoy. Although you may find "Beowulf" extremely exciting, it's probably not the best poem to choose for instilling an appreciation of poetry, at least not initially.

Finally, is the selection appropriate for reading aloud? Some selections will be too complex for your students to understand when hearing it read aloud. It may contain too many words they don't understand. The style could be too complex. For a variety of reasons, some literature is simply not appropriate for oral presentation.

## ACTIVITY C.3

Choose a concept you would teach. Choose the grade level you'll teach. Choose a teaching method—lecture, discussion, or use of small groups. Return to the literary selections you listed in activity C.2. Choose one of these to introduce or develop the concept.

Analyze the selection by answering the following questions.

Is the selection worth your time and effort? Why?

Is the selection appropriate for the grade level? Why?

Is the selection appropriate for your purpose and situation? Why?

Is the selection appropriate for oral presentation? Why?

---

### The Audience—Your Students

It's June, and it's over
The quizzes, the tests—
they passed them all.
But I never found time to get to know them.[3]

Too often we fail to really get to know our students. If we want to be effective communicative readers, we must know our audience—their attitudes, beliefs, likes, and dislikes. Only when we really know our students can we accurately determine what selections are appropriate for them.

In addition to analyzing your students prior to the actual oral reading, you'll need to analyze them as you are reading and adapt accordingly. For example, if students are straining to hear you, you'll need to talk louder. If the oral reading is to be successful, it will be necessary to monitor the reactions of your students. This will be difficult if you never look up from your material!

Finally, post-analysis is important. Ask for reactions from your students. Did they enjoy the reading? What did they learn? Ask them questions to determine if you fulfilled your purpose.

---

### ACTIVITY C.4

Return to the selection you chose in activity C.3. Will it be appropriate for the students you'll teach? Why or why not?

---

## PREPARING THE SELECTION

Now that you've chosen a selection that is suitable for you and your students, it's time to prepare the selection for reading.

## Understanding the Selection

Preparation of the selection begins with a thorough understanding of the selection. What is the mood of the selection? What conflict exists? Who are the characters? What is the point of view of the selection? What is the theme? Does knowledge of the author's background or other works by the author help you to understand the selection? What images are created? What literary techniques, such as alliteration, metaphor, metonymy, hyperbole, or onomatopoeia are used? Put yourself into the selection by considering such questions as, "How would I feel? What would I say? What would my reactions be?"

## Cutting the Selection

Sometimes you will find a selection that fits your purposes perfectly except that it is too long. If this is the case, the selection must be "cut." Cutting a selection must not impair its purpose, attitude, atmosphere, or total impact. What to cut:

1. When possible, cut whole incidents which are not essential to understanding the portion you will read.
2. Cut out characters who are not essential to the part you will read.
3. Cut any description unnecessary to the setting of the mood.
4. Cut any repetition unless it is necessary for emphasis, or for some other obvious reason.
5. Cut the "he said's" and descriptions of action or manner of speaking: "Gary looked up shyly." Imply the action with voice, movement, gestures, or facial expression.
6. Cut profanity or any element which may offend your audience.

---

### ACTIVITY C.5

Below is a selection.[4] Analyze the selection until you are sure you understand it. Then cut the selection. Compare your cutting with that of another classmate. Discuss why you cut the selection in the way you did.

### I Was Sure to Follow
*by Beth Pearson Cooper*

My gimlet eye zeroed in on Rob and Bill sneaking around the corner of the house.

"Hey, you guys!" I called cheerily all in a breath, "Me and Pink git to go help fetch the cow 'cause Mama said we could!"

The boys stopped, disgusted. They hated Me and Pink, Rob and Bill did, and there was no doubt about it.

Bill narrowed his eyes and hissed, "Geez, you cry babies make me wanta throw up! Why don'tcha ever mind yer own beeswax!"

"Yeah," Rob growled, "Me and Bill, we can't never do nothin' or go nowhere but what yer right on our heels. An' one of these days yer gonna be plenty sorry!"

Both boys glowered at Me and Pink so fiercely that if looks could kill we would have met our demise right then and there. But we weren't worried. We'd heard that threatening lingo too many times before. Besides, we held the winning ace in the hole—my Mother had said we could go.

Me and Pink were six years old that summer and I will call us that now as I did then although I had been told a thousand times to say "Pink and I." I was a fat little girl in a cotton sunsuit with my hair chopped off above the lobes of my ears. Pink, whose given name was David Eugene, was a cousin visiting all the way from the City of Angels, Los Angeles, California.

Pink was a whole inch shorter than I, and skinny, and he smelled little boy good, like castile soap and sunshine. Everybody called him Pink because he was crazy about what he called pink bean soup, a concoction of navy beans cooked with tomatoes and ham hock that was standard fare those hard time years. Pink ingested barrels of the stuff.

Pink's hair was bleached white from the sun and it stuck up in back like Alfalfa's in "Our Gang" comedies. He had at least half a million freckles and he was my favorite cousin. I loved him even though he was dizzy as a June bug. I knew for a fact he was loony. Else he never could have stood to leave his home in Los Angeles, right next door you might say, to movie stars like Mickey Rooney and Judy Garland and be content to spend the summer in a dusty backwoods village in North Missouri. The very idea was beyond me! But when I asked him about it, Pink thought a bit, spit on his thumb, crossed his heart and hoped to die and said, "Well, hell! I like it here in Missouri a damn sight better than California any day of the damn week!" Pink swore an awful lot but I noticed he never did within the hearing of the mothers.

Rob was Pink's brother and Bill was another cousin and they were four years older than Me and Pink. Being that much advanced in age, the two of them fairly radiated savoir-faire. They did wicked, secret things Me and Pink were always trying to copy. Such as rolling cornsilk cigarettes in newspaper which they smoked in a rickety tree house high up among concealing leaves. Naturally Me and Pink thought they were the living end while they considered us to be a disaster.

The cow we were to fetch was named Josephine and she was beautiful. Her coat was white with brown spots and her soft velvety ears and great liquid eyes captured our trembling hearts. Me and Pink usually got to ride her home, spraddled across her broad back that tickled our knobby knees digging into her sides, while Rob and Bill prodded her along. "Git on, Josephine! Hi! Hi! Git along now!" But Josephine, having a mind all her own, never planned to hurry—she preferred to munch her way home.

This most lovely of bovines, Josephine, belonged to Bill's parents and it was at their home the entire family—aunts, uncles and cousins of all sizes—had gathered to honor the visiting Californians.

In winter Josephine dwelt luxuriously in a snug shed down the slope back of the house. But in summer she was pastured at the end of a country lane near the edge of town and it was Bill's chore to milk her and drive her to pasture in the morning and back again at night. These excursions were highlights of the day to Me and Pink and we looked forward to tagging along.

I would like to make it clear right here and now that Rob and Bill never once begged us to go with them. And this time they ran down the road slapping their thighs and galloping like horses. They were Tom Mix and Gene Autry riding to head the rustlers off at the pass and they yelled, "HYAH! HYAH!" hoping Me and Pink would give up the chase just this one time and stay at home.

Pink scoffed derisively at their retreating backsides, "Hells bells! Lookit 'em go!" he said. "They oughta know they ain't never gonna git rid of us that damn easy!"

It was late in the afternoon and just plain hot. You could see heat waves shimmering in the distance but Me and Pink didn't mind. We were used to it.

We were unusually carefree because we had somehow managed to stay out of trouble all the day long. Which was a star-spangled miracle in itself for Pink was a wizard at getting us into spankable mischief and exactly like Mary's little lamb "everywhere cousin Pink went I was sure to follow."

We ambled along and scuffled our bare feet in the dust. We picked dandelions pregnant with scraggly seed and scattered it upon the lawns of rich and poor alike, happily ensuring a bumper crop of dandelions the following spring.

It being supper time there drifted upon the air the delicious aroma of someone frying potatoes in bacon fat. Since Me and Pink were nearly always hungry it made our stomachs churn and we broke into a run to catch up with Rob and Bill at the pasture gate.

For some reason Rob and Bill had undergone a miraculous change of heart that Me and Pink would have been hard put to believe had we stopped to think about it. Acting with splendid politeness they held open the wooden gate and graciously ushered us through. Then they pulled the gate closed behind them and dropped a board into a slot shutting us securely inside Josephine's pasture.

Bill grinned, winked slyly at Rob and singsonged, "Won'tcha step into my parlor said the spider to the fly?" And the two of them snickered at a private joke Me and Pink couldn't be expected to understand.

There was always the devil of a time catching Josephine. She was a young heifer and loved to tease. She would lope about the pasture staying out of reach and playing the coquette until she grew weary of the game. Then, suddenly shy, she would butt her head against us and want to be scratched behind her ears.

But Me and Pink, taking advantage of Rob and Bill's expansive attitude, were in no mood for Josephine's shenanigans.

"C'mon, Pink!" I cried. "Let's you and me go lookin' for toads." and we grabbed up some sticks and ran over to a farm pond and started poking in the mud. My daddy had showed us how to stroke a toad on its head to make it "sing." Daddy said it was the male or the female, one or the other, that "sang." I never did remember which sex could be induced to perform this remarkable feat but sometimes they would give a kind of creaky bumble and sometimes not.

To tantalize me Pink hummed "La Cucaracha" under his breath. For days I had implored him to teach me the words and he'd always refused. But suddenly, out of the kindness of his heart, he declared he'd do it. I could barely believe my ears!

"Now lissen close," he said. "These're Spanish words and you gotta git 'em just right. They go like this—'La Kook a raw cha, la kook a raw cha—'"

Happily oblivious to everything around us Me and Pink didn't notice that Rob and Bill had corralled Josephine and led her to where we squatted on the brink of the pond.

"Say, Bill," Rob cooed confidently, "I betcha these two little brats would like a nice swim on such a hot day, don't you?"

"Maybe they would at that!" Bill agreed.

Now Me and Pink were not stupid and we recognized instantly the danger of our position. We tried to scramble away but it was too late.

Dispassionately, like the cold-blooded fiends we always knew them to be, Rob and Bill pushed us into that indescribable mess.

It might well have been the shock of our lives up to that point! Never in a hundred years would we have ventured into that filth on our own.

The summer had been one of severe drought with not so much as a single drop of rain falling for weeks and weeks so that there was little more to the pond than a layer of stagnant water over festering mud, the whole covered with scrabby green scum that stank something terrible. And it was into this horrid putrification Me and Pink flew headfirst, sprawling on all fours.

We struggled soggily out of the muck in slow motion like spawning prehistoric fledglings, wiping slime from our eyes and sputtering it from our nostrils. We were completely swaddled in a cocoon of ooze. Too stunned to merely cry, we crawled up the clay banks of the pond dripping gore, clambered over the pasture gate slipping and clutching at the boards and headed for home squalling loud enough to be heard a mile away.

Pink was so furious he was in a fit. He screamed, "Damn ya sonzabitches! I'll gitcha fer this! I'll gitcha if it's the last thing I ever do!"

Awe stricken, gasping and hilarious, Rob and Bill watched our humiliating escape, observing the scheme to get even with Me and Pink for dogging their every step culminating in a howling, no pun intended, success.

Never being ones to suffer in silence, Me and Pink shrieked louder as we neared our destination to bring the mothers and aunts rushing to see what we had got into this time.

I suppose everyone has at least one excitable aunt and ours was Aunt Ola. She didn't let us down but began her usual screechy "Hoo! Hoo! Hoo!" in a reedy voice like a moonstruck owl which added to the bedlam considerably.

Pink controlled himself enough to sob the explanation for our contaminated condition. "Those damn guys, Rob and Bill, they pushed us in the damn pond!" I heard him say the taboo word and I quaked in my bones for Pink. "He's sure gonna catch it now!" I thought. But nobody else seemed to hear which was a good thing I guess.

Me and Pink stunk so bad everyone gagged and held their noses while we were shepherded around to the back of the house where our mothers filled galvanized washtubs with water and collected old towels for a bath in the yard. The foul likes of us wouldn't be allowed to sully our aunt's pristine bathroom!

My mother and Pink's were mad as old wet geese! Looking for all the world like medieval witches, they gingerly snipped our ruined clothes off with sewing shears and burned them right before our astonished eyes, meanwhile muttering all sorts of evil incantations against Rob and Bill. Pink suggested a day or two of Chinese water torture would be fitting punishment and they agreed which lifted our spirits a good deal. But as it turned out Rob and Bill didn't even get a whipping. Those two boys were smart. They didn't show up until the worst of the mothers' wrath was spent so all they ever got was a harsh scolding. Which didn't disappoint Rob and Bill so that you could notice it but made Me and Pink pretty sad.

It took a lot of scrubbing and three changings of water to get us clean. But at last we were clothed in soft pajamas and hysterical Aunt Ola, who could nonetheless be counted on in an emergency, rubbed our legs and arms with her homemade rose scented glycerol lotion that stung in the scratches but soon left us feeling pampered and soothed. And all the while she was doing it she babbled—"I-declare-I-wouldn't-be-a-bit-surprised-if-the-both-of-you-don't-come-down-with-typhoid-fever-or-somethin'-dreadful-bein'-dunked-in-a-nasty-old-pesthole-like-that-those-boys-need-the-tarnation-whipped-out-of-them-you-poor-little-darlings—" etc. etc. Me and Pink could tell she was getting all worked up to hoot again.

At supper Aunt Ola hovered over us protectively, clucking like a mother hen with newly hatched chicks while her manner toward Rob and Bill was "decidedly chilly with no appreciable change in sight." So the ordeal hadn't been such a total loss, after all.

Me and Pink were so tired we didn't protest when we were sent to bed soon after dark. The night was smotheringly warm and we were allowed to spread sweet smelling quilts on the floor where it might be a bit cooler. Not a single wisp of breeze stiffed the ruffled curtains. And from where I lay I could see the Big Dipper high in God's Heaven, timeless and reassuring. Somewhere beyond the inky Missouri night lurked a bright dawning, impatient to herald another adventuresome day just for Me and Pink. In spite of preceding events of the day, my world was definitely intact.

Still, I was restless. Something nagged at my consciousness like an unfinished melody. There was some meaning to the day I didn't quite understand. Suddenly into my six year old brain flashed a revelation—a spark of truth! Rob and Bill did not always desire the company of Me and Pink! "I reckon," I mused to myself drowsily, "we better not tag after them all of the time." And so, having determined that bit of wisdom, I clutched my shredded ego to my breast along with an equally tattered one-eyed teddy bear and slept.

The next morning, as I recall, Me and Pink were taking turnabout in Bill's tire swing and I was letting the old cat die. No, that is not exactly true. Actually I was Dale Evans and my weary horse staggered and slowed as I desperately sought Roy Rogers to warn that a misguided posse was hot on his trail. "I ben thinkin', Roy,—er, Pink," I said, "an' I ain't ganna always tag along after Rob and Bill to fetch the cow."

I glanced at Pink to see how such a novel idea would appeal to him but Pink was not there. John Wayne was, though. Tall, silent, strong. His steely eyes scanned the menacing horizon. A hard hand drifted down and casually caressed his holstered gun, making sure it was there should he have need of it. Deliberate and calm he spat into a mound of dust at his feet. He hitched up his pants. At last he spoke. "Me neither, Ma'am!" he drawled feelingly. "Not e-ver-y damn time!"

So I have to surmise that Pink had learned the same lesson as I—that lesson being that my presence, charming and stimulating though it might be, is not indispensable to other people's happiness or peace of mind. It has stood me in good stead. Through the years I've discovered that no matter how close the relationship, whether between husband and wife or parent and child or friend and friend, each person needs time to be alone. Time to plan and to dream. Time in which to come to know the most cantankerous, complex person of all, oneself.

Looking back, I believe I learned almost everything really important those childhood years. Some lessons I've had to relearn time and again but valuable things like how to give and accept love and how to get along with my fellow travelers on this spinning orb, these things I learned in the bosom of that large, wonderful, loving family. I was a fortunate child.

All of the old ones are gone, the aunts and uncles, the mothers and fathers, and Me and Pink are the older generation now. Isn't that strange?

Bill is gone, too. Destined to never become older than twenty-one years of age, he died in a bomber over Germany in World War II. And Rob, no less a casualty of that terrible holocaust, wanders the face of the earth a homeless creature, with not wife nor child nor brother knowing his whereabouts for months at a time.

Yes, I remember them all and I loved them fiercely. Or to be more exact, I love them. For as long as I live, every one of them lives, too, in my heart.

---

## Determining How the Selection Should Be Read

When you've completed any necessary cutting, you're ready to determine "how" the selection should be read. The answer to "how?" is found in the meaning of the selection.

You'll use your voice and body to communicate the meaning of the selection. Voice changes can be used to communicate anger or joy. Posture and facial expression can help create a mood. Movement and gesture can help create a character.

Read the poem "Pam" on page 395. In order to create images in your audience's mind you would need to recall the smells and sounds of summer, the sights of a street you may have skipped along at age nine, the joy of your own childhood play pretending, the taste of a lollipop.

When you recall such things, your voice, facial expressions, gestures, movement, etc., will reflect the images in your own mind. As a result, you will be better able to communicate these images to your audience.

Put yourself into the selection by considering such questions as, "How would I feel? What would I say? How would I react?"

## Marking the Script

Each of us should develop a system of marking the selection to indicate how the material should be read. Below are a few suggestions.

1.  A diagonal line to indicate a pause—the more lines between the words, the longer the pause
2.  A curved line connecting words that should be read without stopping
3.  Solid underlining to indicate words to be stressed
4.  Broken underlining to demonstrate a faster pace is needed
5.  A dash to indicate the continuation of a thought from one line to another
6.  Notations to designate movement, gesture, facial expression, etc.

Examine the selection below. Notice how the marking system is used.

*Pam* [5]

Her ponytail bounces—
As moccasined feet/
<u>Hop</u> <u>skip</u>
And jump skip [Make voice reflect movement]
<u>The leaf shaded street.</u>

Clad in checkered blue shorts—
And a white midriff top/
A band aided hand—
Flaunts an iced lollipop. [Raise hand up as if holding a lollipop]

She has sun-blessed complexion.
She has eyes trusting grey.
She has a pert nose—
And curved mouth/
<u>Enchantingly</u> gay.

She lives play pretending—
This bewitched elf of mine/
For the whole world
Is <u>magic/</u>
When a lady/
Is nine.

---

## ACTIVITY C.6

Mark the selection you've chosen using the system presented, or using one of your own invention.

---

## Introducing the Selection

In order to prepare your students for the communicative reading you'll need to introduce the material you'll read. The introduction to communicative reading has the same functions as any introduction. These are to (1) gain the attention of the audience, (2) tell the author and title of the selection, and (3) establish a favorable atmosphere for the performance.

## ACTIVITY C.7

Read the following poem. Write an introduction to this poem. Share your introduction with the class. Discuss how the different introductions could affect student's perception and reception of the poem.

### The Spaces in Between

This house of mine has a Person—
You can't see it, but it's there—
It fills this house to bursting
And its heartbeat is everywhere.
You shrug a bit and laugh and say,
"My sense is not so keen.
I only see the walls and doors
And spaces in between."
Yes, there are doors and window sills
And walls that can be seen.
But the soul of this house dwells within
Those spaces in between!
And there you have the answer
It's not the things you see
That makes my pulse leap with joy
And means so much to me.
Rather, it's the laughter that
Rings out within these walls,
And the love that's here and happiness
And, the sadness that befalls
At times to every house. And so it is that all
These unseen things combine to mean
That the being of this house
Lives in the spaces in-between.
Yes, this house has a soul.
Don't glance with such chagrin,
For the soul of this house is composed
of all of those who dwell herein.[6]

## ACTIVITY C.8

Now write an introduction to the selection you chose in activity C.3.

## DELIVERING THE SELECTION

You've done your job as a communicative reader of literature well so far. Now you arrive at the actual moment of sharing your material with your students. Perhaps the most important concept to remember is that you should interpret the material and not "act it out." It is fine to use gestures, movement, and voice variation as long as they do not distract from the reading itself. Anything that calls attention to the reader rather than to the reading should be avoided.

Facial expressions can be very effective in communicative reading. You can indicate that you expect a humorous response by a sly grin or twinkle in the eye, for example. The mood of the selection, be it sadness, joy, or confusion, can be communicated effectively through facial expressions representing these emotions.

Be direct. Although you are reading to your students, you need to maintain a great deal of eye contact with them. Eye contact allows you to gauge how your students are receiving the reading, and enables you to make any necessary adjustments. Obviously, there may be some selections, or parts of selections, that don't need direct eye contact. If seclusion or privacy is being communicated, for example, indirect eye contact is probably more effective than direct eye contact. Once again, the selection determines how much eye contact is necessary. However, more selections will profit from direct than indirect eye contact.

Don't leave your students "hanging." We've all been in the situation of being unsure when a speaker has finished. Such experiences are frustrating. When you finish your reading, make a definite concluding action so the listeners will know the reading is over. For example, pause and close your book.

## IN SUM

In this section I've discussed the role of communicative reading of literature in the educational environment. General guidelines for selecting, preparing, and delivering literary material were outlined.

**ACTIVITY C.9**

In a microteaching situation, present the selection you've prepared. Have your "students" evaluate your presentation using the evaluation form presented below.

*Communicative Reading Evaluation Form*

Name _____

Type of Literature _____

Title of Selection _____

Author _____

|   |   | *Excellent* | | | | *Poor* |
|---|---|---|---|---|---|---|
| 1. | Introduction | 5 | 4 | 3 | 2 | 1 |
| 2. | Appropriateness of vocal responsiveness | 5 | 4 | 3 | 2 | 1 |
| 3. | Appropriateness of physical responsiveness | 5 | 4 | 3 | 2 | 1 |
| 4. | Communication of mood, emotion, and thought | 5 | 4 | 3 | 2 | 1 |
| 5. | Appropriateness of selection | 5 | 4 | 3 | 2 | 1 |
| 6. | Clarity of ideas expressed | 5 | 4 | 3 | 2 | 1 |
| 7. | General effectiveness | 5 | 4 | 3 | 2 | 1 |

*Comments:*

Total Score _____

## NOTES

1. M. Twain, *The Adventures of Huckleberry Finn* (New York: Harper and Row, 1923) 2.

2. A. Cullum, *Blackboard, Blackboard on the Wall, Who Is the Fairest One of All?* (New York: Harlin Quist, 1978) 60.

3. B. Cooper. Used by permission of the author.

4. Cooper.

5. Cooper.

6. Cooper.

## SUGGESTIONS FOR FURTHER READING

Aggert, O., and E. Bowen. *Communicative Reading.* New York: Macmillan, 1963.

Ecroyd, D. *Speech in the Classroom.* Englewood Cliffs, NJ: Prentice Hall, 1960. Chapter 6.

Lee, C., and F. Galatti. *Oral Interpretation.* 5th ed. Boston: Houghton Mifflin, 1977.

Parrish, W. M. "Getting the Meaning of Interpretation." *Southern Speech Journal* (1968): 186–198.

Robinson, K., and A. Becker. *Effective Speech for a Teacher.* New York: McGraw-Hill, 1970.

Tway, E. *Writing Is Reading: 26 Ways to Connect.* Urbana, IL: ERIC, 1985.

# STORYTELLING
# IN THE CLASSROOM

## INTRODUCTION

*One dollar and eighty-seven cents. That was all. And sixty cents of it was in pennies. Pennies saved one and two at a time by bull-dozing the grocer and the vegetable man and the butcher until one's cheeks burned with the silent imputation of parsimony that such close dealing implied. Three times Della counted it. One dollar and eighty-seven cents. And the next day would be Christmas.*

So begins O'Henry's story *The Gift of the Magi.* As a child I was mesmerized every time my mother read or told me this story. The story remains a favorite of mine. Perhaps it appeals to me because I am a romantic. Perhaps it appeals to me because I have always coveted beautiful long thick hair, and so I can understand the sacrifice Della makes. Perhaps I love this story simply because it is a wonderful story.

We may not all be as eloquent a storyteller as O'Henry, but we are all, nonetheless, storytellers. We tell stories every day. The parent asks the child "What did you do in school today?" The wife asks her husband (and the husband asks his wife!), "How was work today?" The college student calls home, "You'll never guess what happened!" The point is, humans are storytelling animals. We tell stories to make sense of our lives, to share our experiences, and to share ourselves.

Fisher[1] indicates that the essential nature of human beings is that they are the storytelling animal—the "homo narran." Other writers concur. For example, Heilbrun[2] says we live our lives through our text. In other words, we are the stories we tell. These stories create a "witchery"—even making the mundane significant.[3] It is through stories that we become "in cahoots" with one another.[4]

Storytellers Ellin Greene and Laura Simms asked children, "What would happen if there were no stories in the world?" The children gave some very perceptive answers as recorded in the *Chicago Journal*, May 26, 1982:

"People would die of seriousness."

"When you went to bed at night it would be boring, because your head would be blank."

"There wouldn't be a world, because stories make the world."

---

### ACTIVITY D.1

Think about the events of today. What incident(s) stands out in your mind? What makes it memorable?

---

## VALUE OF STORYTELLING

Each of us lives by stories. The stories we "buy into" shape us, give our lives meaning and direction. It is not, however, merely the content of these stories that is important. Perhaps more important is the process of storytelling—the dynamic learning experience that the occasion of storytelling makes possible. This is no doubt true because in the process of storytelling, one human reaches out to another in a direct and positive manner.

Jack McGuire makes a strong argument for the educational value of storytelling:

*Within the necessarily artificial climate of a classroom environment, storytelling is alive, intimate, and personally responsible in a way that the majority of contemporary educational processes are not. In fact, it can be easily claimed that no other educational process comes as naturally to our species. Throughout humankind's preliterate history, storytelling remained the preeminent instructional strategy. By casting information into story form, ancient instructors accomplished several purposes: they rendered that information more entertaining and memorable (for themselves as well as their pupils); they made that information more relevant to their pupils' lives, because it was already grounded in a recognizably human context; and they expressed themselves not simply as experts but as creative, living beings, which helped their pupils to understand, trust, and emulate them more effectively.[5]*

Several researchers have examined the positive effect of using storytelling as a teaching strategy,[6] and teachers are increasingly using this strategy.[7] Why? No doubt the reason relates to the value of storytelling.

Noting the rapid decline of language skills over the past two generations, child psychologists and educators are now actively championing storytelling as an ideal method of influencing a child to associate listening with pleasure, of increasing a child's attention span and retention capacity, of broadening a child's vocabulary, and of introducing a child to the symbolic use of language. The specific educational and social benefits of storytelling from the child's point of view are numerous and well documented. In addition to increasing a child's vocabulary, concentration, and ability to think symbolically and metaphorically, storytelling's values also include:[8]

- building a child's sensitivity to various forms of syntax, diction, and rhetoric
- helping a child to recognize patterns in language and in human experience
- stimulating a child's overall powers of creativity
- providing a child with problem-solving and decision-making exercises
- strengthening a child's capacity to form objective, rational, and practical evaluations
- assisting a child to develop skills in dialogue and cooperative interpersonal behavior
- familiarizing a child with the symbols, artifacts, and traditions that are part of his own cultural heritage
- introducing a child to the symbols, artifacts, and traditions that characterize the cultural heritages of others with whom she shares the world

Perhaps most important, storytelling is fun. Storytelling is not a spectator sport. The listener and teller are united in the building of the story. The listener may engage in one or more types of participation: ritual, coactive, bantering, predictive, and eye contact.[9]

## In Defense of Telling Stories

*"I tell a lot of stories. Stories are nails that I hammer into the wall. On those nails I can hang up the whole, usually highly abstract, conceptual stuff of a philosophy course. If there are no nails in the wall, all the stuff falls down and will be forgotten. But if there are stories, illustrations, visualizations, they will not be forgotten; and contained in the stories there are the problems and the concepts. Years later students will remember the stories and because of the stories, still understand the concepts."*
—Jacob Amstutz, philosophy professor emeritus, University of Guelph. Reprinted with permission from *Teaching Forum*, November 1987.

## STORYTELLING TECHNIQUES

### Choosing a Story

When choosing a story, look for one which has

- simple, yet colorful language (repetitions, rhymes, catchphrases)
- simple, well-rounded plot
- limited number of well-delineated characters
- single theme, clearly defined
- suspense
- fast tempo and excitement

Most importantly tell a story you *really* like. If you choose a story you like, your ability to remember it and tell it convincingly are enhanced.

---

### ACTIVITY D.2

Choose a story to tell. It may be one you have read or heard. It may be a personal story. Why will this story be a good one to tell?

---

### Learning a Story

Beginning storytellers often try to memorize a story word for word. This is neither necessary nor desirable (unless there is a repeated phrase or rhyme which is central to the story). Memorizing a story leaves no room for your individual additions and nuances. What should be remembered is the sequence of events and sequence of images created in your mind. When learning a story, the following sequence is helpful:

- Read the story over several times.
- Close the book and try to see the sequence of the story in your mind.
- Open and read the story again, this time for the words that will add color to your telling (i.e., descriptive, concrete words that describe shape, color, design, etc.).
- Repeat the same process of visualizing the story in your mind.
- Now write out, draw, or outline the story (whatever suits you).
- Retell the story in your own words, out loud so you can hear whether it pleases the ear.

- Tell the story to a friend, or record it.
- Retell the story until you are pleased with your "performance."

## Tips for Telling

You've prepared well. It's now time to tell your story to an audience—your students. Following the guidelines below will greatly enhance your chances for success:[10]

- Rapport is everything! Eye contact is essential. Each listener should feel that the story is being told just for him.
- Image! The tale teller must create vivid images for herself if she wants listeners to see them too. See the pictures and people you are describing. Encourage your audience to imagine with all five of their senses.
- Use vocal variety; predictability is death. Be sure to vary tone, rhythm, pitch, volume, and intensity. Use silences and pauses which will give your listeners a time to imagine.
- Whenever possible, give the storytelling a sense of occasion. Use ritual (light a candle, share an object, close your eyes for a moment) to transform an environment into a private place for storytelling.
- Capture your audience with a well-baited hook. Make them eager to hear the story before you begin the telling.
- Leave your listeners with a "button." Give your story a sense of closure.
- Relish the language. Find the characteristic words which give this story its special flavor. Enjoy the alliterations, the onomatopoeia, and the other devices of language.
- Be selective. The artist knows how little he needs to tell the story. Choose words, characters, and events carefully.
- Enthusiasm is a key ingredient for effective storytelling. As Winifred Ward said, "Tell it with zest!"

### ACTIVITY D.3

Tell a story you have chosen and prepared to this class. Using the evaluation sheet below, ask your classmates to evaluate your storytelling.

## Storytelling Evaluation

Name of storyteller: _____  Date: _____

Name of evaluator: _____

1.  <u>Specifically,</u> what did you like about this story?

_____

_____

_____

2.  How did the storyteller use language, voice, gestures, and body movement to help you create a mental image of the characters, setting and time?

_____

_____

_____

_____

3.  List five things you think the storyteller did that made her story enjoyable to the listener.

   a. _____

   b. _____

   c. _____

   d. _____

   e. _____

4.  What suggestions for improvement would you make to this storyteller?

## IN SUM

On the mornings you tell us about the night before,
you're like one of us.
The dress you bought,
or a movie you saw,
or a strange sound you heard.
You're a good storyteller, teacher, honest!
And that's when I never have to be excused.[11]

Storytelling can have a positive influence in the classroom. It can be a way to "connect" with students. As a result, storytelling can enhance learning.

### Storyteller's Creed

I believe that imagination is stronger than knowledge.
That myth is more potent than history.
That dreams are more powerful than facts.
That hope always triumphs over experience.
That laughter is the only cure for grief.
And I believe that love is stronger than death.[12]

## NOTES

1. W. R. Fisher, "Narration as a Human Paradigm," *Communication Monographs*, 51 (1984): 1–22.

2. C. Heilbrun, *Writing the Women's Life* (New York: W. W. Norton, 1989).

3. V. Nell, *Lost in a Book: The Psychology of Reading for Pleasure* (New Haven: Yale UP, 1988).

4. R. Coles, *The Call of Stories: Teaching and the Moral Imagination.* (Boston: Houghton Mifflin, 1989).

5. J. McGuire, "Sounds and Sensibilities: Storytelling as an Educational Process," *Children's Literature Association Quarterly* 13 (1988): 6.

6. S. J. Holladay, "Narrative Activity and Teacher Effectiveness: An Investigation of the Nature of Storytelling in the Classroom," SCA Convention, Boston, 1987; J. Nussbaum, M. Comadena, and S. Holladay, "Classroom Verbal Behavior of Highly Effective Teachers," *Journal of Thought* 22 (1987): 73–80; V. Downs, M. J. Manchoochehr, and J. Nussbaum, "An Analysis of Teachers' Verbal Communication Within the College Classroom: Use of Humor, Self-disclosure, and Narratives," *Communication Education* 37 (1988): 127–141; and P. Cooper, "Looking into Classrooms: Storytelling as a Teaching Strategy," SCA Convention, New Orleans, 1988.

7. P. Cooper, "Using Storytelling to Teach Oral Communication Competencies K–12," SCA Convention, San Francisco, 1989; N. Holmes, "We're All Storytellers," *Learning 88* (Feb. 1988): 82–84; E. Medina, "Enhance Your Curriculum Through Storytelling," *Learning 86* (1986): 58–61; N. Mikkelsen, "Literature and the Storymaking Powers of Children," *Children's Literature Association Quarterly* 9 (1984): 9–14; N. Moses, "Telling Tales Pays Dividends in Class," *Chicago Tribune*, 1 May 1988, Sec. 9: 3, 6–7; F. Reinehr, "Storytelling," *Teachers and Writers Magazine*, 18(3) (Jan./Feb. 1987): 1–7; R. C. Roney, "Back to the Basics with Storytelling," *The Reading Teacher* (1989): 520–523; H. Rosen, "The Importance of Story," *Language Arts* 63(3) (March 1986): 226–237; M. Schwartz, "Connecting to Language Through Story," *Language Arts* 64(6) (Oct. 1987): 603–610; and "Telling Tales in School: A Revival of the Oral Tradition in the Nation's Classrooms," *Teacher* (Feb. 1990): 30–33.

8. J. McGuire, *Creative Storytelling* (New York: McGraw Hill 1985) 13–14.

9. N. Livo and S. Reitz, *Storytelling Process and Practice* (Littleton, CO: Libraries Unlimited, 1986).

10. I am indebted to Rives Collins, Assistant Professor of Theatre at Northwestern University and a professional storyteller, for these ideas.

11. A. Cullum, *The Geranium on the Windowsill Just Died But Teacher You Went Right On* (New York: Harlin Quist, 1971).

12. R. Fulghum, *All I Really Needed to Know I Learned in Kindergarten* (New York: Villard Books, 1988) viii.

## SUGGESTIONS FOR FURTHER READING

Blaustein, R. "A Guide to Collecting Family History and Community Traditions." *From the Brothers Grimm* 2 (1989): 4–8.

Boscov, R. "Storytellers." *Dramatics* (1985): 39–41.

Clark, E. C., M. Hyde, and E. McMahon. "Developing Instruction in Oral History: A New Avenue for Speech Communication." *Communication Education* 30 (1981): 238–244.

Cohan, S., and L. Shines. *Telling Stories: A Theoretical Analysis of Narrative Fiction.* New York: Routledge, 1988.

Gross, A., and M. Batchelder. "Storytelling: A Process Approach to Speaking Skills." *Integrating Speaking Skills into the Curriculum.* Ed. S. M. Nugent. Boston: New England Association of Teachers of English, 1986.

Kamler, H. *Communication: Sharing Our Stories of Experience.* Seattle, WA: Psychological Press, 1983.

Kirkwood, W. "Storytelling and Self-Confrontation: Parables as Communication Strategies." *Quarterly Journal of Speech* 69 (1983): 58–74.

Lakoff, G., and M. Johnson. *Metaphors We Live By.* Chicago: U of Chicago P, 1980.

Norton, C. S. *Life Metaphors: Stories of Ordinary Survival.* Carbondale, IL: Southern Illinois UP, 1989.

Pellowski, A., and L. Sweet. *The Family Storytelling Handbook.* New York: Macmillan, 1987.

Smith, J. N. *Homespun: Tales from America's Favorite Storytellers.* New York: Crown, 1988.

Zeitlin, S., A. Kotkin, and H. Baker. *A Celebration of American Family Folklore.* New York: Pantheon, 1982.

### Organizations

The National Association for the Preservation and Perpetuation of Storytelling.
  A membership organization that sponsors conferences, workshops, and the *National Storytelling Magazine* and a newsletter; and provides members with technical assistance in becoming or finding a storyteller. For more information contact: NAPPS, P.O. Box 309, Jonesborough, TN 37659.

# INSTRUMENTS FOR SYSTEMATIC OBSERVATION

## FLANDERS

The authors present ground rules to aid the user in categorizing behaviors correctly. These are outlined below.

1. When not certain in which of two or more categories a statement belongs, choose the category that is numerically farthest from category 5.
2. If the primary tone of the teacher's behavior has been consistently direct or consistently indirect, do not shift into the opposite classification unless a clear indication of shift is given by the teacher.
3. The effect of a statement on the pupils, and not the teacher's intent, is the crucial criterion for categorizing a statement.
4. If more than one category occurs during the three-second interval, then all categories used in that interval are recorded; therefore, record each change in category. If no change occurs within three seconds, repeat that category.
5. Directions are statements that result (or are expected to result) in observable behavior on the part of children.
6. When the teacher calls on a child by name, the observer ordinarily records a 4.
7. If there is a discernible period of silence (at least three seconds), record one 10 for every three seconds of silence, laughter, board work, etc.

8.  When the teacher repeats a student answer, and the answer is a correct answer, this is recorded as a 2.

9.  When the teacher repeats a student idea and communicates only that the idea will be considered or accepted as something to be discussed, a 3 is used.

10. If a student begins talking after another student (without the teacher's talking), a 10 is inserted between the 9s or 8s to indicate a change of student.

## *Tally Sheet*

| | | | | |
|---|---|---|---|---|
| 1. _____ | 26. _____ | 51. _____ | 76. _____ | 101. _____ |
| 2. _____ | 27. _____ | 52. _____ | 77. _____ | 102. _____ |
| 3. _____ | 28. _____ | 53. _____ | 78. _____ | 103. _____ |
| 4. _____ | 29. _____ | 54. _____ | 79. _____ | 104. _____ |
| 5. _____ | 30. _____ | 55. _____ | 80. _____ | 105. _____ |
| 6. _____ | 31. _____ | 56. _____ | 81. _____ | 106. _____ |
| 7. _____ | 32. _____ | 57. _____ | 82. _____ | 107. _____ |
| 8. _____ | 33. _____ | 58. _____ | 83. _____ | 108. _____ |
| 9. _____ | 34. _____ | 59. _____ | 84. _____ | 109. _____ |
| 10. _____ | 35. _____ | 60. _____ | 85. _____ | 110. _____ |
| 11. _____ | 36. _____ | 61. _____ | 86. _____ | 111. _____ |
| 12. _____ | 37. _____ | 62. _____ | 87. _____ | 112. _____ |
| 13. _____ | 38. _____ | 63. _____ | 88. _____ | 113. _____ |
| 14. _____ | 39. _____ | 64. _____ | 89. _____ | 114. _____ |
| 15. _____ | 40. _____ | 65. _____ | 90. _____ | 115. _____ |
| 16. _____ | 41. _____ | 66. _____ | 91. _____ | 116. _____ |
| 17. _____ | 42. _____ | 67. _____ | 92. _____ | 117. _____ |
| 18. _____ | 43. _____ | 68. _____ | 93. _____ | 118. _____ |
| 19. _____ | 44. _____ | 69. _____ | 94. _____ | 119. _____ |
| 20. _____ | 45. _____ | 70. _____ | 95. _____ | 120. _____ |
| 21. _____ | 46. _____ | 71. _____ | 96. _____ | 121. _____ |
| 22. _____ | 47. _____ | 72. _____ | 97. _____ | 122. _____ |
| 23. _____ | 48. _____ | 73. _____ | 98. _____ | 123. _____ |
| 24. _____ | 49. _____ | 74. _____ | 99. _____ | 124. _____ |
| 25. _____ | 50. _____ | 75. _____ | 100. _____ | 125. _____ |

11. Statements such as, "Uh huh, yes, yeah, all right, okay," which occur between two 9s are recorded as 2 (encouragement).
12. A teacher joke, which is not made at the expense of the children, is a 2.
13. Rhetorical questions are not really questions but are merely part of lecturing techniques and should be categorized as 5s.
14. A narrow question is a signal to expect an 8.
15. An 8 is recorded when several students respond in unison to a narrow question.

The numbers from the coding sheet can then be recorded on a 10 x 10 matrix like that pictured here.

## Work Matrix

|  | 1 | 2 | 3 | 4 | 5 | 6 | 7 | 8 | 9 | 10 |  |
|---|---|---|---|---|---|---|---|---|---|---|---|
| 1 |  |  |  |  |  |  |  |  |  |  |  |
| 2 |  |  |  |  |  |  |  |  |  |  |  |
| 3 |  |  |  |  |  |  |  |  |  |  |  |
| 4 |  |  |  |  |  |  |  |  |  |  |  |
| 5 |  |  |  |  |  |  |  |  |  |  |  |
| 6 |  |  |  |  |  |  |  |  |  |  |  |
| 7 |  |  |  |  |  |  |  |  |  |  |  |
| 8 |  |  |  |  |  |  |  |  |  |  |  |
| 9 |  |  |  |  |  |  |  |  |  |  |  |
| 10 |  |  |  |  |  |  |  |  |  |  | Matrix Total |
| TOTAL |  |  |  |  |  |  |  |  |  |  |  |
| % |  |  |  |  |  |  |  |  |  |  |  |

The tallies are paired, and then recorded on the matrix. The first number in the pair designates the appropriate horizontal row; the second number in the pair designates the appropriate column. For example, assume the first six categories in your observation were:

$$
\begin{array}{rl}
1. & \dfrac{10}{\phantom{0}} \\[4pt]
2. & \Big( \dfrac{5}{\phantom{0}} \Big) \\[4pt]
3. & \dfrac{5}{\phantom{0}} \\[4pt]
4. & \Big( \dfrac{4}{\phantom{0}} \Big) \\[4pt]
5. & \dfrac{8}{\phantom{0}} \\[4pt]
6. & \Big( \dfrac{4}{\phantom{0}} \Big)
\end{array}
$$

The first pair (10, 5) would be tallied in row 10, column 5 of the matrix. Pair two (5, 5) would be in row 5, column 5 and so forth. These six tallies would appear as follows in the matrix.

## Work Matrix

|        | 1 | 2 | 3 | 4 | 5 | 6 | 7 | 8 | 9 | 10 |              |
|--------|---|---|---|---|---|---|---|---|---|----|--------------|
| 1      |   |   |   |   |   |   |   |   |   |    |              |
| 2      |   |   |   |   |   |   |   |   |   |    |              |
| 3      |   |   |   |   |   |   |   |   |   |    |              |
| 4      |   |   |   |   |   |   |   | I |   |    |              |
| 5      |   |   |   | I | I |   |   |   |   |    |              |
| 6      |   |   |   |   |   |   |   |   |   |    |              |
| 7      |   |   |   |   |   |   |   |   |   |    |              |
| 8      |   |   |   | I |   |   |   |   |   |    |              |
| 9      |   |   |   |   |   |   |   |   |   |    |              |
| 10     |   |   |   |   | I |   |   |   |   |    | Matrix Total |
| TOTAL  |   |   |   |   |   |   |   |   |   |    |              |
| %      |   |   |   |   |   |   |   |   |   |    |              |

Once the tallies are entered on the matrix, the sequence, the amount, and the pattern of verbal communication in the classroom can be analyzed. The steps in this analysis are as follows:

1. Check the matrix total in order to estimate the elapsed coding time. Number of tallies multiplied by 3 equals seconds; divided by 60 equals minutes.

2. Check the percent of teacher talk, pupil talk, and silence or confusion, and use this information in combination with . . . (average of about 68 percent teacher talk, 20 percent pupil talk, and 11 or 12 percent silence or confusion).

3. . . . [Examine] the balance of teacher response and initiation in contrast with pupil initiation.
   a.  Indirect-to-direct ratios; useful for matrices with over 1,000 tallies
       (1) i/d ratio: 1 + 2 + 3 divided by 6 + 7
       (2) I/D ratio: 1 + 2 + 3 + 4 divided by 5 + 6 + 7.
   b.  TRR (teacher response ratio): teacher tendency to react to ideas and feelings of pupils. 1 + 2 + 3 times 100 divided by 1 + 2 + 3 + 6 + 7. Average is about 42.
   c.  TQR (teacher question ratio): tendency to use questions when dealing with content. Category 4 times 100 divided by 4 + 5. Average = 26.
   d.  PIR (pupil initiation ratio): proportion of pupil talk judged initiation. Category 9 times 100 divided by 8 + 9. Average close to 34.

4. Check the initial reaction of the teacher to the termination of pupil talk.
   a.  TRR89 (instantaneous teacher response ratio): teacher tendency to praise or integrate pupil ideas or feelings when student terminates. Add cell frequencies in rows 8 and 9, columns 1, 2, and 3 times 100 divided by tallies in rows 8 and 9 columns 1, 2, 3, 6, and 7. Average is about 60.
   b.  TQR89 (instantaneous teacher questions ratio): teacher tendency to respond to pupil talk with questions compared to lecture. Add cells (8 – 4) + (9 – 4) times 100 divided by (8 – 4) + (8 – 5) + (9 – 5). Average is about 44.

5. Check the proportions of tallies to be found in the "content cross" and "steady state cells" in order to estimate the rapidity of exchange, tendency toward sustained talk, and content emphasis.
   a.  CCR (content cross ratio): concerns categories most concerned with content. Calculate the percent of all tallies that lie within the columns and rows of 4 and 5. Average is close to 55 percent.

b. SSR (steady state ratio): tendency of teacher and pupil talk to stay in same category. Percentage of all tallies in 10 steady state cells (1 – 1), (2 – 2), etc. Average is around 50.

c. PSSR (pupil steady state ratio): tendency of pupils to stay in same category. Frequencies in (8 – 8) + (9 – 9) cells times 100 divided by all pupil talk tallies. Average around 35 or 40.

## GRANT AND HENNINGS

The inventory is presented below. Although it is stated in terms of self-analysis, it could be used by another teacher to observe you. It might be useful for you to complete the inventory and then have another teacher observe you, completing the inventory "on the scene" as you teach. You could then compare your view with the observer's.

### Part I

What kinds of motions tend to predominate in my nonverbal teaching style?

#### A. Conducting

How do I control participation, focus attention, and obtain attending behavior?

|  | Very Typical | Typical | Atypical |
|---|---|---|---|
| 1. *To indicate who the participant is, I:* | _____ | _____ | _____ |
| smile at the participant | _____ | _____ | _____ |
| focus my eyes on the participant | _____ | _____ | _____ |
| orient my body in the direction of the participant | _____ | _____ | _____ |
| nod at the chosen participant | _____ | _____ | _____ |
| point at the participant with finger, hand, stick, chalk, microphone, book | _____ | _____ | _____ |
| walk toward the participant | _____ | _____ | _____ |
| hand the pointer, chalk, book, microphone to the participant | _____ | _____ | _____ |
| touch the participant | _____ | _____ | _____ |
| other:_____ | _____ | _____ | _____ |

|  | Very Typical | Typical | Atypical |
|---|---|---|---|
| 2. *To rate a student's participation, I:* | | | |
| use facial expressions: smiling, frowning, grinning, wrinkling my brow, raising my eyebrows | _____ | _____ | _____ |
| shake my head | _____ | _____ | _____ |
| shrug my shoulders | _____ | _____ | _____ |
| clap my hands | _____ | _____ | _____ |
| make the OK sign with my fingers, forming an "O" by touching thumb to forefinger | _____ | _____ | _____ |
| put my hands to my face | _____ | _____ | _____ |
| hold my head | _____ | _____ | _____ |
| scratch my head | _____ | _____ | _____ |
| write the correct response on the board or on a chart | _____ | _____ | _____ |
| pat student on back | _____ | _____ | _____ |
| move my hand from respondent to another student who has hand up to respond | _____ | _____ | _____ |
| other:_____ | _____ | _____ | _____ |
| 3. *To respond to a student's participation, I:* | | | |
| use facial expressions | _____ | _____ | _____ |
| shake or nod head | _____ | _____ | _____ |
| walk toward or away from the participant | _____ | _____ | _____ |
| point or wave hand | _____ | _____ | _____ |
| write something on the board | _____ | _____ | _____ |
| other:_____ | _____ | _____ | _____ |
| 4. *To regulate the speed of classroom interaction, I:* | | | |
| beckon to child to continue | _____ | _____ | _____ |
| wave at child to stop | _____ | _____ | _____ |
| select motions of different speeds | _____ | _____ | _____ |
| other:_____ | _____ | _____ | _____ |

|  | Very Typical | Typical | Atypical |
|---|---|---|---|

5. *To focus student attention on a significant point in the lesson, I:*

| | Very Typical | Typical | Atypical |
|---|---|---|---|
| write the significant point on the board | _____ | _____ | _____ |
| underline a word or words written on the board | _____ | _____ | _____ |
| point to each word written on the board | _____ | _____ | _____ |
| write over each word written on the board, perhaps with colored chalk | _____ | _____ | _____ |
| point to a related chart, bulletin board display, or picture | _____ | _____ | _____ |
| point to a location on map or globe | _____ | _____ | _____ |
| point to the actual object | _____ | _____ | _____ |
| hold up the actual object | _____ | _____ | _____ |
| point to a person being discussed | _____ | _____ | _____ |
| point to a picture or statement projected by an audiovisual device | _____ | _____ | _____ |
| put words or letters into a pocket chart | _____ | _____ | _____ |
| attach word cards or pictures to the chalkboard using magnets or masking tape | _____ | _____ | _____ |
| hold up word card or picture | _____ | _____ | _____ |
| add the key ingredient to a demonstration I am doing | _____ | _____ | _____ |
| other:_____ | _____ | _____ | _____ |

6. *To get the attention of the total class or portion of the class, I:*

| | Very Typical | Typical | Atypical |
|---|---|---|---|
| close the door to indicate the lesson is beginning | _____ | _____ | _____ |
| flick the lights | _____ | _____ | _____ |
| tap a desk bell | _____ | _____ | _____ |
| pull down a chart or map | _____ | _____ | _____ |
| pick up a textbook or lesson plan book or record book | _____ | _____ | _____ |
| walk to the front-center of the room | _____ | _____ | _____ |

| | Very Typical | Typical | Atypical |
|---|---|---|---|
| survey the class, making eye contact | _____ | _____ | _____ |
| stand at attention | _____ | _____ | _____ |
| hold up my hand | _____ | _____ | _____ |
| play a note on the piano | _____ | _____ | _____ |
| arrange my chair or stool and sit down | _____ | _____ | _____ |
| tap fingers or pencil on desk | _____ | _____ | _____ |
| other:_____ | _____ | _____ | _____ |

7. *To get the attention of a misbehaving child or group of children, I:*

| | | | |
|---|---|---|---|
| orient my body toward and focus my eyes on the inattentive student(s) | _____ | _____ | _____ |
| frown or raise eyebrows at misbehaving student(s) | _____ | _____ | _____ |
| shake my head at the misbehaving student(s) | _____ | _____ | _____ |
| snap fingers in direction of misbehaving student(s) | _____ | _____ | _____ |
| clap hands | _____ | _____ | _____ |
| walk toward the misbehaving student(s) | _____ | _____ | _____ |
| touch misbehaving student(s) | _____ | _____ | _____ |
| sit down near misbehaving student(s) | _____ | _____ | _____ |
| touch object misbehaving student is touching | _____ | _____ | _____ |
| other:_____ | _____ | _____ | _____ |

## B. Acting

How do I use bodily motion to clarify and amplify meanings?

1. *To emphasize meanings, I:*

| | | | |
|---|---|---|---|
| use motion of my head | _____ | _____ | _____ |
| use facial expressions | _____ | _____ | _____ |
| use motions of my feet | _____ | _____ | _____ |
| use motions of my entire body | _____ | _____ | _____ |

|  | *Very Typical* | *Typical* | *Atypical* |
|---|---|---|---|
| 2. *To illustrate a concept, an object, or a* *process, I:* | | | |
| use motions of my hands | _____ | _____ | _____ |
| use motions of my head | _____ | _____ | _____ |
| use facial expressions | _____ | _____ | _____ |
| use motions of my feet | _____ | _____ | _____ |
| other:_____ | _____ | _____ | _____ |
| 3. *To illustrate even more completely,* *I use role playing motions to:* | | | |
| pretend I am an object | _____ | _____ | _____ |
| imitate an animal | _____ | _____ | _____ |
| pretend I am a particular character | _____ | _____ | _____ |
| pretend I am a puppet character | _____ | _____ | _____ |
| other:_____ | _____ | _____ | _____ |

## C. Wielding

In what ways do I manipulate objects, materials, or other parts of the environment when children are not expected to focus on my motions? What kinds of materials do I tend to manipulate?

|  | *Very Typical* | *Typical* | *Atypical* |
|---|---|---|---|
| 1. *I tend to manipulate:* | | | |
| chalk and chalkboard | _____ | _____ | _____ |
| books or workbooks | _____ | _____ | _____ |
| audiovisual equipment | _____ | _____ | _____ |
| paper, pens, or pencils | _____ | _____ | _____ |
| flow pens and charting paper | _____ | _____ | _____ |
| pictures or cards | _____ | _____ | _____ |
| materials related specifically to the teaching of my discipline | _____ | _____ | _____ |
| other:_____ | _____ | _____ | _____ |
| 2. *During the lesson, I focus my eyes on* *written materials:* | | | |
| my lesson plans | _____ | _____ | _____ |

|  | Very Typical | Typical | Atypical |
|---|---|---|---|
| the teacher's manual | _____ | _____ | _____ |
| the students' books | _____ | _____ | _____ |
| reference books | _____ | _____ | _____ |
| material recorded on chalkboard | _____ | _____ | _____ |
| numerals of the clock | _____ | _____ | _____ |
| other:_____ | _____ | _____ | _____ |

3. *Teacher-oriented wieldings I delegate to students are:*

| | | | |
|---|---|---|---|
| distribution and collection of materials | _____ | _____ | _____ |
| setting up equipment | _____ | _____ | _____ |
| putting material on board or bulletin board | _____ | _____ | _____ |
| reading questions that other students answer | _____ | _____ | _____ |
| other:_____ | _____ | _____ | _____ |

4. *I manipulate or wield materials:*

| | | | |
|---|---|---|---|
| before students come into the room | _____ | _____ | _____ |
| while students come into the room | _____ | _____ | _____ |
| while students are performing some other task | _____ | _____ | _____ |
| just before using the material | _____ | _____ | _____ |
| during the actual use of the material | _____ | _____ | _____ |
| other:_____ | _____ | _____ | _____ |

## D. Personal Motions

How do I use motions that are more of a personal nature than they are instructional?

1. *Motions I make that are related to my clothing are:*

| | | | |
|---|---|---|---|
| adjusting my tie or bow | _____ | _____ | _____ |
| adjusting my collar | _____ | _____ | _____ |
| straightening jacket | _____ | _____ | _____ |
| pulling down sweater or skirt | _____ | _____ | _____ |

|  | Very Typical | Typical | Atypical |
|---|---|---|---|
| tucking in blouse, sweater, or shirt | _____ | _____ | _____ |
| other:_____ | _____ | _____ | _____ |

2. *Motions I make in the classroom that are aspects of my own personality are:*

|  | Very Typical | Typical | Atypical |
|---|---|---|---|
| pushing back hair | _____ | _____ | _____ |
| pulling on beads, necklace, locket, etc. | _____ | _____ | _____ |
| adjusting glasses | _____ | _____ | _____ |
| placing hands in pockets | _____ | _____ | _____ |
| jiggling coins in pocket | _____ | _____ | _____ |
| twiddling with ring | _____ | _____ | _____ |
| curling hair around finger | _____ | _____ | _____ |
| scratching head, nose, neck, leg | _____ | _____ | _____ |
| other:_____ | _____ | _____ | _____ |

3. *My physical motions that might be called mannerisms because I repeatedly make them are:*    _____    _____    _____

## Part II

How does my nonverbal activity relate to my verbal activity?

1. To communicate meaning, I use nonverbal motion without any verbal accompaniment.    _____    _____    _____

2. I use nonverbal motion in my classroom to support my verbal remarks.    _____    _____    _____

3. I use nonverbal motion in my classroom to support other nonverbal activity.    _____    _____    _____

4. I use verbal remarks without nonverbal accompaniment.    _____    _____    _____

## Part III

How do I carry on classroom activity? I generally:

|  | Very Typical | Typical | Atypical |
|---|---|---|---|
| sit at the teacher's desk | _____ | _____ | _____ |
| sit on the teacher's desk | _____ | _____ | _____ |
| sit on stool | _____ | _____ | _____ |
| sit on a student's chair | _____ | _____ | _____ |
| sit on floor | _____ | _____ | _____ |
| lean on the chalkboard | _____ | _____ | _____ |
| lean on a desk | _____ | _____ | _____ |
| stand at the front of room | _____ | _____ | _____ |
| stand at the side or rear of room | _____ | _____ | _____ |
| move up and down the aisles | _____ | _____ | _____ |
| move from group to group | _____ | _____ | _____ |
| move from child to child | _____ | _____ | _____ |
| move across the front of room | _____ | _____ | _____ |
| move from desk to chalkboard | _____ | _____ | _____ |
| move around the outside edge of the room | _____ | _____ | _____ |
| sit at a table with the students | _____ | _____ | _____ |
| other:_____ | _____ | _____ | _____ |

## Part IV

What are the general characteristics of my nonverbal classroom behavior?

### A. Acuity Level

Consider the number of nonverbal clues you tend to generate in a classroom. Are you very active, active, not too active? Plot yourself on the following activity continuum:

very active                              active                        not too active

├─────────────────────────┼─────────────────────────┤

### B. Speed of Motion

Consider the nonverbal motions you make in the classroom. Do you tend to move rapidly? Do you tend to move rather slowly? Plot yourself on the following activity continuum:

rapid                                    medium                              slow

├─────────────────────────┼─────────────────────────┤

### C. Size of Motion

Consider the nonverbal motions you make. Do you tend to make such large motions as gestures of the hand? Or do you tend to make such small gestures motions as a nod or smile? Plot yourself on the following size continuum:

large                              medium                              small

|————————————————————————————|————————————————————————————|

### D. Personal Motions

Consider the personal motions you use in a classroom. Do you use many personal motions? Do you use a minimal number of personal motions? Plot yourself on the following continuum:

many personal motions                              few personal motions

|————————————————————————————|————————————————————————————|

### E. Verbal/Nonverbal Orientation

Consider the nonverbal activity and the verbal activity that you carry on in the classroom. Do you have a nonverbal orientation in your teaching? Do you have a verbal orientation? Plot yourself on the following verbal/nonverbal continuum:

verbal                              verbal/nonverbal                              nonverbal

|————————————————————————————|————————————————————————————|

### F. Clarity of Communication

Consider these questions:

- Is my bodily stance communicating what I want it to communicate? Is my manner of sitting communicating what I want to communicate?

- Is my manner of walking communicating what I want it to communicate?

- Is my gesturing communicating what I want to communicate?

- Are my facial expressions communicating what I want to communicate?

- In terms of these questions plot yourself on the following clarity of communication continuum:

motion communicates                              motion does not
what is intended                              communicate what is intended

|————————————————————————————|————————————————————————————|

## TEACHER BEHAVIORS INVENTORY*

### Instructions to Student

In this inventory you are asked to assess your instructor's specific classroom behaviors. Your instructor has requested this information for purposes of instructional analysis and improvement. Please try to be both thoughtful and candid in your responses so as to maximize the value of feedback.

Your judgments should reflect that type of teaching you think is best for this particular course and your particular learning style. Try to assess each behavior independently rather than letting your overall impression of the instructor determine each individual rating.

Each section of the inventory begins with a definition of the category of teaching to be assessed in that section. For each specific teaching behavior, please indicate your judgment as to whether your instructor should increase, decrease, or make no change in the frequency with which he exhibits the behavior in question. Please use the following rating scale in making your judgments:

1 = almost never
2 = rarely
3 = sometimes
4 = often
5 = almost always

### Clarity: method used to explain or clarify concepts and principles

| | |
|---|---|
| Gives several examples of each concept | 1 2 3 4 5 |
| Uses concrete everyday examples to explain concepts and principles | 1 2 3 4 5 |
| Fails to define new or unfamiliar terms | 1 2 3 4 5 |
| Repeats difficult ideas several times | 1 2 3 4 5 |
| Stresses most important points by pausing, speaking slowly, raising voice, and so on | 1 2 3 4 5 |
| Uses graphs or diagrams to facilitate explanation | 1 2 3 4 5 |
| Points out practical applications of concepts | 1 2 3 4 5 |
| Answers students' questions thoroughly | 1 2 3 4 5 |
| Suggests ways of memorizing complicated ideas | 1 2 3 4 5 |
| Writes key terms on blackboard or overhead screen | 1 2 3 4 5 |
| Explains subject matter in familiar colloquial language | 1 2 3 4 5 |

* *The Teaching Professor*, (October 1988): 3-4.

## Enthusiasm: use of nonverbal behavior to solicit student attention and interest

| | |
|---|---|
| Speaks in a dramatic or expressive way | 1 2 3 4 5 |
| Moves about while lecturing | 1 2 3 4 5 |
| Gestures with hands or arms | 1 2 3 4 5 |
| Exhibits facial gestures or expressions | 1 2 3 4 5 |
| Avoids eye contact with students | 1 2 3 4 5 |
| Walks up aisles beside students | 1 2 3 4 5 |
| Gestures with head or body | 1 2 3 4 5 |
| Tells jokes or humorous anecdotes | 1 2 3 4 5 |
| Reads lecture verbatim from prepared notes or text | 1 2 3 4 5 |
| Smiles or laughs while teaching | 1 2 3 4 5 |
| Shows distracting mannerisms | 1 2 3 4 5 |

## Interaction: techniques used to foster students' class participation

| | |
|---|---|
| Encourages students' questions and comments during lectures | 1 2 3 4 5 |
| Criticizes students when they make errors | 1 2 3 4 5 |
| Praises students for good ideas | 1 2 3 4 5 |
| Asks questions of individual students | 1 2 3 4 5 |
| Asks questions of class as a whole | 1 2 3 4 5 |
| Incorporates students' ideas into lecture | 1 2 3 4 5 |
| Presents challenging, thought-provoking ideas | 1 2 3 4 5 |
| Uses a variety of media and activities in class | 1 2 3 4 5 |
| Asks rhetorical questions | 1 2 3 4 5 |

## Organization: ways of organizing or structuring subject matter

| | |
|---|---|
| Uses headings and subheadings to organize lectures | 1 2 3 4 5 |
| Puts outline of lecture on blackboard or overhead screen | 1 2 3 4 5 |
| Clearly indicates transition from one topic to the next | 1 2 3 4 5 |
| Gives preliminary overview of lecture at beginning of class | 1 2 3 4 5 |
| Explains how each topic fits into the course as a whole | 1 2 3 4 5 |
| Begins class with a review of topics covered last time | 1 2 3 4 5 |
| Periodically summarizes points previously made | 1 2 3 4 5 |

## Pacing: rate of information presentation, efficient use of time

| | |
|---|---|
| Dwells excessively on obvious points | 1 2 3 4 5 |
| Digresses from major theme of lecture | 1 2 3 4 5 |
| Covers very little material in class sessions | 1 2 3 4 5 |

Asks if students understand before proceeding to next
topic                                                                1 2 3 4 5
Sticks to the point in answering students' questions                 1 2 3 4 5

**Disclosure: explicitness concerning course requirements and
grading criteria**
Advises students as to how to prepare for tests or exams             1 2 3 4 5
Provides sample exam questions                                       1 2 3 4 5
Tells students exactly what is expected of them on tests,
essays or assignments                                                1 2 3 4 5
States objectives of each lecture                                    1 2 3 4 5
Reminds students of test dates or assignment deadlines               1 2 3 4 5
States objectives of course as a whole                               1 2 3 4 5

**Speech: characteristics of voice relevant to classroom teaching**
Stutters, mumbles, or slurs words                                    1 2 3 4 5
Speaks at appropriate volume                                         1 2 3 4 5
Speaks clearly                                                       1 2 3 4 5
Speaks at appropriate pace                                           1 2 3 4 5
Says "um" or "ah"                                                     1 2 3 4 5
Voice lacks proper modulation (speaks in monotone)                   1 2 3 4 5

**Rapport: quality of interpersonal relations between teacher
and students**
Addresses individual students by name                                1 2 3 4 5
Announces availability for consultation outside of class             1 2 3 4 5
Offers to help students with problems                                1 2 3 4 5
Shows tolerance of other points of view                              1 2 3 4 5
Talks with students before or after class                            1 2 3 4 5

# TEACHER COMMUNICATION RATING SCALE*

Teacher name _____        Date _____

School _____              Evaluator _____

Grade Level _____         Student Teacher? _____

Certified? _____

* Thanks to Dr. Phil Barklund and Dr. Don Black of Central Washington University, Ellensburg, WA,
who developed this instrument.

This evaluation form follows the Speech Communication Association's newly developed description of teacher communication competencies. It can be used as a basis for observation in evaluating the classroom communication skills of student teachers to determine the presence or absence of these communication skills.

It is suggested that the following criteria for rating each item be followed for consistency in using this instrument.

Let a #1 rating mean . . . . Behavior did not appear in this observation.

Let a #2 rating mean . . . . Opportunities for behavior were present, but student did not demonstrate the behavior at the appropriate time.

Let a #3 rating mean . . . . Behavior demonstrated occasionally.

Let a #4 rating mean . . . . Behavior demonstrated consistently, effectiveness average.

Let a #5 rating mean . . . . Behavior demonstrated consistently with obvious skill.

Column #6—Confidence of judgment. In observing a teacher for a short period of time, not all behaviors may be judged with equal confidence. Column #6 asks the rater to give a confidence level for the judgment of the indicated skill.

- Rating of 1 indicates low confidence in judgment. There were low levels of the observed behaviors.
- Rating of 2 indicates average confidence in judgment.
- Rating of 3 indicates high confidence in judgment.

## TEACHER'S COMMUNICATION RATING SCALE

Ratings do not need to be made in the order presented here. In some instances, the rating for a behavior may be done during the observation. In other instances, the rating may need to be done at the completion of the observation to ensure an adequate sample.

I. INFORMATIVE MESSAGES
   a. Sending
      1. Structures informative messages effectively by using devices such as initial partitions, transitions, internal summaries, and concluding summaries.

| 1-NR | 2 | 3 | 4 | 5 | 6-CJ |
|------|---|---|---|---|------|

2. Amplifies information effectively through the use of verbal and audiovisual supporting materials.

| 1-NR | 2 | 3 | 4 | 5 | 6-CJ |
|------|---|---|---|---|------|

3. Asks effective questions to assess student understanding of information given in lectures.

| 1-NR | 2 | 3 | 4 | 5 | 6-CJ |
|------|---|---|---|---|------|

4. Presents information in an animated and interesting way.

| 1-NR | 2 | 3 | 4 | 5 | 6-CJ |
|------|---|---|---|---|------|

b. Receiving
   1. Is able to identify main point of student comment.

| 1-NR | 2 | 3 | 4 | 5 | 6-CJ |
|------|---|---|---|---|------|

   2. Can identify structural patterns or problems of informative messages.

| 1-NR | 2 | 3 | 4 | 5 | 6-CJ |
|------|---|---|---|---|------|

   3. Can evaluate the adequacy of verbal supporting materials.

| 1-NR | 2 | 3 | 4 | 5 | 6-CJ |
|------|---|---|---|---|------|

   4. Can formulate questions that probe for the informative content of messages.

| 1-NR | 2 | 3 | 4 | 5 | 6-CJ |
|------|---|---|---|---|------|

   5. Can distinguish messages which are delivered in an animated manner and those which are not.

| 1-NR | 2 | 3 | 4 | 5 | 6-CJ |
|------|---|---|---|---|------|

II. AFFECTIVE MESSAGES. Teacher should demonstrate competence in sending and receiving affective messages (i.e., messages that express or respond to feelings).

a. Sending
   1. Expresses positive and negative feelings about self to students.

| 1-NR | 2 | 3 | 4 | 5 | 6-CJ |
|------|---|---|---|---|------|

2. Expresses positive and negative feelings about students to students.

| 1-NR | 2 | 3 | 4 | 5 | 6-CJ |
|------|---|---|---|---|------|

3. Expresses opinions about classroom content, events, and real world occurrences.

| 1-NR | 2 | 3 | 4 | 5 | 6-CJ |
|------|---|---|---|---|------|

4. Demonstrates interpersonal openness, warmth, and positive regard for students.

| 1-NR | 2 | 3 | 4 | 5 | 6-CJ |
|------|---|---|---|---|------|

5. Demonstrates energy and enthusiasm when relating to students.

| 1-NR | 2 | 3 | 4 | 5 | 6-CJ |
|------|---|---|---|---|------|

b. Receiving
   1. Recognizes verbal and nonverbal cues concerning student feelings.

| 1-NR | 2 | 3 | 4 | 5 | 6-CJ |
|------|---|---|---|---|------|

   2. Invites students to express feelings.

| 1-NR | 2 | 3 | 4 | 5 | 6-CJ |
|------|---|---|---|---|------|

   3. Is nonjudgmental in responding to student feelings.

| 1-NR | 2 | 3 | 4 | 5 | 6-CJ |
|------|---|---|---|---|------|

   4. Asks open-ended questions in response to student expressions of feelings.

| 1-NR | 2 | 3 | 4 | 5 | 6-CJ |
|------|---|---|---|---|------|

   5. If necessary, offers advice tactfully.

| 1-NR | 2 | 3 | 4 | 5 | 6-CJ |
|------|---|---|---|---|------|

III. IMAGINATIVE MESSAGES. Teacher should demonstrate competence in sending and receiving imaginative messages (i.e., messages that speculate, theorize, or include fantasy).

a. Sending
   1. Uses vivid descriptive language.

| 1-NR | 2 | 3 | 4 | 5 | 6-CJ |
|------|---|---|---|---|------|

2. Uses expressive vocal and physical behavior when creating or recreating examples, stories, or messages from exemplars.

| 1-NR | 2 | 3 | 4 | 5 | 6-CJ |
|------|---|---|---|---|------|

b.  Receiving
1. Responds to imaginative messages enthusiastically.

| 1-NR | 2 | 3 | 4 | 5 | 6-CJ |
|------|---|---|---|---|------|

2. Is nondirective when encouraging student creativity.

| 1-NR | 2 | 3 | 4 | 5 | 6-CJ |
|------|---|---|---|---|------|

IV.  RITUALISTIC MESSAGES. Teacher should demonstrate competence in sending and receiving ritualistic messages (i.e., messages that serve to maintain and facilitate social interaction).

a.  Sending
1. Demonstrates appropriate behavior in performing everyday speech acts such as greeting, turn-taking, and leave taking.

| 1-NR | 2 | 3 | 4 | 5 | 6-CJ |
|------|---|---|---|---|------|

2. Models appropriate social amenities in ordinary classroom interaction.

| 1-NR | 2 | 3 | 4 | 5 | 6-CJ |
|------|---|---|---|---|------|

3. Demonstrates competence when participating in or role-playing interviews, conversations, problem-solving groups, legislative groups, and public ceremonies.

| 1-NR | 2 | 3 | 4 | 5 | 6-CJ |
|------|---|---|---|---|------|

b.  Receiving
1. Recognizes when students perform everyday speech acts appropriately.

| 1-NR | 2 | 3 | 4 | 5 | 6-CJ |
|------|---|---|---|---|------|

2. Recognizes appropriate and inappropriate performances of social amenities.

| 1-NR | 2 | 3 | 4 | 5 | 6-CJ |
|------|---|---|---|---|------|

3. Recognizes competence and incompetence when students participate in interviews, conversations, problem-solving groups, legislative groups, and public ceremonies.

| 1-NR | 2 | 3 | 4 | 5 | 6-CJ |
|------|---|---|---|---|------|

V. PERSUASIVE MESSAGES. Teacher should demonstrate competence in sending and receiving persuasive messages (i.e., messages that seek to convince).

   a. Sending
      1. Can differentiate between fact and opinion.

| 1-NR | 2 | 3 | 4 | 5 | 6-CJ |
|------|---|---|---|---|------|

      2. Can recognize audience factors which may encourage or constrain acceptance of ideas.

| 1-NR | 2 | 3 | 4 | 5 | 6-CJ |
|------|---|---|---|---|------|

      3. Offers sound reasons and evidence in support of ideas.

| 1-NR | 2 | 3 | 4 | 5 | 6-CJ |
|------|---|---|---|---|------|

      4. Recognizes underlying assumptions in one's own arguments.

| 1-NR | 2 | 3 | 4 | 5 | 6-CJ |
|------|---|---|---|---|------|

      5. Demonstrates a preference for reason-giving over power moves when interacting with students.

| 1-NR | 2 | 3 | 4 | 5 | 6-CJ |
|------|---|---|---|---|------|

   b. Receiving
      1. Recognizes own bias in responding to ideas.

| 1-NR | 2 | 3 | 4 | 5 | 6-CJ |
|------|---|---|---|---|------|

      2. Questions the adequacy of reasons and evidence given.

| 1-NR | 2 | 3 | 4 | 5 | 6-CJ |
|------|---|---|---|---|------|

      3. Evaluates evidence and reasons presented.

| 1-NR | 2 | 3 | 4 | 5 | 6-CJ |
|------|---|---|---|---|------|

      4. Recognizes underlying assumptions in arguments of others.

| 1-NR | 2 | 3 | 4 | 5 | 6-CJ |
|------|---|---|---|---|------|

# Credits

Dwight Allen and Kevin Ryan, *Microteaching*, 1969, Addison-Wesley Publishing Company, Inc., pages 1–3, 39–41. Reprinted with permission.

E. Amidon and E. Hunter, from *Improving Teaching: The Analysis of Classroom Verbal Interaction* by Edmund Amidon and Elizabeth Hunter. Copyright 1966 by Holt, Rinehart and Winston, Inc. Reprinted by permission of Holt, Rinehart and Winston, Publishers.

Rob Anderson, from *Students as Real People*, copyright 1979, reprinted by permission of the publisher, Hayden Book Co., Inc.

W H. Auden, from "Some Thirty Inches from My Nose." Copyright 1965 by W. H. Auden. Reprinted from *W H. Auden Collected Poems*, edited by Edward Mendelson, by permission of Random House, Inc.

A. A. Bellack. Reprinted by permission of the publisher from A. A. Bellack, H. M. Kliebard, R. I. Hyman, and F L. Smith, Jr., *The Language of the Classroom*. (New York: Teachers College Press, copyright 1966 by Teachers College, Columbia University. All rights reserved.)

Rodney Borstad, from "Why Teach?" *Wisconsin Journal of Speech* (September 1971):20. Reprinted by permission of the publisher.

Mary Bozik, from "Teaching Students to Listen to Teacher Talk," *Teacher Talk* 7 (Spring 1989):2. Reprinted with permission.

John K. Brilhart, from *Effective Group Discussion*, 5th ed. Copyright © 1986 Wm. C. Brown Publishers, Dubuque, IA. All Rights Reserved. Reprinted by permission.

J. E. Brophy, from "Synthesis of Research on Strategies for Motivating Students to Learn," *Educational Leadership* 45, no. 2 (October 1987). Reprinted with permission of the Association for Supervision and Curriculum Development and Jere E. Brophy. Copyright © 1987 by the Association for Supervision and Curriculum Development. All rights reserved.

Jere E. Brophy and Thomas L. Good, from *Teacher-Student Relationships*. Copyright 1974 by Jere E. Brophy and Thomas L. Good. Reprinted by permission of Holt, Rinehart and Winston, Publishers.

N. F. Burroughs, P. Kearney, and T. Plax, from "Compliance-Resistance in the College Classroom," *Communication Education* 38 (July 1989): 221–223. Reprinted with permission.

Sunny Decker, from *An Empty Spoon*, Copyright 1969. Reprinted by permission of the publisher, Harper & Row, Publishers, Inc.

Michael Dunkin and Bruce Biddle, from *The Study of Teaching*. Copyright 1974 by Michael Dunkin and Bruce Biddle. Reprinted by permission of Holt, Rinehart and Winston, Publishers.

Ned Flanders, *Analyzing Teaching Behavior*, 1970, Addison-Wesley Publishing Company, Inc., pages 98–106. Reprinted with permission.

Gerhard E. Frost. Reprinted from *Bless My Growing* by Gerhard E. Frost, copyright 1974, by permission of Augsburg Publishing House.

N. L. Gage and D. C. Berliner, *Educational Psychology*, second edition, Fig. 17.5, p. 378. Copyright 1979 by Rand McNally College Publishing Company.

Haim Ginort, from *Teacher and Child*, Copyright 1972. Reprinted by permission.

William Glasser, from *Schools Without Failure* by William Glasser, M.D. Copyright 1969 by William Glasser. Reprinted by permission of HarperCollins, Publishers.

Thomas L. Good and Jere E. Brophy, from *Looking in Classrooms*, Second Edition. Copyright 1978 by Thomas L. Good and Jere E. Brophy. Reprinted by permission of HarperCollins, Publishers.

B. Grant and D. Hennings. Reprinted by permission of the publisher from Grant and Hennings *The Teacher Moves: An Analysis of Non-Verbal Activity* (New York: Teachers College Press, copyright 1971 by Teachers College, Columbia University. All rights reserved.), pp. 126–133.

Rod Hart, from *Lecturing as Communication: Problems and Potentialities*, copyright 1973. Reprinted by permission.

David W. Johnson, from *The Social Psychology of Education*, copyright 1970. Reprinted by permission of the author.

David W. Johnson, *Reaching Out: Interpersonal Effectiveness and Self Actualization*, 1972, p. 125. Reprinted by permission of Prentice-Hall, Inc., Englewood Cliffs, New Jersey.

D. Johnson and F. Johnson, *Joining Together: Group Therapy and Group Skills*, 1975, pp. 7, 157–158, 405, 415. Reprinted by permission of Prentice-Hall, Inc., Englewood Cliffs, New Jersey.

J. E. Jones and J. W. Pfeiffer. Reprinted from: J. E. Jones and J. W. Pfeiffer (eds.), *The 1973 Annual Handbook for Group Facilitators*. San Diego, CA: University Associates, 1973. Used with permission.

Patricia Walsh, "Third Grade Arithmetic by the Window." Reprinted by permission of the author.

John Wenburg and William Wilmot, from *The Personal Communication Process*, copyright 1973. Reprinted by permission of the publisher, John Wiley & Sons, Inc.

L. R. Wheeless, from "An Investigation of Receiver Apprehension and Social Context Dimensions of Communication Apprehension," *The Speech Teacher* 24 (1975):261–68. Reprinted by permission of Speech Communication Association.

B. Wood, from *Development of Functional Communication Competencies: Pre-K-Grade 6*, copyright 1977, pp. 2 and 5, and *Development of Functional Communication Competencies: Grades 7–12*, Copyright 1977, p. 2. Reprinted by permission of the publisher, ERIC Clearinghouse on Reading and Communication Skills.

# INDEX